GETTING EQUAL

GETTING EQUAL

The history of Australian feminism

Marilyn Lake

ALLEN & UNWIN

Copyright © Marilyn Lake 1999

All rights reserved. No part of this book may be reproduced or transmitted in any form or by any means, electronic or mechanical, including photocopying, recording or by any information storage and retrieval system, without prior permission in writing from the publisher.

First published in 1999
Allen & Unwin
9 Atchison Street, St Leonards NSW 1590 Australia
Phone: (61 2) 8425 0100
Fax: (61 2) 9906 2218
E-mail: frontdesk@allen-unwin.com.au
Web: http://www.allen-unwin.com.au

National Library of Australia
Cataloguing-in-Publication entry:

Lake, Marilyn.
    Getting equal: the history of Australian feminism.

    Includes index.
    ISBN 1 86508 137 X.

    1. Feminism—Australia—History. 2. Women—Australia—History.
    3. Women—Australia—Social conditions. I. Title.

305.420994

Set in 11/13 pt Goudy by DOCUPRO, Sydney
Printed in the United States of America

10 9 8 7 6 5 4 3 2 1

For Sam, with love

CONTENTS

Acknowledgments	viii
Abbreviations	x
Introduction	1
Part I Women in a New World	**17**
1 The power of the ballot	19
Part II Building a Woman-Friendly Commonwealth	**47**
2 The creation of a welfare state	49
3 The rights of mothers	72
4 The independence of women	87
5 Campaigning for Aboriginal rights	110
Part III Feminist Modes of Doing Politics	**137**
6 The non-party ideal	139
Part IV Equality With Men	**165**
7 The right to work	167
8 No discrimination on the grounds of sex or race	191
9 An end to woman's role	214
10 Liberation on our own terms	231
11 The institutionalisation of feminism	253
Conclusion	277
Notes	283
Index	305

ACKNOWLEDGMENTS

The research on which this book is based has been greatly assisted by large and small grants from the Australian Research Council; I wish to thank the ARC for this financial support and the research assistants employed thereby. Their conscientious work, over a period of some ten years, has been crucial to the making of this book and it is a source of great pleasure to me that a number of them have, in the meantime, become historians employing research assistance themselves. I thank Katie Holmes, Penny Russell, Esther Faye, Glenda Sluga, Kate Gray, Heather Gunn, Monica Dux, Catriona Elder, Liz Conor, Cathy Colebourne and Ruth Ford.

In 1996, my colleagues, Susan Magarey, at the University of Adelaide and Ann Curthoys, at the Australian National University, and I were jointly awarded an ARC grant to undertake a research project specifically on the history of Women's Liberation in Australia since 1968. Some of the material in the final chapters of this book derives from research for that project; for their productive labours, often working in difficult circumstances, I thank Ruth Ford, Heather Gunn, Liz Conor, Liz Dimock, Judith Tom, Tristan Slade, Kate Borritt, the late Sarah Zetlein, Ann Genovese, Inara Walden and Deb Worsley-Pine. I also thank Sarah Squire, indexer extraordinaire, for her gracious, conscientious work in meeting a tight deadline. Like all historical works, this book builds on the collective scholarship of others, especially, in this case, the work of feminist historians over the last thirty years. Although limits of space mean that I cannot, either in the text or in the notes, do justice to the work of individuals, I want to acknowledge their findings as crucial to my own.

I have been fortunate during the last ten years to work at La Trobe University, where I could combine teaching in History and Women's

Studies, a happy and stimulating conjuncture—and many of the arguments in this book have been clarified in the course of explaining them to students and colleagues. For providing an academic environment conducive to research, I also wish to thank Alan Frost, Rhys Isaac, John Salmond and the Vice-Chancellor, Michael Osborne, who have supported my work and the project of Women's Studies more generally.

Around Australia many people have graciously responded to enquiries or provided me with relevant material. I am grateful to Pamela Gatenby, Faith Bandler, Dianne Davidson, Susan Ryan, Jill Matthews, Shirley Castley, Martha Macintyre, Zelda D'Aprano, Ann Pengelly, Dame Rachel Cleland, Sue Rickard, Fiona Paisley, Jan Roberts, Deborah McCulloch and David Dutton. I also wish to thank the staff at the National Library of Australia, the Battye, Mortlock and Mitchell Libraries for their courteous assistance in locating relevant manuscript materials. At Allen and Unwin I wish to thank Elizabeth Weiss and Karen Ward for their patience and support.

Writers owe a special debt to those who engage with their ideas and I offer particular thanks to such colleagues and friends: Carmel Shute, Mary Crooks, Judy Smart, Pat Grimshaw, Stuart Macintyre, Henry Reynolds, Tim Rowse, Katie Holmes, Joy Damousi, Diane Kirkby, Barbara Caine, Hilary Charlesworth, Kim Rubenstein, Marian Sawer, Meaghan Morris, Tom Stannage, Chilla Bulbeck, Patricia Crawford, Richard White, Jim Walter, Stephen Garton, Susan Magarey and Ann Curthoys. Colleagues in distant places have been especially generous in this regard. For their intellectual comradeship and the warmth of their hospitality my thanks go to Mary Maynard, Alice Kessler-Harris, Karen Offen, Cora Kaplan, Sonya Rose, Gisela Bock, Martha Vicinus, Catherine Hall, Sonya Michel, Linda Kerber, Sally Alexander, Joan Scott, Ida Blom, Karen Hagemann, Barbara Hobson and all the participants in the 'Recognition Struggles' symposium, Barbara has managed to lure to Stockholm University.

At home, in Armadale, where the writing takes place, I am inspired and touched by the fierce independence and loving kindness of my girls, Kath and Jess (and grateful to them for sometimes allowing me to use the computer and the phone), but my most important debt is to my husband, Sam, whose support—intellectual, emotional and material—has in a real sense made this work possible.

ABBREVIATIONS

ACT	Australian Capital Territory
ACTU	Australian Council of Trade Unions
AFWV	Australian Federation of Women Voters
ALP	Australian Labor Party
ANU	Australian National University
AWNL	Australian Women's National League
BCL	British Commonwealth League
CR	Consciousness Raising
CWA	Country Women's Association
DIY	Do It Yourself
EEO	Equal Employment Opportunity
ERI	Equal Rights International
FECCA	Federation of Ethnic Community Councils of Australia
FILEF	Federazione Italiana Lavoratori Emigrati e Famiglia
FTYC	First Ten Years Collective (Archive)
ILO	International Labor Office
IWD	International Women's Day
IWSA	International Women's Suffrage Alliance (later the International Alliance of Women for Suffrage and Equal Citizenship and later again the International Alliance of Women)
IWY	International Women's Year
JP	Justice of the Peace
LL.B.	Bachelor of Laws
ML	Mitchell Library
MLA	Member of Legislative Assembly
MP	Member of Parliament
MWLA	Melbourne Women's Liberation Archive
NCW	National Council of Women

NESB	Non-English Speaking Background
NHMRC	National Health and Medical Research Council
NLA	National Library of Australia
NWCC	National Women's Coordinating Council
ODI	Open Door International
OSW	Office of the Status of Women
UA	United Associations (of Women)
UAW	Union of Australian Women
UN	United Nations
USA	United States of America
USSR	Union of Soviet Socialist Republics
VD	Venereal Disease
VEWOC	Victorian Employed Women's Organisations Council
VWCM	Victorian Women Citizens' Movement
WAAC	Women's Abortion Action Committee
WAC	Women's Action Committee
WCTU	Woman's Christian Temperance Union
WEA	Workers' Educational Association
WEB	Women's Employment Board
WEL	Women's Electoral Lobby
WL	Women's Liberation
WNPA	Women's Non-Party Association (of South Australia)
WOC	Women's Organising Committee (of the Australian Labor Party)
WPA	Women's Political Association (formerly Women's Federal Political Association)
WPEL	Women's Political Education League
WSG	Women's Service Guild
WSL	Womanhood Suffrage League
WSPU	Women's Social and Political Union
YWCA	Young Women's Christian Association

INTRODUCTION

THE POWER OF FEMINISM

'Feminism was a cult so deep that one lost oneself in it, and it was a power which pushed the true feminist along.'[1] Feminists were empowered by feminism. Such was the simple, but perceptive insight of Linda Littlejohn, sometime president of the United Associations (of Women) (UA) in New South Wales and described in 1935 by the Melbourne *Herald* as 'Australia's leading feminist'.[2] For Littlejohn, feminism was a movement, a set of ideas, a collective force—not merely an individual persuasion, not something one did for one's self. Littlejohn worked with a variety of feminist organisations, at home and abroad. In 1935, she was not only well known in Australia, as the *Herald* suggested, she also became prominent internationally, when elected president of the Geneva-based Equal Rights International. Today, however, few Australians would know her name or the local and international organisations for which she worked. Linda Littlejohn, like much of feminism, has effectively been written out of history.

With her shingled hair, elegant attire and bold style, Littlejohn was a thoroughly modern woman. A wife and a mother of four, she worked professionally as a radio broadcaster, in which capacity she was invited to deliver a paper to the BBC on 'radio and the woman listener'. By the early 1930s, her radio and press work had made her a household name, and she was much in demand as a public speaker, addressing around one hundred meetings in 1930 alone. A founding member (with labour movement activist Muriel Heagney) of Open Door International, formed in Berlin in 1929 to promote 'the Economic Emancipation of the Woman Worker', Littlejohn was indefatigable in her pursuit of equality for women. Her admirers praised her 'engaging and vital personality'; others called her 'forceful'.[3] She herself, as we have seen, attributed her uncommon energies to the force of feminism itself. Women today might be thankful that feminism has so empowered feminists, for there has been much work to do. Linda Littlejohn was an uncompromising equal rights feminist—heroic and unsentimental— but sixty years on we know that equality will get us only so far. This book is a study of the power of feminism, but also of the limits to equality.

THE LIMITS TO EQUALITY: FROM CHARLOTTE McNEILLY TO HEATHER OSLAND

In 1877, Charlotte Elizabeth McNeilly went to court in Sydney in an attempt to gain a divorce from her husband, who had, she said, terrorised her and their five children over a period of several years. Moreover, when she had tried to earn her own living as a teacher, he had confiscated her earnings, which under law he was entitled to do. Before 1879, in New South Wales, and until later dates in other colonies, married women were legally debarred from ownership of property, and denied inheritance and custody rights. Marriage robbed women of their individuality and it made them vulnerable to daily abuse. But divorce was not easy to obtain. The grounds differed for men and women; whereas a husband need only prove adultery, a wife had to prove adultery coupled with another ground, such as cruelty.

McNeilly, who had been married twenty-six years, recounted in terrible detail a series of violent acts her husband had committed against her and her children:

> four years ago her husband threatened to take her life with great violence, and took up a meat fork and chased her all over the room, threatening to murder her. Her son interfered, and for a week after she was in danger of her life . . .
>
> Once he blacked and bruised her body by kicks, and on another occasion he nearly choked her, leaving marks on her neck for several days. While he was trying to choke her, the child cried, and he violently pushed a stick down the child's throat, tearing lumps of flesh off and nearly choking the child. He made broth for the child which afterwards died.[4]

She also brought evidence of her husband's adultery before the court, which she needed to do, but in the end the judge was unconvinced that the petitioner had established her case, which was dismissed with costs.

In the nineteenth century, Australian women lacked basic political, civil and economic rights. Denied access to most professions and unable to earn a living wage in those occupations to which they were admitted, such as teaching, nursing, factory work and domestic service (the largest employer of female workers), the vast majority of women were forced to find a husband to provide them with a livelihood. Marriage, however, rendered women even more powerless as it robbed them of the right to own property, the right to refuse sexual access to their bodies and the right to custody of their children. Not until 1934, in New South Wales, did married women have custody rights to their own children recognised in law. Not until 1981, in New South Wales, did rape in marriage become a crime.

Since the late nineteenth century, feminist activism over several decades has been effective in substantially improving women's position in society and in marriage. We now enjoy freedoms unimagined by our grandmothers and mothers. But the goal of equality remains elusive, and the recent case of Heather Osland highlights the ways in which marriage, economic dependence and mothers' continuing responsibility for children render women vulnerable to male power still. At the time of writing, Heather Osland is serving a gaol sentence for murder because she assisted her son to kill her brutal husband before he killed them.

Like McNeilly's husband, Frank Osland terrorised his wife and children over a period of several years. Heather Osland was beaten, kicked, dragged by the hair, threatened with razor blades and had her head held under water. The sexual abuse included vaginal, oral and anal rape. The psychological abuse included being subjected to strict rules, being stalked and, like Charlotte McNeilly, having to watch violence against her children and pets. Frank Osland ripped the heads off budgerigars in front of the children. She had tried to leave many times, but her husband had followed her, smashing down doors, stalking her, making threats to chop the children into little pieces and send them to her in the post. Fifty per cent of women killed in domestic homicides are killed while leaving their partners or after having left.[5]

Fearing she or her children would be killed, Heather helped her son kill her husband. Although her son was eventually acquitted on the grounds of self-defence (it was he who dealt the fatal blow), Heather was found guilty of murder. In appeals to the Court of Appeal of the Supreme Court and the High Court, the argument that she was provoked and acted in self-defence was rejected, in part, because the planning involved rendered it a premeditated act. Feminist analysis of the Court decisions has made the point that the legal defences of 'provocation' and 'self-defence' are themselves masculinist, in that they privilege men's behavioural patterns: provocation being said to occur, for example, when a man flies into a jealous rage and kills his wife's lover, and self-defence when a man responds on the spot to a violent attack in a bar. Thirteen years of abuse were not considered by the court to constitute provocation; Heather's fear that her husband would kill her did not make her act one of self-defence.

The Osland case has highlighted the problematic nature of equality for women: women have equal access to the law, but what if its categories, constructs and interpretations are based on men's experience of the world? Women now have, for the most part, equal access to the professions and public life, but what if these have been built around the assumption that their occupants are free from the responsibilities of children and daily life? Women are eligible to sit in the national parliament, but what if the founding fathers chose to locate it hundreds of kilometres away from the cities where most people live with their families? Women are now free to go out into the world as independent citizens, but what if the pervasive fear of male violence keeps them shut indoors?

Decades of feminist activism have won women equal rights to participate in social, economic and political life in Australia, but equality has meant participating on men's terms, which assume that workers and citizens are autonomous, mobile and free from domestic responsibilities. It should not be surprising, then, that women in waged work still earn on average only 65 per cent of what men earn (or 79 per cent if total full-time earnings are compared), that over 70 per cent of part-time workers are women, that some 93 per cent of the recipients of the supporting parent's benefit are mothers, that only 9 per cent of university professors are women and that we remain dramatically underrepresented in the national and State parliaments. Equality is a necessary, but limited, goal. The problem with the pursuit of equality is that, while admitting women to the world of men, it reinforces the idea that men's way of organising the world is natural.

Significantly, in the long history of the women's movement in

Australia, feminists were more likely to name 'independence' and 'freedom', rather than 'equality', as their goals. Alert to the many married women subject to the gross or petty tyranny of husbands and the degradations of economic dependence for them and their daughters, feminists have long championed economic independence for women. In 1903, Rose Scott presented a paper on 'The Economic Independence of the Married Woman' to the post-suffrage Women's Political Education League of which she was president. Scott, like other leaders of the women's movement, was inundated with letters from women detailing their plight, women like Florence Roberts, who wrote of her husband: 'He simply would have me be his slave not his wife. He said he would make me obey him, he would make me do just what he chose or murder me. He would teach me who he was'.[6]

In 1921, Henrietta Greville, the first woman president of the Workers' Education Association (WEA), inspired by related developments in England, declared: 'All over the world today, the cry goes up for the Economic Independence of the Married Woman'.[7] In the mid-1920s, Victorian labour organiser Jean Daley wrote a column in the union journal *Woman's Clarion*, in which she observed darkly that women 'who economically depended on men, moulded themselves to his desire'. Her conclusion? 'Every mother should strive to make her daughter self-supporting.'[8] In the late 1930s, Jessie Street, president of the United Associations, produced a pamphlet called *Income for Wives How It Can Be Managed or The Economic Independence of Married Women* in which she called the right to an income 'the very foundation of human liberty'.[9]

Feminists generally advocated a combination of different reforms to achieve economic independence: legislation to require husbands to share their family wage and to grant ownership to wives of household savings; motherhood endowment and later a supporting parent's benefit; the public provision of child care; and equal pay or the rate for the job. As it became clear that the only way women would enjoy their own income was by following men into the labour market, so 'equality'—in wages, opportunities and conditions—became feminism's defining goal. Feminists were still demanding equal status and opportunities for women—at work, in public life, on juries—when Women's Liberation erupted onto the scene in the 1970s. Interestingly, many of the leading feminists of the interwar period—Jessie Street, Bessie Rischbieth, Ada Bromham, Mary Bennett, Constance Cooke—died in the decade between 1960 and 1970, as if to make way for the new wave about to break on the shore. Women's Liberationists were largely oblivious of the older feminists' passing, however, and ignorant of their lives and work. As a young feminist and post-graduate student in History in the early 1970s, I shared that ignorance—but how might we have known better? Why weren't we told?

HISTORY'S OBLITERATION OF THE FEMINIST PAST

Until the 1970s, the writing of Australian history was marked by the absence of women. This was no accident, nor was it an easily corrected oversight. For, as the public record of men's deeds, history rested on—in fact required—the invisibility of women. History was the self-conscious record of the white men who made the nation. Women, Aboriginal or non-Aboriginal, did not figure in Australian history books because, it was said, when justifications at last became necessary, we hadn't done anything. When finally national histories did notice the existence of women in the past, as in F. K. Crowley's *New History of Australia*, published in 1974, we had a short index entry between 'wombats' and 'wool'. Of course, neither wombats, nor women, nor wool were thought to have a political history, although readers were apprised of wool's importance to the political economy.

Professional historians did not—until feminists started writing in the 1970s—accord Australian women activists the dignity of being historical and political actors. Accounts of Australian politics, similarly, were (and are) blind to the decades of political activity undertaken by women. That women were leading theorists and practitioners of citizenship, that they were outspoken advocates of proportional representation, a welfare state, Aboriginal citizenship, the custody rights of Aboriginal and non-Aboriginal mothers and the importance of international law seemed to be of no consequence to the men who documented, and still document, our political history. It was as if political women had never existed.

THE PAST CONFRONTS THE PRESENT

Some of those who had been active since the 1920s lived on into the 1960s and 1970s, carrying the memory of their political work into the present, bearing witness to what had gone before. Determined that the history of feminism would be remembered, they deposited their rich collections of papers into national and State archives and, as with Bessie Rischbieth's *March of Australian Women*, offered first-hand accounts of their long campaigns for sexual equality. Most of the older feminist organisations, such as the Australian Federation of Women Voters (formed in 1921) and the United Associations (of Women) (formed in 1929), continued into the 1970s, and although utterly disregarded, they and their records testified to the fact that feminists had been active throughout the century.

To the extent that Women's Liberationists were aware of their hard-working predecessors, they were usually considered an embarrassing legacy to be overcome, rather than a tradition with which to connect. Whereas earlier feminists had acted as exemplary citizens, Women's Liberationists were self-styled revolutionaries, scornful of the politics of reform and the respectability of reformers. The issue that most clearly separated the new politics from the old was sexuality: Women's Liberationists were the first Australian feminists to declare that they had sexual rights, rights as sexual subjects, as lesbians, bisexuals and heterosexuals. For decades Australian feminism had operated on the assumption that sexual freedom was invariably harmful for women, that women's advancement as citizens necessitated the disavowal of sexual desire. These dramatically different understandings of the relationship between sexual freedom and political equality came into collision in an historic encounter in Adelaide, in 1974.

In June that year, in the pages of the Adelaide *Advertiser*, Ellinor Walker, an eighty-year-old veteran of post-suffrage feminism, took on a young woman in her twenties, Ann Pengelly, about recommendations to abolish various laws dealing with sexuality. Walker was secretary of the South Australian branch of the League of Women Voters, originally founded as the Women's Non-Party Association in 1909, which she had joined in 1914 aged twenty-one, becoming the proud editor of its newsletter, the *Non-Party News*. Sixty years later, still actively involved in feminist politics, Walker was moved to write to the press to correct the dangerously wrong-headed views expressed by a young woman espousing the ideal of sexual liberation. Pengelly was president of the South Australian branch of Young Labor, the youth arm of the Australian Labor Party (ALP), and she would later become president of the South Australian branch of the ALP and stand (unsuccessfully) as a Labor candidate in the South Australian State elections.

To the Young Labor president, women's liberation meant sexual liberation. Accordingly, she advocated the complete decriminalisation of sexual relations, recommending that 'carnal knowledge, prostitution, the age of consent and laws dealing with homosexuality [be] abolished from the statute books'.[10] Feminists in the League of Women Voters were aghast. Cherished reforms were under attack. For decades, their organisation had argued that it was women's use as 'creatures of sex' that produced their oppression; and that sexual promiscuity could only reinforce the degradation of women and the contempt in which they were held by men. For as long as Ellinor Walker had been politically active, feminist associations had promoted 'an equal moral standard', by which they meant that men should become as chaste as women were expected to be. Only then might men be persuaded to respect women as equal citizens. As the Australian Federation of Women Voters put it, meeting in Adelaide in 1936, men and women had to 'uphold the same human personality [and] sexual discipline' and the 'traffic in women and all forms of third party exploitation of vice should be considered as a legal offence and punished as such'.[11] This was the feminist wisdom that was dramatically called into question by the young woman who was president of the Young Labor convention in 1974.

When Ellinor Walker read about the proposal to decriminalise prostitution, she wrote in agitation to the *Advertiser* to defend the current law, which punished not the prostitute, but her male beneficiaries, the traffickers in women's bodies. Her letter called up her long association with international feminism:

> Present legislation thus implements the opinion of highly qualified investigations carried out by the League of Nations and the United Nations and already expressed in an important United Nations Convention. These all totally condemn legalised brothels and the regulation of prostitution. To ignore their findings would not be modern rationality, but a return to the very worst of old-fashioned and wholly discredited notions.[12]

To veterans of the women's movement such as Ellinor Walker, feminism in its modern 'liberated' guise seemed dangerously misguided. Yet most Women's Liberationists were blithely ignorant of the fact that feminists like Walker and the international feminism of which she spoke had ever existed. We could not have known that Marguerite Dale, Australia's first woman delegate to the League of Nations (and the first woman to be appointed from any of the Dominions), served as a member of its

Traffic in Women committee—an appointment described rather optimistically by Bessie Rischbieth, president of the Australian Federation of Women Voters, which had nominated Dale, as 'an epoch-making event in the annals of the women's movement'.[13] Marguerite Dale was also a feminist playwright, who, in her play *The Mainstay* penned the memorable line: 'You have only to scratch the feminist to find the female underneath'.[14]

CORRECTING COMMON MISCONCEPTIONS

University courses in the 1970s were silent about Australian feminism's long past and continuing present (and they still are for the most part). But a little learning quickly produced several new misconceptions:

1. that there have been but two waves of feminism with a long lull in between
2. that although Australian feminists were among the first in the world to achieve basic political rights they didn't do anything with the vote
3. that Australian feminists failed politically because they largely failed to win election to parliament
4. that Australian feminists were only concerned to advance the interests of white, middle class, career women

One of the aims of this book is to correct these popular misconceptions. For the moment I shall address each briefly in turn.

Have there been just two waves of feminism with a long lull in between?

Contrary to the popular idea that the women's movement languished with the achievement of the vote, feminism in Australia flourished in the interwar years, decades that, in many ways, could be characterised as the golden age of the woman citizen. Older organisations, such as the National Council of Women and the Woman's Christian Temperance Union, were joined by new feminist groups self-consciously aimed at promoting women's status as citizens: the Women's Service Guild in Western Australia (1909); the Women's Non-Party Association in South Australia (1909); the Victorian Women Citizens' Movement

(1922); the Feminist Club (1914) and the United Associations (of Women) in New South Wales (1929); the Women's Non-Party Political League in Tasmania (1909); and the federal body, the Australian Federation of Women Voters (1921), to which the State groups were affiliated.

It was a period of mass mobilisations. So, for example, when in 1923 a conference was organised by the National Council of Women in the then federal capital of Melbourne to defend the 5 pounds Maternity Allowance from a cost-cutting federal government, hundreds of women from all classes and parties travelled there from around the country, non-party feminists joining women from the Labor party to press (successfully) for retention of the allowance as the mother-citizen's basic right. Feminists were also active in the 1930s, forced, in the context of escalating attacks on female employment, to defend women's right to work. Muriel Heagney, under the auspices of Open Door International, wrote *Are Women Taking Men's Jobs?* and was instrumental in establishing the Council of Action for Equal Pay. When the New South Wales government passed legislation banning married women from work as teachers and lecturers, concerted feminist resistance finally succeeded in having the legislation repealed.

In the 1940s, feminist intervention was effective in having the new child endowment paid to mothers rather than fathers and in having workers taxed as individuals rather than as couples. The first Women's Charter conference in 1943, organised by Jessie Street as president of the United Associations to plan for a post-war order based on justice and equality between the sexes, was attended by delegates from ninety-five women's organisations. During the 1950s and into the early 1960s, feminists continued to lobby with considerable success for key reforms—for the right to sit on juries, for an end to the marriage bar in the Commonwealth public service and for equal pay (achieved by New South Wales teachers in 1958). Even as the tide went out, waves continued to roll in, but the more narrowly feminism focussed on public life, the less it seemed to speak to the mass of young women.

From the mid-1960s, new connections were made with rebellious university students. In 1965, in a much-publicised protest, Merle Thornton and Ro Bognor chained themselves to a foot-rail in the Regatta Hotel in Brisbane in support of their demand for the right to drink in the public bar with their male university colleagues. In 1969, Zelda D'Aprano, an older working-class woman from a migrant background, also invoked the English tradition of suffragette militancy, by chaining herself to the Commonwealth Building in Melbourne to protest against women's lesser pay rates. In *The Female Eunuch*, Germaine Greer, who had left Australia to study in England in 1964, urged her contemporaries to cast off the sexual passivity of the castrate, 'to embrace and stimulate the penis instead of *taking* it'.[15] These rude, unruly protests, with their assertions of women's sexual, drinking and economic rights, represented a sharp break in style with a feminist tradition that had been closely allied with the temperance movement and had cultivated the respectability expected of exemplary citizens. It was thus bizarrely appropriate when Ellinor Walker, invited in 1973 to address a Women's Studies seminar at Flinders University on the history of suffrage, decided to go dressed in period costume, styling herself, as she was no doubt seen, as a relic from a long-gone age.

Did women really do nothing with the vote?

To the contrary, they were active and effective citizens. Post-suffrage feminists articulated the idea of Australia as a welfare state and did much to bring it into being. They envisaged an ethical state, one that would service human needs rather than maximise profit. 'The Country whose chief ambition is the Almighty Dollar', said Rose Scott, 'is the meanest country on Earth'.[16] In 1921, the feminist temperance campaigner and motoring enthusiast Ada Bromham stood as the 'Social Welfare' candidate in the 1921 Western Australian elections, the election in which Edith Cowan, endorsed by the Nationalist party, became the first Australian woman to win parliamentary office. Although on different political tickets, Bromham and Cowan shared a commitment to putting human welfare, especially maternal and infant welfare, first. At her opening campaign address, Bromham's banner proclaimed: 'Women will help to create protective legislation for the factory, the home, and as between nation and nation'.[17]

Like other Australian political progressives, feminists looked to the state to play a key role in bringing about conditions of freedom and equality between citizens. Feminists well knew that if women were to participate as equals in paid work and public life, then the state would have to assume responsibility for much of the caring work traditionally done by women. They knew, too, that if women were to go freely into the public world of men, then the state would need to protect them from men's violence, just as they needed to be freed from it in their homes. While working to enhance women's independence, feminists thus also addressed the realities of human interdependence: the dependence of the old, the young, the sick and the frail on the care of others. Hence their advocacy of motherhood endowment, to provide mothers with economic independence while they cared for their children. Feminists were not successful in achieving this particular aim —no group of men, neither trade unionists, nor government nor the labour movement could countenance such a challenge to the authority of husbands.

Post-suffrage feminists' major political achievement was to create a maternalist welfare state—with an array of infant and maternal welfare centres, women's hospitals, children's courts, maternity benefits and eventually child endowment. They won restrictions on the availability of alcohol which they considered vital to securing women's wellbeing in the home, they raised the age of consent and they were active on film censorship boards. They also secured the appointment of women to a range of protective positions in the state bureaucracies, so that women and girls need never fall into men's hands. Women were appointed for the first time as police, doctors, lawyers, factory inspectors, magistrates, Justices of the Peace, gaol matrons, welfare workers—not as a matter of equal job opportunities, but to promote the welfare and security of girls and women. The fact that earlier generations of feminists worked for reforms in 'frameworks now thought unprogressive', as historian Jill Roe has noted, seems to have made it more difficult for feminists today to recognise their political achievements.[18]

Is women's political history a history of failure?

Of course not. Because post-suffrage feminists hardly featured in the masculine domain of parliamentary politics until recent years, it is commonly concluded that their political history is a history of failure. But such a view tells us more about current preoccupations with party political representation than it does about the aims of women at the time and their ideas about the purpose and nature of political power. Feminist organisations believed that women shared particular experiences and responsibilities that required separate political representation. They concentrated on the distinctiveness of being women, emphasising their condition as mothers, as prostitutes, as economic dependants, as the bearers of unwanted children, as unpaid domestic drudges. They demanded recognition of the sanctity of their bodies in, for example, age of consent legislation, the principle of voluntary motherhood, opposition to the compulsory testing of prostitutes and the demand for harsher penalties for white men sexually abusing Aboriginal women.

To achieve their distinctive political program, post-suffrage feminists developed their own mode of doing politics, eschewing for the most part the traditional male-dominated political parties in favour of mobilising women at the grass roots level. Post-suffrage feminists saw the whole *raison d'être* of their enfranchisement as the development of their own policies and perspectives. Believing that they should operate as a new and independent force in politics, they were determined advocates of non-party politics. As Rose Scott observed, more than once, the whole point of the vote was 'to bring a new element into Political Life. Not to accentuate the quarrels of men'.[19] Women, she said, should not become men's 'catspaws in politics', sentiments echoed by Vida Goldstein in Victoria, who stood on five occasions as an independent feminist candidate for the Senate. But women's aspirations to independent representation were no match for the strength of the two main parties. The non-party approach was more effective in shaping policy than in producing politicians.

To maximise the effectiveness of the collective resource of the vote, post-suffrage feminists' most characteristic political activity was to circulate candidates of all parties at election time to win their support for feminist policies. Nowhere was 1970s feminism's ignorance of the work of its predecessors more evident than in the assumption of the Women's Electoral Lobby that its now legendary 1972 canvassing of federal election candidates was unprecedented, in Australia at least. Australian feminist organisations had, in fact, been sending questionnaires to election candidates in Australia since the granting of suffrage at the beginning of the century. This was a key mode of doing politics for a political movement that determined to remain independent of the established parties, deciding on its own platform and priorities and placing its demands on the political agendas of all parties. Women's political power was thought to reside in the wise and collective use of the ballot, not in the advancement of individual aspirants to office. Post-suffrage feminists recognised that a strong and independent women's movement was always necessary to achieve real reform.

Were feminists only interested in white, Anglo, career women?

No. In fact, the maternalist orientation of the women's movement between the wars led feminists to champion the rights of Aboriginal women—and these feminists were the first organised political group to oppose the removal of Aboriginal children from their mothers, to criticise what Mary Bennett called 'the official smashing of family life' in Aboriginal communities. Feminist agitation on the international stage, with charges that Australian governments were condoning the slavery of Aboriginal people, led to the appointment of a Royal Commission in Western Australia at which a number of representatives of the Women's Service Guild, in conjunction with Aboriginal women, gave evidence. 'Under the law', Ada Bromham told the Commission, 'the mother has no rights over the child'.[20] Aboriginal women, feminists argued, had rights as individuals and as mothers. Bennett and Bromham, as well as Edith Jones (the second president of the Victorian Women Citizens' Movement), Constance Cooke (a South Australian feminist), and others lobbied in Australia and overseas for recognition of Aboriginal citizen rights, for the return of land, for education, for an end to the sexual abuse of Aboriginal women.

The Australian Women's Charter drawn up during World War II contained twenty-six recommendations addressing the oppressed condition of 'Aboriginal and coloured people'. Its principal author, Jessie Street, was an Australian delegate to the founding conference of the United Nations, and subsequently served as vice-president of the Commission on the Status of Women. In Australia, in the late 1940s, she became a key exponent of the Universal Declaration of Human Rights' emphasis on the principle of non-discrimination. In exile overseas during the Cold War in the early 1950s, she worked with the Anti-Slavery Society to bring the condition of Aboriginal people to the attention of the United Nations—although she was unable to attend the General Assembly, having been denied a visa by the United States government who deemed her a Communist sympathiser. On her return to Australia, she joined with Faith Bandler and Pearl Gibbs, who had, in 1956, formed the Aboriginal–Australian Fellowship in Sydney, Shirley Andrews in Victoria, Ada Bromham in Queensland and other women and men to press for a referendum on Aboriginal citizenship.

The concerns of 1970s Women's Liberation however—with its emphasis on sexism, sex roles and sexual rights—were less in tune with the needs of Aboriginal women, who pointed to what Pat O'Shane called the irrelevance of 'the white women's movement' to those who suffered most acutely from racism. Many migrant women shared this view. Although Women's Liberationists secured government support for bodies such as the Working Women's Centre, which strove to meet the specific needs of migrant women at the workplace, and International Women's Year funded initiatives such as the Migrant Women's Centre, many women of non-English-speaking background saw the women's movement as exclusionary, concerned only with the advancement of Anglo women. Aboriginal and migrant women often established their own services and organisations, working with and within their communities.

Clearly, feminism has its limits as a politics of emancipation, and white Anglo women have had to come to terms with the fact that their priorities are not always or often shared by migrant women, who might speak languages other than English, abide by different cultural and religious values and are often discriminated against on the basis of their appearance. Indigenous women, too, might find other issues more pressing: for example, land rights and the reconstitution of family, culture, languages and community life. For many Asian women in Australia, racism—not sexism—constitutes the most daily and searing oppression. White feminists have had to acknowledge the privilege of our whiteness and our advantage, along with that of non-Aboriginal men, as the beneficiaries of Aboriginal dispossession. We have had to come to terms with the fact that feminism might not be the most appropriate or urgent politics for all women; that feminism is, in the words of Australian post-colonial theorist Ien Ang, a 'limited political home'. For different oppressions are differences not necessarily of degree, but of kind.

FEMINISM AS A POLITICAL ACHIEVEMENT

Given the differences between women, the wonder is, perhaps, that the women's movement achieved such coherence and effectiveness over such a long period of time, building a mass politics that succeeded in winning so many political, civil, economic and social reforms. These reforms include political rights; mothers' custody rights; age of consent legislation; infant and maternal welfare centres; women's hospitals; maternity benefits; the appointment of women JPs, police and magistrates; the appointment of women to juries; the criminalisation of rape in marriage; government-subsidised child care centres; the establishment of female refuges and rape crisis centres; the supporting parent's benefit; equal pay; and affirmative action programs. For, despite what post-suffrage activists liked to believe, women are not a natural political constituency. Feminism is a politics, not an effect of biology.

The feminist movement itself should thus be seen as a major political achievement, its ideas, its mode of doing politics and outcomes constituting an important part of Australian political history. Its distinctive insights and analyses—elaborated in its own newspapers, journals, plays, films, radio broadcasts and books—comprise an important, if usually overlooked, strand of Australian political thought. In presenting a history of feminism in Australia over a period of more than one hundred years, this book is a study in political history, an analysis of the political movements brought into being by the demand for sexual equality and an end to women's oppression. In documenting the richness and complexity of what has gone before, my hope is that we might be more clear-sighted about what remains to be done, so no woman will suffer the series of abuses that women such as Heather Osland have suffered.

PART I
WOMEN IN A NEW WORLD

1
THE POWER OF THE BALLOT

RAISING THE WOMAN QUESTION IN THE AUSTRALIAN COLONIES

When the Woman Movement as it was called, emerged in the late nineteenth century as a major political force in the Australian colonies, it was the condition of married women that most captured its imagination. No Australian woman enjoyed basic political rights, but married women were subjected to particular tyrannies. Denied the right to own property and the right to custody of their children, married women were also denied sovereignty over their bodies. Marriage involved an exchange: men enjoyed conjugal rights of sexual access to their wives in return for which women were promised maintenance. In the late nineteenth century Australian families often included large numbers of children (in the 1870s women bore an average of seven children), and this effectively increased wives' dependence on their husbands or left them poverty-stricken if they were deserted, which was commonly the case. Repeated childbearing also left thousands of women with debilitating injuries or in permanent ill health.

If a husband were improvident, unreliable, violent or a drunk, then women and children suffered. In the early 1890s, Sydney's only Female Refuge admitted 1169 women and 691 children in just one month. If women remained or returned home, they were subject to men's sexual demands, which, according to Louisa Lawson, turned many a bedroom into a Chamber of Horrors:

> A nerve of iron truly must be possessed by frail women, who are expected to endure nightly this horrid ordeal, and put a cheerful

face upon it in the morning, well knowing that this is her fate so long as her power of endurance holds out. How often does the patient wife quietly steal from the Chamber of Horrors to seek shelter by the bed of her sleeping children, content if but allowed to sit in peace until day brings temporary respite.[1]

If husbands wandered, they might bring venereal disease back to the marriage bed. Women began to demand self-possession. They wanted to be able to live freely and independently, while attending to their responsibilities as mothers. The degradation of wives and the burden of mothers became major preoccupations of feminists such as Louisa Lawson and Rose Scott, who sought a wide range of reforms to give married women property, custody and inheritance rights and to protect little children.

Louisa Lawson, one of the early leaders of the movement in New South Wales, opened club rooms for women in Sydney, where they might meet and talk about their problems. She later recalled: 'That was when I saw the best side of women—the weary, sad-eyed things who used to come in and tell tales of violent husbands and dreary homes. I dreamed always that I would fight and struggle and better things for women'.[2] Lawson also established a journal, the *Dawn*, (also the title of the journal founded by the Women's Service Guild in Western Australia in 1920) and began to campaign publicly for women's rights, especially the right to vote, because in the ballot lay the power to change relations between men and women and ultimately to create a better world.

In an address in 1891, recorded in her papers as the 'first public speech' made in connection with womanhood suffrage in New South Wales, Lawson declared: 'If we are responsible for our children give us the power and sacredness of the ballot, and we will lift ourselves and our brothers to a higher civilisation'.[3] Like many in the Woman Movement, Lawson justified her political demands by referring to the responsibilities of motherhood; and she identified the aim as a higher civilisation. The Woman Movement placed itself self-consciously in the vanguard of the mission to establish white civilisation in Australia. Feminists' identity as British, civilised and white provided the crucial underpinnings for their assumed rights as reformers. Their status as white women gave them their authority to speak, and for good and ill feminists assumed that they spoke for all women. Feminism was and is a politics of representation.

Louisa Lawson was a member of the group that established the Womanhood Suffrage League in Sydney, in 1891, to secure the franchise for women upon the same conditions as those that applied to men. Its motto was 'Equality is Equity'. Other founding members included Dora Montefiore, Rose Scott and Maybanke Wolstenholme. Three years earlier, Lawson had established the *Dawn*, a self-declared journal for Australian women, 'their journal and mouthpiece'. Designed as a paper in which women could 'express their opinions on political and social questions which [involved] their interest', the journal was allied to the Dawn Club, established in 1889 to aid 'the social advancement and industrial independence of women'.[4] Earlier, in 1887, Lawson had founded the short-lived *Republican* to argue the case for Australian independence from Britain. 'The hour of manhood is at hand',[5] declared the first editorial, but already it was the Woman Question that had captured Louisa Lawson's imagination.

Like many Australian suffragists Lawson was an ardent nationalist, committed to the project of building a new society in the New World—which as 'pioneers', they assumed to be rightfully theirs. She had been born in Mudgee, New South Wales in 1848, the second of twelve children, educated at a national school but later forced to stay at home to care for her siblings. Her father was a station hand. She married a gold miner turned selector, but ultimately she left her husband and moved with her children to Sydney, where she became involved in movements for political and social reform. During the 1880s she wrote a good deal of nationalist verse, penning poems such as 'Australia', 'Australia Felix', 'Sweet Australia' and 'An Australian Song', whose words spoke the pride and defiance of the colonial:

> And we can render scorn for scorn,
> And laugh at all the sneers,
> While in our veins there runs the blood
> Of Austral's pioneers.
>
> *Chorus*
> For we hail from a land that is great and grand,
> And the pride of the Southern Sea;
> 'Tis a sunny land, 'tis a golden land,
> And the home of the brave and the free.[6]

Australia was a land of promise for the pioneers, and although political radicals such as Lawson were sympathetic to the oppressed condition of Aboriginal people, they could not acknowledge that their own national home-making required the removal of the original owners and the destruction of their culture.

As a feminist, Lawson wanted (white) women's contribution to nation-making recognised. In her poem 'The Women of the Bush' she wrote:

> Ah how I bless the pioneers
> The women lost to fame,
> Who braved the bush for strenuous years
> To make Australia's name.[7]

The problem was that the achievements of 'the pioneers' rested on the removal of people already here; 'the pioneers' were also the agents of the dispossession that had left Aborigines suppliants in their own land. Lawson urged her readers to identify with the plight of Aboriginal women, who were 'wives and mothers like ourselves'. White women should show 'consideration and kindness' by 'sympathising in their troubles, alleviating as far as possible, their hardships, and honouring their womanhood as we honour our own'.[8] She nevertheless consoled herself with the evolutionary conceit that Aborigines were but 'poor remnants of a dying race'. Lawson was thus able to assert solidarity with Aboriginal women, while absolving herself and her people of responsibility for their condition.

The conceptualisation of women as a group in the late nineteenth century was, in part, the product of their collective exclusion from political life. Leaders of the Woman Movement also argued, however, that their sex had a distinctive perspective based on shared experiences and interests (as mothers, as creatures of sex, as domestic drudges) which necessitated political representation. In the pages of the *Dawn*, arguments were advanced for womanhood suffrage, dress and diet reform, temperance, the appointment of women to public office and woman's right to paid work.

A new ideal of woman was promoted: she would be strong, healthy, practical, self-sufficient and independent. The *Dawn* argued for the importance of sensible clothes and a nutritious diet: the 'world would be none the worse for a robuster, healthier, stronger type of woman'. Corsets were denounced for their injurious effects: 'We laugh at the Chinese women with their poor useless bandaged feet, and all the while we are tying up ourselves and laming much more important organs than feet, viz, lungs'.[9] Lawson exemplified the ideal of independence in her own life, having left her husband in western New South Wales to move to Sydney, where she initially supported herself and her children by washing and sewing clothes and taking in boarders. By the late 1880s, her foray into publishing and printing was proving a commercial success, despite ongoing harassment from the male Typographical Association.

The *Dawn* published testimonials from like-minded women in other colonies. Henrietta Dugdale wrote from Camberwell, in Victoria, of her elation at having been freed, at age eighteen, from her corset, that 'vile instrument of torture'. Fifty years later she was strong and independent:

> I run and swim with thorough pleasure . . . I do a great amount of garden work, nearly all that is needed in the house and generally walk 2 or 3 miles daily, sometimes double that distance . . .[10]

Henrietta Dugdale, a twice-married secularist, had long been interested in the Woman Question. A member of both the Australian Secular Association and the Eclectics (formed to discuss controversial subjects), she published her Utopian novel *A Few Hours in a Far Off Age* in 1883, in which she imagined free, strong and unconstrained women joined with men in companionate marriages. In this future woman-friendly society—brought into being by women's enfranchisement—war, drunkenness and prostitution were unknown.

The following year, 57-year-old Dugdale joined forces with Annie Lowe and others to form the Victorian Women's Suffrage Society: until that time, she later claimed, she had been the only woman in Victoria to publicly advocate the right of woman to her share in political power. In the 1880s, Melbourne was prosperous and lively, the largest city in Australia, supporting a cosmopolitan intellectual community of writers and reformers. But it also sustained a culture of sexual violence, and it was the failure of public authorities to adequately protect women from such assaults that was one of the precipitating factors in the formation of the Victorian Women's Suffrage Society. 'The laws for offences against property were very severe, but for brutal offences against women they were not', the fifty women and twenty men who attended the first public meeting were told.[11] Or as Louisa Lawson observed matter-of-factly in her first public speech: 'Here in Australia it is considered more a crime to steal a horse than ruin a girl'.[12]

As in the other colonies, suffragists in Victoria were joined in their campaigns for women's rights by the Woman's Christian Temperance Union (WCTU), which had been formed in Victoria in 1885 and expanded into fifty-seven branches by 1891, the year in which Victorian women secured a major victory with amendments to the Crimes Act, which raised the age of consent from twelve to sixteen years and defined incest, for the first time, as a criminal offence. The WCTU attracted large numbers of adherents in the Australian colonies, women determined to take seriously their role as guardians of the home, to protect themselves and their children from the harms associated with excessive alcohol consumption—violence, sexual abuse and poverty. The decentralised, grass roots basis of WCTU organising provided a valuable resource for the Woman Movement, evident in the thousands of signatures gathered for the 'monster petitions' collected to demonstrate women's desire for the vote, to give the lie to those who charged that the mass of women were not interested in their rights.

In Melbourne, 22-year-old Vida Goldstein was one of the canvassers for the petition of 1891, when 30 000 signatures were collected. In its scale and the way it captured the public imagination, it was an event that prefigured the massive Women's Electoral Lobby survey of political candidates carried out some eighty years later in 1972. Goldstein claimed that it was the largest petition ever presented to the Victorian parliament and that 'tremendous interest was aroused when the bulky document was carried by several attendants into the Legislative Chamber'. She praised the industry of the canvassers, as they walked from door to door with paper and pencil, in city and suburbs, ever ready to engage in political debate. But, she claimed, there was little opposition: 'Wherever the workers went they found the great majority of women in favour of the vote, and of being on a footing of equality with men in every respect'.[13] The petition did not achieve its immediate aim, however, and indeed its very size and the connection so graphically drawn between suffrage and temperance might well have consolidated the political opposition to women's suffrage in Victoria, where activists were forced to wage the longest campaign of all.

In South Australia, meanwhile, Mary Lee, a devout Christian and member of the Ladies' Social Purity Society, was the third speaker at a meeting held in 1888 to form the Women's Suffrage League in that colony. Lee, a widow and a mother of seven children, had only recently migrated from Ireland; when she embarked on her South Australian career as a proselytiser for women's rights she was sixty-four years old. Women in South Australia, she ventured, simply asked for the 'modicum of power' necessary to secure the rights of women. Like members of the Woman Movement in other colonies, Mary Lee saw the right to be free from unwanted sexual advances as central to women's rights more generally and, as with many fellow activists, her first public campaign had been to lobby to have the age of consent raised to sixteen years, a reform achieved in South Australia in 1885.

A keen advocate also of workers' rights, Lee drew a connection between women's sexual exploitation and their sweated working conditions. She became secretary of the Working Women's Trade Union, established in 1890 to improve working conditions in the clothing industry. In her work towards women's enfranchisement, Lee was joined by members of the WCTU, local branches having been established in Adelaide by United States 'world missionary' Mary Leavitt in 1886.

The American headquarters of the WCTU despatched a second ambassador to the Australian colonies in 1892. Jessie Ackerman was a dynamic speaker and organiser whose tour included the newly settled areas of Western Australia, where she founded six new branches of the WCTU and organised the first Colonial Convention. In a deputation to the Premier of that colony newly prosperous from the discovery of gold, members presented a petition asking that the moral welfare of the country be given the same consideration as its material welfare. From the beginning, a suffrage department was established within the WCTU to lobby for votes for women, for the political power necessary to secure their major goal of 'the protection of the home'. During 1894, members gathered so many signatures for their women's suffrage petition that they needed a mile (1.6 km) of cloth to contain them.

Their campaign was bolstered by proselytising visits from Elizabeth Nicholls, a leader of the WCTU in South Australia, and by the growing perception that the influx of men to the 'eastern goldfields' in the 1890s posed particular problems for the raw, new colony. Women—white, British, Christian women—were necessary to refine and civilise Western Australia and to check masculine extravagance. In June 1898, Ada Throssell, secretary of the Northam branch of the WCTU, wrote to the Premier, Sir John Forrest, to persuade him of the political wisdom of introducing women's enfranchisement in 'our common country':

> I am sure you have recognised that there are special reasons existing in this colony that render the concession of the franchise to women of the utmost importance to stable government. I need only mention the fact of the great disparity between the sexes: to show that the addition of women to the electoral roll would go far to minimise the extravagant demands likely to result from a large unsettled male population possessed of political powers.

... It seems passing strange that while a woman is thought fit to rule an empire; she should be denied a vote in a democratic country. A ready affirmative to women's request would, I earnestly believe, be a most tactful act at this particular juncture in our history.[14]

Talk began to spread around Perth of women's plans, and Mrs G. O. Ferguson, president of the WCTU, hastened to reassure the Premier that women would do nothing untoward: 'we really don't mean to agitate only we mean to get the vote'.[15]

In Queensland, too, the WCTU was the major force behind the campaign for women's suffrage in the 1890s. A male-dominated frontier colony like Western Australia, Queensland had an economy based on pastoral and mining industries employing a largely itinerant population of male workers. Press publicity accorded cases of sexual violence, such as the brutal rape of Jane King by Charles Muller in Maryborough in 1887, suggested that women and girls were in need of special protection: the short-lived Queensland Women's Suffrage League, formed in 1889, had as a major goal the raising of the age of consent, which was achieved in 1891. By then, the local WCTU had grown to include seventeen branches, most of which became active in the pursuit of women's political rights as well as in the campaign to abolish alcohol consumption. As in Western Australia, the masculine frontier culture of Queensland was perceived as dangerous and threatening to women, whose sense of vulnerability rendered them responsive to the WCTU's emphasis on home protection, to what American historian of the WCTU Suzanne M. Marilley has called the 'feminism of fear'.[16] Agnes Williams, the colonial vice-president of the WCTU in Queensland and wife of a clergyman, was a leading campaigner, noted as 'perhaps the best-known speaker in the State'.[17] The temperance women were joined in their campaign for political rights by other activists, such as Leontine Cooper and Emma Miller, both associated with the emergent Labor party. The early development of the Labor party in Queensland meant that the suffrage struggle there was quickly entangled with party politics, much to the consternation of fiercely non-party feminists such as Rose Scott from New South Wales, who undertook a speaking tour of the northern State in 1903 to impress on enfranchised women the necessity of steering clear of men's parties and platforms.

In Tasmania, too, the WCTU was resuscitated by the visit of the dynamic Jessie Ackerman in 1892, when over twenty new branches were formed. The organisation encouraged women to take up public questions, insisting that it was their Christian duty to work in the public domain for social reform ('none has the right to be a modest violet').[18] The demand for women's suffrage was a logical consequence of this commitment. In 1894, Ethel Searle read a paper advocating political rights for women at the State conference of the WCTU and in 1896, following rejection of suffrage legislation by the Legislative Council, she helped organise petitions to parliament signed by 2273 'female residents of Tasmania'.[19] At the same time, ladies' literary societies were also debating the merits of women's suffrage; but when Ida McAulay (the rifle-shooting wife of the professor of Mathematics at the University of Tasmania) spoke in favour of women's suffrage in 1899 on behalf of the Itinerant Society, she noted with concern that she was the only member to champion this cause so dear to her heart. It was selfish, she claimed, for privileged women to ignore the plight of their 'less fortunate sisters' and as for the fear that the franchise would take women out of their sphere: 'I believe that a woman's sphere is just what she chooses to make it'. When the Tasmanian parliament granted women the vote in 1903, McAulay referred with feeling to 'our long struggle for political freedom extending over more than twenty years'.[20]

Women's suffrage was achieved on a colony by colony basis: South Australia led the way in 1894, Western Australia followed in 1899. New South Wales granted women the vote in 1902, Tasmania in 1903, Queensland in 1904 and Victoria, finally, in 1908. The federal franchise was extended to all white women in 1902, on the principle that as women in South Australia and Western Australia could already vote on a State basis, federation should not prevent them from voting in federal elections. And if women in those States could vote at federal elections, then consistency demanded women in other States be granted the same rights. The inclusion of the appropriate clause in the federal Constitution was claimed as an achievement by the suffragists who presented a petition incorporating this demand to the 1897 Federal Convention in Adelaide.

The federal politicians who extended the federal suffrage to women in 1902 specifically denied it to Aboriginal Australians (and other non-whites) in those States where they had not previously been eligible to vote; namely Queensland and Western Australia, where most Aborigines happened to live. Racist sentiment among the founding fathers of the new parliament of White Australia ensured the exclusion of the majority of Aboriginal Australians from political rights and recognition as citizens.

In the colonies of New South Wales, South Australia and Victoria, however, Aboriginal men had been formally entitled to vote on the same grounds as other men. That was as it should be, according to Rose Scott, who in her 'Reply to Miss [Edith] Badham' in 1895 defended the enfranchisement of Aboriginal Australians because:

> they are human beings with an interest in their country and its laws and on this same principle is there any logical reason for depriving the women of the country of the same privilege?
> . . . the accident of Race or Color cannot interfere with the Principle involved in one man one vote and the right of the people to govern themselves.

According to Scott, self-government was a basic human right; 'the sex of a human being [was] like Race or Color a secondary matter'.[21]

DEFINING THE WOMAN'S MISSION IN POLITICS

Although suffragists such as Scott, who with Louisa Lawson was a founding member of the Womanhood Suffrage League in 1891, argued that women were entitled to the vote because they were human beings like men, they also assumed that their enfranchisement would bring new values into social and political life, because of their different social position and experience. Winning the vote was not just a matter of abstract justice, but was necessary to the building of a better society. Whereas fathers taught their sons how to fight and defend themselves, mothers taught them to cultivate their affections and practise generosity. This balance of values was also needed in public life, as Scott explained:

> I can imagine no more effectual way of raising the tone of Public Opinion, of purifying its moral sentiments, than by imparting into Public life the woman's influence and something of that tenderness, refinement and Purity for which women are especially noted.[22]

Although a childless spinster all her life, Scott, like other women of her generation, spent many years taking care of relatives (especially her mother and nephew), and she assumed that women as a group shared such capacities and commitments. Caring for people was a noble occupation; it was women's degrading dependence on men, their relegation to the 'House of Bondage', that was the problem.

Born into a large family on the rural property of 'Glendon' near Singleton in New South Wales in 1847, Scott inherited at the age of thirty-two a sum sufficient to provide an independent income, a home in Sydney and freedom from the need to marry. She also inherited the care of her mother and nephew, which provided ongoing responsibilities that would shape her political philosophy about the primary duty of love. Scott's brand of feminism could not encompass self-advancement at the expense of others, so when Ibsen's shockingly modern play *A Doll's House* was staged in Sydney in 1890, she declined to applaud Nora walking out on her home and family. Scott was impressed by Ibsen's attempt to sympathise with the condition of women, but deplored his suggestion that Nora had to save herself by forsaking her children:

> Ah Nora, Nora, it was at this point you failed, it is noble to be oneself but a self without sympathy for the views of others or their grief and misery what sort of self is that? To forsake her children in order to learn her duties to them and to be a better mother to them was a mistake . . . How much do we hear nowadays of women's and men's rights? Real progress is not the acquisition of more rights but the better performance of duties.[23]

Selfishness was, for Scott, the worst of moral and political failings, selfishness as displayed in Drink, Gambling and Immorality and expressed in party political government. It was this masculine culture that would be combated by the enfranchisement of the 'national motherhood of women'. Arguing against the federation of the colonies (because it would remove power to 'a faraway national parliament' beyond the reach of women), Scott proposed instead a federation of men and women:

> Then and then only will you temper the selfish spirit of anarchy and violence that is growing up in this country . . . Then and then only will you bring about a Socialism of Love and Unselfishness men and women together doing what now they can never do apart . . .[24]

Scott brought into being her vision of men and women conferring on all things when she turned her home into a 'salon' to which she invited a range of influential and informative people: politicians, writers, artists, academics, public servants, judges, lawyers and businessmen. The exercise of personal influence was Scott's preferred mode of doing politics and she was deeply hostile to the professionalisation of politics in parties. As Judith Allen has pointed out in her biography of Scott, her Friday night 'salons' became the stuff of legend, with participants recalling that 'the great questions of the day were debated there and that the course of politics, social reform and social mores were shaped by the deliberations transpiring in Scott's "salon"'. Allen elaborates:

> Issues debated there included free trade versus protection, industrial legislation, socialism, taxation, Utopianism, nationalism and republicanism, capital punishment, public charities and their administration, temperance, Australian literature and literary criticism, Australian art and exhibitions and urban social problems including slums, contagious diseases, prostitution, illegitimacy and juvenile delinquency.[25]

The most important issue for Scott was women's sexual degradation at the hands of men, whether the woman be married or unmarried, wife or prostitute. Prostitution was symbolic of women's condition as sex slaves, yet it seemed to be of little interest to socialists interested in other forms of exploitation. 'Oh how many would be reformers strain at a gnat and swallow a camel! To them the sweating system that injures a poor woman's body seems more terrible than the system which directly destroys her self-respect . . .'. Men divided women into good and bad to suit themselves. Purity was but 'a garment in which women should be clothed or otherwise as suits man's pleasure or otherwise'. It was left to women to attend to 'our common womanhood' and lead their fallen sisters 'out of the Land of Impurity, the House of Bondage'. Certainly 'bad women' would vote if women were enfranchised, but they were no worse than the men whose demand for degradation created its supply. Men must learn respect for women, who would be permitted in turn to acquire self-respect: 'Man should no longer be as he too often is the sole aim and object of woman's existence!'[26]

Scott and other suffragists believed that women should become independent of men. Enfranchisement meant self-government, politically and symbolically. Freedom was the oft-stated goal, a freedom defined in opposition to slavery. 'Woman has been a slave too long', wrote Scott in a paper outlining 'Why women want the vote'. 'She has belonged to her parents, and belonged to her husband and now at length she demands that she should belong to herself! And that she should have the Freedom to choose her own duties in the world and not have them chosen for her!'[27] As Louisa Lawson wrote in the *Dawn*, in 1890, women owed it to themselves and their children to demand their liberty:

> To claim the full rights and privileges of thinking, self-respecting, free human souls is to undermine a thousand wrongs and humiliations, to render themselves the more beloved for their apparent audacity and to, at the same time, secure the best conditions for their children.[28]

Women needed the vote, Scott and Lawson agreed, to better defend themselves and their children. They also needed it to effectively reform men.

REFORMING MASCULINITY

In the eyes of the nineteenth century Woman Movement, Australian masculinity was a problem. In order for women to become autonomous and self-determining, men would need to change their ideas about what it was to be a man; they would have to become more like ideal women—chaste, pure, loving, selfless, temperate, restrained, companionate. This was the radical vision of equality promulgated by nineteenth century feminists.

Australian frontier conditions had encouraged a certain style of masculinity which was deleterious to women and children, and not just in Queensland or Western Australia. Australian nationalist culture celebrated a particular model of manhood—eulogising in print and paintings the Lone Hand, the mobile, independent, seasonal worker, freed from the trammels of domesticity. His unencumbered lifestyle enabled him to indulge in distinctive leisure pursuits—casual sex, gambling, smoking and drinking deep. This model of manhood was influential in urban Australia, too. In Sydney, both Rose Scott and Louisa Lawson deplored the fact that boys were taught by 'public opinion' that it was manly to know life, to 'drink, to gamble and to be immoral, encouraging immorality in others . . .'.[29] It was regarded as a miracle, said Lawson, should a boy grow to man's estate and escape the contaminations of vice which daily example made familiar: 'To be able to smoke, swear, drink and gamble like a man is the Alpha and Omega of his infantile dreams'.

Women were, of necessity, in the front ranks of the battle against intemperance, gambling and impurity, but were denied 'the only weapon with which to fight'.[30] This vision of the empowered woman combating the male serpents of vice was vividly depicted in a well-known cartoon published in the Sydney *Woman's Suffrage Journal* in 1891, drawn by B. E. Minns, 'artist of this city, who has very kindly given his services for the benefit of the cause'. It showed a distressed mother clutching her baby, her other little ones cowering behind her as the serpents advance from four male figures, representing variously 'Whiskey', 'Seduction', 'Gambling' and 'Cruelty'. The mother is unable to reach the weapon (the ballot) with which she could strike the serpents down, because chained as she is to the 'woman's sphere', it lies beyond her grasp.[31]

Encouraged by the temperance movement, many women attempted individually to persuade men to change their ways—to take the pledge of abstinence—efforts that were regularly mocked in the pages of men's magazines such as the *Bulletin* in Sydney and the *Bull Ant* in Melbourne. A cartoon in the *Bulletin* in 1888, for example, featured one 'Mr Smile' sitting up at a bar, being fed his drink by an obliging barman wielding a spoon. The caption explained: 'Mr Smile often promised his wife he would never raise a drop of liquor to his lips again, but, though he has not broken the promise, the whisky gets there just the same'.[32] By the 1880s, private protests against men's selfish indulgence had merged into public campaigns.

In Melbourne, Bessie Harrison Lee became a popular target for masculine satire, as when she featured in a cartoon on the front page of *Bull Ant* magazine, pictured as a leading spoiler of men's pleasures. Bessie Lee campaigned against Drink. Born in 1860, young Bessie Vickery had been raised by her uncle's family in a small, male-dominated mining community in the isolated country of south east Victoria. Her mother had died when Bessie was eight, but at nineteen she was rescued from her harsh existence in the mining town by an offer of marriage to Harrison Lee, a handsome young railway worker from Melbourne—the city in which the couple would make their home. Bessie Harrison Lee became an energetic worker for the temperance organisation the Victorian Alliance, and president of the Richmond branch of the WCTU. In the course of her temperance activism she became a convert to the cause of women's political rights. In local option polls, held to determine whether a municipality should be 'dry', she quickly realised, any man (the drunkard, the wife beater, the seducer) could cast a vote, but all women were denied it. A vote, she later wrote, meant 'power to express an opinion on the burning question of the day where it would carry weight and do most good'.[33]

In her work with women, Bessie Harrison Lee was struck by the misery and oppression experienced by those forced to bear and rear the large families that were the consequence of men's sexual indulgence. The only solution was for the community to revise its ideas about the nature and purpose of marriage. For her, a truly companionate marriage was one lifted to a higher plane, no longer seen as the vehicle for the gratification of men's lusts. Husbands needed to practise self-restraint and recognise that women had a right to 'voluntary motherhood', interpreted as the right to be free from men's sexual advances. To most in the Woman Movement (Brettena Smyth was a notable exception) the availability of contraceptives only exacerbated the difficulties of marital relations, confirming women's status as degraded creatures of sex.

'The sufferings and patient endurance of numbers of women first forced the matter on me', Bessie Harrison Lee reported in her best-selling book, *Marriage and Heredity*, published in 1893. In visiting women in their homes she had learnt at first hand that men's sexual licence could have deadly consequences for their wives. One woman she encountered was already critically ill:

> Her constitution was utterly undermined with the burden and care of a large small family. By the united skill of doctors and nurses she was brought back from the very brink of the grave; but the doctor warned her husband that her life would pay the forfeit of any indiscretion on his part. Three months later our bitter tears fell on the grave of that gentle woman, who had been as surely murdered as any other victim of man's passion. Had she not been his wife, he would have been arrested for outrage and murder; being his wife, the law could do nothing, and we, who loved her, could only stand helplessly by and mourn the patient victim of degraded marriage.[34]

In its critique of relations between husbands and wives, the nineteenth century Woman Movement posed a radical challenge to men's sexual prerogatives and prevailing ideas about the meaning of marriage. Men could no longer be confident of their 'conjugal rights'.

Bessie Harrison Lee set out the terms of the challenge in a letter to the Melbourne *Herald* on 8 October 1888:

> My advice to those who cannot afford a family is not to have one. Marriage should be a union of souls, a sweet companionship, a mutual help and sympathy; but marriage, as it is, has been degraded to the most unholy gratification of men's worst desires and the result is—little children coming unwished for, and unprovided for, a burden rather than a blessing, wearying alike to the ill-paid father and the overworked mother. A man and a woman before marriage are expected to be pure; let them remain so after marriage, living together in the holiest, best of all unions.[35]

The *Bulletin* was savage in its masculinist response, commenting that the 'well-known champion of "Women's Rights", Mrs Harrison-Lee (with a hyphen) had solemnly painted a frigid picture of polar moonbeam happiness by marriage according to the tenets of the Abelites':

> After reading this letter over one would naturally ask: 'Why marry at all?' Or, why should not women marry each other, the old maid joined in icy wedlock to the other old maid?
>
> . . . We are told that in Heaven there is neither marriage nor giving in marriage. The cynical man will admit that that would be Heaven indeed.[36]

In Melbourne, the *Bull Ant* also reacted to the threat posed to men's liberties by feminist plans for a new social order. When feminists argued that railway workers should not be allowed to drink on the job, the paper commented on the deputation with nervous humour:

> Last week a deputation of 'lovely women' which realises that the staple article of food for men in these parts, is drink with a bite in it and who are fully alive to the fact that man, as aforesaid, possesses a good appetite and is on deck every time the liquor is to be had, waited on the Minister . . . Things in general are pretty bad now, but what life would be like with this class in the ascendant, it isn't good for the mind of man to dwell upon . . .[37]

In its confrontation with the masculinist values of Australian nationalists, feminism was cast as a dangerous threat to men's freedom, but the political contest had broader implications for the emerging nation: masculinists and feminists were engaged in a struggle for control of the national culture. The *Bulletin* held out against womanhood suffrage until 1899.

It was feminists' desire to make men behave more like women that made many politicians prone to prevaricate, as this somewhat droll report of a deputation from the Womanhood Suffrage League to New South Wales Premier George Reid in 1894 suggested:

> The deputation made a long struggle for the last word, during the course of which it was urged that the object of women in asking for the franchise was to reform men. This is just the point he is dubious about. He does not know, in the first place, that he wants any reforming; and anyhow, he would rather look after that business himself. He does not seek by legislation to reform woman; he minds his own business and leaves her to do the same. Under the laws, woman is left at liberty to have her own club, her billiard room, her whiskey bar, or her latchkey, just the same as he is. If she does not avail herself of these things, it is only because her unwritten code forbids them. The question is, how much of this one-sided code does she want to put into print against man for the purpose of 'reforming' him? Would she lead him off from the Scylla of whiskey and tobacco by forcibly running him against the Charybdis of scandal and tea?[38]

Clearly, the prospect of women winning political power was a daunting one for men of the world, but nowhere did the consequences seem more serious than in their own homes.

In their critique of sexual relations between men and women, Australian feminists focussed, in particular, on the vulnerable condition of the wife. Their political agenda was less concerned than that of English feminists with the plight of the single woman; the different demographic situation in Australia, with men outnumbering women, meant that the vast majority of Australian women—including feminists—married at some point in their lives. Marriage was most women's fate: feminists were preoccupied with its tyrannies and humiliations. Although the adverse publicity provoked by Lizzie Ashton's statement that marriage should be abolished—it was 'a failure [and] a lamentable one'—led her to withdraw from the Womanhood Suffrage League Council, her critical attitude was not unusual in her circles.[39]

To many in the Woman Movement, marriage had become a cover for sexual violence. An article in the *Woman's Voice* in 1895 quoted a lady physician to the effect that when young women fell into marriage they suffered what was 'essentially rape . . . husbands quote Paul on the need for obedience of the wife and his "marital rights"'. A WCTU organiser was reported as saying that 'the common prostitute is far freer than the wife who nightly is the victim of the unholy passion of her master, who frequently further inflames his brain by imbibing stimulants'.[40] Louisa Lawson in calling for the passage of the divorce amendment bill in New South Wales in 1892 asked her readers to consider the plight of 'The Drunkard's Wife', who every night faced the prospect of the beast in her bedroom, the unleashing, as Rose Scott put it, of the 'animal in man'.

Economic independence was crucial to their escape from bondage. For middle class women, education became increasingly important as one path to freedom. And teaching and writing both provided valuable sources of income.

WOMEN DESIRE TO BE EDUCATED

In 1914, Maybanke Anderson writing as 'Lois' in the *Sydney Morning Herald* took issue with the continual charge that women had not done anything with the vote. After pointing to numerous social reforms, Lois returned to her main argument that more important than the question of whether women had done anything with the vote was whether the vote had done anything for women, and she concluded: 'the vote is a teacher, and women desire to be educated'.[41] Late nineteenth century feminists were hungry for knowledge and read avidly about the position of women in different parts of the world. They referred to the works of British authors such as John Stuart Mill and Frances Power Cobbe and the Americans Frances Willard and Charlotte Perkins Gilman. The proliferation of feminist journals (*Dawn*, the *Woman's Suffrage Journal*, *Woman's Voice*, the *Woman's Sphere*) and women's literary societies during the 1890s served to educate women and stimulate radical thinking, as well as providing opportunities for publication, debate and public speaking. In 1890, the Women's Literary Society became the first women's group in Sydney to meet at night, allowing working women such as Maybanke Wolstenholme, its first secretary, to attend its meetings. The advanced views of several of its members did not please some, however. The young writer Ethel Turner was moved to comment after a meeting in 1891 that discussed the topic of women's suffrage: 'It is horrid to see the way some of them go on about their rights and wrongs, it's old fashioned of me I suppose but I do think it would take from the womanliness of a woman to be in Parliament'.[42]

In 1894, the Karrakatta Club was formed in Perth as an extension of the St George's Reading Circle, attracting about forty members, including Madeleine Onslow and Edith Cowan. The new club's purpose was explicitly political, promoting women's 'mutual help and self-improvement'. Its aim was educative and its business divided into four departments: Hygiene; Literature; Artistic; and Legal and Educational. Madeleine Onslow, as first president, insisted on members speaking at meetings and presenting papers in order to gain confidence to speak in public, which continued to be an ordeal for many women. Women's suffrage was one of the most debated subjects at their meetings, and Edith Cowan presented a radical paper on women's right to economic independence; their dependence on men, she said, was a waste of their mental and physical powers and they should seek congenial employment. There was much spirited argument. In Hobart, the suffragist Ida McAulay was a leading light in the Itinerant Society, formed in 1894 when a group broke away from the Hamilton Literary Society. Their topics for discussion included literary subjects, writers, famous women and women's suffrage. McAulay also formed a women's rifle club.

Younger women began to acquire a more institutionalised education, taking advantage of the new secondary schools established during the last decades of the nineteenth century to prepare girls for university and thus the professions and public life. Such a school was Presbyterian Ladies College, founded in Melbourne in 1875, from which Vida Goldstein matriculated with honours in 1886. In Adelaide, the Advanced School for Girls performed a similar function. The first woman to graduate from an Australian university, however, had been schooled at home. Bella Lavender, who took out a Bachelor of Arts degree from the University of Melbourne in 1883, and a Master of Arts in 1885, later secured work as a secondary teacher. After graduation she taught at Loreto Convent in Ballarat and was then appointed principal of the university classes at the Ballarat School of Mines, where she promoted the importance of higher education for girls in fitting them for work in the world.

Her independent attitudes did not stop her marrying, however. In 1891 she took to herself an 80-year-old husband (she was thirty-three) to whom she bore a son. In Bendigo in the 1890s she became an officebearer in the local Women's Franchise League, while running University College there between 1898 and 1903. A committed socialist feminist, who became an active member of the Women's Federal Political Association and a supporter of Vida Goldstein's bid for the

Senate in 1913, Bella Lavender, by then known by her married name of Guerin, nevertheless opted to join the Labor party, whose dismissive attitudes towards women members she then spent years fighting.

The educational achievements of Bella Lavender and other women graduates in Melbourne were made possible partly through the efforts of reformers such as C. H. Pearson, the first headmaster of Presbyterian Ladies College. He had been closely associated with the movement for the higher education of women in England, where there was more pressure than in Australia for single women to find professional careers to support themselves. In Melbourne, he and his successor Andrew Harper became determined supporters of girls' right to matriculate and take out degrees at the university. In 1880, five of the six university council members who voted to admit women to all degrees (except Medicine) were themselves teachers. At the University of Sydney, the decision to enrol women was influenced by the persistent advocacy of the chancellor, Sir William Manning. Both the University of Sydney and the University of Adelaide admitted women in 1881, with other universities accepting women on equal terms with men as they were established; the University of Tasmania followed suit in 1890. At the University of Sydney, the Women's College became in 1892 the first women's college in the British Empire to be fully affiliated with a university. The first principal was the remarkable graduate from London University, social reformer and friend of Rose Scott, Louisa McDonald, who became active in education at all levels from kindergarten through to university. She was an ardent feminist, committed to educating women to take their place in each and every sphere of life. She would later fall into dispute with Scott about the advisability of educating girls in domestic arts, which McDonald considered a dangerous trap.

At the same time, a less elite path to education was developed by the pioneers of adult learning such as Maybanke Wolstenholme (later Anderson), who had been active in the Sydney Women's Literary Society and a founding member of the Womanhood Suffrage League. In 1892, she helped establish the Australasian Home Reading Union under the auspices of the Literary Section of the Australasian Association for the Advancement of Science. She also contributed to setting up the Free Kindergarten Union, and in 1894 established the journal *Woman's Voice*.

Born Maybanke Susannah Selfe in Surrey, England in 1845, May, as she was called by the family, emigrated with her mother, father and two brothers to Australia when she was nine years old. Married at twenty-two—and possibly already pregnant—May Wolstenholme bore seven children to her first husband, of whom only three sons survived into adulthood. Infant mortality was high in Sydney in the late nineteenth century and parents like the Wolstenholmes were forced to witness the slow, agonising deaths of their infants from common diseases such as tuberculosis. May Wolstenholme assuaged her grief in verse; her personal experience informed her early advocacy of child welfare and sex education in the service of voluntary motherhood. Her marriage deteriorated as her husband drank away the family income and in 1879, following the passage of the Married Women's Property Act in the New South Wales parliament, May Wolstenholme had the title of her home, 'Maybanke' transferred from her husband's name to her own. Henceforth, she would be the legal owner of any future earnings, derived at first from turning her spacious home into a boarding house and then from her work as a teacher. By 1883, she was headmistress of a private girls' school based in her home.

In 1892, following the passage of the Divorce Amendment and Extension Act, she was able finally to petition for a divorce on the basis of 'three years of desertion'. May Wolstenholme earned her own living, but like Henrietta Dugdale, Bessie Harrison Lee and Bella Lavender Guerin, she also remarried. Her new husband, Francis Andersen, was a professor of Philosophy at the university and eleven years her junior; they shared literary and political interests and had worked together in 1892 to establish the Australasian Home Reading Union (AHRU), which by 1893 had attracted 2000 members distributed throughout 106 reading circles. As her biographer Jan Roberts has observed, Maybanke Wolstenholme's work for the AHRU was linked to that for kindergartens by the philosophy of social regeneration through lifelong education and by providing a bridge between the worlds of the working class and the rich.

The 1890s were extremely busy years for her, but by 1897 Maybanke Andersen had resigned from her position on the council of the Womanhood Suffrage League to concentrate on extending women's political reform into the federal arena. She made a major contribution to sending the petition from the Womanhood Suffrage League to the 1897 Federal Covention in Adelaide, asking that the new Constitution provide for equal political rights for men and women. In South Australia, where women enjoyed full political rights, Catherine Helen Spence, a champion of proportional representation or 'effective voting', achieved fame by standing as a candidate for election to the Convention, becoming the first woman to stand for political office in Australia. She was unsuccessful. In all their campaigns for civil and political rights at this time, feminists had perforce to look for support from sympathetic men. Frederick William Holder, the South Australian delegate to the Federal Convention, who steered women's suffrage into the Draft Federal Constitution, was one such man.

WORKING WITH AND AGAINST MEN FOR VICTORY

Although the nineteenth century Woman Movement focussed on the need to reform men, it also needed male sympathisers to grant women political power. Clearly its critique of particular models of masculinity did not apply to all men and fortunately not all men took the criticisms personally. The movement's most basic goals—the vote, married women's property Acts, raising the age of consent, temperance, amendments to divorce legislation—depended on legislative support. In South Australia this was forthcoming, in the person of Dr Edward Stirling, an admirer of John Stuart Mill and professor of Medicine at the University of Adelaide, who had admitted women to his classes before they were able formally to enrol. In 1885, as a new member of the House of Assembly, he had introduced a motion recommending the extension of the franchise to women, but only to propertied women; although its terms were unacceptable to many supporters of womanhood suffrage and to the newly formed Trades and Labour Council, Stirling's motion and subsequent bill served to open up the whole issue for public debate. In 1888, the Women's Suffrage League with Dr Stirling as president, Mary Lee and Hector McLennan as co-secretaries and Rosetta Birks as treasurer began its campaign for the vote for women on the same grounds as men. Its platform specifically disavowed any interest in women standing for election to parliament.

In 1889 and 1890, Robert Caldwell introduced new legislation for womanhood suffrage, but again it did not give the vote to all women. The Women's Suffrage League, strengthened by the addition to the executive of 66-year-old Catherine Spence, was adamant that all women must have the vote. Following elections in 1893, the new liberal government led by Charles Kingston promised legislation enfranchising women, but complicated matters by providing for a referendum. Elections in 1894 returned a liberal majority to the upper house, a happy outcome for proponents of womanhood suffrage; this was achieved that same year, but not without last-minute complications that inadvertently resulted in South Australian women becoming the first in Australia to win not just the vote, but also the right to stand for parliament. A reactionary bid to derail the legislation by adding a clause enabling women to stand for election failed, and suffragists won more than they had bargained for.

In the other colonies, suffragists were forced into a similar round of deputations, petitions, lobbying, manoeuvring and shifting political alliances with politicians who were given to evasion, prevarication and changes of mind. In New South Wales, the support of Labor man Arthur Rae, who persuaded the ALP to add female suffrage to its platform in 1896, was important, as was that of Liberal politician William Lyne, who had changed his mind in favour of women's suffrage by the time he became Premier in 1899. A bill introduced by his government passed the lower house in 1900, but was rejected by the Legislative Council. Not until 1902, after women had been granted the federal franchise, did the upper house pass legislation giving New South Wales women the vote in State elections. The long years of campaigning took their toll: the Womanhood Suffrage League was beset by internal dissension and the joyful celebrations were somewhat marred by ideological and personal conflict. By 1902, Labor sympathisers Annie and Kate Golding together with Nellie Martel had left the Womanhood Suffrage League to form a new organisation, the Women's Progressive Association, which held a separate victory celebration.

When the Womanhood Suffrage League held its 'joy meeting' in September 1902, some were dismayed that veteran suffragist Louisa Lawson, who had joined the Golding sisters and Nellie Martel in their breakaway group, was not invited to sit with the special guests, including many men, on the crowded platform—a rebuff Margaret Windeyer sought to rectify by personally leading the aged and frail Lawson forward to the front of the hall where space was made and Rose Scott presented her with one of her bouquets. Just as the political campaign itself had generated strains and tensions in the Woman Movement, so did the ensuing contest for recognition and acknowledgment. Rose Scott recalled the heart-rending struggle and called for mutual generosity in their hour of victory:

> The price of Freedom is always sacrifice. Hope deferred hath often made the heart sick. There have been days of despair, and hours of heartache, and worse still, a knowledge of human nature one would rather have been without . . . let us realise how wonderful is this Flower of Freedom which has blossomed for the women of Australia this year! Are we to rush around like so many puny children, crying out, one 'it is mine, I saw it first!', another 'it is mine, I touched it first'. Oh foolish and blind! a thousand unseen influences have gone to sustain those hidden roots.[43]

The sources of support were indeed various, but so were the forces of opposition.

In Victoria, opposition was formalised in the Anti-Suffrage League, formed in 1900 by Freda Derham and Carrie Reed, both daughters of Assembly members, who were able to gather 22 978 signatures for a petition against women's suffrage which they submitted to the Victorian parliament. They received support in turn from the liquor trades, who everywhere felt directly threatened by the prospect of enfranchised women. Opposition was most concerted and effective in the Legislative Council, which regularly turned back legislation passed in the Legislative Assembly. In Victoria, a total of eighteen bills were submitted to parliament before women's suffrage was eventually achieved in 1908.

The difficulty experienced by Victorian suffragists in winning the vote was due in part to the very strength and vociferousness of their movement. During the 1880s and 1890s, organisations calling for the granting of political rights to women multiplied. In 1888, Brettena Smyth left the Victorian Women's Suffrage Society to form the Australian Women's Suffrage Society, her main aim being to promote the usefulness of contraceptives in freeing women from excessive childbearing. Advertising items such as the 'best female French contraceptives' had just been declared legal and the enthusiastic Smyth became an effective publicist, writing books with titles such as *Love, Courtship and Marriage* and *Limitation of Offspring*—which was a best-seller, going into eight editions. Popular with the reading, middle class public, Smyth's activities were viewed less favourably by most feminists, for whom free sexual relations were the basis of women's degradation, not to be encouraged. Measures that encouraged the 'animal in man' could never be conducive to the advancement of women. It was a male member of the Australian Women's Suffrage Society, however, who first introduced a bill into the Victorian parliament to remove all sex disabilities in regard to voting. Dr William Maloney, a socialist medical practitioner known for his bohemian flair and advanced views, was elected as a candidate of the Workingmen's Political League to the Legislative Assembly in 1889. He submitted his bill supporting women's suffrage, which lapsed for want of support.

Suffragists next placed their hopes with James Munro, a temperance Premier, to whom they presented their monster petition of 30 000 signatures. Criticised for linking the suffrage bill with a proposal to abolish plural voting, Munro let the latter go forward without the other, but neither measure was then successful. Frustrated at their lack of progress, suffragists decided to regroup, forming the United Council for Woman Suffrage in 1894 to co-ordinate the activities of the many interested associations, of which there were thirty-two, including the Victorian Lady Teachers' Association, the Central Methodist Mission and the Trades Hall Council. The activism of Clara and Alice Weekes in the Victorian Lady Teachers' Association, which had been formed in 1884 in support of equal pay and opportunities for women teachers, was influential in linking feminism with industrial issues in ways not so apparent in campaigns in other colonies. 'When suffrage is granted to women', proclaimed the annual report of the Victorian Lady Teachers' Association in 1898, 'the claims of the female teachers will receive greater consideration'.

The leading strategist and first president of the new organisation was Annette Bear, whose father's death at his vineyard, Chateau Tahbilk, had prompted her to return from England to be with her mother. John Pinney Bear had served as a Legislative Councillor in Victoria between 1863 and 1878. Annette was the oldest of eight children, well educated, independent minded, trained as a social worker in London, where she was a member of the sexual purity organisation, the National Vigilance Committee. In 1894, at the age of forty-one, she founded the United Council for Woman Suffrage and she also married William Crawford, a solicitor, becoming Annette Bear-Crawford.

Bear-Crawford was an energetic and capable campaigner for that 'most effective instrument for improving the conditions of life', the vote, but she also worked for related reforms—raising the age of consent, and securing women's appointment as factory inspectors, as supervisors under the Infant Life Protection Act and on schools' boards of advice.[44] Her concern with the effects of men's predatory sexual habits was characteristic of Australian engagement with the Woman Question: she worked for the appointment of women to public office, not to win equal professional opportunities for her sex, but to keep vulnerable women and children out of men's hands. She helped launch the Society for the Prevention of Cruelty to Women and Children, and with the Goldsteins and others organised the Queen's Willing Shilling Fund in 1897 to establish the Queen Victoria Hospital for Women, but died of pneumonia on a trip to London before the hospital opened.

In her political role as a public speaker, Bear-Crawford was a mentor to Vida Goldstein, who worked as paid organising secretary of the United Council for Woman Suffrage between 1899 and 1901. The following year Goldstein went as Australian delegate to the International Woman Suffrage Conference in Washington, where she delighted other delegates with her youthful confidence. Her position as organising secretary was filled by Lilian Locke, a Labor party member whose platform performances, according to the Brisbane *Worker*, were 'as fiery as her hair'.[45]

In 1903, Goldstein stood for the Senate as an independent candidate, endorsed by the newly formed Women's Federal Political Association, but her candidacy produced new tensions in the Woman Movement, between women loyal to the Labor party and non-party women, and between members of the WCTU, some of whom disapproved of enfranchised women standing for parliament. Goldstein was opposed by a combination of Liberal, conservative and Labor candidates, but with a respectable 51 497 votes she came fifteenth in the election. Her defeat might have been instructive, an early indication of the barriers posed to independent feminist candidates by the already entrenched party system. But the leading suffragists drew a different lesson from their political experience: it was their first-hand knowledge of dealing with male politicians, their encounters with so much evasiveness, deception, lack of principle and conviction that strengthened so many, like Goldstein and Scott, in their determination to eschew party politics and strike out on their own.

But still Victorian women did not have the vote for State elections and they faced staunch opposition with the election of the conservative politician Thomas Bent as Premier, who suggested on several occasions that enfranchised women would add to the electoral success of his Labor opponents. In 1906, suffragists received support from a Men's League for Women Suffrage which sent a deputation to Bent urging the granting of adult suffrage; women's activity continued unabated. Finally, Premier Bent announced that he had changed his mind and introduced a government bill in support of women's suffrage. When it reached the Legislative Council, Goldstein wrote sixty-one letters to members of parliament on its behalf. On 18 November, 1908 women crowded the galleries to listen to the debate, about to witness their final triumph. On 7 December, they held their victory celebrations, which honoured in particular the early campaigners Annie Lowe and Henrietta Dugdale Johnson, and Dr William Maloney who had introduced the first bill for women's suffrage into the Victorian parliament almost twenty years before.

PART II
BUILDING A WOMAN-FRIENDLY COMMONWEALTH

2
THE CREATION OF A WELFARE STATE

THE ADVENT OF THE MOTHER-WOMAN'S WORLD

The major achievement of post-suffragist feminists in Australia was the creation of a maternalist welfare state, a development anticipated when they gathered to celebrate their 'double victory' in Sydney in 1902. Granted the State and federal vote in the same year, enfranchised women in New South Wales were urged by Rose Scott to note the full significance of this 'Flower of Freedom', which had lately blossomed in their land. She emphasised the profound political and social transformations expected to ensue:

> Make no mistake! Accept no petty local, short sighted victory for women. Its possibilities are for all nations and for all time! And its birth at the beginning of the 20th century heralds to a world oppressed with poverty, suffering and sin, the advent of the mother-woman's world with loving heart and sheltering arms . . .[1]

In winning political rights, especially the right to vote, feminists had acquired the power to shape the infant Commonwealth, to mould a caring, protective, nation state, one oriented to securing human welfare rather than to maximising the power of 'the Almighty Dollar'. 'The country whose chief ambition is the Almighty Dollar', said Scott, 'is the meanest country on Earth'.[2]

According to leaders of the campaign, such as Scott, Louisa Lawson and Vida Goldstein, women would imbue the polity with the values of heart and home, with that spiritual quality Woman's Christian Temperance Union (WCTU) leader Frances Willard referred to as 'mother-heartedness'.³ The enfranchisement of women gave political voice to 'the National Motherhood of women' in Rose Scott's words.⁴ Australian feminists shared this understanding with many of their counterparts overseas, but the creation of the new Commonwealth in 1901—the virtual coincidence of the inauguration of a nation state and the granting of (white) women's political rights—provided a distinctive nationalist context for the development of feminism in Australia.

Australian feminists were self-conscious nation-builders: from the beginning they were engaged in forging a new social and political order, wanting to 'guild up the glory of a grand New World'.⁵ Feminists in Australia, then, were not simply concerned with the advancement of women; they aimed to use their new political status to shape a Commonwealth of which they were proud to be a constituent part. 'Australia offers such tremendous possibilities', wrote West Australian feminist Bessie Rischbieth to veteran United States activist Carrie Chapman Catt in 1924, 'it is the youngest of the great continents in development and a comparatively small population makes it possible to sow the seed now of the sort of civilisation women of all countries dream about'.⁶ Rischbieth believed that feminism was an expression of an evolutionary force which laid the basis of a 'new citizenship'.

Bessie Rischbieth was the magisterial president of the Australian Federation of Societies for Equal Citizenship, formed in 1921 and shortly to change its name to the Australian Federation of Women Voters (AFWV). Born in Adelaide in 1874, the child of working class parents, and raised in the progressive household of her uncle, the theosophist politician William Rounsevell, Bessie Earle was brought up to take an interest in politics and social reform. Her marriage in 1898 to the wealthy merchant Henry Rischbieth changed her circumstances and place of residence as she moved interstate to live in a grand mansion, Unalla, in the glossy Perth suburb of Peppermint Grove. The couple had no children (although her niece, now Dame Rachel Cleland, lived with them for periods of time) and in the early years of the new century the energetic Bessie embarked on a sixty-year career as a feminist citizen activist.

A beautiful woman, blessed with presence and stamina, but who could sometimes seem cold and aloof ('fire and ice' as her niece recalled), Rischbieth aspired to a position of leadership in the world-wide women's movement. She was a founding member of the Perth feminist organisation the Women's Service Guild (WSG), established in 1909, and her political commitments to service and the spiritual uplift of humanity were profoundly shaped by her theosophical beliefs, which had been strengthened by the visit to Perth in 1908 of Annie Besant, a world leader of the theosophical movement. In the human basis of citizenship were sown the seeds of a new spirit of co-operation, in which there was no place for barriers of sex, race or class; in citizenship the human consciousness of oneness could find full expression. A trip to London in 1913 intensified Rischbieth's commitments to theosophy and feminism. Listening to the public lectures by the American, Charlotte Perkins Gilman left her enraptured: 'Mrs Gillman [sic] then came on and she spoke oh! will I ever forget her great address'.[7] But although she was a passionate advocate of 'unity of purpose' as 'the heart of the new citizenship for women', Rischbieth's own ambitions could be divisive.[8] Her career was marked by a poignant tension between her idealistic belief in the unity of humankind and the ongoing alienation of feminist allies caused by her relentless drive for political pre-eminence. Edith Cowan, Mrs Iles, Mary Montgomerie Bennett, Ada Bromham, Constance Ternente Cooke, Jessie Street—all would in due course be banished from her court.

The inauguration of the new Commonwealth fired feminist ambition. 'Perhaps never since the world began', wrote Isobel G. Noar in *Woman's Sphere*, 'had women such a grand field for patriotic action as you, the enfranchised women of Australia'.[9] Feminists shared a conviction that women's accession to political rights would change the world because women brought a distinctive point of view to their engagement with public life. This conviction was articulated over four decades by activists ranging from Rose Scott in forming the Women's Political Education League (WPEL) in the first years of the century, to Bessie Rischbieth presiding over the formation of the Australian Federation of Women Voters in the 1920s, to Jessie Street working with the United Associations (UA) to draft a charter for Australian women in the 1940s.

These feminists believed that women shared distinctive values and priorities that, once translated into government policy, would create a different type of state—a welfare state. Explaining what she hoped to achieve with a new federal organisation in the 1920s, Bessie Rischbieth spoke of an 'army of Australian women organised thus to make the vote more effective by helping to establish a human basis of welfare in this great new land'. Working together women could 'create new channels whereby human welfare shall play the first and great part in our social system'.[10] The Australian Federation of Women Voters, a self-consciously nationalist organisation, adopted the slogan 'An All Australian Outlook'. It had three planks:

1. This Federation shall be non-party and non-sectarian in policy.
2. Shall promote equality of opportunity, status and reward between men and women.
3. Shall uphold an equal moral standard for men and women.

Feminists across Australia endorsed this non-party approach to securing their joint aims of equality for women and a welfare state for Australia. In 1925, an election leaflet was produced in support of the (successful) feminist candidate in the New South Wales State election, Millicent Preston Stanley, an executive member of both the Feminist Club, formed in Sydney in 1914, and the Australian Federation of Women Voters. It argued:

> Men's training tends to direct their interest to business (which covers trade, commerce, industry, work, wages, profits). Women's training tends to direct their interest to Social Welfare (which covers health, food, housing, care of children, care of sick, care of poor, preservation of family and home life). To take care of the Social Welfare, women must be in Parliament.[11]

The United Associations, formed in Sydney from an amalgamation of the Women's League, the Women's Service Club and the Women Voters' Association in 1929, and itself a constituent society of the AFWV, explained the difference women's political power would make to national life in these terms:

> Woman's point of view is not the same as man's. Her sense of values is different, she places a greater value on human life, human welfare, health and morals. The changed attitude of people to these questions which has taken place in countries where women have the vote can be attributed to the more direct influence of women. It behoves women to use their power, to the fullest extent possible to bring greater security and happiness into the lives of the whole community.[12]

The UA's aims and objects were:

1. To achieve by legislation, administration, organisation or any other means considered advisable a real equality of status, oportunities and liberties for men and women.
2. To secure equal pay for equal work and equality for men and women in all laws, rules and regulations.

3. To improve the legal status of mothers.
4. To promote an equal moral standard for men and women.
5. To support the candidature of qualified men and women for public office, who shall have pledged themselves to support constitutional methods and who shall be endorsed by the Council.
6. To promote the welfare of children.
7. To promote the study of Social, Political and Economic questions.
8. To promote international peace and understanding and to foster the League of Nations.

A special two-day conference organised by the UA in Sydney in 1934, 'For the Review and Planned Extension of the Essential Social Services' congratulated the State for its commitment to baby health centres, day nurseries and kindergartens and recommended the use of unemployment relief to effect greater integration of district nurses into other municipal health services. In 1936, the triennial conference of the Australian Federation of Women Voters, meeting in Adelaide, reaffirmed the view that government should work as an ethical force, 'to secure peace, freedom and justice and well-being for all'. One of the Federation's numerous resolutions aimed at securing the community's wellbeing called for a federal scheme for health and employment insurance to include 'the principle of equal contributions and equal benefits for both sexes'.[13]

The feminist approach to creating a new social order initially drew on and emphasised women's acknowledged duties and capacity as mothers. Feminists usually ascribed this distinctive capacity to training and experience, not nature. Many of those who invoked this maternalist orientation, such as Bessie Rischbieth, Vida Goldstein and Rose Scott, were not mothers themselves, but felt keenly that their sex had a responsibility for the human welfare of the nation state. Another maternalist without children was Ada Bromham, a motoring enthusiast and businesswoman who, at the age of forty-one, stood as the Social Welfare candidate (endorsed by the Women's Service Guild) for the seat of Claremont in the 1921 Western Australian State election.

Born in 1880, Ada Bromham had moved with her working class family to Western Australia from Victoria at the age of thirteen; she worked as a school monitor, then as a doctor's receptionist, and later took a position as an assistant in Thomas Smith's drapery business, rising to become a partner. Active in social reform, she was smart, good looking and articulate. With her shingled hair, simple dress and Oakland car, purchased in 1916, she presented the image of a thoroughly modern woman. One of her pleasures was to drive her car, which she serviced herself, across the Nullarbor Plain.

Her political views were also advanced; Bromham was socialist in sympathy, influenced no doubt by her early tutelage in a Labor household, and her political activism—which spanned a period of some five decades—included support for temperance reform, trade unionism, and the rights of Aboriginal people as well as of women. In 1952, as a member of the Chinese–Australia Friendship Society, she joined a peace delegation to Peking (Beijing); on her return she had all her literature confiscated by the Department of Customs. Five years later she responded to an invitation from Jessie Street to join the campaign for a referendum to make Aboriginal welfare a federal responsibility.

During World War I, Bromham had helped form a Women's National Movement to campaign for new restrictions on alcohol, but by 1918 the members had decided to merge with the Women's Service Guild, which agreed to add a prohibition plank to its platform. In the election campaign in 1921 Bromham, a non-party feminist candidate, was referred to in the press as the 'Social Welfare candidate'. When she opened her campaign in the Princess Hall, to prolonged applause, she began by speaking about the difference that women's participation would make to government. A large white banner adorning the stage proclaimed the candidate's promise of welfare through protection: 'Women will help to create protective legislation for the factory, the home, and as between nation and nation, because they belong to the great human movement which includes equally men and women'. In her speech, Bromham told electors:

> There were fundamental reasons why a woman was particularly fitted to fill a position in the legislature. A man government was a government of all the people in the interests of man, not because men intended it to be so, but because from generation to generation, man had been trained commercially and it was his nature to put business first and human welfare second. Women put human welfare first and business second. (Applause.) Man was the creator. He thought and acted in terms of the wealth which he created. Woman thought and acted in terms of human beings which she brought forth and cared for. (Applause).[14]

Bromham was a popular candidate. Her opening campaign address attracted an audience of some 700 electors, who seemed to appreciate her wit as well as her political views:

> They heard a great deal at election time about finance. Each candidate stressed the financial outlook. They said the country wanted hard-headed men to do things. The state had them right along, eighty such, fifty in the Assembly, thirty in the Council—(Laughter)—and the only consolation the people had was an ever growing deficit and an ever increasing burden of taxation. (Applause). It was really wonderful what men did when one came to think of it. (Laughter).[15]

On the primary vote Bromham came second in a field of six candidates. She was defeated on the fifth distribution of preferences by a Nationalist candidate, J. Thompson, who was Mayor of Claremont. In the same election, Edith Cowan, also a Nationalist party candidate, won the seat of West Perth to become the first woman to win a seat in an Australian parliament. Cowan's victory and Bromham's defeat could be read as a portent: the dominance of the two-party system in Australian politics would mostly prove an insurmountable barrier to the aspirations of non-party feminists seeking political office. But Cowan, too, was a maternalist: she had long worked for child welfare, kindergartens and playgrounds and her first piece of legislation provided equal inheritance rights to the mothers of adult children who died intestate.

In creating their version of a maternalist welfare state, Australian feminists sought to combine a liberal emphasis on the sanctity of the individual with a recognition of human interdependence and a call for collective provision and state regulation. The history of the welfare state in Australia has usually been represented as a masculine project, the work of a group of 'new liberals' intent on civilising the relationship between capital and labour, their finest achievement the conciliation and arbitration system, which placed working men's needs ahead of employers' desire for profit. The Harvester judgment of 1907, which enshrined the right of white men (whether married or single) to a family wage—sufficient to keep a wife and children—and the introduction of old age and invalid pensions in 1908 laid the basis for a new form of social citizenship. This 'new liberalism' was shaped by the teachings of the English theorist T. H. Green, who promoted the idea of an ethical state providing 'positive liberty', an idea taken up in Australia by key figures such as Prime Ministers Alfred Deakin and

Andrew Fisher, intellectuals Francis Anderson and Walter Murdoch and president of the Arbitration Court H. B. Higgins, who presided over the deal between capital and labour that has been called the New Protection.

Political history has paid little attention, however, to the parallel attempt by feminists in Australia to create an ethical state for women. As with the men's project, liberal or non-party women (Rose Scott, Vida Goldstein, Bessie Rischbieth and Ada Bromham) were joined by Labor women activists (Lilian Locke-Burns, Jean Daley and Muriel Heagney) in demanding that the state adopt the role of protector. The major difference was that women activists expected their ethical state to provide protection for women from predatory and exploitative men. They made a particular case that the state should support those who worked as mothers, providing them with an income which would free them from a demeaning dependence on husbands. It was this commitment to the independence of mothers, their desire to end the despotic power of husbands, that brought feminists into direct conflict with liberal and labour men who wanted to secure, not just the male citizen's industrial rights, but also his conjugal rights to women's domestic and sexual services.

The independence of the married woman was a key goal for feminists between the wars, but they also worked for social recognition of the work of caring. Feminists argued that the labour performed by mothers was crucial to national welfare and that motherhood should be accorded political and economic status. Their campaigns for recognition of mothers—Aboriginal and non-Aboriginal—as political subjects with rights are discussed in the next two chapters.

In Australia, feminists looked to the state to provide the conditions for women's freedom—positive liberty—by protecting them from predatory and violent men and the forces of intemperance, selfishness and vice. Their campaigns were animated by a profound sense of the harm that men's sexual licence did to women and girls. It was a politics that spoke to widespread experience of venereal disease, degradation and debasement; unwanted pregnancies, poverty and ill health. The sexualisation of women increasingly evident in the wider culture seemed inimical to the advancement of women as citizens. In a letter to a friend about the painter Norman Lindsay, Rose Scott remarked that although he was considered a genius by some, his paintings suggested he might more appropriately be regarded as 'a sex maniac': 'His women have no souls only bodies', she wrote. 'To me his women are degrading. Sex dominates his pictures.'[16] Like other well-known feminists, Scott received numerous letters from women detailing the miseries inflicted on them as a result of men's personal tyranny and their unrestrained indulgence in 'animal passion'.

To understand women's apprehension of sexual danger and the threat that men posed to girls and women, it is important to contextualise feminists' views in their anxieties about unrestrained masculine power. Feminist discourse, in the first decades of the twentieth century, spoke to a profound sense of feminine vulnerability: in homes, at the workplace and on the streets. At a time when venereal disease was widespread and dire in its effects, when 'illegitimate' pregnancies spelt shame and social ostracism for women, when public drunkenness was common and sexual assaults well publicised, and when almost all women and girls depended on a man's goodwill for their survival, feminists highlighted women's need for 'protection'. Feminist visions of freedom spoke of a yearning to be free from masculine assault.

Thus, in the new Commonwealth, women activists campaigned for male sexual control and for legislation to raise the age of consent, outlawing men's sexual access to young women and girls. 'In West Australia', Rose Scott was pleased to report, 'women had the vote a year when they got the age of protection for young girls changed from 14 to 16 and that is one of the first steps [enfranchised] women take'.[17] As president of the post-suffrage Women's Political Education League, formed in 1902, she led campaigns in New South Wales to raise the 'age of protection' from fourteen to seventeen years—that was the question, she said, which above all others 'should be nearest our hearts'. In Victoria, the Women's Federal Political Association (later, the Women's Political Association or WPA), formed in 1903, demanded that the age of consent be raised from sixteen to twenty-one years for both sexes. In that State, the number of carnal knowledge cases heard in the Supreme Court had increased from just twelve between 1880 and 1885 to 116 between 1886 and 1900, an increase due in part to the increase in the age of consent from twelve to sixteen in 1891. But opposition to these reforms was strident, and in the event Scott had to settle for an 'age of protection' of sixteen in New South Wales and Goldstein for seventeen in Victoria.

Feminists also sought longer gaol sentences for men convicted of assault against women and children. Arguing that women should 'use the vote to protect themselves and their children', Vida Goldstein as secretary of the Women's Federal Political Association pointed out that the 'traces of our Common Law which gives a man the right to chastise his wife are still seen in the utterly inadequate penalties inflicted on men for brutal assaults on their wives, as contrasted with the severe penalties for assaults on men'.[18] In Western Australia, feminist outrage was provoked in April 1916 by the sexual assault of a five-year-old girl, who was then infected with venereal disease. Because the assailant was a juvenile, he was sentenced to just eighteen months' imprisonment. The Women's Service Guild passed a resolution: 'That we as a band of women of WA feel strongly that attention should be drawn to the utterly inadequate sentence imposed on offenders against little children'.[19] Echoing Louisa Lawson's observation of twenty years before about the relative value in Australian culture of horses and women, the resolution concluded that 'property seems of more value than human life'. A public meeting was called, with fifteen organisations—including the National Council of Women, the WCTU and the Labor party—sending representatives. They demanded various amendments to the Criminal Code, including a provision that the minimum sentence be not less than five years and that the United States' example of segregating the unfit be considered with a view to the implementation of similar measures in Western Australia. However, when a deputation waited on Premier John Scaddan to put their proposals to him, he suggested that the problem lay not with the perpetrators of sexual assault, but with their victims: children should not be allowed to roam the streets 'getting themselves molested'.[20]

'MOTHERS OF ALL THE CITY'

Central to the creation of a maternalist welfare state was the appointment of women to a range of positions in the state as police, gaol matrons, factory inspectors, school inspectors, magistrates, Justices of the Peace, lawyers and doctors. Feminists asked for these appointments not in terms of 'equal opportunity' in employment, but to secure the protection of women and girls, to prevent them from falling into men's hands. The Women's Political Association in Victoria explained how its goal of protection would be achieved through appropriate 'supervision':

> Wherever women and children are in subjection, supervision by women is necessary and women should vote to secure the

appointment of women as inspectors of asylums, boarded out children, hospitals, schools and gaols.[21]

In New South Wales, feminists were successful in having police matrons appointed to the central city lock-up; but as Rose Scott, in her capacity as president of the WPEL, pointed out in a letter to the Inspector-General of Police in 1904, women prisoners at other venues were still at risk:

> When the three Police Matrons now at Central were appointed it was understood that all Women prisoners would in future be conveyed to the Central. This does not appear to have been possible . . . I find that hundreds of women during the year lie in the cells at the Water Police Station, Darlinghurst, Paddington, Randwick . . . night after night attended to by men constables only. To obviate this state of affairs, degrading alike to men and women, we do earnestly implore you to appoint more Police Matrons . . . [women are] entitled to that measure of decent protection and care from their own sex which is without question accorded to women in hospitals and gaols of the country.[22]

In her presidential address of 1904 she was pleased to report that 'through the sympathy of Mr Garvin, the new Inspector-General of Police, one more Police Matron was appointed to the Water Police Station'.[23]

The vision of a maternalist welfare state, with women occupying key positions in the bureaucracy, was definitive of this phase of feminism. It was a politics concerned above all to end the 'degradation' of women, which was how women's subordinate status was commonly conceptualised in these years, as was made clear in Scott's presidential address to the WPEL. After reporting on their success in securing the appointment of more police matrons, Scott continued:

> Gladly did we welcome the appointment of Miss Duncan as our Lady Factory Inspector; of Miss Ferguson as a Sanitary Inspector; and we have to thank the late Government for appointing Dr Mary Booth as a Lecturer on Hygiene to the Public Schools, and Dr Agnes Bennett to care for the poor women lunatics. In Victoria, women can practise as lawyers, and in Tasmania we see only this week a bill passed to that effect—while in New South Wales, our lady barrister, who has attained to the dignity of an Ll.B. is not as yet legally qualified to practice. How much better it would be if poor women who, for the sake of their children and

their own safety are compelled to ask for a legal separation or a divorce, could confide all their wretchedness to one of their own sex.[24]

Not until 1918, with the passage of the Women's Legal Status Act, were women lawyers permitted to practise in New South Wales.

When feminists exchanged interstate news, they invariably reported on their latest victories in having their State staffed by women personnel. Following a lecture tour of Brisbane, Scott 'noted with pleasure that there were women doctors in every hospital in Brisbane and women were on all the Hospital Committees there'.[25] In 1906, Catherine Spence wrote from Adelaide, happy to report to Sydney friends that she and her co-workers had 'succeeded in getting an excellent paid probation officer, Catherine Cooke and her first work—she only began 1st May—is admirable. In fact we have in the Dept. four admirable women'.[26]

When Edith Cowan visited Sydney during the war she brought news of the success of feminists in the west in getting women appointed to a variety of public offices charged with the welfare of women and children. Interviewed by a local newspaper she enthused:

> The conditions under which the Women's Prison existed have been improved to an almost incredible extent. I remember going with some other members of the Women's Service Guild to see that prison about three years ago and I brought away an impression that robbed me of sleep for many nights . . . Now we have police matrons at the Women's Prison . . .[27]

The Women's Service Guild, Edith Cowan continued, was also successful in securing the appointment of women as health inspectors and as members of hospital boards.

From 1921, the Women's Service Guild lobbied in Perth for the appointment of a 'lady doctor' to examine women candidates for the Commonwealth public service; at first the politicians refused, deferring to the judgment of the Public Service Commissioner. The feminists persisted: 'we do not intend to let the matter drop, because we consider our demand so reasonable and so important and so inexpensive'. The Public Service Commissioner maintained his objections: 'there had been no general demand'. The campaign finally met with success two years later, following the visit of the Prime Minister to Perth, who received a deputation on the matter. Jubilant feminists reported in the

Dawn: 'This request has been granted . . . applications are being invited for a woman medical officer to undertake this duty'.[28]

In all States feminists argued 'the necessity for police women': 'a woman's voice, a woman's hand subdues; a man's voice, a man's hand infuriates'. Policewomen, said the *Woman Voter*, journal of the Women's Political Association, were required so that they might patrol the streets and make arrests when necessary, 'but more particularly to act as guardians of women and young people, who frequently get into trouble because there is no motherly person at hand to warn and advise them in moments of danger'.[29]

The campaign for the appointment of women police was joined by the Woman's Christian Temperance Union and the National Council of Women. Success came in 1915 when the first female officers were appointed in Victoria, New South Wales and South Australia. There were ten policewomen working in South Australia by 1924, when Helen King visited Senior Policewoman Miss Cocks to report on their work for the *Dawn*. She was full of praise:

> the preventive and protective work that may be accomplished by enlightened and good women in their official capacity as police is difficult to estimate, nor is it sufficiently appreciated by the parents in the cities in whose interests noble and unselfish services are being rendered to the community.[30]

The Women's Non-Party Association in South Australia listed policewomen's duties in the 1920s as follows:

1. To patrol streets, parks and open places and to deal with loitering and soliciting.
2. To undertake observation of theatres, dance halls, cinemas, show grounds, railway stations, markets.[31]

The young needed to be protected from 'contaminating influences' and these maternalist feminists made the welfare of children a major priority.

As Alice Henry, the Australian feminist working as a trade union organiser in the United States, saw it, women's citizenship—their entry into public life—restored them to their 'true position of maternal supervision', which as individual mothers of individual children they had lost both because of industrialisation and the state assuming responsibility for education:

> But because the mother can no longer oversee her own child all the time, the mothers of all the city should be able to do so. This

they can do only through the vote and through their being placed in administrative positions in the legislature, on boards of schools, recreation parks, and as police women and matrons.[32]

Speaking to a meeting of the WPEL in Sydney in 1903, Rose Scott insisted that 'in gaining the Woman's Vote the first great thought had been to help the children and our own sex . . . As an instance of this three bills entirely affecting children were . . . before the legislature— the State Children's Bill, the Infants' Protection Bill and the Girls' Protection Bill'. Two years later, Scott gloried in their political success: 'This year shines out like a new star, a constellation of hope fulfilled and glorious triumph when we consider the difference that the women's vote has already made'. Three bills that were 'upon our programme, Bills dealing very especially with the interests and Protection of Women and Children have now become the law of the land'.[33] One of these was the so-called State Children's Bill (the Neglected Children and Juvenile Offenders Act), which made provision for 'neglected children' to be dealt with in separate children's courts—'as women', Scott commented, 'this Bill appeals to us greatly, making as it does provision for removing children from the contaminating influences of police courts and gaols'.[34] In her enthusiasm to protect children, Scott seemed oblivious of the coercive implications of the legislation, of the vulnerability of working class and Aboriginal families to having their children removed from their care. The other two pieces of legislation hailed as feminist victories were the Habitual Criminals Bill and the Infants Protection Bill, the latter requiring deserting fathers to pay maintenance for their children. Further measures sought by the WPEL included provision for mothers' equal custody rights and legislation preventing fathers being able to will their estates away from their wives and children, leaving them penniless. Mothers' rights to custody of their children would not become law in New South Wales until 1934.

Feminists defined freedom from sexual harassment (to use a contemporary term) as the precondition for full citizenship, yet it is arguable that the feminist politics of protection, by dwelling on men's power and women's helplessness, worked to reinforce women's sense of vulnerability. At the discursive and perhaps practical levels, feminists produced the violable bodies that they then sought to protect and govern. The violability of women was invoked to justify the appointment of women as protectors, but women as a whole remained the protected sex. The capacity for self-defence remained formally and informally the preserve of men.

SAVING THE SONS

It was men's duty as citizens to defend their country (and citizen training schemes had prepared boys for this duty), but there was much opposition to the state endorsement of slaughter. The outbreak of World War I saw many feminists—especially those associated with Vida Goldstein in the Women's Political Association, such as Adela Pankhurst, Jennie Baines and Cecilia John—direct their energies into pacifist campaigns and the anti-conscription movement, all in the name of a responsible motherhood. The WPA was at the forefront of opposition to the war, resolving as early as 7 August 1914:

> This Association hopes that women everywhere, the lifegivers of the world will work henceforth with one mind to destroy the perverted sense of national honour and demand that international disputes shall be adjusted by arbitration. This Association resolves to cable to the President of the International Women's Suffrage Alliance, asking that women of all nations be urged to support the actions of President Wilson and plead for immediate arbitration.[35]

As chair of the Australian Peace Alliance, Goldstein toured Australia in 1915 with Pankhurst and John, setting up branches of a new, militant, Women's Peace Army, in Sydney and Brisbane as well as Melbourne. Cecilia John, a celebrated contralto, often opened meetings with a well-known anti-war song, which was deemed to be so effective a statement against war that it was outlawed under war precautions regulations as 'prejudicial to recruiting'. She sang:

> I didn't raise my son to be a soldier
> I brought him up to be my pride and joy,
> Who dares to put a musket on his shoulder
> To kill some other mother's darling boy?

In Brisbane, John and Pankhurst found a dedicated worker for the cause of peace in Margaret Thorp, whose home was visited by Military Intelligence in a fruitless search for copies of the printed song lyrics.

In their opposition to the war, feminists laid the basis of an enduring tradition of feminist pacifism, which also found expression in the Sisterhood of International Peace, formed in 1915 and later to become the local branch of the Women's International League for Peace and Freedom, which was first known as the International Committee for Permanent Peace at the Hague Congress in 1915.

During the conscription campaigns of 1916 and 1917, which divided Australian society into acrimonious camps, both sides appealed to women in their capacity as mothers. Pro-conscriptionists asked that voters allow the government to send reinforcements to assist the boys already there. Anti-conscriptionists, including feminists such as Goldstein and Pankhurst, and Labor women such as Alicia Katz, Annie O'Brien and Emma Miller, portayed the Yes vote as a 'blood vote', as in the famous leaflet that appealed directly to mothers:

> 'Why is your face so white, Mother?
> Why do you choke for breath?'
> Oh I have dreamt in the night, my son,
> That I doomed a man to death.

Kathleen Hotson, a South Australian feminist and pacifist, declared that women must 'put an end to the reign of brute force' because 'we shall have no faith in womanliness, in wifeliness, motherliness, if women cannot do this'; while Jennie Scott-Griffiths, a Sydney feminist and socialist, also linked her anti-war activities with her feminist vision more generally: women needed to challenge the political, social and economic conditions that male dominance had created—a world in which nations slaughtered the sons, lovers and husbands of women.[36] Pankhurst and Goldstein constantly invoked women's maternal responsibilities as peace makers, Goldstein asking:

> What can a boy think of the mother who teaches him one thing, and then countenances this legalised murder? The time has come when the women, the mothers of the world shall refuse to give their sons as material for shot and shell.[37]

As leading anti-war campaigners, Goldstein and Pankhurst had their writings heavily censored and their political activities closely monitored by Military Intelligence. In 1919, Goldstein travelled to Switzerland where she represented Australia at the women's peace conference in Zurich—and she stayed away for three years.

Meanwhile in Perth, debates over the war and conscription had split the Women's Service Guild, even as Bessie Rischbieth initially tried to steer a neutral course. Proceedings became acrimonious at the general meeting in December 1916 when it was ruled that the WSG could not support a visit to Perth by noted anti-conscription speaker Adela Pankhurst. Labor women protested 'at the lack of tolerance shown by the Guild in refusing to hear a fellow woman whose views might be divergent', but their views were deleted from the minutes at the request of Amelia MacDonald, an ardent pro-conscriptionist.[38] The following year the Labor Women's Organisation arranged a meeting for Pankhurst to speak at the Trades Hall. When Rischbieth nominated for presidency of the WSG that year she made clear her pro-conscriptionist views: 'much as she detested war she felt we were in honour bound to stand by those men who had gone forward to help the Empire and we must see this great national crisis through as a Commonwealth'.[39] She was re-elected unopposed, while all but one of the Labor women who stood for executive positions were defeated. Rischbieth proved adept at marginalising her opponents.

In their mission to protect the home—specifically to protect women and children—feminists since the nineteenth century, especially those in frontier societies, had placed much emphasis on the ravages wrought by alcohol: the poverty, the sexual abuse and violence that destroyed homes as a result of men's drinking. The free availability of alcohol was seen as a threat to women's security and freedom. Post-suffrage feminists continued to be active in the Woman's Christian Temperance Union and the Anti-Liquor Leagues and, as in Ada Bromham's case, they set up new prohibitionist organisations. They also incorporated temperance objectives into the platforms of already existing feminist groups.

The commitment to temperance—indeed to prohibition—was a powerful unifying force among post-suffrage feminists. Possibly not until the emergence of Jessie Street did a leading feminist enjoy a drink. The advent of World War I, with the increased demand for economy and national efficiency and the absence of hundreds of thousands of men at the front provided the right political circumstances to push for new liquor restrictions. Feminists were also concerned about the availability of alcohol to the boys in the defence forces, the effects of which seemed to be graphically demonstrated in the mutiny of sections of the Australian Imperial Force at Liverpool, New South Wales, in early 1916. All States implemented six o'clock closing during the war, most by the passage of referenda in electorates, many of which were newly dominated by women. Feminist groups were also active in local option polls, lobbying residents of their municipalities to vote 'no license'. Newsletters reported regularly on temperance successes throughout the country, as when a newly formed branch of the Women's Service Guild in Camberwell, Victoria, advised in 1921 that in a recent local option poll 'many of their members canvassed on a house-to-house basis with the excellent result that the district went "dry"'.[40] Much of Camberwell has remained 'dry' ever since.

Throughout Australia women mobilised to curb the availability of alcohol. The South Australian branch of the WCTU was pleased to report that as a result of its pressure, the government had stopped its practice of allowing liquor advertisements to be displayed at railway stations. In March 1919, in Perth, a Parade of Mothers of returned servicemen was held to lobby the Premier to save their sons from drink, and two years later the *Dawn* reported 'an historic march of women', held in conjunction with the annual congress of the Women's Service Guild, to the Perth Town Hall:

> By far the largest procession of women ever held in this State assembled at the Railway Station on Friday afternoon, April 29 and marched from there through the main streets to the Town Hall where a 'Women's Rally' was held in furtherance of the No License Poll on the following day . . .
> It was a great event and it was indeed gratifying to see women from all sections of the community present.[41]

In 1922, Bessie Rischbieth visited Sydney, where she was a guest of the Women's Club and met the president of the Feminist Club, Millicent Preston Stanley, who was 'a powerful speaker and out on the prohibition platform'.[42] That feminists were so closely identified with temperance in the interwar years undoubtedly contributed to their kill-joy image among many Australians at the time, and subsequently. To many of their critics during these years, feminists were not self-serving careerists, as enemies would later depict them, but wowsers bent on destroying other people's pleasures.

THE CITIZENS OF THE FUTURE

Child welfare, as Ada Bromham insisted in her 1921 election campaign, was the woman reformer's foremost plank. It was a priority in tune with the times as political leaders and newspaper columnists—in the wake of the war that took some 60 000 Australian lives—vied with each other in paying tribute to 'His Majesty the Baby'. Feminists determined to turn this maternalist rhetoric to women's advantage, insisting that state resources be invested in maternal and child welfare, women's hospitals and maternity benefits.

The establishment of separate children's courts, first introduced in South Australia, was always listed by feminists as one of their most significant political achievements, as when the 1906 conference of the International Women's Suffrage Alliance in Copenhagen was informed about the activities of enfranchised women in Australia:

> What is it they vote for? . . . the questions they take up, the measures they get passed. Well, they take first Local Option or some measure for minimising the drink evil, then children's courts, the care of neglected and feeble minded children, a more scientific method of treating habitual criminals, the closing of drink bars on election days and, as regards legislation for women specially, equal divorce laws, the raising of the age of consent and the Testator's Maintenance Act (preventing a husband from willing away his property from his wife and family).[43]

South Australia held pride of place in feminist accounts of their work on behalf of children. The pioneering path laid down by Caroline Clark and Catherine Spence in establishing the 'boarding out system', which enabled impoverished but respectable (white) mothers to keep their children with them, had been followed by the formation of the State Children's Council. Subsequent achievements were elaborated in a glowing tribute to the extent of the regulatory apparatus produced by the Women's Non-Party Association of South Australia in the 1920s:

> From the work so begun has grown the present State Children's Department with its numerous foster-mothers, its Receiving Homes, Reformatories, Children's Courts and the great army of officials, inspectors, probation officers, matrons and others who carry on this magnificent work . . . The Mothers' School, now known as the Mothers' and Babies' Health Association has carried on its work along the lines of similar child welfare societies which are now well established throughout the world. There are now 42 centres for weighing babies in the Metropolitan area, as well as several pre-natal clinics.[44]

The report emphasised the practical results of feminist reform efforts, attributing the dramatic lowering of the infant mortality rate (with the exception of New Zealand and the Netherlands 'the lowest in the world') to this women's work for mothers and children. The report also recorded the appointment of professional women to key positions in this extensive welfare regime: Dr Gertrude Halley as Medical Inspector of Schools in 1913 and 'a woman who is a Doctor of Philosophy' appointed as Child Psychologist. This was Dr Constance Davey, who as a Catherine Helen Spence scholar had studied at the University of London, where she had received her doctorate. In 1926 she introduced psychological services for school children in South Australia.

In Western Australia the Women's Service Guild reaffirmed its commitment to child welfare at its annual conference in 1921:

> Believing that in the children of the community are the foundation stones of our national edifice, we urge the extension of child welfare and we consider no present sacrifice too great if, by that sacrifice, we may build up a good and virile nation.[45]

In 1925, its recorded achievements included reforms for women and children—free kindergartens, the Child Welfare Bureau, the Women's Immigration Auxiliary Council, the Young Women's Christian Association (YWCA) in Perth, the King Edward Memorial Hospital, the League of Nations Union, better conditions in the Old Women's Home, women on hospital boards, women police, children's courts and public conveniences for women.

The nationalist identifications of the feminist project in the early Commonwealth shaped its policies and priorities. Dr Roberta Jull, the well-known feminist (and mother of writer Henrietta Drake-Brockman), became something of a role model in Western Australia in her position as State School Medical Officer. In a speech on women's work in the new nation, she drew the explicit connection between children's health and national greatness with a dramatically simple example. Deploring the prevalence of tooth decay among school children she asked: 'How can we build a healthy and efficient nation if the teeth are bad?'[46]

Child welfare was not just in the national interest, however—it was an international obligation. Since 1922, when the playwright Marguerite Dale was appointed, Australian feminists had been attending the League of Nations as (substitute) delegates, the first women delegates to attend from the Dominions. A major topic of debate in Geneva was the traffic in women and children and children's welfare more generally. In 1925, the League of Nations Assembly, supported by Australia, had determined that children had rights, including the rights:

1. To be fed and cared for in health and in disease, whether born in or out of wedlock;
2. To have an opportunity to develop normally, both physically and mentally.

When she attended the League of Nations as substitute delegate in 1930, Dr Roberta Jull had an opportunity to make a close study of women's work in this field in other countries and was able to conclude that Australia's infant welfare clinics and children's hospitals led the field.

Feminists believed that the community, especially children, also needed to be protected from the harmful influences thought to flow from sexually explicit literature and from that new form of entertainment, moving pictures. Assuming that the sexualisation of the culture endangered children and retarded women's bid to be taken seriously as equal citizens, feminists lobbied for the appointment of film censorship boards and the appointment of women to them. However, recognising the popularity and potential of the entertainment provided by moving pictures—by 1927 there were 1240 picture theatres in Australia and attendances in Victoria alone were estimated at 18 000 000 annually—they stressed the importance of a positive response through building up repositories of educational films and establishing good film leagues. In 1927, feminists around Australia gave evidence to the Royal Commission appointed by the federal government to enquire into the film industry. In Melbourne, Edith Jones, president of the Victorian Women Citizens' Movement, recommended the establishment of a national film studio, the appointment of a federal censorship board including women members, a classification 'suitable for children' and an Australian films advisory committee on which women, educational authorities, the Australian film industry and picture theatre proprietors would be represented. In Perth, representatives of the Women's Service Guild also urged the establishment of censorship boards composed equally of men and women, a tightening up of censorship of films, advertisements and posters and more frequent screenings of educational films.

To advise mothers on how best to raise their children—to protect their bodies as well as their minds—women reformers set up baby health centres and mothers' schools, which during World War I were gradually subsidised by State governments and became maternal and infant welfare centres. The death of infants from gastro-intestinal diseases was still relatively common—between 1918 and 1921, for example, 2175 babies died during the summer months just in metropolitan Melbourne. The new clinics addressed mothers' real anxieties, as well as adding to their workload. For a time, medical women and trained nurses envisaged the clinics as a women's public health service operating independently of doctor-controlled hospitals; but like midwives, maternity nurses were quickly brought under medical control, and their practice limited to strictly non-medical procedures.

With the establishment of State departments of infant and maternal welfare in the 1920s, professional women were put in charge of their operations, with Dr Vera Scantlebury Brown appointed Director of Infant and Maternal Welfare in Victoria (part-time because married) and Dr Elma Sandford holding the equivalent position in New South Wales. By the end of the decade a mass public health program was in place—there were eighty maternal and infant welfare clinics in New South Wales, for example, and 120 in Victoria—a substantial victory for the feminist project of shaping the Commonwealth as a maternalist welfare state. Their achievement was evident in national statistics. Between 1900 and 1930 infant mortality dropped from over 100 to under fifty deaths per 1000 live births.

Increasingly, the qualified women being appointed to positions as 'welfare workers' were—as a result of women's admission to higher education from the 1880s and the lobbying of organisations such as the National Council of Women—professional graduates from the universities. They staffed State Departments of Education, Health and Infant Welfare as well as filling new positions in department stores and large manufacturing companies. Margaret Thorp worked as paid secretary to the Young Women's Christian Association before joining Anthony Hordern's store in Sydney to organise a welfare department—and cultural and sporting clubs—for their 3000 employees. Eleanor Hinder, a B.Sc. graduate from the University of Sydney, became founding secretary of the Australian Federation of University Women in 1922, while working as the welfare supervisor of Farmers' and Co. By the late 1920s, Hinder had gone to work with the YWCA in Shanghai, from which base she became, in 1928, organising secretary with the Pan-Pacific Women's Conference in Honolulu. Dr Grace Boelke was founder and then executive member of the Professional Women Workers' Association of New South Wales when she joined the Berlei company in Melbourne as medical director, and was appointed convenor of the Standing Committee on Health of the National Council of Women. Margaret Cuthbertson, the first factory inspector in Australia, worked from 1920 as a welfare officer in Myers, where Dr Margaret Andersen was medical officer. Women doctors became influential in public health debates in Australia and in the formulation of national policy on infant and maternal welfare, but their investment in their expertise and the application of scientific knowledge to solve social problems increasingly brought them into conflict with feminists concerned about the individual rights of mothers as citizens, as occurred in the 1920s' debate over the future of the Maternity Allowance, a conflict discussed in the following chapter.

Post-suffrage feminists in Australia were maternalists in two senses: first, in the way they conceptualised their political mission as a matter of securing the protection and care of the vulnerable and defenceless members of the community; and second, in their discursive construction of the mother as a rights-bearing political subject, a figure equivalent to the worker in labour movement discourse. What distinguished feminist discourse from other versions of maternalism was, first, a concern to protect women and children from sexual degradation and violence and, second, their representation of the mother as a political subject with rights—equal custody and inheritance rights, an entitlement to state services and appropriate health care and, above all, the right to economic independence. As maternalist citizens, they spoke for the vulnerable in society, especially in regard to the needs of children; as feminists, they demanded recognition of women's rights as self-determining individuals, with a right to independence from men. In the context of a patriarchal society, which enshrined men's power as husbands, fathers and breadwinners, these goals would prove increasingly difficult to reconcile.

3
THE RIGHTS OF MOTHERS

THE RIGHT TO MOTHER

Women's claims to rights as mothers were asserted on the basis of their status as citizens—their status as independent self-governing individuals. Feminists invoked a maternalist discourse to radical ends, insisting that child-bearers were rights-bearers. Feminists demanded that women be treated 'as persons and not as a sex' (as labour organiser Jean Daley put it in 1927 in her column 'Woman to Woman' in *Woman's Clarion*, the journal of the Female Confectioners' Union) and that in whatever employment—as banker or factory hand, statesman or mother—the woman should be paid for 'her work as an individual'.[1] Most important, mothers needed the economic support that would secure their capacity and right to mother.

During the 1920s and 1930s, the rights of mothers came to be articulated in quite distinctive political and class contexts—but the belief that women had rights as mothers proved a powerfully unifying principle among women activists between the wars. Feminists attempted to establish mothers' custody rights in divorce courts in opposition to the exclusive legal rights of husbands; while labour movement women insisted on the rights of working class mothers to keep their children, in opposition to the new claims by the state to the guardianship of those deemed 'neglected'. Mothers thus articulated their 'rights' against the assumed rights of husbands *and* of the state. As English writer Sarah Benton has said, we use the language of rights when the question of power is in contention. It is our word, she says, for disputing power that is exercised over us—the language of rights is a language for claiming or reclaiming power.[2] Post-suffrage feminists claimed rights for mothers in an attempt to enhance their economic, political and social power.

Outrage at the mother's lack of legal rights to the custody of her own children was one of the reasons women joined the nineteenth century Woman Movement, as recorded by Dora Montefiore, one of the founders of the Womanhood Suffrage League, in her autobiography *From a Victorian to a Modern*. When her husband died in 1889 she consulted the family lawyer about his will and was informed that as her husband had made no provision for the guardianship of her children, they could remain with her. Mothers had no custody rights in law. She was amazed, telling the lawyer 'You don't know how your horrible law is insulting all motherhood'. And from that day, she declared, 'I was a suffragist and determined to alter the law'.[3] Not until 1916, with the Testator's Family Maintenance and Guardianship of Infants Act did widows automatically become their children's legal guardians, and not until 1934 in New South Wales (and 1940 in South Australia) did women with husbands still alive win equal custody rights in law.

Labor party women also put mothers' custody rights on the political agenda in Australia when they were forced to defend working class mothers against the intrusions of an increasingly child-oriented state, against having their children taken away. From the 1890s and into the first decade of the Commonwealth, Australian governments—spurred on by philanthropists and, ironically, by activists in the Woman Movement—passed a range of laws aimed at removing 'neglected children' from the contaminations of their own families and communities. Thus did George Guillaume, Secretary of the Neglected Children's Department in Victoria, proclaim that the 'rescue' and 'regeneration' of neglected children was 'one of the most sacred and pressing duties of any State', and leading South Australian reformer Caroline Clark confirmed that it was a grave mistake to leave young children to be raised in 'the hotbed of their own moral disease'.[4]

In this discourse on the 'neglected child', it was clear that it was working class children who were thought to be at risk, as legislative definitions of neglect expanded to include children who spent too much time on the streets, in the company of drunkards and prostitutes, or took on paid work at too young an age. The state's interest in the child as future citizen threatened mothers least able to care for their offspring in the ways stipulated by the expanding state agencies. There was concern, however, about the wisdom of removing children from their families into the care of strangers, which led, as we have seen, to the institution of 'boarding out' schemes, whereby poor but respectable (white) mothers, mainly widows, were paid to care for 'neglected' children in their own homes. There were other strategies to assist working class women keep their children. Women's organisations such as the National Council of Women began to set up crèches to enable working class mothers to take paid work without courting the charge of neglect.

In response to these developments, the labour movement began to call for a mothers' pension fund to provide the money to enable all working class mothers, whether married or unmarried, to care for their own children. A mother had a right to care for her own child and a progressive, democratic state should secure this right. Working class women held no illusions about the emancipatory character of paid labour—in a factory or shop for example—especially if combined with the arduous work of caring for home and family. Paid work was usually exploitative and exhausting and working class mothers were among the most overworked of citizens. According to their foremost champion, labour organiser Muriel Heagney, they gave 'an infinitely greater service than those of most other sectors of the community'.[5] Hence her use of the term 'working mothers', to refer not to women who combined paid work with motherhood, as in today's usage, but to distinguish working class mothers who did all their own domestic work from middle class women who employed 'help'.

Like Ada Bromham, Heagney was born in the 1880s and raised in a Labor party household. Unlike Bromham, she retained a fierce loyalty to the Labor party and followed her mother and father into the Richmond branch in Melbourne. She worked as researcher, writer and organiser for trade unions and the Labor party from the first decade of the century until she helped form the Council of Action for Equal Pay in 1937. Labor women knew that working class mothers were overworked as well as underpaid, but in the early 1920s they were confident that progressive social change was at hand. In 1919, labour organiser Lilian Locke-Burns, then sixty years old, issued a manifesto entitled 'State Provision for Mother and Child' in the journal *Labor Call*, in which she heralded the day when 'One Woman One Job' would be the general rule, for then 'a mother will not be expected to combine half a dozen occupations to the serious detriment of herself and of the children'.[6] How to secure the economic independence of mothers without jeopardising their health through overwork: this was the pressing issue for Labor women.

They argued that an income from the state was the citizen-mother's right, and they found in party leader Andrew Fisher a receptive audience. In 1912, as Prime Minister, Fisher introduced the Maternity Allowance of 5 pounds, a one-off payment equivalent to around five weeks' wages for a working woman, on the birth of a child. Fisher explained the grant in terms of the entitlements of citizenship: it was 'to protect the present citizens of the Commonwealth and to give to coming citizens a greater assurance that they will receive proper attention at the most critical period in their lives'. 'Statistics show', he added, drawing a common parallel between masculine and feminine forms of citizenship, 'that maternity is more dangerous than war'.[7] Cynical conservative critics observed that the Prime Minister was simply wooing recently enfranchised women voters, which was testament indeed to the power of the woman's vote!

Labor women rejoiced at their political success, and they were especially pleased that unmarried mothers were also to receive this radically innovative benefit. Jean Daley, one of the leaders of the campaign, had herself given birth to an 'illegitimate' baby just six years before and knew the social stigma and material difficulty associated with this peculiarly feminine shame. Born in Victoria in 1881, Daley, like Muriel Heagney, grew up in a Labor household; her western district father was a member of the Australian Shearers' Union. She went to live and work in Melbourne, but at the age of twenty-five, still single, she became pregnant. Blessed with supportive parents, Daley was able to return home with her baby to Wallacedale, where he would be raised by his grandmother. Back in Melbourne, Daley became a dedicated union organiser and member of the Women's Organising Committee (WOC) of the Australian Labor party. In 1912, the Committee passed a heartfelt resolution congratulating the Prime Minister on his 'noble and wise act' in introducing the Maternity Allowance 'conferring this instalment of the mother's maternal rights'. They anticipated that the next instalment would be a 'pension', by which they meant an income from the state.[8] When critics attacked the Maternity Allowance for apparently endorsing unmarried motherhood, saying that the extension of civil rights to 'those who have become mothers before they have become wives' violated 'the law of marriage which the state exists to safeguard', the WOC 'on behalf of the working class women of Victoria' angrily denounced the 'foul slanders levelled at our class'.[9]

Although the Maternity Allowance extended to unmarried mothers, this Labor legislation specifically excluded non-whites from the benefit:

mothers who were 'Asiatics' or 'Aboriginal natives of Australia, Papua or the islands of the Pacific' would not receive the payment. Labor women, who were strongly committed, like the men in the Labor party, to the White Australia policy, let the racist exclusions pass without comment. Non-party feminists, such as Vida Goldstein in the Women's Political Association, denounced the 'colour bar': 'It is the White Australia policy gone mad. Maternity is maternity whatever the race . . .'.[10] The rights of mothers, in other words, were universal. This emphasis on 'the common status of motherhood', to use Ada Bromham's phrase,[11] would be the distinctive message of non-party feminism in Australia, as expressed by the Women's Political Association and then the Victorian Women Citizens' Movement in Victoria, the Women's Service Guild in Western Australia, the United Associations in New South Wales and the national body, the Australian Federation of Women Voters.

THE COMMON STATUS OF MOTHERHOOD

In pursuit of the mother's right to economic independence, non-party feminists joined Labor women in their campaigns for a range of economic benefits. The effectiveness of this cross-class political alliance was demonstrated at the large 1923 women's conference in Melbourne, organised to defend the Maternity Allowance, which cost the nation 700 000 pounds a year and was targeted by a cost-cutting Nationalist government. In 1921, at the behest of the government, the National Council of Women in Victoria sponsored a report on the Maternity Allowance by three female medical experts: Dr Constance Ellis, who ran a general and obstetric practice in Malvern and worked as honorary pathologist at the Queen Victoria Hospital, Dr Mabel Baillie and Matron Andersen, also of the Queen Victoria Hospital. They concluded that the benefit was wasteful, extravagant and ineffective from a personal and national viewpoint. Feminists and Labor party women objected that such criticism missed the point, that the Maternity Allowance contained 'the vital principle of recognising the services rendered to the State by the mothers of the community' and that it was 'every mother's right to claim the Allowance'.[12] The following year, however, the federal government appeared to endorse the findings of the report and raised the possibility of achieving large savings by subjecting the allowance to a means test, or replacing it with a more restrictive scheme. But faced with mounting feminist protest, the government decided to defer action until after the next election.

Early in 1923, Bessie Rischbieth, president of the Australian Federation of Women Voters, was moved to observe in the *Dawn*:

> the Federal Treasurer, with the help of the Commonwealth Committee of the British Medical Association have apparently made up their male minds that the present maternity allowance must go, and they suggest an alternate scheme which, it is claimed, will cost less and be more beneficial.
>
> All these arrangements appear to be assuming concrete shape, without any idea on the part of the Federal authorities of obtaining the consent of the mothers of Australia who have directly handled this benefit since 1912.[13]

The idea that mothers were political subjects with rights whose 'consent' had to be obtained for changes that affected them was no doubt new to the government.

Rischbieth was pleased to report, further, that organised women were making arrangements to hold a nation-wide conference in Melbourne to discuss the issue and hopefully support the view that 'the present allowance by reaching *every* mother under *all* circumstances has the advantage of establishing a common status of motherhood which must not be lost sight of'.[14] The Maternity Allowance was one of the few benefits paid to women as mothers; it was every mother's right to claim the benefit and, contrary to the view of many medical experts that the money would be better spent on providing services, mothers had the right to determine the right and wise use of the money. Additional medical services should supplement the allowance, rather than replace it.

The conference took place in March amid much publicity. It was organised by the National Council of Women and delegates from 120 women's organisations throughout the Commonwealth packed into the Melbourne Town Hall. The *Age* newspaper considered it a major political event for Australian women: 'It is safe to say that the majority of women in the Commonwealth have given more thought to Melbourne [the site of the federal parliament] this week than ever before'. The reporter considered the most significant aspect of the proceedings to be the unanimity of women: 'one representative woman said that it had broken down barriers that until last week were believed to be impregnable'.[15] The barriers referred to were those of class and party: the conference was notable for the political agreement between Labor women and non-party feminists, but Victorian Labor women, to whom this cause was so dear, were in attendance in defiance of their party's ruling that they should not attend. In the event, Nelle Rickie went as a representative of the Trades Hall Council, Jean Daley (oddly) as representative of Labor Organisations in Western Australia, May Francis on behalf of the Socialist Women's League and Muriel Heagney represented the Clerks' Union.

Heagney delivered a powerful paper in support of the allowance called 'Has the Maternity Allowance Failed?', in which she refuted the popular idea that it was a mere 'Baby Bonus'. It had been introduced not to improve the birth-rate, but rather to assist the citizen-mother at a time of particular hardship: 'the Maternity Allowance has not failed to achieve its purpose. On the contrary, it has been a godsend to almost every mother who has claimed it'. But more was needed. To deal with the high levels of infant and maternal mortality, the government must ensure for every mother:

> good housing, continuous income, freedom from arduous toil, medical care, and attention and everything else that is conducive to the production of healthy children, whilst retaining her own health and vigour.

Her research work for the Basic Wage Royal Commission had brought her into contact with 'scores of workers' wives in each of the capital cities' and she knew that these basic rights were lacking among a very large section of the community.[16]

Heagney recommended the retention of the Maternity Allowance, the establishment of a Public Maternity Scheme available to all mothers irrespective of their social condition, and the introduction of a system of motherhood endowment. Her paper was very influential among other women at the conference. Her position was supported by M. Jamieson Williams, president of the Women Citizens' Association in New South Wales, who stressed that it would be a retrograde step to withdraw the 'first recognition of the value of the mother to the community', and by M. W. MacCallum, president of the New South Wales branch of the National Council of Women, who stressed 'the point of view of the individual mother' and 'the mother's personal rights'. Whether she chose to spend the money on medical services, a new outfit, a perambulator or household help was her right: such uses were ' all perfectly legitimate . . . and in addition suit the needs of the individual as a stereotyped institutionalism would not do'. Edith Cowan, member of the Legislative Assembly in Western Australia, the first Australian woman in parliament, attending the conference as a representative of the National Council of Women, argued that the allowance should be retained: it had been given to women as 'a recognition of their motherhood'. Irene Longman, representing the National Council of Women in Queensland, said that rather than abolishing the allowance, the government should double it.[17]

Women's mobilisation in support of the idea that the mother had political and economic rights forged a powerful political solidarity. Despite the misgivings of women doctors, such as Dr Edith Barrett who spoke at the conference on behalf of the Victorian National Council of Women report and reiterated the view that in terms of saving mothers' lives the allowance was a complete failure, the conference resolved to inform the Prime Minister that the allowance should be retained and supplemented by 'such projects for mother and child welfare as may be desired in each State'. In Western Australia, the Women's Service Guild concluded triumphantly that until a better scheme 'approved by the mothers of the Commonwealth, is inaugurated, let our slogan be "Hands Off the Maternity Bonus"'. The federal government had suffered a resounding defeat at the hands of organised women.[18]

The Maternity Allowance was again under threat during the 1930s Depression, when the federal government embarked on cost-cutting measures in response to the Premiers' Plan and the visit by Bank of England emissary Sir Otto Niemeyer. Labor Prime Minister Scullin reduced the payment to 4 pounds and introduced a means test. In a letter to the *West Australian* newspaper, Ada Bromham pointed out that no other pensions had been subjected to a salary test: 'The Maternity Allowance alone has been singled out for this treatment'. The more serious offence from a feminist point of view, however, was that

> the splendid principle upon which the allowance was instituted as the right of all mothers has been sacrificed for a problematical monetary saving, which even if possible to realise can never outweigh the moral loss of the national acknowledgment of the common status of motherhood.[19]

But by then it was increasingly evident that it was not just mothers' status as rights-bearing political subjects that was at risk, but also their lives.

THE MOTHER'S RIGHT TO LIFE

One of the disturbing facts registered in the national debate about the Maternity Allowance was the alarming level of maternal morbidity and mortality in Australia. While infant mortality had noticeably declined—the welfare state was working for children—the experience of childbirth for women continued to be dangerous and debilitating. In her paper 'Has the Maternity Allowance Failed?' Heagney had reported that in 1918 one in every 219 married mothers and one in every 123 unmarried mothers died from puerperal causes. These figures pointed to the class dimensions of the problem: 'the relation between economic and social conditions and the high death rate'.[20] In 1924, Heagney produced another paper, this time a research report on the plight of unmarried mothers in Melbourne, a subject 'near to her heart'. She strongly attacked the tendency of the middle class to moralise: 'in every class, race, country and religion there is a vast amount of irregular indulgence, which precludes the vast majority from pointing the finger of scorn at these less fortunate ones'.[21] Rather, a community education campaign was needed to change attitudes, and the state had to provide decent hostel accommodation.

During the 1920s, the high maternal mortality rate—described by the 1925 Royal Commission on Health as a 'grave national danger'—became a major feminist issue in Australia. Consistently worse than in England or Wales, in 1928 it reached its highest level since 1911. Many leading feminists followed the trend of looking to medical solutions, even as some began to suspect that it was the increased medicalisation of childbirth itself, facilitated by the Maternity Allowance, that was contributing to the mortality rate. Millicent Preston Stanley, executive member of the Feminist Club and successful candidate for the 1925 New South Wales election, campaigned for the establishment of a Chair in Obstetrics at the University of Sydney. When the University created a Chair in Veterinary Science and approved instruction in horse obstetrics, she commented: 'if the university is able to grant the means in the case of the horse, it should be equally able to grant "horse-rights" for women'.[22] Upon election to the New South Wales parliament, Preston Stanley immediately secured a suspension of Standing Orders to move that the recommendations of Dr E. Sydney Morris in his report on the 'Causes and Prevention of Maternal Mortality and Morbidity' be put into effect. Believing that maternal mortality was a question that 'transcended all party politics', she followed Morris in demanding that the government increase the number of maternity hospitals, establish maternity homes with post-natal clinics in town and country, introduce legislation making puerperal infections notifiable and ensure that more training in obstetrics was provided for all medical students. Success came with the establishment of a Chair in Obstetrics at the University of Sydney.

During the 1927 conference of the Australian Federation of Women Voters, meeting in Sydney, delegates angrily denounced authorities in general and doctors in particular for their failure to address and deal with maternal mortality. Women from the Feminist Club, the Citizens' Association, the Women's Union of Service, the Housewives' Association, the Women's League, the Professional Women Workers' Association, the Racial Hygiene Centre and the Country Women's Association joined together in urging the University of Sydney to increase its endowment to Obstetrics and to extend clinical training and research. To continue with their campaign they formed a Standing Committee for the Reduction of Infant and Maternal Mortality, which collected over 4000 signatures for a petition calling for the appointment of a Royal Commission to investigate causes contributing to maternal mortality and the appalling morbidity of women giving birth and to enquire into infant mortality.

In 1929, the Department of Health appointed Dame Janet Campbell, Senior Medical Officer for Maternity and Child Welfare in the Ministry of Health in London, to investigate maternal and child welfare in Australia. Her report commended Australia's measurable progress in child welfare: 'The steady reduction of the infant death rate in Australia from 96 per 1000 at the beginning of the century to 52 in 1928, is an achievement to be proud of'. The 'steady and almost uninterrupted rise' in maternal mortality, on the other hand, was alarming. And it was not just the deaths:

> for every woman who dies as a result of child-bearing many others are injured more or less seriously, more or less permanently. It is impossible to measure accurately this morbidity and the consequent amount of illness and suffering which women are called upon to endure. We can only guess at it from the records of gynaecological hospitals, though we know enough to be sure that in many ways this physiological disability and the resulting loss of health and strength is an even more serious matter than the actual mortality.[23]

Campbell applauded the political work of women's organisations for 'calling attention to this matter', but her recommendations, which focussed on returning maternal care and childbirth to the control of midwives—Campbell was one of several investigators to notice that the nation's high maternal mortality rate was exacerbated by doctors spreading infection in hospitals—were ignored by the government, which preferred to tie initiatives in this area to the advancement of the medical profession and its institutions. Not until the 1940s, with the introduction of antibiotics, was maternal mortality in Australia brought under control.

The extended discussions that occurred in Australia in the 1920s about infant and maternal welfare highlighted the ambiguities of the feminist maternalist project—while there had been considerable success in creating a welfare state for infants and children, the results were not so impressive to those concerned about the welfare of adult women. It became all too evident that the state was more responsive to demands for an increase in resources for babies and children—the future citizens—than to improving the wellbeing of current women citizens. The debate over the Maternity Allowance saw feminists insisting on mothers' rights as citizens and individuals, but these were increasingly threatened by the primacy accorded in public discourse to the rights of the child. Authorised to enter the public domain as the protectors of children, feminists found that in the longer term the cause rebounded on them, as the welfare of children became the justification to undermine the rights of mothers. This tension in feminist maternalist politics was dramatised by the Emelie Polini case in New South Wales, in which a mother lost custody of her child because she intended to pursue her career as an actress abroad. The case formed the basis of a play called *Whose Child?* written by Millicent Preston Stanley.

MOTHERS' CUSTODY RIGHTS

Aboriginal mothers lost custody rights to their children under a series of so-called Protection Acts passed by colonial governments in the nineteenth century and by the States in the twentieth century. In New South Wales, for example, legislation in 1909 extended the Neglected Children and Juvenile Offenders Act of 1905 to specifically provide for creation of a new 'Board for the Protection of Aborigines' authorised to remove and control Aboriginal children deemed to be 'neglected'. An amendment in 1915 extended its powers providing that:

> The Board may assume full control and custody of the child of any aborigine, if after due enquiry it is satisfied that such a course is in the interest of the moral or physical welfare of the child.
> The Board may thereupon remove such child to such control and care as it thinks best.
> The parents of such child so removed may appeal against any such action on the part of the Board to a Court as defined in the Neglected Children and Juvenile Offenders Act, 1905, in a manner to be prescribed by regulations.

In States such as Western Australia, Chief Protectors of Aborigines became the legal guardians of Aboriginal people with tyrannical powers over every aspect of their lives. Everywhere legislation empowered police to remove children from their families and communities, regardless of their parents' wishes. Aboriginal mothers used all means in their power to oppose their children's removal, sometimes hiding them, taking to the bush and sometimes protesting to the authorities. In South Australia and Western Australia, as will be discussed in the next chapter, feminists campaigned and lobbied authorities in support of Aboriginal women's claims to the custody of their children.

In South Australia, the Royal Commission on Aborigines in 1913–14 was told by one Aboriginal mother that although they wanted their children educated, they did not want them 'to go too far away'. Matthew Kropinyeri, an Aboriginal man, told the Royal Commission that the removal of Aboriginal children was 'an unequalled act of injustice'. When further legislation in 1923 empowered the Chief Protector to remove Aboriginal children from their communities for the purposes of education or training, Kropinyeri wrote on behalf of the mothers of the Point McLeay and Point Pearce mission stations, that 'the army of motherhood has taken up their position in opposition to the bill'.[24] Despite concerted protests, by Aboriginal and non-Aboriginal women, most Aboriginal mothers did not enjoy standard custody rights until as late as the 1970s, and many not even then.

Although white women enjoyed the political status of citizens, the Australian family remained a patriarchal institution, in that only husbands were endowed with the rights of guardians. This glaring inequality usually only became evident when fathers died or parents separated or divorced, but the injustice was always keenly felt. As the

Non-Party News, the journal of the South Australian Women's Non-Party Association, put it in 1924:

> By the very laws of Nature the bond existing between mother and child must perforce be stronger than that between father and child. Yet, in the eyes of the obsolete law on the question of child-guardianship, a mother has no authority over her own children, except by the courtesy of her husband.[25]

In the same year, the feminist Agnes Goode, endorsed as a Liberal candidate for the unwinnable Labor seat of Adelaide in the State election, explained that she wanted to tidy up the 'unravelled ends of laws': in relation to custody, for example, a married woman did not 'own half her child'.[26] Her work as a Justice of the Peace had brought this inequality to her notice. For example:

> On the bench, the other day, we had to decide on a case which concerned a woman who obtained a legal separation from her second husband. By the law, that woman had to hand over her own children to the husband, their stepfather, unless we expressly gave an order giving her their guardianship![27]

Also in 1924, in Sydney, Patricia Mary Ellis, known by her stage name of Emelie Polini, petitioned for custody of her two-year-old daughter, who had lived with her paternal grandmother following her parents' separation. As Polini's husband had failed to maintain his family, she supported herself and her daughter through her work as an actress, but she wished to go abroad for a period of time and take her daughter with her. She was a 'gifted and successful' actress with not a 'breath of suspicion' against her character—as Justice Harvey put it—but Emelie Polini lost her case.

In his ruling, Justice Harvey made the reason clear: the mother 'had never allowed her maternal affection to interfere with the call of her profession'.[28] In pursuing her profession, she had forfeited her rights as a mother. He explained that if Polini

> were settling down in a home in Australia I should be of the opinion that it was clearly a case in which the custody of the child should be shared between them turn and turn about.[29]

The ruling against Polini provoked outrage from feminists who embarked on a long campaign for equal custody rights for men and women. It was clear that marriage consolidated men's patriarchal rights at women's expense. Unmarried mothers had more rights to their children than married ones: 'the unmarried mother has full legal right in her child and no man can take it away from her'.[30]

This observation was made in a play *Whose Child?* written by the leader of the campaign for mothers' equal custody rights, Millicent Preston Stanley, and staged in the Criterion Theatre by J. C. Williamson's in 1932. In the play, the mother, Margaret, asserts her right to custody by invoking in her favour the law of nature and the law of God; the father replies that he has on his side 'all the laws of men'. In pressing the mother's claim, several characters in the play emphasise the bodily specificity of motherhood and point to the differences in the meaning of fatherhood and motherhood. Alice, the domestic help, voices this wisdom in working class dialect:

> A woman can nearly die bringin' her baby into the world, then it aint hers—a man can be a thousand miles away, when his brat's born—but he owns it—even if he don't know he has it.

The mother in the play, upon losing custody of her child, is permitted to put her case before the bar of parliament, where she speaks, somewhat histrionically, as the voice of all 'legally bereaved women', calling up the drama of embodiment, life and death, which was motherhood:

> have you forgotten that my body was your first cradle—my breast your first pillow—my arms your first world—my love your first shield. Have you forgotten that Nature has welded the mother and her child into one spirit and one flesh through the great drama of birth—or if remembering, how justify the law which has sundered so often and so pitilessly, the mother from the child.

When asked why mothers' rights should be placed ahead of fathers', the main character's ringing answer echoed all those post-war rhetorical flourishes of national statesmen on behalf of their dead, but most notably Prime Minister W. M. Hughes' response to American President Woodrow Wilson. When challenged at the Versailles conference to say why Australia, as a Dominion, should receive full representation, Hughes allegedly replied: 'I speak for 60 000 dead, Mr President and you?'. When asked why mothers' custody rights should take precedence over fathers' rights, the protagonist Margaret tells the parliament:

> Gentlemen the answer is simple and sufficient—by the right of their dead—by the right of their wounded. In this country 10,000 women have died in one generation in bringing their children

into the world and 10,000 more have been maimed in the same time in the same cause.

Shall parliament then dare to maintain that the paternal rights are superior to the rights of those who pay this terrible toll . . .

> . . . because she has cradled the race within her body—borne it upwards upon the rungs of her soul—lived for it—died for it—I proclaim mother right the highest moral law and on that principle I take my stand . . .[31]

As a result of a massive feminist mobilisation, which included several deputations representing some seventy women's organisations (speaking, in the Attorney-General's estimation, for around 70 000 women) the legislation providing for equal custody rights was finally passed in 1934, but it was not the victory feminists had hoped for. As Heather Radi has noted in her study of this case, 'the Act denied that any right resided in the mother, as mother':

> It formally acknowledged that a mother's wishes should count equally with a father's, but it explicitly stated that the welfare of the child was the 'first and paramount consideration'.[32]

And what became clear was that there were different expectations of mothers than of fathers. A mother's right to custody of her own children was conditional on her being not an exemplary citizen, but a good woman: white, married, chaste and economically dependent on a husband. Motherhood had become—partly as a result of feminism's own efforts—an exacting business, and the priority accorded by the state to children's welfare served to lock mothers into an ever more demanding 'role'. Feminists continued to insist, however, that motherhood should not lock women into a degrading dependence on men.

4
THE INDEPENDENCE OF WOMEN

WOMEN AND ECONOMICS

As a suffragist, Rose Scott had received numerous letters from married women such as that by Florence Roberts detailing the 'conjugal misery' inflicted by her husband:

> He simply would have me be his slave not his wife. He said he would make me obey him, he would make me do just what he chose or murder me. He would teach me who he was.[1]

To Scott, the sexual coercion that she believed was consequent upon women's economic dependence in marriage made it a profoundly problematic institution. As her biographer, Judith Allen, has noted, her understanding of women's position was strongly influenced by the writings of the American Charlotte Perkins Gilman, whose short stories she had discussed in the 1890s and whose book, *Women and Economics*, was published in 1898. In a paper delivered in 1903, called 'The Economic Independence of the Married Woman', Scott had emphasised the moral and psychological effects on wives of men's enforcement of their conjugal rights: 'how much degradation and insult (even unintentional) may a woman have to endure because economically she is dependent on her husband!'. As Allen has commented, for Scott the struggle to alter the position of wife from degraded sexual slave to self-governing partner was central to the struggle for women's citizenship.[2]

With the granting of political rights to women, Australian feminists became preoccupied with the anomalous status of the citizen-wife, marriage appearing as an anachronistic form of personal bondage and bodily oppression ('sex slavery') in a modern democratic polity. In the nation-building context of the early Commonwealth, Scott, like most feminists who followed in her path, argued for the economic independence of married women in their capacity as the mothers of the nation, as citizens and workers. As mothers, women were the hardest of hard workers, always on call, 'always ready to manage, nurse and attend to the numerous wants of those who are constantly appealing to her'. As mothers of future citizens, women performed work of vital civic importance: they ought not be forced to neglect this vital role in order to earn economic independence in the labour market. The mother had 'a right to an Independent position inside the home'.[3] Whereas Scott argued that legislation should entitle the wife to a share of her husband's income, her successors, influenced by Labor and socialist ideas circulating in Britain, began to advocate a scheme of motherhood endowment, an income paid by the state to women in their capacity as workers and citizens.

Importantly, Scott's full-time political activism, like that of many middle class feminists during this golden age of the woman citizen, was made possible by her own economic independence. Bessie Rischbieth enjoyed a similar position, initially as a wife of businessman Henry Wills Rischbieth and then, from 1925, as his wealthy widow. But like Scott, Rischbieth was also persuaded of the necessity of women's economic independence by the analyses of women's subordination offered by Charlotte Perkins Gilman, whom she heard speak in London in 1913, when visiting with her husband. She was enraptured. Gilman was 'wondrous, so powerful and so sweet to look at. A woman of forty five with a most logical brain'. Gilman expounded her view that human evolution had produced societies where 'emphasis is laid on "sex" to the detriment of our whole civilization'. For women to be treated as 'humans first' the 'whole economic condition of women must change': women had to become economically independent of men.[4]

Rischbieth became a convert to Gilman's teachings. Describing a meeting of the Women's Social and Political Union (WSPU) to family back in Perth, she wrote:

> Mrs Gillman [sic] then came on and she spoke oh! will I ever forget her great address. All along her own line of scientific research of the masculine feminine powers of nature and their absolute equality. Also of the sociological evolution and the way gradually the woman has been made dependent. I am bringing out some of her books. She is the most definite teacher and the most

scientific I have heard on the ethical side of the woman movement.[5]

(The Perth bookseller, Albert and Son Ltd., would later advertise that C. P. Gilman's book *Women and Economics* was available for purchase.)

During her stay of several months in London, Rischbieth came to passionately identify with the ongoing campaigns of the militant suffrage struggle there, attending weekly meetings of the WSPU and protest meetings about the Cat and Mouse Act. 'Oh this is an interesting place', she wrote to her niece Alice, 'and an interesting age to live in'.[6] Listening to Mrs Pankhurst speak, 'so weak and so ill' from her hunger strike, Rischbieth felt 'her backbone growing longer, as though you gained courage and freedom from her'. Disturbed by the militants' advocacy of law breaking, Rischbieth, was, nevertheless, unwavering in her support: 'There is no doubt this movement is the real thing from the very opposition it is arousing'.[7] Somewhat astonished by her own radical enthusiasm and endorsement of political militancy, this very respectable Australian woman worried about what people back home might think. To her sister, 'very dear Olive', she confided, 'I don't think you had better in any way say much about my letters outside just immediate friends it is so difficult for most folks to understand the present movements . . .'. Clearly anxious, she added in jocular vein, 'Don't you think the authorities would chuck me into prison if they could read my epistles'.[8]

The influence of analyses such as Gilman's, which stressed the importance of economic independence to women's emancipation, was evident in the priority given to 'freedom' and 'independence' rather than 'equality' in Australian feminist discourse in the interwar period. The alternative to independence was 'sex slavery', in or out of marriage. Such degradation might befall any woman without an independent means of survival. In Melbourne, Angela Booth drew the connection between prostitution, venereal disease and women's status in her book *The Payment for Women's Work* published in 1918, an extended argument for the necessity of equal pay: it was low rates of pay that forced women into unwise marriages, irresponsible parenthood and work as prostitutes.

An early member of the Women's Political Association, Booth disagreed with its anti-war stance ('there is a peace that can be worse than any war'), and after her resignation she gravitated to more conservative political company, becoming a member of both the

Nationalist party and the Australian Women's National League. During the war, Booth had agitated against the freer availability of contraceptives for soldiers, supporting, instead, sex education to teach boys and men the virtues of abstinence and self-control. A key speaker at the 1916 conference organised by the Workers' Educational Association (WEA) of New South Wales on 'The Teaching of Sex Hygiene', she lectured on the dangers of prostitution to 200 delegates from over forty organisations and representatives from government departments. Working class women were being depraved to gratify men's lusts; married men, who were the prostitutes' clients, took the disastrous contaminations back to their families, thereby spreading 'disease, sterility, deformity and death'. Booth advocated a number of feminist reforms: equal pay, sex education, the entry of women into public life and the inculcation of a single moral standard.[9]

Angela Booth knew that her forthright advocacy of women's rights would earn her opprobrium. In her pamphlet *The Necessity for Woman Awakening to her Political and Civic Duties*, she referred to the fate of Sappho, the leader of 'a woman's movement' in ancient Greece, who had 'determined to do her best to raise the position of her sex'.

> There is no doubt Sappho was an innovator—a voice calling on her sex to break through their baneful restrictions and so endeavour to arrive at their development. If we need further proof of this we shall find it in the attacks made upon the character of Sappho by the comic poets of a later date—a vilification which was pursued until the name of Sappho had become a synonym for lasciviousness: but vilification is the price all women pay who take their place in the van of progress of their sex.[10]

Thus, while Melbourne poet and law graduate Lesbia Harford was fantasising a life as the sexual Sappho—('Greece my land, not this! There the noblest women. When they loved, they would kiss')"[11]— Angela Booth was attempting to rehabilitate Sappho as a maligned feminist heroine.

Vida Goldstein also condemned the medical profession's proposal to curb the spread of venereal disease by making contraception more widely available and early marriage more acceptable:

> Boiled down to bald conclusion it means that women are still to be regarded primarily as sex creatures; they are to be on hand in numbers, indigent, unskilled of hand and brain, to be chosen by

men as sex mates, not even primarily as mothers for the race, but as outlets for the sexual impulses and alleged needs of men.

Her alternative proposal was that: 'A greater degree of independence must be striven for; marriage must be placed on a higher plane; men must make themselves more worthy of women of exalted ideals'.[12]

During the 1920s and 1930s, feminists stressed that all women—middle class and working class, married and unmarried, Aboriginal and non-Aboriginal—should enjoy economic independence. This was the precondition of true equality and freedom. 'All over the world today', proclaimed *Australian Highway*, journal of the Workers' Educational Association (WEA) in 1921, 'the cry goes up for the Economic Independence of the Married Woman'. 'Why should a woman forfeit the measure of economic independence which is hers prior to matrimony', asked the editor and first woman president of the WEA, Henrietta Greville, long-time labour organiser (born, like Locke-Burns, in the 1860s) and Labor party candidate for the federal seat of Wentworth in New South Wales in 1917.[13]

Jean Daley agreed. Mothers should raise their daughters to be self-supporting, she advised in her column in *Woman's Clarion* in 1925, for women who depended on men 'moulded themselves to his desire'. The real problems for women occurred when they had children, however. 'The truly equal and happy marriage is often the one in which both husband and wife are wage earners', she wrote. 'When children come, however, they complicate the situation.' Until mothering was 'regarded as national work and paid for as such, some period of dependence is inevitable for the working class woman'.[14] Hence the necessity for motherhood endowment. In Western Australia, Mary Montgomerie Bennett, the leading campaigner for Aboriginal rights, related the appalling abuse suffered by Aboriginal women to their being deprived of their land and economic resources. 'Economic dependence', she wrote in a letter to Bessie Rischbieth in 1932, 'is the root of all evil'.[15] As a teacher, Bennett hoped to educate Aboriginal women and girls in the craft skills that would enable them to become self-supporting. Across the country and across class and party lines, economic independence was inter-war feminists' central animating vision.

In her 1919 article, 'State Provision for Mother and Child', her manifesto for working class mothers, Lilian Locke-Burns made a heartfelt plea for their economic independence. As observed earlier, Labor women held no illusions about the emancipatory nature of paid employment, especially when combined with caring for a home and family. That was the route to exhaustion, drudgery and premature aging. The 'working mothers of Australia', as labour movement activist Muriel Heagney called this large constituency, wanted less, not more work, and 'One Woman One Job' was the slogan devised to publicise their demand for shorter hours. But as citizens, as mothers performing vital national work, they also asserted their right to an income that would secure their economic independence.

Locke-Burns put the case for extending the existing services for mothers and children through the provision of a state income for mothers. She commended the Commonwealth's evolution as a maternalist welfare state:

> In no other part of the world, as far as one can ascertain, is so much being done by the State in the way of providing for mothers and children as in the Australian Commonwealth. And yet how far we are still from a proper realisation of the value of the child as an asset of the State, and how little we realise the true position the mothers of the community would occupy in a properly-organised social system where the economic independence of women was fully recognised and assured![16]

Lilian Locke-Burns wanted to put mothers on the same economic basis as women who gained their fulfilment in other fields, such as journalism or business:

> we have also to recognise that, if a woman desires and chooses motherhood, she should be as economically free, as little dependent upon others as the well paid woman who has climbed to the top of the ladder in the scholastic, commercial, literary or any other arena of her own choosing.[17]

Working class mothers had a right, like middle class women, to an income of their own.

To conceptualise this preoccupation with the condition of wives and mothers as a conservative tendency in the history of feminism, as a perpetuation of 'traditional roles', which some have done, is to miss the revolutionary character of the demand for the economic independence of mothers.[18] Motherhood endowment as a recognition of 'a minimum income as an individual right' was expected to bring—in Muriel Heagney's words—'revolutionary changes in the relations of husband and wife'.[19] Feminists invoked maternalist discourse to disconnect the category of 'mother' from 'wife', which was seen as a demeaning and sexualised status of dependency, at odds with the independence and self-determination promised by citizenship. Post-suffrage feminists saw that so long as men's citizenship rights included conjugal rights—to their wives' bodies and domestic services—wives' status as self-determining citizens would always be compromised.

An independent income paid to mothers in recognition of their work was necessary to end the 'sex slavery' of women. As Nelle Rickie, delegate of the Theatrical Employees' Union to the Victorian Trades Hall Council (and Honorary Secretary of the Socialist and Communist women's group) argued in *Labor Call*:

> The economic dependence of woman on man is sex slavery—the only slavery that exists today. Woman will be a sex slave until such time as the community, and not the individual father and husband, is responsible for the provision of the necessities of life for the rising generation—until such time as there is Childhood and Motherhood Endowment.[20]

For women, the degradation of economic dependence was experienced in especially personal and sexualised ways.

THE CONTROL OF THEIR OWN BODIES

The political activism of feminists as citizens spoke to women's experience of sexual embodiment. Thus, not surprisingly, feminists theorised the rights attached to citizenship in different ways than men, interpreting the promise of individuality as a condition of bodily integrity and personal inviolability. For women, they said, the right to the sanctity of the person was 'the most fundamental reform of all'.[21] Men were more likely to see in the status of citizen guarantees of liberty defined against the power of the state, demanding freedom of speech, assembly and movement. Feminists looked to freedom from masculine, specifically conjugal, tyrannies. No longer, they insisted, were women to exist 'for the service and convenience of men'.[22] No longer should men have a right to enforce their conjugal rights over their wives. (Although the legal right existed in fact until the passage of legislation criminalising rape in marriage in the 1980s.) In insisting on their inviolability, feminists affirmed the right of women to control their bodies. As Edith Jones, president of the Victorian Women Citizens' Movement in the mid-1920s and dedicated campaigner for Aboriginal rights, put it, 'If a woman, whether black or white, has not the control of her body, she is a slave'.[23]

Feminists' preoccupation with the sanctity of the person was reinforced by their engagement with the League of Nations, specifically its Convention on Slavery and ongoing concerns about the 'traffic in women and children'. In 1927, the *Dawn* acclaimed the publication of the first part of the experts' report on the 'traffic in women and children':

> While for many years the scare of the White Slave Traffic has haunted women and girls who have read lurid stories of assault and abduction, very little has been known of the actual facts of the trade or how the market is organised.

The extent of the report's reach was also noted:

> The fact that Part 1 of the Experts' Report has gone into four editions and that 5000 copies have already been sold and distributed—a record for any League of Nations publication—proves that people are alive to the need for knowledge on this question.[24]

M. Jamieson Williams, president of the New South Wales branch of the Woman's Christian Temperance Union (WCTU) and Australian delegate to the League of Nations in 1927, wrote excitedly to Ada Bromham to report that the Fourteenth Assembly had strengthened the Slavery Convention by accepting the proposal to set up a permanent advisory commission of experts, including one woman. The conceptual framework in which the League of Nations formulated human rights—the emphasis on self-determination, rather than equality, and the understanding that the 'self' invoked in the promise of 'self-determination' was constituted in sexual and cultural difference—shaped the feminist emphasis on the importance of self-possession.

Their belief that women's use and abuse as 'creatures of sex' lay at the heart of their subordination meant that the demand for an 'equal moral standard' was a prominent plank on the platforms of most feminist citizens' organisations, including the Women's Service Guild, the Australian Federation of Women Voters and the United Associations. An 'equal moral standard for men and women is as necessary and important as equal legal, economic or equal anything else', said Rose Scott as president of the post-suffrage Women's Political Education League. Jean Daley, working to organise women workers, agreed:

'the double standard of morality . . . has been at the root of most women's troubles in the past'.[25] Women, like men, had to demand recognition as persons and as individuals.

The right to control one's body meant freedom from unwanted sexual advances, in or out of marriage. Feminists expected that this would be achieved through a change of attitudes, an acceptance of the equal moral standard, whereby men would come to exercise the same standards of purity and self-control expected of women. The principle of the sanctity of the person was invoked by feminists to defend women against unwanted sexual advances and pregnancies as well as the contaminations of venereal disease. One correspondent wrote about her horror of venereal disease to *Labor Call* in 1923:

> Gonorrhea is a disease of excess and uncleanliness and excess in married life means anything causing bad health to the woman, such as over child-bearing, over-work on the land and all the troubles caused by want of rest and attention before and after childbirth. I feel very strongly on the subject of marriage and have always advocated the 'economic independence of women'.[26]

In feminist discourse the link between women's right to control their bodies and their economic independence was taken for granted. To achieve the equal moral standard, however, men's attitudes to women also needed to change. Men needed to adhere to the standards of purity advocated for women. Thus feminists urged the introduction of sex education, especially for boys, and opposed the various States' efforts to introduce legislation providing for the compulsory detention and medical inspection of prostitutes. Such regulations simply encouraged the view that men had a right of access to women's bodies.

Unlike some of their counterparts in England and the United States, Australian post-suffrage feminists neither advocated sexual freedom for women nor supported the availability of artificial contraceptives in terms of a woman's right to sexual pleasure; such devices, it was assumed, would only encourage men to indulge their animal instincts and use women as 'sex slaves'. In a related argument, Rose Scott opposed the pro-natalist demand for an increased population; such calls merely clothed 'the desire for liberty to be freely licentious'. The quality of the population, not the quantity, was what mattered and women must assert 'the right to the control of their own bodies as well as their souls, so that the children of the future may have a nobler environment, physically, mentally and morally, before and after their birth'.[27] The right to control their bodies meant women's right to refuse the unwanted sexual advances of men.

Contraceptives only began to be tolerated as a protective measure for women against venereal disease and/or to protect the 'health of the race' by preventing the unfit from breeding, as explained by the Racial Hygiene Congress in Sydney in 1929. In 1930, Jessie Street was the only Australian to attend the International Birth Control Conference at Zurich, when she became a subscriber to the London-based Birth Control International Information Centre and a convert to the idea of contraception as an aid to women's health. In 1934, she wrote to Edith How Martyn, Honorary Secretary of the National Birth Control Association in London to report: 'A Birth Control clinic has been started in Sydney and has been running for about a year. The Organisation which started it [the Racial Hygiene Association] has been in existence for some time doing educational work for the prevention of venereal disease'.[28] One of the clinic's most ardent proponents in Sydney and London was Australian feminist Ruby Rich, whose talks to English women about 'women's work for racial hygiene' in Australia reportedly made many of them 'really long to try and pay a visit'.[29] Some feminists were more eugenicist in outlook. Angela Booth figured as a prominent member of the Victorian Eugenics Society in the 1930s, but in her last publication *Voluntary Sterilisation for Human Betterment*, published in 1938, she was careful to distinguish between her advocacy of voluntary sterilisation and the compulsory sterilisation she knew to be practised in Nazi Germany.[30] Jessie Street had urged Australian doctors to play a role in making contraception more widely available. One enthusiastic proponent was Dr V. H. Wallace in Melbourne whose assistance led a grateful patient in Brunswick, Victoria, to report exultantly that his method of contraception (a diaphragm) had given her 'more satisfaction and happiness than [she] had ever thought possible'.[31] It was a viewpoint unrepresented in organised feminism in these years, which continued to worry that sexual freedom meant women's degradation.

Women's major defence against the degradation of 'licensed and unlicensed vice' was seen to lie in their achievement of economic independence. Hence the singular concentration on this goal. 'The economic dependence of women is responsible for the double standard of morality that now obtains in our society', observed labour organiser Jean Daley, 'and this attitude of men has been at the root of most women's troubles in the past and every mother should strive to make her daughter self-supporting'.[32] Following a similar logic, Muriel Heagney argued that it was women's lack of economic independence that drove so many 'to make unsatisfactory sex alliances as a means of subsistence'.[33] In this discourse on sexual degradation, feminists could not imagine sexual pleasure as a woman's right. Not until the late 1960s did feminists in Australia put sexual rights on their political agenda.

SEX ANTAGONISM IN THE LABOUR MOVEMENT

Middle class and working class women joined together in their insistence on the importance of economic independence for women. In 1913, in Melbourne, the Women's Political Association (whose platform included the goal of equal pay) was addressed by trade unionist Ellen Mulcahy, who discussed possible industrial and political strategies to achieve equal pay, specifically for women clerks and typists. For some years, the Victorian Lady Teachers' Association, led by Clara Weekes, had campaigned for equal pay for women teachers, and they had received support from the Women's Post and Telegraph Association, the Women Public Servants' Association, the Women Caterers' Union, the National Council of Women and the Women Typists' Association.

The case for equal pay was also made at the Women's Industrial Convention, held in September 1913 in response to the Arbitration Court decision of 1912 (the Rural Workers' Union case) that endorsed one wage rate for men and another for women. Women delegates thought that it was an act of gross injustice that single men were awarded the same rate as married men, yet female breadwinners went unprovided for. 'The time had arrived in the Commonwealth of Australia', declared the chairwoman of the Convention, 'when women . . . [having] been raised to the dignity of citizenship . . . must organise industrially and politically'.[34] Speakers such as Sarah Lewis, from the Hotel and Caterers' Union and one of the organisers of an equal pay rally in Melbourne in July that year, insisted that women workers did the same quality and quantity of work as men. She assumed that those present

> as workers in the industrial field did know something about the work done by men and women, and that they were all seized with the justice of women receiving the same payment as men—that is, of women receiving a decent living wage which would prevent

them from being, as some of them were at present, with only sixpence between them and destitution.[35]

The Convention resolved that the State government should proceed towards equal pay by eliminating the word 'sex' from the Factories Act, and appropriate legislation was introduced into parliament by Labor MLA Slater, which lapsed for want of support. In any case, because male trade unions invariably defended their right to a higher wage in terms of their responsibility to support dependants, labour movement women concluded that they must devise alternative principles of wage fixation that made provision for dependants in quite different ways. As Muriel Heagney put it, they had to 'challenge the existing theoretical basis of wages'; by recognising the right of every individual to an income, 'we will be driven inevitably to reconstruct our whole policy on wages'.[36]

To achieve the economic independence of all women—for those who laboured at home as well as those working in shops, factories and offices—women activists in the labour movement began to consider ways of disconnecting the payment of wages from the need to make economic provision for persons temporarily unable to enter the labour market, namely mothers and children. They joined non-party feminists in espousing the principle that all individuals, all citizens, had a right to an individual income. They were strengthened in their resolve by the intervention of A. B. Piddington, chairman of the 1919 Royal Commission on the Basic Wage, who in a memorandum to the Prime Minister and a subsequent booklet *The Next Step A Basic Family Income* argued that a wage for a married couple only, supplemented by a scheme of child endowment, would be fairer to workers with families. Income would go where it was intended to go and where it was needed. Some women in the labour movement welcomed his proposal, but considered it didn't go far enough. They wanted to secure not just the welfare of children, but also the independence of women. Labor party men considered it went too far, because it threatened to reduce some men's wages to 'rear other men's children': 'under the Piddington proposal the majority of the male adult workers are to have their standard of life lowered one eighth'. His scheme was denounced by men in the labour movement as not in the interests of the working class.[37]

In a bid to reconstruct the whole sytem of wages, Labor party and socialist women developed a three plank platform of interrelated goals: equal pay, motherhood endowment and child endowment. Each reform necessitated the other. The dismantling of the family wage and the introduction of motherhood and childhood endowment constituted their major strategy in the 1920s to achieve equal pay or the rate for the job. 'The reforms of motherhood and childhood endowment are . . . bound up with the demand for equal pay for the sexes', explained Nelle Rickie, an executive member of the Victorian Socialist party in 1918–19, founding member of the Communist party in 1921 and delegate to the Victorian Trades Hall Council in 1923.[38] An official with the Theatrical Employees' Union, described as a frail, but very earnest and well-educated socialist speaker, Rickie was involved in putting a claim for equal pay to the Theatrical Managers' Association. Equal pay or the rate for the job (and not the sex) meant that workers would be paid as individuals. The higher wage for men could only be justified because they were expected to make provision for their wives and children. Childhood and motherhood endowment, conceptualised as two different measures, would make this rationale redundant. Thus to feminist activists in the 1920s, the goal of equal pay for the sexes logically necessitated motherhood and childhood endowment.

But at the same time, labour movement women emphasised the justice of remunerating mothers for their death-defying travail. 'Every mother', said Muriel Heagney, 'like Hercules in the quest of Alcestis, has been down into the Valley of the Shadow and wrestled there with death in order to bring a young life into the light of day'. She continued:

> Twenty-four centuries ago, a mother, in the play, Medea, claimed that her lot was harder even than a soldier's. 'They say that we women live a sheltered life in the home while men go forth and fight with the spear. They reason ill. For I would rather thrice confront an enemy with my shield than once bring forth a child'.[39]

Motherhood entailed courage, but also hard work, for which women weren't paid. It was precisely the entry of large numbers of single working class women into the labour market (in Victoria, by the 1920s, one in every three factory workers was female) that highlighted what Daley referred to as 'the slavery of the married woman'.[40] The more common it became for single women to enter paid work, the more problematic was married women's penury.

The feminist program to reorganise the wage system was hammered out in prolonged and at times acrimonious debate at the Victorian Trades Hall Council during the 1920s, when a number (but not all) of the women set out to persuade their male comrades of the justice and wisdom of the feminist cause. (Alicia Katz, for example, whose husband had been tarred and feathered during World War I because of his anti-conscription stand, defended the family wage.) The starting point for the champions of women's independence was the fact that women were now 'a permanency in industry'; equal pay was needed to prevent female workers undercutting male wages, but it was also a matter of justice. Nelle Rickie reported on the progress of the debate in September 1923:

> the matter was discussed in the Trades Hall Council. Some old-fashioned people thought that the discussion should have been along lines of the glory of motherhood etc., but, fortunately, there were enough ready to face the real issue. A decision was arrived at to demand equal pay for the sexes right throughout industry.[41]

Rickie, by then secretary of the Socialist and Communist Women's group, elaborated on the way that equal pay would be complemented by childhood and motherhood endowment.

> That is, we are demanding that the State must provide the full maintenance, general education and technical training of every child, till the earning age; also, the full support of mothers while they are rearing children . . . The last Easter Conference decided to get on with a scheme for motherhood and childhood endowment and there we remain, evidently exhausted with our effort in coming to a decision.[42]

Nelle Rickie's and Muriel Heagney's ideas built on the socialist critique of dependence—the general critique of 'wage slavery' and Ferdinand August Bebel's writings on the particular oppression suffered by the working class woman, 'the slave of the slave'. But they aroused spirited opposition among labour movement men keen to see the family basis of wages retained and not at all convinced by 'the modern feminist viewpoint of this question'. However, during 1923 and 1924 Rickie's views seemed to have won the day and some men thought twice about questioning their political correctness. One dissident reported: 'Several members of the Trades Hall Council, who had the courage to express their views, were taken to task over an alleged unscientific attitude of this phase of industrial life'.[43]

But labour movement men were not backward in voicing their opposition, characterising Rickie's views as 'claptrap', and charging feminists with ruining even the Eight Hours Day commemoration by including a float advocating motherhood endowment. One irate critic, 'a mere man and a Unionist' thought the time had come to put a stop to the spread of feminist propaganda, at least in the labour movement. In February 1924, John Newton wrote to *Labor Call*:

> When the movement foolishly allowed Mrs Nelle Rickie and a few misguided enthusiasts to put a 'Motherhood Endowment' display in the last Eight Hours procession, they should have expected the present propaganda. For twelve months now there has been insistent propaganda for 'women's freedom', 'the economic independence of women' claptrap has been going on insistently and insidiously. The Trades Hall Council has foolishly adopted the sentiments of Mrs Rickie, and it seems inevitable that there will be a change in the adjustment of wages . . .

But, Newton insisted, the family basis of wages had to be maintained: 'a man must receive sufficient so that a wife need not go to work. The home must be preserved . . .'.[44] Whereas feminists spoke on behalf of the 'mother', their male opponents referred to the duties of the 'wife', her 'duty to husband and children'. And when labour movement men paid lip service to the desirability of motherhood endowment, they usually meant child endowment, a measure of which was first introduced by the Labor government in New South Wales in 1927 after years of lobbying there by Labor women, such as Annie Golding, Kate Dwyer and Mrs Seery. Child endowment was one thing, the economic independence of wives was a much more threatening prospect.

Women on the left found themselves in increasingly tense relations with their male comrades in these years. Expected to repudiate feminism as a bourgeois deviation (feminists fomented 'sex antagonism' and thus drove a wedge into the working class), they were often silenced by the demand for solidarity. 'Labor women are loyal to their men', stated an editorial in *Labor Call*. 'They will work with their men.'[45]

Another argument erupted in 1923 between Labor party men and women, at the annual conference of the Victorian branch of the ALP, over the ruling of the central executive that the Women's Organising Committee could not attend the Maternity Allowance conference called by the National Council of Women in March 1923. Lizzie Wallace said that the central executive had inflicted 'an unmitigated humiliation on the Labor women by preventing them from attending' and Nelle Rickie, who had gone as a representative of the Trades Hall

Council, also said it was humiliating to her to be met with the remark 'Oh, I thought you labor women were pulled off the conference'. Male conference delegates defended the decision, reminding their women who was in control: the Women's Organising Committee was 'an adjunct of the ALP and it had not the power to do anything the conference did not want'. Moreover, 'Labor women should not confer with people who opposed the maternity allowance when Labor introduced it and who declared that it was a premium on immorality'.[46] The women's motion of regret was, nevertheless, carried. As discussed earlier, Victorian trade unionist women Jean Daley, Muriel Heagney and Nelle Rickie did in fact attend the Maternity Allowance conference, representing other bodies, and were able to participate in the cross-class and cross-party alliance that ensured the survival of that cherished citizen-mother's benefit.

Labor women were expected to put their class loyalty before sex solidarity. Feminism was accused of being a middle class indulgence. Many feminists were, indeed, identified with the Nationalist party in politics—Edith Cowan in Western Australia, Millicent Preston Stanley in New South Wales, Agnes Goode in South Australia and Eleanor Glencross in Victoria. Labor women could see, however, that men's insistence on 'class solidarity' was often an alibi for male domination, and while they disclaimed a feminist identity ('I have never been a feminist', 'I am not a man-hater'), they deployed a distinctly feminist discourse. For despite men's doctrine, 'years of experience' in political life had demonstrated, as Jean Daley said, that there was after all 'a woman's point of view in politics' and it enabled Daley to see that 'it is [men's] fear of losing their dictatorship, that makes them resent independent women'.[47] Daley was an indefatigable, if unappreciated, worker for the Labor cause and accepted preselection as Labor candidate for the unwinnable seat of Kooyong in the federal election of 1922.

Daley's readiness to identify publicly with the feminist cause was encouraged by the visit of Alice Henry, who returned temporarily from the United States in 1925. Born in Melbourne in 1857, Henry had worked as a journalist for several years before embarking on an overseas tour in 1905 at the age of forty-eight. This led to a career in the United States as lecturer and writer, ultimately as editor of the journal of the National Women's Trade Union League, in which capacity Henry was able to promote the two causes of labour reform and the advancement of women. When she returned in 1925, nearly seventy years old, she was a respected figure in the American women's and trade union movements and at the height of her career, having published two books, *The Trade Union Woman* (1915) and *Women and the Labor Movement* (1924) during the previous decade.[48] Addressing meetings in Melbourne in 1925, she urged the importance of combining unionism and feminism within the one movement. At this time, Jean Daley was working as a trade union and Labor party organiser and was keen to embrace this double identity: 'woman would no longer be a slave for [man] but rather insist on being a comrade; and she will find, too, pleasure in being a woman's woman also . . . in foregathering with her own sex, in fighting with them to gain the right of development in education, in civil and political life'.[49]

Inspired by Alice Henry's visit, working women in Melbourne formed a Women's Trade Union League modelled on the organisation for which Henry worked in the United States. Delegates from thirteen unions attended a meeting in July 1925, which adopted a platform aimed at increasing women's participation in their individual unions and on public tribunals. They also resolved to obtain for 'girls and women equal opportunities with boys and men in trades and technical training, and pay on the basis of occupation and not on the basis of sex'.[50] Its constitution was framed to attend to the sensitivities of their male comrades: no one eligible to join a union who had not done so would be permitted to join the League. But masculine anxieties were not so easily assuaged and the League did not thrive. 'I am not a man-hater', declared Daley wearily the following year, 'but I pity man because he cannot see woman as an equal doing an equal share in the world, but sees her rather as an inferior being because she is doing different work'.[51] She continued her different work as a 'woman's woman' in her capacity as women's organiser for the Victorian branch of the ALP, a position to which she was appointed in 1926.

A REVOLUTION IN THE FAMILY?

The campaigns for mothers' rights and women's economic independence came together most radically in the proposal for a federal scheme of motherhood endowment. Labor women were again challenged by their male comrades about where their loyalties lay when they joined non-party feminists in supporting motherhood endowment and equal pay at the Royal Commission, appointed by Nationalist Prime Minister Stanley

Melbourne Bruce in 1927, to enquire into the feasibility of introducing a federal scheme of motherhood and/or childhood endowment. Feminists were pleased when after concerted lobbying one of their number, Mildred Muscio, a distinguished university graduate and president of the New South Wales branch of the National Council of Women, was appointed as a Royal Commissioner. Also appointed was John Curtin, future Prime Minister, who would be elected in 1928 as Labor member of the House of Representatives for the seat of Fremantle. The larger political context of the enquiry—Bruce's desire to reduce the cost of wages and dismantle the federal arbitration system—put Labor party women in a difficult situation, as the feminist advocacy of an income for mothers was increasingly construed as an attack on male living standards and labour solidarity. Muriel Heagney was perhaps speaking specifically to Curtin when, as a witness, she reminded Commissioners that the policies of motherhood and childhood were not in fact the invention of anti-Labor forces, but had first been taken up by the labour movement in the 1890s.

An ardent champion of working class mothers—'working class mothers give an infinitely greater service than those of most other sections of the community'—Heagney told the Royal Commission that in her view 'there should be a payment to the mother, altogether independent of the father's wages'. In response to further questioning, she clarified that she was indeed advocating the independence of women, not just the greater support of children. 'I think that the family income should be based on individual needs ultimately, that the mother would ultimately draw an income for her services as home-maker and not as wife'. But even the payment of child endowment was a step in the right direction, for it 'could not fail to increase [the mother's] importance in the home and also in the community'.[52]

Other Labor women supported her in this claim. Lena Lynch, secretary of the Women's Central Organising Committee of the New South Wales branch of the Labor party, condemned the family basis of wage fixation: 'in the Industrial Court women and children are not recognized as individuals at all, they are just appendages to men . . . endowment recognizes the women citizens and the child. It is an individual right which is passed over by the Industrial Court'.[53] Labor women were frequently put on the defensive, however, by questions about the relationship between the basic wage—men's wage—and the proposals for family endowment. There was constantly the suggestion that the introduction of endowment—the redistribution of national income from men to women—necessitated the lowering of men's wages.

Labor men who appeared as witnesses opposed any suggestion of a transfer of income from wallet to purse. 'The single men of Australia', declared E. H. Baker, general secretary of the Western Australian branch of the ALP, 'would not stand for it'.[54]

Non-party feminists such as Jessie Street, president of the Feminist Club in 1927, were under no obligation to cater to the sensitivities, or bow to the intimidation, of men. Street pointed to the unfairness and inefficiency in a system that paid the family wage to all men, regardless of whether they had family responsibilities, regardless of whether they were fathers of ten or young bachelors, who might squander the extra amount in drinking or gambling. Large numbers of men received the family wage 'on false pretences'.[55] Meanwhile, thousands of families headed by women lived in poverty. In response to Royal Commissioner Curtin's suggestion that even the single man needed a higher wage to pay for domestic services—'that is to say the mending of his apparel, the cleaning of his room, and house keeping services'—Street insisted that wages should be paid for work done, not to meet social responsibilities. Wage fixing should take the man as 'an industrial unit', not a social unit. Her recommendation was straightforward: 'I would like to see the basic wage fixed for the individual, irrespective of sex and irrespective of social responsibilities'.[56] The rate for the job would be supplemented by motherhood and childhood endowment.

Irene Maud Longman, president of the National Council of Women in Queensland, also advocated women's right to economic independence, whether they worked in the labour market or at home. That was 'the trend of the present day' and there was no point in holding back from it. 'We felt that if this could be hastened it would be for the good of the community.' Astonished Commissioners questioned Longman about her advanced 'theory':

> Your theory is that the State should pay the wife for services rendered to the State?
>
> Yes, we say that her services to the State are as great as those of the man; and, therefore, that those services should be paid for as an independent economic unit.
>
> . . .
>
> Women could live apart from their husbands? That is an alteration of existing conditions?
>
> Yes, absolutely. It is revolutionary, and that is what we wish.[57]

The Royal Commissioners were not about to preside over a revolution in family relations, however. Recognising that motherhood endowment—'the idea of treating the wife as a separate economic unit on the pay-roll of the state'—would, in bypassing the husband, introduce 'a very powerful solvent' into 'family life as we know it', the Majority Report refused any scheme of family endowment, tending to blame mothers for any shortcomings in the conditions of family life.[58] A Minority Report by John Curtin and Mildred Muscio recommended child endowment as part of a scheme that would preserve the family wage. Mindful of threats to men's status in the family, they, too, rejected arguments for motherhood endowment: such a proposal would 'revolutionise the organic unity of the family and involve a financial contract which the State would effect with wives and children in their individual right, apart from the husband and father'.[59] But that is precisely what feminists like Street and Longman had in mind.

THE SERVICES OF WIVES AND MOTHERS CANNOT BE MARKETED

Feminists had succeeded in putting the case for the remuneration of mothers' work on the political agenda and they had popularised the idea that all women as citizens should be accorded economic independence. They were not successful, however, in winning their goal. The economic independence of mothers was not to be. Their campaigns had, moreover, provoked a political backlash among men on the left fearful about the threat to their wages. At the same time, feminists' emphasis on women's responsibilities as mothers shaped a discursive context in which these very responsibilities could be used against women, cited as a reason for confining them to home duties and dependence on their husbands. These ramifications would become clearer with the onset of the Depression, the spread of unemployment and the escalation of attacks on women's entry into the labour market, which forced feminists to articulate women's 'right to work'.

On the other hand, the attacks on women's paid labour during the Depression also reinvigorated the campaign for an income for those who worked at home. If women were justly rewarded for the work they already did, many would not need or want to seek employment beyond the home. Feminists continued to make the point that women working at home had a right to economic remuneration. In the first of a series of pamphlets issued by the United Associations of Women (UA) in the 1930s, whose title, *Income for Wives How It Can Be Managed or The Economic Independence of Married Women*, echoed that of Rose Scott's paper delivered some thirty years before, Jessie Street presented an historical account of married women's distinctive condition of servitude. She explained:

> The right of all men, with the exception of lunatics and criminals, to sell their labour for the highest price, has been recognised since the abolition of slavery 100 years ago. The recognition of the right of women to do so is much more recent, and, judging from various statements heard and read today, women and married women in particular, are in danger of having taken from them this right, which is the very foundation of human liberty . . .
>
> Just as working men appreciate the right to their own money, so should wives appreciate a similar right. How can we make it possible for a wife who is working in her own home to have the right to her own money?[60]

Street advocated legislation requiring men to hand over a share of their family wage to its intended beneficiaries. A report of a radio 'debate' staged by feminists on station 2GB spelt out the full dimensions of the degradation of the wife's position under existing law:

> She is not entitled to any money, for housekeeping or for any other purpose. The husband may order all the supplies for the house itself. Indeed he may even order or buy his wife's clothes and she had no cause for complaint. So long as he houses, clothes and feeds her at a standard in keeping with his income, he need not give her a penny piece, and she can do nothing about it.
>
> Do you mean to say that a wife is not entitled to enough money to even buy her own clothes and other personal necessities?
>
> That is just what I do mean.
> She—is—not—entitled—to—any—money—whatever—for—any—purpose—whatsoever.[61]

In a later pamphlet called *Woman as a Homemaker*, Jessie Street argued that a mother's work, 'the most indispensable and important work done anywhere by anyone', should be rewarded by the state: 'the adequate remuneration by the State of the work of homemakers would satisfy the desire of the homemakers for economic independence'.[62] By being denied an income, homemakers were 'deprived of their independence and liberty'. In the final pamphlet in the series, on *Child Endowment*, similar arguments were made, but with a new emphasis on the national interest. In the event, a federal scheme of child endowment was introduced by the United Australia party government in 1941, with an amendment incorporating the UA recommendation that the endowment be paid to mothers, rather than to fathers, as initially proposed. Motherhood endowment as recommended by feminists for some twenty years was never granted—as ever, politicians seemed more responsive to arguments about the needs of children than to those about the rights of women.

The difficulty entailed in convincing men of the value of women's domestic work was evident in the derisory response of Professor F. A. Bland, professor of Public Administration at the University of Sydney, to the suggestion of a group called the Wives' and Mothers' Union that the 'vast army of unpaid workers' should be remunerated by the state. The women insisted on the reasonableness of their claim:

> No sane person can ignore the claim of wives and mothers if only as essential workers who perform such a multitude of vital household tasks and who also risk their lives in motherhood and are responsible for bringing into existence, maintaining and caring for the most important product of mankind—human beings.

Professor Bland said that such proposals caused him 'great hilarity': 'Services can have an economic value only when they are marketed. The services of wives and mothers cannot be marketed—they are above all price'.[63] Increasingly, it became clear that equality would only be achieved on men's terms, by following men into the labour market. Women would need to go out to work. Significantly, the second in the UA series of pamphlets, *The Justice of Equal Pay and Equal Opportunity*, registered this fact, outlining an argument for women's right to equality of employment in the public service:

> Women are making their contribution as taxpayers, and that in itself should go a long way to entitle them to the fullest freedom on terms of equality to every post which the State has to offer and which they can fill with reasonable success in the service of the community.[64]

Clearly, if women were to achieve economic independence they would need to disavow sexual difference and become workers just like men. This would become the new path to the elusive goal of equality.

5
CAMPAIGNING FOR ABORIGINAL RIGHTS

A CALL TO THE WOMEN OF AUSTRALIA

In March 1932, Mary Montgomerie Bennett, a teacher and passionate campaigner for Aboriginal rights, was entertained at the headquarters of the Women's Service Guild (WSG) in Perth, where she urged those present to take up the cause of the oppressed condition of Aboriginal women in Western Australia. She had spent most of the previous year exploring the Kimberley and working on missions in the area, including at Forrest River, and had been horrified at what she saw. She asked the members of the Women's Service Guild to make a commitment:

> Will you affirm the right of the aboriginal woman to the sanctity of her person and ask for definite reforms for her protection—two of these reforms should be the appointment of married protectors of high character and qualifications and of a doctor as a travelling protector?

The WSG accepted Bennett's offer to pay for a leaflet detailing the conditions of Aboriginal women and recommended reforms. This leaflet became *A Call to the Women of Australia to Demand an Honourable Native Policy*.[1]

In this leaflet, which reflected a mixture of her anthropological interest in Aboriginal culture and its special relationship to land, the feminism espoused by Edith Jones and Constance Cooke, and the Christian belief shared by all three, Bennett emphasised the importance of land and education for Aboriginal people and of encouraging them to maintain 'the many admirable elements in their own culture'. But 'the most important fundamental reform of all' she emphasised was 'the right of women to the sanctity of the person'. For, Bennett explained, it was a deplorable fact that Western Australian 'women Natives and Half-castes' had 'neither human rights nor protection against irresponsible white men'. To 'ensure this protection' Section 43 of 'The Aborigines' Act' had to be amended to provide harsher penalties for white men engaging in sexual relations with Aboriginal women not their wives.

Bennett's suggestion that Aboriginal women's rights could be upheld by offering them better protection represented an extension of the maternalist strategy that feminists espoused generally in these years in pursuit of a welfare state. Similarly, the analysis that located the oppression of Aboriginal women in the violation of their bodies by rapacious men, with its concomitant demand for recognition of the 'sanctity of their person', was an extension of the feminist demand for an equal moral standard. Travelling through the north west of the State, Bennett was appalled at the extensive evidence of the 'white slave trade in black women'. She noted the slave labour conditions in which Aboriginal employees were forced to work without wages, but in her view the chief sufferers in this regime of coercion were the women. 'The worst thing I have seen', she wrote, 'is the attitude of the average white man to native women—the attitude not of the mean whites, but of the overwhelming majority of white men. In the North-West it is so much the accepted thing for white men to abuse native women that it is the custom of the country'.[2]

Mary Montgomerie Bennett had arrived in Western Australia in 1930. Though she had lived in England most of her life, she had grown up in Australia, the devoted daughter of Queensland pastoralist Robert Christison, whose sympathetic treatment of local Aborigines she extolled in her biographical tribute to him, *Christison of Lammermoor*, published in 1927. In the same year, while living in London, her growing conviction that she must devote her life to improving the conditions of Aboriginal people was given new force when she went to hear 45-year-old Constance M. Ternente Cooke, a member of the Aborigines' Welfare Committee of the Women's Non-Party Association in South Australia, deliver the annual address to the Anti-Slavery Society. Like Mary Bennett and Ada Bromham, who would become lifelong friends and political allies, Cooke was born in the 1880s.

A founding member of the Aborigines Protection League and a Justice of the Peace, Cooke had long taken an interest in Aboriginal welfare, and the Women's Non-Party Association had added the 'furtherance of the welfare of aboriginal women and children' to its list of stated objects in 1927. According to Travers Buxton of the Anti-Slavery Society it was Cooke who brought the question of the treatment of Aborigines to their attention 'in the first instance'.[3] She also introduced Bennett to the gentlemen who ran the Society—John Harris and Travers Buxton—but they were somewhat alarmed by her energy and passion. Bennett was intense, eloquent, righteous. She was an avid researcher, assiduously documenting the history and legal status of Aborigines, investigating the relevant legislation and international conventions, sending volumes of documentary material to newspapers and other opinion makers in London and attempting to establish 'a study circle of Australian ladies'.[4]

By 1928, Bennett had become convinced, in her imperial way, that there was a 'need for a firm policy in Australia in regard to the Aborigines'.[5] As a Britisher and a Christian, Bennett insisted that Aborigines, 'our native race', were 'our responsibility'. She lobbied the Anti-Slavery Society unceasingly; she was 'most earnest', the gentlemen noted, 'and indeed, indefatigable in her work for the Australian natives'.[6] When the Rev. C. E. C. Lefroy suggested that Bennett be invited to become more closely involved with the Society's work by joining their Committee, their parliamentary secretary John Harris took fright:

> I hardly think it would be wise to ask Mrs Bennett to attend our Committee Meeting on Thursday. She is so full of, and keen on, her object that I feel sure she would take up a good deal of our time.
> ... You suggested to me that Mrs Bennett might be proposed as a member of our Committee, Mr Harris and I had already thought of this. I think, however, this had better stand over for the present. Our Treasurer thinks we have already too many women members, and I myself think that our Committee is quite large enough in numbers.[7]

Meanwhile, Bennett had met Edith Jones, a friend of Constance Cooke, who had been involved in a combination of feminist and missionary work in Australia.

Edith Jones had recently returned to Britain with her husband, the Anglican clergyman Rev. John Jones, from Victoria, where he had been Anglican vicar for East St Kilda. Described by the *Dawn* as 'a true feminist, with a clear vision and a broad outlook',[8] she was one of the first women Justices of the Peace in that State and the second president of the Victorian Women Citizens' Movement. In that capacity she had offered herself for preselection in the 1925 federal elections, until pressured to withdraw her candidature by her husband's vestrymen. Feminists recorded their regret that the churchmen's action thus prevented 'an enthusiastic and gifted woman citizen from seeking a share in the national councils where the mother-voice is too long silent in this land of ours'.[9] Bennett was keen for Edith Jones to add her voice to her own at the meetings of the Anti-Slavery Society. She recommended her extensive experience and qualifications to Harris:

> She is the founder of the Women's Auxiliary of the Australian Board of Missions and was the chairman of the girls' department of the Young Women's Christian Association for Australia and New Zealand. She was on the National Council of Women, on the Social Hygiene Committee, one of the first women Justices (when she did a vast amount of work in the children's courts) and for several years was President of the Victorian Women Citizens' Movement.

Bennett went on to say that she had asked the British Commonwealth League (BCL), a London-based feminist organisation working for women's equality as citizens throughout the Commmonwealth, to invite Jones to speak to their annual conference about Aboriginal women, 'the very women who most need help'.[10] Expressing the sensitivity to imagined slights and the quickness to take offence for which she would become known, Bennett observed that if the BCL did not invite Jones to speak 'it would be a snub to the Australian women who have been and are collaborating with Mrs Jones in this great work'. To Harris she added: 'I think your Society might also avail itself of Mrs Jones' experience and support with great advantage'.

Bennett was especially impressed by Jones' political activity in support of Aboriginal rights in Australia: she had given evidence to the 1927 Royal Commission on the Constitution, advocating federal responsibility for Aboriginal affairs—a reform that would not eventuate until 1967—and in 1929 Jones had attended (as a representative of the Victorian Women Citizens' Movement) the federal conference called to consider the report by J. W. Bleakley, Chief Protector of Aborigines in Queensland, on the condition of Aborigines in the Northern Territory. There Jones had made an impact by drawing attention to the sexual abuse of Aboriginal women, demanding that the government institute reforms that would safeguard Aboriginal women's bodily and personal integrity, demanding recognition of their right to 'the sanctity of the person', the cause that Bennett would ask feminists in Perth to support when she addressed them in 1932.[11]

At the 1929 conference of 'representatives of missions, societies and associations interested in the welfare of Aborigines' called to consider the Bleakley report, Edith Jones emphasised that not only did there need to be more protectors of Aborigines, there needed, more specifically, to be women protectors, preferably 'medical officers'. Jones' analysis drew on the discourse provided by the League of Nations report on the traffic in women and children and the Convention on Slavery. This provided an enormously influential framework in which interwar feminists explained the oppression of women. 'If a woman, whether white or black', said Jones, 'has not the control of her body she is a slave . . . Some of these black women are slaves. Their bodies are not subject to their own discretion'. Jones' motion to the conference recommending the appointment of women protectors was supported by her friend Constance Cooke, who argued that the '30,000 aboriginal and half-caste women and children' in Australia needed representation by women, who could 'understand their needs perhaps far better than men, however kindly disposed they might be'.[12] The motion was carried unanimously, but with little effect. Seven years later, writing on behalf of the Anti-Slavery Society to Prime Minister Joseph Lyons, who was visiting Britain, Jones was still arguing the case for the appointment of women protectors.

When Jones first returned to live in England with her husband, appointed vicar of Marlborough in 1929, Bennett urged the gentlemen at the Anti-Slavery Society to avail themselves of her unusual experience and rhetorical skills: 'she is an effective *most* able speaker'.[13] Bennett herself, meanwhile, had experienced a series of setbacks in her mission of reform. She could not get letters she had written to the *Times* newspaper published—'I think the letters would be far more effective if they were rather shorter and contained fewer enclosures', advised Sir John Harris.[14] Furthermore, when she delivered a paper to the feminists at the British Commonwealth League in 1929, she had met with a hostile response, a defensiveness among some of the Australians present. Sir John Harris explained in a letter to Constance Cooke, the secretary, Chave Collison, 'being an Australian objected to her criticising the Federal Government'.[15] This nationalist defensiveness was a portent; by the mid-1930s Bennett's agitation about the treatment of Aborigines —especially her ongoing charges that Australia was condoning slavery—

would lead to considerable tension between Australian feminists, caught as most were between conflicting loyalties to their sex and their nation.

In London in 1930, Bennett published her book *The Australian Aboriginal as a Human Being* and she and Edith Jones both gave papers to the annual conference of the BCL. Jones had indeed impressed the gentlemen at the Anti-Slavery Society and she soon became the most active member of their Australian Aborigines Sub-Committee, pursuing the goal of the appointment of qualified women to 'protective' positions in the administration of Aboriginal welfare. This was the recommendation she took to the BCL conference in 1930. Bennett used the forum to charge Australia with condoning slavery, charges that were publicised in the *Manchester Guardian*. Australians were breaking the Convention on Slavery, she said, in three ways: 'employers were using forced labour on private property, they were refusing to pay wages to working natives, and they were removing natives from their tribes and families to work in Darwin'. 'It was a disgrace', Bennett added, 'that native women should be placed at the disposal of white men'.[16] Bennett had urged the Anti-Slavery Society to make a formal complaint to the League of Nations, a suggestion the Society passed on to sympathisers in Australia, notably Constance Cooke and the Rev. W. Morley of the Association for the Protection of Native Races in Sydney. The news story in the *Manchester Guardian* based on Bennett's claims about slavery in Australia was taken up in Perth by the *Dawn*, the journal of the WSG, which proclaimed that 'never in history' had the welfare of indigenous peoples received such publicity as at that moment, at the very heart of the Empire.[17]

Bennett was proving an effective publicist for the cause of Aboriginal rights, as she had hoped, but wanting to help in more direct and immediate ways she had decided to return to Australia, to 'throw herself into the actual work amongst the Aborigines'.[18] On arrival in Western Australia, in 1930 she went to the south west to visit the people of Gnowangerup, taking her spinning wheel and large weaving frame. Bennett planned to use her artistic training and teaching skills to teach indigenous people crafts, thus helping them to become self-supporting. She was heartened by the initial response. 'The people of Gnowangerup took readily to the weaving which she taught them and were able to create designs and arrange colours in a wonderful manner.'[19]

Back in Perth, in November, Bennett attended a 'pleasant informal luncheon' arranged by members of the Women's Service Guild, at which she spoke about her work. She praised Aboriginal people for their intelligence, their capacity for hard work and their fine physiques. 'The Aboriginals are not depraved', said Bennett, 'they are deprived'. She intended to challenge the conventional wisdom that they were a dying race—to assure their future, she stressed, a constructive policy was needed and more reserves—land set aside for their exclusive use. But at this early stage her emphasis was on education. Only with effective teaching might Aborigines 'improve their conditions and live more comfortably'.[20]

By that time, however, large sections of public opinion seemed to have abandoned the view that 'these races were necessarily doomed', as T. H. Buxton had observed to the Australian High Commissioner in London in 1927. The resultant public debate about the condition of Aborigines that erupted in the 1930s was, for a time, shaped by a distinctively feminist discourse, an influence that was most clear in the public attention given to the particular, sexualised exploitation of Aboriginal girls and women. Feminist engagement in campaigns for Aboriginal rights, like their engagement in other movements for women's rights in these years, was animated by an anxiety about male sexuality and its harmful consequences for girls and women. Feminist concerns were also evident, however, in the case they made for recognition of the rights of Aboriginal mothers, especially their right to the custody of their children. In the steps taken to formulate 'a constructive and honourable native policy' in these years, feminists often led the way.

RIGHTING HISTORICAL WRONGS

In 1930, Constance Cooke presented a paper on 'The Status of Aboriginal Women in Australia' to the Pan-Pacific Women's Conference in Honolulu. The first such conference had been held in 1928, with Australian Eleanor Hinder, then based in Shanghai, as organising secretary. The conferences attracted large numbers of delegates from countries bordering the Pacific, including the United States, China, Japan, New Zealand, Canada, the Philippines and Korea. Alarmed at the prospect of adverse international publicity about the conditions of Aborigines, the Australian government demanded a right of reply to Cooke's paper, which was printed in the published reports. In her paper, Cooke provided an extensive survey of the position of Aboriginal people in each State in Australia and in the Federal Territory, preceded by an historical account of how these shameful conditions had come about. It was a history of Australian settlement that was neither peaceful nor glorious, an early version of what came to be called in the 1990s, 'black arm band' history.

The settlement of Australia, said Cooke, was characterised by 'two great wrongs': first the settlers took the land, then they took the women.

> The first great wrong was when the original inhabitants were deprived of all their lands by the legal device of declaring them the property of the Crown. Women, as well as men, were relegated thus to the position of serfs.
> . . . The second great wrong to the race has been the interference of the white man with the native women.[21]

Having requested a copy of Cooke's paper beforehand, the Minister for Home Affairs prepared, in response, two papers in defence of his administration: (1) 'Comments by Commonwealth Government in regard to statements respecting aboriginals in North Australia and Central Australia made in the paper "Status of Aboriginal Women"' and (2) 'A general statement regarding action taken by the Commonwealth Government for the welfare of aboriginals in North Australia and Central Australia'. Cooke reported on the government reaction in a letter to Sir John Harris, at the Anti-Slavery Society:

> The Minister of Home Affairs asked the Australian Committee to allow him to see my paper on 'The Status of Aboriginal Woman'. He then asked that a statement from the Federal Government be read at the same time at the Conference. This was impossible as it was a lengthy statement of the excellent laws (not enforced) and also of the policy of the Govt. However my paper and the statement are being printed in 'The Report of the Proceedings of the Conference' and I shall endeavour to use that statement as a lever to get the laws enforced. On the whole I felt that the trip to Honolulu had been worth while; I did a good deal of spade work . . .[22]

The unenforced laws referred to by Cooke related to the penalties to be inflicted on white men who sexually abused Aboriginal girls and women.

The development of feminist policy relating to Aboriginal rights in the 1920s and 1930s focussed on securing the better protection of Aboriginal girls and women through increased penalties for male sexual abuse; replacing police protectors (themselves often the abusers) by 'qualified women'; helping Aboriginal women to become economically independent through education and training; and granting to Aborigines the full rights of citizenship, including custody rights, education and most importantly, sufficient land in their own country, free from the incursions of marauding white men.

Drawing on already familiar discursive frameworks, feminists argued that Aboriginal land and women's bodies should be rendered inviolable. Like white women, they should be offered the protection of the 'law of the land' and like white women they should never be allowed to fall into men's hands. At the same time Aboriginal culture and traditions, not injurious to women, should be respected and maintained. Cultural difference was not threatening to these activists, who interpreted their special capacity for mothering, not as an artificially imposed 'role' (as would become conventional wisdom in the 1970s), but as an evidently important occupation which society, as it was organised, did not properly remunerate. Feminists in the 1920s and 1930s assumed sexual and cultural difference as givens.

After arriving in Australia, Mary Bennett briefly felt optimistic. She wrote to Rischbieth thanking her for entertaining her to lunch and finding 'a volunteer to cope with our really serious native problem'. That volunteer was Ada Bromham, who in 1930 was president of the Women's Service Guild. 'I am so glad to find Miss Bromham regard things seriously', said Bennett, 'and I have written fully to her and long to hear that things are in a way to being put on a just basis and largely through the *women*'.²³ Bromham would become a lifelong friend and political ally, writing the preface to Bennett's last book in the 1950s.

During 1931 and 1932, Bennett persuaded a number of other local feminists, including Bessie Rischbieth, president of the Australian Federation of Women Voters (AFWV), to take up the cause. In March 1931, Rischbieth wrote to Western Australian Senator George Pearce, Minister for Home Affairs, about a proposed big game hunt—'an invasion into the territory of the original owners of this country'—in the Northern Territory, asking that the proposed Arnhem Land Reserve be gazetted as soon as possible:

> We realise that the time is fast approaching when there will not be an acre of land in the Northern Territory or anywhere else in Australia which is not overrun by the white man and thereby the nomadic life for any native is doomed. We would therefore esteem

it a favour if the Minister would inform us if it is the Government's intention to proclaim Arnhem Land a Reserve for Aboriginals or just what is the intention of the Government in regard to reserving territory for native use before it is too late.[24]

The WSG had also lobbied for the government for amendments to Section 43 of the Western Australian Aborigines Act, as suggested in Bennett's *Call to the Women of Australia*. On an earlier occasion, although similar amendments had passed the lower house, they were blocked by the Legislative Council, thrown out by the squatters. Bennett denounced their conflict of interest to Rischbieth: 'I grew up in squatterdom and most of my friends are squatters, so I know their case through and through, but this does not blind me to the fact that a party to a case ought not to be judge in his own cause. And of course you have the squatter interest represented in your Guilds and very properly'. Mrs Joyner, she said, had told her personally that 'her people had pioneered the Kimberleys and been murdered by the natives'.[25] Within three years, Rischbieth's own links with the social and political establishment would contribute to growing tensions between Bennett and herself.

By the beginning of 1932, Bennett was working with superintendent Rev. R. S. Schenk and Mrs Schenk at the Mt Margaret Mission, near Kalgoorlie. She derived considerable solace and satisfaction from the work of Mrs Schenk, who had been trained in raffia work at the Arts and Crafts School in Melbourne and was teaching the girls and women to become self-supporting. In April 1932 she wrote rapturously to Rischbieth:

> Ever since I have been here I have been longing for you to see this place, and the department of the work which particularly appeals to me—an Australian woman's work for native women. It is grand, beautiful! an inspiration! And since you cannot be here and see it for yourself, I am sending you a little raffia brooch made by a girl here . . .[26]

Bennett elaborated the feminist credo: the solution to the indigenous women's problems lay in economic independence. Sexual slavery was the result of women's economic dependence. The raffia work gave the girls not just the joy of creativity and self-respect, but also a 'way of earning a living honestly': the money earned from the sale of the articles went back to the workers. 'It is enough', said Bennett, 'that the women and girls can be self-supporting and are self-supporting. Economic dependence is the root of all evil'.[27]

Attempting to subvert the racist stereotype that portrayed native women as inherently lascivious and promiscuous, Bennett insisted on the Aboriginal girls' 'instinctive passion for purity'. In seeking to reclaim Aboriginal women as 'ready for a position of respect and independence', Bennett and like-minded feminists followed a logic that demonised male sexuality, black or white. Male sexual desire was the serpent that needed to be cast out of Eden. Just as Vida Goldstein castigated the oversexed males of her day for leading white women inexorably into the pit of dependence and degradation, so Bennett despaired that the lusts of men entrapped Aboriginal girls and women, whichever way they turned. So she recounted the stories of her two brooch makers. Linda had never visited the white men's camps, but was 'betrothed in infancy to an old man, a witch doctor, and a dirty old man at that. She loathes him but some years back he took her, and there is no escape for her'. Theresa was also 'betrothed from babyhood to an old native man whom she loathed, but she only escaped from him to fall into the hands of an aged white prospector called Graham, who kidnapped her . . .'.[28]

In the public domain, Bennett's indictment of settlers' greed and rapacity had become ever more scathing. In March 1932, she wrote a letter to the *Australian Board of Missions Review*, which was republished in the *West Australian*, denouncing both the greed of pastoralists for taking up 'vast leases' in the north and also the government for sanctioning this injustice:

> If the squatters would, as an act of mercy, surrender a small proportion of their thousand-mile sheep walks and cattle runs, or if the Government would, as an act of justice, reclaim a small proportion of these vast leases for the natives' use, and at the same time secure human rights to them, the process of extermination of our native race would cease. It pays the white man to dispossess the natives of their land wholesale, because the Government permits them to impress the natives as labour without paying them . . . Practically all the work of the white people throughout the Kimberleys and in some other parts of Western Australia and the Federal Territory is done by unpaid natives.[29]

In addition, Aboriginal women were subject to systematic sexual abuse by white men, the 'white slave trade in black women', in order to earn the wherewithal for them and their families to survive.

These new 'Allegations of Slavery', as the subheading in the *West Australian* characterised the story, provoked an impassioned debate in the Western Australian press and in the government. The nationalist writer Ernestine Hill defended the men of the outback as the 'most fair-minded and open-hearted people one could find anywhere—the Australians who matter most'. If promiscuous sexual relations between white men and Aboriginal women constituted a crime, it was a crime 'that should be charged, not to the men of the North, but—shall I say it?—to the women of the South, who leave them to live and die alone uncared for and unthought of, shouldering the white man's burden for Australians of the future'. Aboriginal Australians could scarcely be credited with 'exalted ethics' and in any case the race was 'doomed in the march of our civilisation'. It would be pointless to pay them for labour, moreover, because 'in the handling of money the native is a dupe and a fool'.[30]

Bennett responded with a renewed attack on masculine rapaciousness: 'it was time the wickedness of the white men was charged to them, instead of, as Mrs Hill seeks to charge it, to their black victims in the north west and the white women in the South West'. Those men were, moreover, hardly the national heroes Hill liked to suggest: 'White men who abuse defenceless black girls are not usually the type who make a home for a wife. Many of them have wives whom they have deserted'.[31] Rev. R. S. Schenk, superintendent of the Mt Margaret Mission where Bennett worked, denounced pastoralists more generally, adducing 'five facts' about the destructive and exploitative nature of the industry:

(1) The pastoral industry robs the natives more than any other industry—of their land.
(2) The pastoral industry, more than any other, has been responsible for the slaughter of natives.
(3) The pastoral industry has bred most half-castes.
(4) The pastoral industry has been helped by free native labour more than any other.
(5) Pastoralists show the least desire to establish the native race.[32]

Feminist criticism of the exploitative white man was, once again, opening up questions about the legitimacy of settlement itself.

In her contribution to this debate, Ada Bromham applauded the fact that 'the conspiracy of silence so long observed, regarding the treatment meted out to the Aborigines of our state' had been broken;

that those who had so long condoned injusice were 'on the offensive' was a welcome indication that a public conscience was at last being awakened. She then returned the discussion to the rights of Aboriginal women, echoing Bennett's argument in A *Call to the Women of Australia* that Aboriginal women needed 'a full measure of protection and encouragement in their own culture' as well as the 'rights common to other women'. White women had a special responsibility to work for justice for their 'dark sisters', for they had 'neither human rights nor protection against the irresponsible white man': 'Legislation protects property of all kinds, but that most fundamental right, the right of woman to the sancity of her own person is denied to the native women of Australia'.[33]

Meanwhile the Acting Chief Secretary, P. D. Ferguson, asked the Chief Protector in Western Australia, A. O. Neville, to investigate the allegations and prepare a response. (A file was opened in the Chief Secretary's department with the title 'Allegations by Mrs. M. M. Bennett in regard to native slavery, inadequate reserves and traffic in native women'.) Neville prepared a statement denying the existence of slavery of any kind. Sometimes breaches of the law occurred, but the department exercised continual vigilance. Armed with these reassurances, the Acting Premier C. G. Latham publicly attacked Bennett and her supporters as 'uninformed persons rushing into print'. The natives on pastoral stations were 'happy and contented'. The Country Women's Association (CWA) took fright at the controversy. Having been approached by WSG State secretary Dorothea Cass to elicit their support for the reforms listed in A *Call to the Women of Australia*, the CWA took the precaution of first seeking Neville's advice. He sent them his response and suggested they think the matter over.[34]

VIOLATED WOMEN AND GRIEVING MOTHERS

Feminist critiques of Western political thought have often made the point that its paradigmatic figures, the liberal individual, the citizen and the worker, though masquerading as gender neutral, are, in fact, masculine in conception. The two figures around whom feminist campaigners for Aboriginal rights mobilised their political campaigns were distinctively feminine: the sexually violated woman and the grieving mother. Mary Bennett's paper 'The Aboriginal Mother in Western Australia in 1933', read to the British Commonwealth League conference in that year, emphasised the distress caused to both the sexually abused woman and the mother robbed of her children. Aboriginal women's position, already subordinate in a 'patriarchal' traditional society, deteriorated dramatically under the impact of 'civilisation'; their current degraded condition was 'the logical conclusion of our own dealings with them'.[35] Bennett's account of the history of white settlement followed the model offered in Cooke's paper to the Pan-Pacific conference some three years earlier, but Cooke's 'two great wrongs' had become for Bennett 'two outstanding facts':

(1) Slow starvation of the natives through our depriving them of all land to live on, and, arising from dispossession and starvation,
(2) Wholesale prostitution of the women; originally 'property' they have now become 'merchandise'.[36]

In the wholesale prostitution of Aboriginal women, according to this analysis, the process of settlement simply put on display the underlying dynamics of the masculine frontier. For interwar feminists the prostitute was the paradigmatic woman; in Australia the plight of Aboriginal women was the plight of all women reduced to their sex.

In her paper on the Aboriginal mother, Bennett also stressed the trauma involved in separating Aboriginal people from their country and families: 'Aboriginals are deeply attached to their own country, and should not be "transported". It would be as reasonable to attempt to solve the problem of the English slums by snatching the children from their mothers and "transporting" them to a settlement in Tenerife or Turkey'. Again she stressed the necessity of returning their land: in Western Australia 'at least 50 native territories [were] needed'.

The effects on mothers and children of being 'hunted' by police intent on removing the children were evident years later:

> These women suffered an agony of fear, and the effects may still be seen in their children. I refer particularly to one of my pupils, a nervy boy with a look of shock. Another half-caste child is nervy and lacking in concentration, and yet another is stunted and timid.
> But Aboriginal women are inarticulate, so they endure all the untold sufferings of serfdom, because we have deprived them of land to live on, and refuse them education, with all the other rights that are founded on education—medical services, wages when they earn them, and a political standing by which they might obtain other rights due to them.[37]

Aboriginal women were given the opportunity to speak for themselves, however, in the following year at the Royal Commission appointed in response to the ongoing feminist agitation in Australia and London. Feminists effectively forced the Western Australian government to Investigate, Report and Advise upon Matters in relation to the Condition and Treatment of Aborigines, and listen to women witnesses, Aboriginal and non-Aboriginal—but the government refused their demand for the appointment of a woman Royal Commissioner, deciding to appoint just one man, Henry Moseley.

Feminist campaigns for Aboriginal rights utilised their international networks to great political effect between the years 1930 and 1935. Constance Cooke's paper at the Pan-Pacific Women's Conference in Honolulu had provoked a lengthy federal government response; ongoing discussions at the British Commonwealth League in London, given extensive publicity in the *Manchester Guardian*, also produced a flurry of official explanations and denials. In 1933, Australian delegate Ruby Rich, described in the *Dawn* as 'a leading Australian Feminist', read Mary Bennett's paper on the Aboriginal mother in Western Australia to the annual conference of the British Commonwealth League, of which she had become an executive member.[38] Rich, a member of the New South Wales United Associations, appointed overseas liaison officer for the Australian Federation of Women Voters from 1930, found herself unexpectedly in the limelight after she had read Bennett's paper on the Aboriginal mother, and Edith Jones had added her own charges. The *Daily News* observed that 'comments in overseas newspapers have created wide interest in Australia's treatment of her aboriginal population'; Bennett had agreed that her controversial paper could be republished and the Minister for Native Affairs had been forced to reply at length.[39]

Shortly afterwards it was announced that there would be a Royal Commission in Western Australia. Bennett's cynical response was published in the *West Australian*. Little had been achieved with Royal Commissions in the past. There was an ongoing problem with police protectors. Of the six currently in employment, she said, all were heavy drinkers and five were immoral. 'Mrs Bennett said she knew a lot about the police because she had to teach their half-caste children'.[40]

The government was on the defensive. Asked by the Minister to comment on the charges made by feminists at the BCL and later, Chief Protector Neville responded:

While I have every admiration for the praiseworthy work of Mrs Bennett, Miss Jones [sic] and others similarly situated, it would appear that the cause of the aborigines cannot be advanced by wild unsubstantiated statements, but Mrs Bennett and others will shortly have an opportunity of stating their cases to the Royal Commission proposed to be appointed . . .[41]

For the time being, it seemed that the feminists had secured a political victory.

In September 1933, Bennett wrote to Rischbieth to thank her for her supportive coverage in the *Dawn* of Australia's 'wicked mishandling of our native race'. She noted that a Royal Commission was promised for Western Australia. 'Mrs Vallence [the State president of the WSG] writes that the Women's Service Guilds are pressing for a woman on the Commission most *important* & I am hoping that Miss Bromham may be one of the members, for she has all the gifts of head and heart & has such a fine record of work in this dept.' Bennett then referred to new legislation for the Federal Territory, prescribing stiffer penalties for the sexual abuse of Aboriginal women there:

> the only new part is prescribing 3 months imprisonment for the aboriginal female victim. This will effectively silence her forever from giving evidence against her oppressor—she is silent now, knowing from grim experience that whoever else goes free, *she*, always & always, suffers.[42]

The following month, Bennett urged Rischbieth to impress on the women's societies that securing justice in the north of Australia had not just moral dimensions, but national and international implications: 'though a wise Aboriginal policy is needed for survival of aboriginal race [sic] it is equally urgent for our own survival in the Pacific. Australia shall understand this . . .'.[43]

NO DEPARTMENT IN THE WORLD CAN TAKE THE PLACE OF A CHILD'S MOTHER

The Royal Commission conducted by Moseley began its hearings in March 1934. As with the federal Royal Commission investigating the feasibility of childhood and motherhood endowment in 1927, feminists rallied to present their point of view, to put their advocacy of mothers' rights on the public record and to articulate their political goals. Most emphasised the injustice and pain inflicted on Aboriginal communities by the policy of child removal.

Ada Bromham told the Royal Commissioner she and her political organisation had worked with Aboriginal mothers in the Brookton area in the south west and they had impressed on her the extent of their needs—ranging from food, blankets and clothing to a school for their children. Bromham argued in particular that Aboriginal mothers should be granted custody rights over their children for 'under the law the mother has no right over the child'. Her comment that the department was too ready to take the children away led to the following exchange:

> That should operate only where it was clear beyond doubt that the child was not being looked after properly?
>
> It is becoming more or less the practice to take the children away. In only eight cases, where the fathers were known, were proceedings taken for maintenance. It has been suggested that the Act has its limitations and needs to be amended.[44]

Bromham also drew attention to the violence of the government settlement at Moore River, which was often the destination of those removed. Her use of evidence supplied by Aboriginal women produced a rebuke from Moseley about reliance on 'hearsay evidence':

> I am not going to listen to hearsay day after day. I have listened to a great deal rather than that anyone should say he or she had no chance of coming before the Commission. It is all very interesting but valueless?
>
> It is an ordeal to come before a Commission of this kind.[45]

Although many prospective witnesses were too intimidated to appear before the Royal Commission, several Aboriginal women—Mary Warmadean, Melba Egan, Annie Morrison, Emily Nannup—did 'courageously present evidence. They spoke about the appalling treatment of the inmates at Moore River, the deprivations, the floggings and inmates running away. They spoke about their pain as mothers in not being able to care for their children. 'They do not get enought to eat', said Annie Morrison. Emily Nannup wanted answers: 'I want to know the reason for my children being taken from me'.[46]

The Aboriginal women's claims were also set out in a document specially prepared for the Royal Commission by the self-styled 'Halfcastes of Broome', who detailed the various ways their daily lives—their access to work, to their children, to marriage—were tyrannised by the Chief Protector and the humiliating legislation that controlled them. The influence of the feminists with whom they prepared this petition was evident in their plea that they be given the freedom to 'rule our lives and make ourselves true and good citizens' and more particularly in their request for the appointment of 'a paid lady Protector' to replace police 'who have more often been our prosecutionists than our protectors'.[47]

Bessie Rischbieth gave evidence to the Commission as president of the Australian Federation of Women Voters. She too criticised the policy of depriving parents of the custody of their children, insisting in response to repeated questioning that more was involved than child neglect:

> You would not cavil at the principle of taking a neglected Aboriginal child any more than at a neglected white child being taken from an improper home?
>
> It goes deeper than that.
>
> You would not join issue with the principle of removal if a child were not properly cared for by the parents?
>
> In most instances I should prefer to see the children left with their parents.
>
> One could imagine cases of sheer neglect in which something would have to be done?
>
> Then we could follow the practice adopted regarding white children.
>
> Where there is no real concern for removal you advocate leaving the children with their parents?
>
> Yes, and I also suggest that the system of dealing with the parents should be improved in order that they might keep their children.[48]

Rischbieth's main political agenda, however, was to present the case for 'nationalisation', which had been AFWV policy since 1927, to submit the recommendation that 'the welfare of the Australian Aborigines be made a Federal responsibility by means of an amendment to the Commonwealth Constitution'.[49] There was a specifically Western

Australian interest in this recommendation. Because the whole of Australia owed a debt of reparation to the Aborigines, that debt should be equally distributed, but under present conditions three States—Tasmania, Victoria and New South Wales—carried 'practically no responsibility'. More importantly, however, Australia had to adopt consistent reforms; there was now 'widespread public interest not only in Australia, but also overseas, which is all to the good, for the eyes of the world are upon us'.[50]

Other feminist witnesses presented evidence—for example, May Vallance, president of the WSG—but none spoke with the eloquent power of Mary Bennett, who also appeared as an accredited representative of the WSG. The influence of feminism on her thinking was then at its height. The deplorable social and economic position of the Aborigines was caused by the 'victimisation of Aboriginal women': the traffic in women and children was the basis of the society's deterioration. The patriarchal ordering of the indigenous society, which often entailed polygamy and child betrothal, was exploited by unscrupulous white men, according to Bennett, to satisfy their unbridled lusts. Masculine sexual licence, whether Aboriginal or non-Aboriginal, led inexorably to the degradation of women. 'A clean and clean living half-white girl called . . . was appropriated by a dirty old witch doctor . . . who is old enough to be her grandfather and whom she loathes . . .'.[51] Although Bennett was a champion of Aboriginal culture, praising the emphasis it placed on family solidarity and reciprocity, she was, nevertheless, adamant that individual choice in marriage was central to women's freedom.

Bennett derived her confidence and authority in making this claim, however, not from feminist principles or her accredited status as witness for the WSG, but from the Christian teaching of 'the intrinsic value of every human being'.[52] Her perspective was that of a missionary and imperialist, but Bennett was also a passionate advocate of human rights and the sanctity of the person. Thus she endorsed missionaries' recommendations that in settled areas 'patriarchal' Aboriginal customs be banned:

> the property status of human beings with its attendant evils of infant betrothal, child-marriage, wife-lending and polygamy, shall be declared illegal; that there shall be one law, the law of the land; that Aboriginal and half-caste girls who need the protection of the law shall obtain it; and that all people shall be free to

make their own lives within the law, and not be handed over to claimants as property.[53]

But Bennett was also clearsighted about the utter destruction of Aboriginal society for which white settlers were responsible. Prostitution, disease and starvation were the logical results of the sub-human conditions in which

> our dispossessed, unrepresented, regulation-governed native race is compelled to exist, under-fed, untaught, uncared for, turned off their native country, turned away from schools and hospitals, described as a 'menace' and treated like vermin instead of what they really are, magnificent potential citizens, whom Australia cannot afford to destroy.[54]

The abuse of Aboriginal women was both a product of and conducive to 'wicked callousness' on the part of white men, who were without natural affection or compassion, indifferent as to whether their children lived or died.

Bennett reserved her most passionate condemnation for the policy of child removal. For 'no department in the world can take the place of a child's mother and the Honourable Minister does not offer any valid justification for the official smashing of native family and community life'. She spoke about the life of terror led by the hunted ones:

> So mothers with infants and individual children and sometimes families are mustered up like cattle and deported to the remote Government native settlement at Moore River, there to drag out their days and years in exile, suffering all the miseries of transportation for no fault but only because the white supplanters are too greedy and too mean to give them living areas in their own districts . . . They are captured at all ages, as infants in arms, perhaps not until they are grown up; they are not safe until they are dead.[55]

Bennett also reported how unsafe Aboriginal women felt in police hands; that in fact the native name for police was 'munda-murrungga' meaning 'iron-hands'. Should an Aboriginal woman dare to register a complaint about a white molester, it would be she who would be punished, sent away from her family and community to a government institution in strange country.

Feminists had forged an effective political alliance with Aboriginal women to draw attention to the systematic nature of sexual abuse on the frontiers of settlement and to the destructive effects on Aboriginal women and children of the policy of child removal. They had successfully made private issues public, but the practice of taking the children away went on, legitimised by Chief Protector A. O. Neville and others as the policy of 'the absorption of the blacks by the whites'.[56] Feminine sentiments about the importance of mother love and choice of marriage partner counted for little in the face of such a determined, masculine, 'science'. At the Royal Commission, Chief Protector Neville was himself allowed to put questions about the science of breeding to Bennett:

> Referring to marriages at the Mt Margaret Mission do you consider it right to marry a half-caste girl to a full-blooded native?
>
> That is entirely a matter for the individuals to decide. It is not a matter for anyone else.
>
> You would not regard it from the ethnological point of view at all?
>
> We do not ask the white to marry ethnologically and why ask the blacks? It is entirely a matter for the man and woman concerned. Any interference would be against the liberty of the subject.[57]

To counter criticism of its policies, the government determination to discredit Mary Bennett as of unsound mind gathered pace, and the release of Moseley's Royal Commission report in 1935, which contained harsh criticism of Bennett, served to exacerbate the growing tensions in feminist ranks over how best to advance Aboriginal rights.

The severity of Moseley's attack on Bennett as a witness became a talking point. 'I consider the Commissioner's criticism of Mrs Bennett's evidence was unjust', her friend Constance Cooke wrote to Travers Buxton at the Anti-Slavery Society. At the same time recriminations broke out between Bennett and Bessie Rischbieth, who echoed Moseley's criticisms about Bennett's unreliablity. Political considerations exacerbated personal differences between the two, both imperious and strong-willed women, used to exercising considerable authority in their own domains: Bennett disapproved of Rischbieth's worldliness, while Rischbieth could not abide Bennett's self-righteousness and her lack of national loyalty.

By the mid-1930s, Bennett frequently expressed the view that white Australians were not fit to rule over indigenous people. In a letter to Travers Buxton at the Anti-Slavery Society she observed:

> The majority of Australians are still poisoned with a strong anti-native bias—the criminal cannot forgive the victim he has wronged . . . But that I believe in God, I should despair, not of the Aborigines who respond magnificently, but of the white people who are certainly not fit to rule over them. Perhaps the day is not far distant when all races whose lands are occupied by others may claim to be under a special mandate from the League of Nations. Nobody could be more cruel, greedy, dishonourable and unjust in their dealings with native races than the British Australians.[58]

On another occasion she wrote that if the immoral traffic in women and children continued it would 'be definitely to the good for Australia to disappear'.[59]

Rischbieth, an ardent nationalist and ambitious citizen politician, networking the upper echelons of society, decided that Bennett was alienating potential supporters. She, too, cast doubt on the substance of Bennett's claims before the Royal Commission, suggesting that the Aboriginal women did not support her evidence, as Bennett claimed. In refuting Rischbieth's charges, Bennett's proprietorial attitude towards Aboriginal people was also evident:

> Mrs Rischbieth is in error in saying that my native witnesses did not support my charges. Melba Egan, Mrs Stack and Mary Warmadean were all fine and spoke with courage and adhered steadfastly to their statements though Mr Moseley bullied . . .
>
> Mrs Rischbieth was not present when these girls and poor Mrs Stack gave evidence so pluckily so she has no evidence at all for saying that they did not support me.[60]

Bennett threatened that if the women's societies in Australia were 'too smug and too self-seeking' to assist her in the project of reforming the condition of Aboriginal women, she would 'seek help outside where ever I can get it not forgetting Japan'. Then in a characteristic move, Bennett referred to her embattled position as one of the few fighters for justice, alongside 'a very very few noble women like Mrs Ternente Cooke and Mrs Vallence, Miss Bromham, Mrs Bryce, Miss Baillie and a few others'.[61] The last named supporter of the cause was Helen Baillie, an activist with Church of England and labour movement connections who had made contact with Bennett and Cooke from around 1933.

Bessie Rischbieth continued, in her capacity as president of the Australian Federation of Women Voters, to lobby for Aboriginal rights, but focussed most of her efforts on her cherished 'nationalisation' policy. She continued to work in consultation with Edith Jones in London, delivering a paper to the BCL in 1935, and attempted to get a hearing at the League of Nations in the same year. This was apparently hampered, however, by her reluctance to address the subject of Australia's appalling treatment of its indigenous people under the heading of 'slavery'. Conflict between Australian feminists over these issues erupted in 1936 in Adelaide, both at the AFWV triennial conference and during feminist preparations for the centenary of white settlement in South Australia, being commemorated that year.

POST-COLONIAL DISSENSIONS

During the 1930s there were three commemorations of settlement in Australia—the State centennials in Victoria in 1934 and South Australia in 1936 and the sesqui-centennial of Australian settlement centred in New South Wales in 1938—which provided feminists with occasions to insist that women's part in nation-building be publicly acknowledged. The problem was that women's work as 'pioneers' and helpmeets on the land rested on the dispossession of the original inhabitants.

In Victoria, a volume of women's writing edited by Frances Fraser and Nettie Palmer, called *The Centenary Gift Book*, contained a remarkable story, 'A Fantasy', by the nationalist and feminist writer Mary Fullerton, who had lived in England since 1914. Her arch and archaic prose seemed appropriate to her self-innocenting account of the displacement of local tribes, the author's bad conscience also evident in her determined invocation of the nationalist conceit that Aborigines were doomed to extinction, destined to make way for the progress heralded by the 'great white men'. Fullerton imagines the moment when the local tribe realises that they are doomed:

> The dark man's kingdom was to pass from his dominion. The great wide bush that their nomadic feet had trod since ocean made it land, would pass to these new lords, these pallid men . . .[62]

In suggesting that Aboriginal men treated their women as drudges and slaves, Fullerton also lent a feminist moral justification to the dispossession.

In Adelaide, a Women's Centenary Committee was formed, under the auspices of the National Council of Women chaired by Adelaide Miethke, to decide on an appropriate contribution to the centenary in that State and the contents of a proposed commemorative collection of writing. Constance Cooke joined the Committee as representative of the Aborigines Protection League and she lobbied to secure 'justice for our original inhabitants' in the form of recognition of Aboriginal women in the centenary volume and the return of land, as a small step towards redressing the 'wrongs of a century'.[63] She forwarded the following resolution from the Aborigines Protection League:

> That a portion of the land that has been taken from the Aborigines should be allotted to them in perpetuity so that they may become self-supporting and enabled to work out their own destinies in their own communities.[64]

She met with little success, however, writing to Travers Buxton in London:

> I have done my utmost to get our Aboriginal women included in the Women's Centenary Council programme. Tomorrow there will be a meeting at the Town Hall at which 80 women's associations will take part. The President's speech is to be broadcast, and I think that she will make reference to our aboriginal women, who should be included with the pioneers.[65]

Cooke was rebuffed in her endeavours. The recommendation on land was rejected and the editors of *A Book of South Australian Women in the First Hundred Years* added insult to injury by inviting the discredited Daisy Bates, arch proponent of the 'dying out' thesis, to write a chapter on 'Our pioneer woman and our natives', which assured her readers: 'Wherever the British woman penetrated the native women benefited by her coming in amongst them . . . That means a great deal to those of us who know that our natives are a dying race'.[66] Cooke withdrew from the Committee. The tensions occasioned by the commemoration highlighted the necessarily ambiguous relationship between nationalism and feminism for women unable to reconcile their proud nationalist identifications with a recognition that their national history rested on a process of dispossession, exploitation and sexual abuse.

Divisions also opened up at the 1936 conference of the Australian Federation of Women Voters in Adelaide, when Cooke attempted to supplement the 'nationalisation' policy in Aboriginal affairs by adding a call for formal recognition of Aboriginal women's equality of status and rights. The president, Bessie Rischbieth, opposed the move, insisting that the conference simply reaffirm the existing (nationalisation) policy. Mary Bennett, presumably informed by Cooke, reported exultantly to Edith Jones in London:

> Now the most wonderful thing happened at the Centenary AFWV Conference. My darling Mrs Ternente Cooke brought forward a Resolution to give citizen rights to Aborigines, but the Board would not accept it, she was asked to re-affirm the Resolution of the preceding Conference dealing with Aborigines and to do it without comment, as Aborigines were not considered to come within 'Equality of Status' etc !!! However Mrs Ternente Cooke protested against this. To my thinking the truly important thing is that an Australian lady has brought forward a Resolution asking for equality of status for Aborigines. This is something to dream of and work for and those who tried to trample her only cut their own throats. Do let Mr Buxton know of this please. He knows Mrs Ternente Cooke and she has made history.[67]

Bennett then referred to the acrimony that by then characterised relations between Rischbieth and her allies on the one hand and those such as Constance Cooke and Ada Bromham, who advocated a more radical commitment to Aboriginal rights. Her own antagonism to Rischbieth was made abundantly clear:

> But this was not all. Mrs Rischbieth is a real rotter and went out of her way to snub Mrs Cooke on every possible occasion. What Mrs Rischbieth is going to find is that her worldly selfishness is not going to get her anywhere except in an impasse. She has been such a beast to two different friends of mine who have taken up work for the natives, and she does try to keep the native out of sight on every possible occasion, though she is much too cunning to show this in front of people like myself who have no other interests except these despised and rejected ones. But it just means that though I haven't quarrelled with her, I shall not refrain from the most offensive things that I can possibly bring home.[68]

Clearly Bennett's passionate identification with the 'despised and rejected ones' led her to simplify complicated and changing political alliances into a clearcut division between the virtuous embattled few and the uncaring vicious majority, but in her judgment about the significance of Cooke's interventions she was surely right. Cooke's call for 'equality' for Aboriginal women rather than their 'protection' represented a historic shift in the relationship between feminists and their 'dark sisters', whose interests they strove so earnestly to represent.

PART III
FEMINIST MODES OF DOING POLITICS

6
THE NON-PARTY IDEAL

EXEMPLARY CITIZENS

Post-suffrage feminists were enthusiastic, even exemplary, citizens; they gloried in the new possibilities of civic and political life and effectively blurred the boundaries between the two. Citizenship was a practice that was valued in itself, not merely as a means to other ends. Feminists wrote and talked endlessly about the responsibilities and duties accruing to their newly exalted position. In 1924, the State executive of the Women's Service Guild in Western Australia exhorted women to recognise 'the power and dignity which the position of full citizenship may mean to them':

> Truly this is the day of cooperation and freedom. Everywhere
> women are waking to the fact that they must combine their forces
> and also prepare themselves for the added responsibilities which
> they are being called upon to bear now and in the future and so
> equip themselves that they may be worthy of their great heritage
> won for them by the pioneers of the Women's Movement.[1]

To equip themselves for their awesome responsibilities, feminist organisations established schools for citizenship (sometimes with the help of 'Professors of the University') and conducted courses in public speaking, debating and running meetings; they stocked bookshops with the latest overseas works and advised when and where League of Nations reports might be available. Feminists wrote and staged plays, they made radio broadcasts, they flocked as witnesses to Royal Commissions, they formed study circles, organised conferences. They were leaders in the League of Nations Union. Feminist organisations provided their branches with syllabuses for study and lists of appropriate lecturers. Feminists took their citizenship seriously. Political action was an extension and an expression of their new civic life.

In their separate organisations they forged a distinctive mode of doing politics suited to their primary purpose of mobilising public opinion to achieve greater freedom and security for women. The achievement of suffrage was followed by the immediate formation of State-based organisations specifically designed to educate women in the use of the vote, notably the Women's Political Association in Victoria, the Women's Political Education League (WPEL) in New South Wales and the Women's Suffrage Association in Tasmania. These groups were succeeded by organisations more consciously concerned to realise the promise of equal citizenship. The Women's Service Guilds in Western Australia, the South Australian Women's Non-Party Association, the Women's Non-Party Political League in Tasmania, the United Associations and the Feminist Club in New South Wales all affiliated with the Australian Federation of Women Voters (AFWV) in the 1920s.

The three main AFWV policies were that the organisation be non-party and non-sectarian, that it promote equality of opportunity, status and reward and that it uphold an equal moral standard for men and women. To differentiate itself from the other national body that sought to represent the interests of women, the National Council of Women (NCW), the Australian Federation of Women Voters always stressed its primary commitment to the feminist goal of obtaining an equal citizenship between men and women.

Feminists' political ideas and practice arose from the domestic circumstances of citizens charged with responsibility for the care of others and the management of the home. Many of the new leaders, such as Jessie Street, Constance Cooke, Edith Waterworth and Linda Littlejohn, were married with children; others cared for parents, younger siblings, nieces and nephews. In most cases their active citizenship was made possible by independent incomes, earned or inherited, and the employment of household help; few if any husbands seem to have shouldered the domestic workload. Edith Waterworth of the Tasmanian Women's Non-Party League raised money for her overseas trips by working as a journalist; Ada Bromham of the Women's Service Guild was a partner in a drapery store; Linda Littlejohn of the United Associations (UA) worked as a broadcaster. The private incomes of Jessie Street, Bessie Rischbieth and others were also crucial in subsidising the movement as a whole.

The feminist perspective on citizenship in these years was shaped by the context of women's responsibilities. As Jill Vickers has pointed out with regard to the equivalent organisations in Canada, 'women whose circumstances precluded a professional political role, nevertheless created organisations adaptable to their life circumstances, in which they exercised leadership and engaged in their own form of political discourse informed by domestic and community needs and values'.[2] Thus did the Women's Service Guild in Western Australia remind potential recruits that politics was highly relevant to them, dealing with 'questions affecting home life, such as housing, health, education, employment and food supplies'.[3]

The meaning of citizenship was extensively theorised by feminists in these years. On the one hand, feminists had high expectations of the personal rewards to be conferred: individuality, economic independence and bodily inviolability were all claimed by women in the name of their citizenship. Enfranchisement offered a new status to women as individuals and persons; they were no longer to be regarded as the appendages or chattels of men. Hence the significance of feminists' preoccupation with the issue of married women's right to retain their own nationality. 'The time had passed', said Amelia Macdonald in a deputation to Prime Minister Stanley Melbourne Bruce, when visiting Perth in 1923, 'when the wife shall be regarded as a chattel of her husband . . . a married woman should have her own individuality'.[4] Macdonald had been active in the Women's Service Guild since its inception in 1909, serving as first treasurer, and like Bessie Rischbieth she was a theosophist.

Citizenship was believed to endow women with the status of individuals, but feminists also emphasised citizenship as a collective resource. Theosophy was influential in encouraging some to attribute a particular significance to citizenship as a 'New Evolutionary Force' ushering in a world characterised by 'unity of purpose' and 'a sense of the inter-relationship of the whole human race'.[5] Theosophy also encouraged feminists' non-party stance. Human solidarity was more important than class, racial or national solidarity. In an article called 'Women's Political Attitude The Value of a Non-Party Basis of Action', Bessie Rischbieth suggested that, as it was generally agreed that the party system simply helped accentuate the political differences of the old order, more progressive lines of action were necessary, an approach that recognised the human basis of citizenship. It was this approach that was uniting women the world over.

> They are fast learning to realise that their common interests as women matter more than what separates. They are pioneers in helping to establish a new conception of real values . . . [the] social welfare platform . . . is far above any class or party.[6]

The United Associations in New South Wales offered a more pragmatic rationale for collective action:

> Women working individually are like voices crying in the wilderness. Women united will be able to use their brains, sympathy, intelligence, energy, foresight, economy and all the capacities they possess for the public good, for the good of the country, as well as for the good of their families.[7]

The exercise of women's political power was conceptualised as a collective endeavour. In their struggle to enhance all women's freedom and security, it was the vote, not seats in parliament, that post-suffrage feminists emphasised as their major political resource. The vote, said Rischbieth, was the 'weapon of the "new citizenship"'.[8] Arguing the need for the new federal organisation, which would become the (significantly titled) Australian Federation of Women Voters, Rischbieth predicted:

> When voters really seriously comprehend that they are the *rulers of the nation*, this will be a vastly different and infinitely better world.[9]

A new federal organisation would 'strengthen the army of Australian women organised thus to make the vote more effective by helping to establish a human basis of welfare in this great new land'.[10] The election of women to parliament, now regarded as such an important goal, was seen in earlier decades as but one expression of a broader and more ambitious conception of civic and political engagement, just one means of inaugurating the new order. Some organisations, in fact, cautioned women against using their new status for self-aggrandisement. The platform of the Women's Service Guild specifically gave as one of its objects: 'to seek public good and not personal advantage'.

A SPECIAL WORK TO DO

Most feminists engaged in the suffrage campaigns in Australia assumed that enfranchised women would bring a new element to political life;

they would represent the distinctive interests of women and children and bring new values to the political domain. 'Women had a special work to do with their vote': this special work was their *raison d'être* as political subjects.[11] They did not seek political rights merely to double the numbers in the existing men's parties. Rather they sought to establish different priorities through a new political discourse on human welfare. As the United Associations put it: 'Woman's point of view is not the same as man's. Her sense of values is different, she places a greater value on human life, human welfare, health and morals.'[12] Committed to the human basis of citizenship and the ideal of an interdependent community, feminists sought, in Ada Bromham's words, to create a political force that would transcend party and sectional interest, bringing together 'human hearts too long separated by class, race or other prejudices'.[13] The non-party strategy was thus integral to the feminist political philosophy and vision.

Conservative women, committed to returning the non-Labor parties to office, formed their own organisations, such as the Australian Women's National League (AWNL), which became the largest non-Labor political group in the country. Dedicated to the anti-socialist cause, its first object was 'Loyalty to the Throne', and although committed to educating women in politics its influential president Eva Hughes believed that ordinary women's 'best power lies behind the throne', guiding 'right-thinking men . . . to act for us—amending laws relating to women and woman's honour'.[14] The AWNL provided a conservative forum for women who wanted to preserve the status quo: in the home, in relations between men and women and in the world at large. Under Elizabeth (May) Couchman's presidency from 1927, the AWNL moved into a closer alliance with the United Australia party, then agreed to subsume its separate identity in return for guarantees of women's representation in Robert Menzies' new Liberal party.

Labor women also eschewed the feminist label in these years and again formed their own organisations, although they frequently co-operated with the feminist associations in particular campaigns. In Victoria and Tasmania, Lilian-Locke Burns (as she became) was an effective 'lady organiser'. In Fremantle, a women's branch of the Labor party called the Women's Political and Social Crusade was formed in 1905, which became the Fremantle Labor Women's League with Jean Beadle as president. Several other Labor women's leagues were formed in the State, their main objects being to secure the return of pledged Labor candidates to the federal and State parliaments and to educate women in industrial and political matters. The first Labor Women's Conference, with Beadle at the helm, was held in 1912, the second in 1927. Meanwhile, in the other States, Labor Women's Organisations were also formed, their members attempting to pursue feminist policies without fomenting 'sex antagonism'. Many Labor stalwarts, such as Jean Daley, Victorian State women's organiser from 1926, gave years of service to the party but achieved little recognition or support. Daley gave vent to her frustration in a public interview just a few months before her untimely death in 1947. 'The men in the Labor movement lack courage', she said. 'They are not interested in organising women and this is a keen disappointment to those of us who have given so many years of service to the movement.'[15]

During Jean Daley's life, feminism was owned by non-party middle class women, who although often associated with the non-Labor cause in politics, in fact had diverse party political allegiances—with Vida Goldstein, Ada Bromham and Jessie Street, for example, on the left; while Millicent Preston Stanley, Angela Booth and Eleanor Glencross supported the Nationalist Federation. Bessie Rischbieth was a very close friend of fellow West Australian, Prime Minister John Curtin, but in the 1950s she became a leading anti-Communist, a politics possibly fuelled by her rivalry with Jessie Street, who was, in turn, close to H. V. Evatt. In 1948, the *Sydney Morning Herald* accused the United Associations of being an organisation 'in which Communists and fellow travellers form a majority or in which they appear to possess influence outweighing their proportion of membership'.[16] The UA vehemently denied the allegations: it was, it continued to insist, non-party. Until the 1970s, when feminism became the cause of Labor women, feminists worked for the most part in their separate organisations, setting their own goals and agenda.

Feminist leaders such as Vida Goldstein, Rose Scott, Bessie Rischbieth and Ada Bromham all wrote and spoke at length about the snare of party politics, but whereas Scott and Goldstein objected to the masculinity and lack of individual conscience in established parties, arguing that 'the hatred of rivals or the thrust for power became the primary motive for political action', Rischbieth and Bromham objected to party politics as inimical to the recognition of human oneness and the human basis of citizenship. A further difference was that whereas Scott and Goldstein set up organisations in opposition to the established political parties, the Australian Federation of Women Voters and its affiliates accepted that 'non-party' might mean 'every party', that their organisations might provide a common meeting ground for women who, despite their political differences, could make common cause as citizens. Indeed, in Western Australia the Women's Service Guild did include prominent Labor women such as Jean Beadle and Henrietta Hooton—but by the late 1920s its emphasis on 'co-operation' had led to the espousal of 'all-party government', with Rischbieth supporting conservative groups such as the 'Who's For Australia League' in their strenuous denunciations of party government. The outbreak of 'anti-political political thought', precipitated by the Depression, spoke to a well-established feminist tradition.

For Scott and Goldstein, active in the immediate post-suffrage years, it was the domination of party politics by men that was the problem. 'Men's point of view in the past had dominated the world and women had been so taken up with the study of man and with the endeavour to please him that they had well nigh forgotten the needs of children.' For Scott these needs—otherwise unrepresented politically—were paramount. Having been wooed herself by the Labor party (as had Goldstein), she deplored the tendency of many women to join the men's parties for their own advantage. Women were 'too ready to follow men and be made their catspaws in politics forgetting that the very *raison d'être* of their possession of the vote is to bring a new element into Political Life'.[17] That element, for Scott, as for her contemporaries, was mother-heartedness: 'The chief mission of women to the world is her Motherhood—to protect and to take care of the race—and not to accentuate the quarrels of men . . .'.[18] Women's place in politics was not that of 'camp followers to a corrupt system of party politics'. The 'blind worship of man and his methods never did any man any good'.[19]

Scott established the Women's Political Education League in 1902 to develop policy for women and children and lobby politicians and other state officials to support their proposed measures. In Victoria, Vida Goldstein formed the Women's Federal Political Association in 1903 (later simply the Women's Political Association (WPA)) for the same reasons and to support her candidature for the Senate. In the journal the *Woman's Sphere*, Goldstein lectured women about the pointlessness of engaging in party politics:

> Women should carry on the fight and the campaign by means of their own organisations, and not by means of any of the existing ones controlled and directed by men. If they do the latter, they must adopt men's methods and men's aims, and simply help in

perpetuating the old order of things. The right of the franchise
will have been bestowed on them for no purpose.[20]

Goldstein noted that immediately women won the vote, all the parties had scrambled to sign them up as members, but if they succumbed to their inducements and joined Labor or Liberal organisations, women would

> justify the sneer which the opponents of woman suffrage have ever made, that once granted the franchise, we would vote just as the men told us to do. Where would be the 'new element' that we were to introduce into politics? Where would be the juster legislation?[21]

Instead women should maximise their political power by keeping men guessing about how they would vote, by setting the agenda, by remaining out of reach of party machinations.

The work of the Women's Political Education League in New South Wales demonstrated well the relationship between feminists' distinctive political agenda and their non-party mode of doing politics. Its record of activity also highlights the energy and commitment of citizen activists such as Scott, whose modest independent means made possible a lifelong dedication to politics. Her famous salon, to which she invited a range of political and intellectual figures, exemplified feminists' attempt to persuade the rest of the world to their point of view. Scott personally lobbied leading politicians such as W. A. Holman, B. R. Wise, E. W. O'Sullivan and Arthur Rae, assisting them to draft legislation and build the necessary political alliances to achieve reform.

Scott worked closely with C. K. Mackellar on his amendment to the Crimes Act to raise the age of consent from twelve to seventeen, arranging to have different branches of the WPEL send petitions to parliament. By August 1903, 'some 50 petition forms had been distributed to Leagues, public hospitals and other institutions, praying for the passing of the Bill, the Coast Hospital alone sending in over 100 signatures'.[22] The parliamentary opposition to this measure—seen by many men on both sides of politics as posing a threat to their sexual liberties—was fierce, however, and the bill did not pass the second reading. In 1909, Scott approached Labor member W. A. Holman for support. He replied:

> Your note to hand this morning. I recognise with you the importance of the Girls' Protection Bill and you may be sure I

will do all possible to interest my fellow-colleagues in it, but of course it is a work of time to get enough interested to make any show; still I think the time is not far distant when something will be done to improve the condition of our children.[23]

Holman's support proved crucial and the legislation was finally passed in 1910, but with the age of consent set at sixteen years, not seventeen as Scott and other feminists had urged.

After a decade's work as citizens, the members of the WPEL had reason to be pleased. Their political effectiveness was evident in the increased 'protection' (and some would say regulation) of children in New South Wales. The League claimed credit for several legislative measures—the Juvenile Smoking Suppression Act (1903), the State Children's Amendment Act (1903), the Infants' Protection Act (1904), Neglected Children and Juvenile Offenders Act (1905), the Police Offences Amendment Act and the Prisoners' Detention Act (both 1908) and the Crimes (Girls' Protection) Amendment Act (1910)—as well as the appointment of women to key administrative positions in courts, gaols, hospitals, schools and factories. The same work occurred in other States. 'Practically every reform that has been won for women and children', wrote Goldstein in the *Christian Science Monitor* in 1918, 'has been initiated through the political action of non-party women'.[24]

With the passage of her most cherished reform, the 1910 Crimes Amendment Act, which raised the age of consent to sixteen years, 63-year-old Scott closed down the WPEL. Just one year before, in 1909, the Women's Service Guild was established in Perth, initially with a similar mission 'to educate women . . .'. Its club-rooms exemplified the civic culture that characterised feminist citizenship in the interwar years. First located in Market Street, later in Murray Street, there was a library and meeting rooms where 'tea, coffee or cocoa' and sometimes lunch were served to members and 'business girls'. The WSG published a monthly journal, the *Dawn*, detailing local, interstate and international feminist news. Members organised a school for citizenship with lectures by Walter Murdoch and others, and they established the local branch of the League of Nations Union, conducted public speaking and debating classes, marched in the streets, organised rallies, spoke on radio and interviewed politicians—a wide range of activities that together expressed 'women's struggle for a wider expression of "citizenship"'.[25] In Sydney, the Feminist Club had established a Women's Club, providing, like their counterparts in Canada and the United States, accommodation for visitors. When the United Associations was formed in 1929, it offered:

> a Club room with a Lending Library, a Board Room and Office at Challis House, Martin Place (Light lunches and teas are available by arrangement). A number of overseas Women's Papers are available free of charge. There is a general meeting every Thursday afternoon at which addresses on topics of general interest are given which are followed by general discussion.[26]

The annual subscription was 10/6; the member's fee 21/-.

Recognising that women in paid work were unable to attend daytime meetings, the UA established a Professional and Business Women's Group, which met in the evenings, as well as the Married Women Teachers' Committee, which fought the ban on their employment. As feminism in the 1930s shifted its focus away from relations between men and women in the home to concentrate more on the position of women in paid work and public life, so meetings and political organising had to take into account the constraints of differently situated women. A meeting to discuss attacks on women's right to work, for example, was organised by Linda Littlejohn for 21 November 1933, at 6 pm.

Feminist organisations between the wars (and by the 1920s their members had generally adopted the feminist label) espoused a characteristic combination of aims and principles: they were non-party, and they stood for an equal moral standard, for an equality of status, opportunities and liberties with men, and for the other reforms (censorship, temperance, the appointment of women police) deemed to be necessary to enable women and girls to live in freedom and security. These aims were interrelated because feminists believed that women's status was undermined by their treatment as 'creatures of sex', that so long as men assumed the right of sexual access to women's bodies, women as a group could never enjoy an equal regard as citizens. Thus did 'good morals' and 'good citizenship' go together.[27]

Feminists were non-party because none of the existing political parties shared their goals and priorities. On issues that concerned them—equality of status and opportunities for women, men's assumed right of sexual access to women's bodies, the harmful effects of alcohol, attacks on women's right to work—the predominantly male membership of the major political parties was divided at best. As often as not, feminist demands were seen to threaten men's liberties and certainly neither political party supported feminist aims as a matter of policy.

Feminists were non-party because they had their own political agenda to pursue, which they hoped to persuade other political forces to support. Accordingly, in 1924, the Women's Service Guild held 'interviews of an interesting nature' at Headquarters with various federal members of parliament in order to inform them 're our position with regard to':

> Child Welfare, Motherhood Endowment, Maternity Allowance, Keeping Canberra Dry, Invalid and Old Age Pensions, Nationality of Married Women, Equal Opportunities in the Federal Service, Free Breakfast Table, Women as Full Delegates to League of Nations Assembly . . .[28]

In Sydney, in 1933, the United Associations circulated a questionnaire to federal election candidates which asked whether they would support a bill providing for proportional representation in the Senate, the restoration of the Maternity Allowance to its former basis, nationality rights for married women, federal control of Aboriginal welfare— 'having full regard to aboriginal tribal laws and customs'—the appointment of a woman inspector of Aborigines, the establishment of a new Ministry of Peace and finally, the principle of complete equality of women and men under the law and in all human relationships.[29]

These modes of doing politics produced results. In 1942, the UA was able to claim credit for the introduction of Child Endowment, with payments made to the mother, and for amendments to income tax legislation, preventing plans for the wife's income to be added to that of her husband for the assessment of their income. In a letter to Treasurer J. B. Chifley, it had been pointed out that such a proposal

> infringed rights which women gained under the Married Women's Property Act, which conferred upon women the right to independent ownership, control and management of their property . . . We consider that in any scheme of taxation, the rights and status of the individual citizen should be preserved.[30]

In 1947, in a membership drive, the UA pointed out that four bills currently being debated in the New South Wales parliament (concerning married women teachers' right to work, mothers' inheritance rights, married women's right to household savings and women's right to serve on juries) were to enact reforms for which the United Associations had worked for many years. The Married Women Teachers and Lecturers Act was repealed in 1947 and, after concerted lobbying by the New

South Wales Teachers' Federation and the UA, equal pay was introduced for teachers in New South Wales in 1958. Among 'advanced' women, New South Wales became known as an 'equal pay State'.

Feminists continued to lobby throughout the 1950s for uniform divorce laws, for federal government ratification of the International Labor Office (ILO) convention on equal pay, for equal pay and opportunities in the public service and for the repeal of Section 49 of the Commonwealth Public Service Act which barred the employment of married women, a goal finally achieved in 1966. In the federal arena, equal pay was formally recognised by Commonwealth Arbitration Court decisions in 1969 and 1972: victories for women that were the culmination of years of political work, undertaken by feminists old and new, who had lobbied, demonstrated, formed deputations, researched and written lengthy submissions—engaging in all the traditional feminist modes of doing politics.

Because their main aim was to change public opinion and win support for their policies, feminists became skilled and indefatigable public speakers. They addressed rallies, engaged in radio debates, presented petitions and spoke to public meetings. When Marguerite Dale returned from her work at the League of Nations in 1922, she made around 100 speeches throughout Australia in six months. Millicent Preston Stanley was renowned as a gifted public speaker who had no rival in her ability to deal with hecklers. Linda Littlejohn made her reputation in New South Wales as a radio broadcaster, but she was also in demand as a platform speaker more generally. During 1930—when she held office as vice-president of the United Associations of Women, and was a member of the Sydney Board of Public Health, director of Crown Street Women's Hospital, a member of the board of the AFWV and of the executive of the League of Nations Union (New South Wales branch), superintendent of the Australian Broadcasting Company's Women's Sports Association and chair of the Maude Royden Study Circle—she managed to give ninety-eight public talks.

SEEKING A VOICE IN PARLIAMENT

Feminist modes of doing politics were effective in securing a range of reforms—equal custody and inheritance laws; raising the age of consent; restricting the availability of alcohol; the censorship of picture shows;

establishing maternal and infant welfare services; securing women's appointment as police, Justices of the Peace, lawyers, magistrates, medical and school inspectors; prison reform; child endowment; and eventually equal pay—but the limits of the non-party strategy in a political system dominated by the two parties were made starkly evident when non-party feminists attempted to win seats in parliament.

In the Commonwealth, (white) women became eligible to stand for parliament in the same year, 1902, as they were granted the suffrage. In the States, with the exception of South Australia, women were not granted the right to stand for parliament until some years after their enfranchisement—in New South Wales and Queensland in 1918, in Western Australia in 1920, in Tasmania in 1921, in Victoria in 1923. In any case, aspiring women politicians were caught in an impossible situation. They were either offered preselection by the major parties in unwinnable seats (Jean Daley stood for the Labor party in Kooyong in 1922) or they faced defeat as Independents. Thus prominent non-party feminist candidates were all defeated—women such as Vida Goldstein who stood five times as a Victorian candidate for the Senate, Ada Bromham who stood in the seat of Claremont in the 1921 Western Australian election, Edith Waterworth who was a candidate for the Tasmanian Non-Party Women's League in the 1921 State election, Eleanor Glencross who stood as an independent Nationalist for the seat of Brighton in Victoria in 1928, the five women endorsed by the United Associations as candidates in the New South Wales election in 1932 and the nineteen Independents sponsored by the Women for Canberra movement in 1943.

Vida Goldstein, herself a socialist, was upset at Labor opposition to feminist candidates and in 1910, when she was again running for the Senate, she rebuked them for their continued hostility:

> It seems to be a human law that the oppressed of one age become the oppressors of the next. The Labor Party sprang into existence because the working class, so-called, was oppressed by the Liberals and Conservatives, who could not understand its interests. Now, having attained political power, a section of the Labor party would oppress all who do not see eye to eye with it on all points,
> instead of leaving them free to work out their political salvation.[31]

But feminists were not free to work out their own political salvation, because they entered a political system not of their own making.

Rather, they were forced to accommodate themselves to the two-party structures already in place at the time of their enfranchisement.

Significantly, the first women to win seats in parliaments were endorsed by the established political parties. In State elections, Nationalist candidates Edith Cowan and Millicent Preston Stanley won seats in 1921 (in Western Australia) and 1925 (in New South Wales) respectively, but both lost their seats when they lost their party preselection after just one term in office. May Holman was the first Labor woman to win a seat in parliament, succeeding in 1925 to her father's seat of Forrest, which she held through four elections. The first women to win seats in the federal parliament, Enid Lyons in the House of Representatives and Dorothy Tangney in the Senate, were also endorsed party candidates—for the United Australia party and the Labor party respectively.

The one notable non-party triumph for feminists was the election of Ivy Weber in the 'dry' seat of Nunawading in Victoria in 1937, her candidature supported by the Woman's Christian Temperance Union and the League of Women Voters (the erstwhile Victorian Women Citizens' Movement). Forty-five-year-old Weber was a wife and a mother of twelve children (although only four were living at home at the time of her election), an advocate of temperance and a photogenic fitness enthusiast. Her campaign focussed on 'Mother, Child, Family, Home and Health' and the right of women to political representation. It was well known, said Weber, 'that political parties have completely ignored the just claims of their women supporters to be given a chance to contest seats under reasonably fair conditions'.[32] But when she attempted to transfer to the federal parliament, standing for the seat of Henty as part of the Women for Canberra movement in 1943, she was defeated, as were all nineteen Independents sponsored by that movement.

The barriers to the election of non-party feminists to parliament were many. Feminists faced not just the opposition of the men who represented the established political parties. In Victoria, Edith Jones, president of the Victorian Women Citizens' Movement, presented herself as a candidate for the federal election in 1925, but the Church of England vestrymen of her husband's East St Kilda parish pressured her to withdraw. Visiting Perth on her way to England, Jones explained that it was important for the 'woman's mind' to be present in the federal parliament, because otherwise legislation would remain 'purely economic'. Issues that particularly concerned her were the 'protection and education and economic use of the aboriginals of the Northern Territory' and the urgent need for a better national health policy. The *Dawn* commented:

> It cannot but be regretted that circumstances should thus prevent an enthusiastic and gifted woman citizen from seeking a share in the national councils where the mother-voice is too long silent in this land of ours.

Indeed, Jones was a 'true feminist, with a clear vision and a broad outlook'.[33]

Reflecting on the election of women to parliament (possibly in response to May Holman's election), the Women's Service Guild emphasised the importance of electing feminists, if women as a whole were to benefit:

> A woman candidate, to be satisfactory must be a 'feminist' in the best sense of the word. She should understand matters relating to the lives of women, both as wives and mothers and workers; and she should believe absolutely in the necessity for equality of status, liberty and opportunity between men and women. A woman candidate that [sic] is shaky on this matter, or not sufficiently imbued with its importance to be able to speak convincingly on the matter will do the movement towards establishing Women in Parliament far more harm than good.[34]

But how to return feminists to parliament?

Feminist leaders realised that to have non-party women represented in parliament, electoral reform was necessary to introduce proportional representation and multi-member electorates. In the first speech to parliament by Australia's first female politician, Edith Cowan announced she would like to amend the Electoral Act to provide for compulsory voting and proportional representation, 'on the lines of the Denmark system'.[35] In South Australia, the advocacy of proportional representation or 'effective voting', which had been Catherine Helen Spence's special cause, had been kept alive by her co-worker, Jeanne Young, who convened a Proportional Representation Group of the South Australian Women's Non-Party Association. Her message was that single member constituencies were undemocratic in that they were only able to represent one side or the other:

> Electoral machinery to be effective should give to the majority in every district the majority of seats. It should, at the same time,

give to the minority in every district that share of representation to which its voting strength entitles it.³⁶

In Western Australia, Victoria and New South Wales non-party feminists unceasingly urged the adoption of this electoral reform. At a meeting of the Victorian Women Citizens' Movement in May 1931, the president, Britomarte James, endorsed the view that only proportional representation, in providing for the representation of 'minorities', would make possible the adequate representation of women candidates. In 1933, the United Associations questionnaire to federal political candidates asked whether they would support proportional representation for the Senate, a reform that was finally introduced by Labor in 1948. The subsequent significantly greater representation of women in the Senate than in the House of Representatives—in 1996 women constituted 30 per cent of the Senate, but only 15 per cent of the House of Representatives—would seem to support the view that proportional representation was good for women's representation.

A NATIONAL AND INTERNATIONAL VOICE

Post-suffrage feminists, for the most part, focussed their demands for reform on State governments and bureaucracies, because they had jurisdiction over matters affecting home life—health, education, the administration of justice, licensing laws and welfare. By 1920, however, many feminists became convinced of the necessity for a federal organisation. There were three reasons for this: first, feminists needed to voice their views at the federal level; second, an equal citizenship demanded national consistency in laws concerning women; and third, feminists needed a national body to represent them at the international level.

The formation of the Australian Federation of Women Voters, initially called the Australian Federation of Women's Societies, was a response to both local and overseas developments, but it was also the result of Bessie Rischbieth's ambition for political leadership in the national and international domain. Rischbieth, as we have seen, had visited London in 1911, when she thrilled to the speeches of the American Charlotte Perkins Gilman and became an ardent supporter of the suffragettes. As it happened, Vida Goldstein was in London in the same year at the invitation of the Women's Social and Political

Union; together with another Australian, Harriet Newcombe, and Lady Anna Stout from New Zealand, Goldstein had formed the Australian and New Zealand Women Voters' Committee, to lobby the imperial conference and the British government about the rights of Dominion women in the United Kingdom, including women's right to maintain their nationality on marriage. This organisation subsequently became the British Dominions' Woman Suffrage (later Citizenship) Union, run by Australians Margaret Hodge and Harriet Newcombe. Rischbieth established links between this organisation and the Women's Service Guild in Perth, but she also sought affiliation with the International Alliance of Women for Suffrage and Equal Citizenship. In 1915, Harriet Newcombe regretted to inform her that the Women's Service Guild was not eligible for affiliation, because it was not itself a national association.

> The WPA [Women's Political Association] is not a national association, either, but Miss Goldstein arranged to pay the affiliation fee for the *whole* of Australia, until a national association was formed. If the Women's Service Guild and the Women's Non-Party Association of South Australia would join with the WPA of Victoria, it would be a glorious beginning of a national association.[37]

Rischbieth seemed disinclined to accept the implied seniority of Vida Goldstein and her organisation, the WPA, in such an arrangement. Goldstein had already offered Rischbieth 'pages' in her paper the *Woman Voter* to report feminist news in Western Australia and South Australia, observing that it was 'very desirable to have uniformity amongst the non-party organizations in each State'. But Rischbieth planned to set up her own national organisation and her own paper to report interstate and international news, which became the *Dawn*.

The first steps towards forming a federal body were taken in Perth, in 1918, at the time of the Triennial Convention of the Australasian Woman's Christian Temperance Union, when Rischbieth together with other members of the Women's Service Guild arranged a meeting of a number of women 'in an individual capacity for a quiet talk over questions immediately affecting Australasian women', as Rischbieth carefully described the gathering in a letter to prospective supporters.[38] She explained that there needed to be better communication about federal issues and co-ordination on matters such as marriage and divorce, health (especially dealing with venereal disease), maintenance, prohibition and the rights of citizenship. She reported further:

> After careful deliberation the following two motions were carried unanimously by those women present acting in quite an individual capacity.
>
> (1) That a consultative Committee of three in each State be selected to act as an 'Advisory Committee'.
> (2) That these three women be selected to form a link for the interchange of acts and opinions on questions affecting women and children, and that each Committee be asked to appoint a convener.[39]

The meeting further resolved that Rischbieth contact the three 'selected' women in each State and invite them to consult with the other two so nominated and let Rischbieth know the results of her deliberations.

Most of the women quickly pointed out that they had no authority to speak on behalf of the women of their State. Edith Waterworth, of the Child Welfare Association in Tasmania, replied that the idea of interstate co-operation was a good one, but Rischbieth's method of setting up the proposed council was not:

> Three women acting without authority from women's societies here would have no standing and what they said would carry no weight. You see although our names were given to you, that is no guarantee that we are the women to voice Tasmanian women's opinions, even privately. But if we were appointed by the Women's Societies to speak for them the position would be unassailable.[40]

From Queensland, Annie Carvosso replied enthusiastically, observing that in times past she had worked hard to establish an interstate National Council of Women, but without result. There might be some resistance to the idea of an independent committee, however. She commented about the recent deportation of Russians from Queensland—'there is a terrible lot of disloyalty here'—and asked: 'What do you think of the cabled information of Russian Free Love? Is there anything Australasian women can do?'.[41] To Australian feminists, Russian 'free love'—or licensed vice—represented the very antithesis of the equal moral standard.

From New South Wales, H. Bennett also reported on her efforts to galvanise the National Council of Women into fresh life and the lack of co-ordination and agreement among the different organisations: 'oh for a leader to wake up our women and shew [sic] them how to organise . . .'. She spoke enviously of the American Women's Clubs: 'personally I think nothing but a combination of women's societies and all classes of women organised under one head is going to pull Australia through'. She was hoping that women would fall into line behind the Feminist Club, but women in other States could have no idea 'how difficult the Sydney women are . . .'.[42] In New South Wales, the desired amalgamation did not take place until ten years later, with the formation of the United Associations under Jessie Street's leadership in 1929. With the emergence of *two* strong leaders in Rischbieth and Street in the 1930s, however, new rivalries were brought into play in feminist politics, exacerbated by the different political sympathies of these doctrinally non-party feminists.

Rischbieth's proposed interstate committee was formed in 1919, but its non-representative status remained a problem. In 1920, Elizabeth Nicholls, a member of the Woman's Christian Temperance Union and the Women's Non-Party Association of South Australia, who had been nominated by the committee to attend the Congress of the International Women's Suffrage Alliance in Geneva, encouraged the idea that Australia should form a national association, which could affiliate with the Alliance and send properly accredited national delegates to the next Congress.

INTERNATIONALISM

The changing status of Australia as a Dominion gave new urgency to the move to form a national feminist organisation. From 1913, Australian feminists had secured representation at the International Women's Suffrage Alliance as part of the British delegation of twelve, nominated by the British Dominions' Woman Citizens' Union, but they had been limited to a maximum of four delegates, rather than the twelve possible for other national groupings. When Australia was given status as an independent nation at the League of Nations from 1919, Australian women became eligible to participate as national delegates—but who would nominate them?

When the Women's Service Guild and the South Australian

Women's Non-Party Association invited their 'sister organisations' to another meeting following the 1921 WCTU Convention in Melbourne, to form a body 'uniting societies in Australia working for Equal Citizenship', they at first conceived of their organisation as a branch of the British Dominions' Woman Citizens' Union. The officers of the resulting Australian Federation of Women's Societies were Bessie Rischbieth (Western Australia), president; Elizabeth Nicholls (South Australia), Jamieson Williams (New South Wales) and Annie Carvosso (Queensland) vice-presidents; and M. King (Western Australia) as honorary secretary.

When Harriet Newcombe, the effusive secretary of the British Dominions' Woman Citizens' Union received the news of the formation of the Australian Federation of Women's Societies, she acclaimed the event as having almost messianic significance. To vice-president M. King she wrote: 'To me it is simply of the highest significance in the history of Australia, and in the history of the Women's movement, that the Women-Citizens of Australia should have federated'.[43] In a further letter to the 'officers' of the new organisation she continued, 'I need not repeat what I have already said about the importance to the whole world, as well as to Australia, of this step. To me it seems that we cannot overrate its importance. Australian women are now brought into the forward line of the great world movement which aims to realise the most deeply cherished ideals of women'.[44] In a note to Rischbieth she made it clear to whom credit was due: 'I have just sent a little interim note to dear Mrs Nicholls, conveying a very inadequate idea of my appreciation of the fine piece of work she has inaugurated for women in Australia, and through them for the women of the world'.[45]

Newcombe cautioned Rischbieth, however, about an ambiguity in her publicity material, where she had referred to the 'Mother-Heart' of the Empire:

> I understand you to mean the grand idea that the 'Mother-Heart' which exists in all women should find expression, as regards the British Commonwealth of Nations in one United Mother-Voice. But in other parts of the world there are some who might misunderstand you, and fancy you meant further consolidation of the Centre of Government in the Mother-city, London, which is often called the Heart of the Empire.[46]

Perhaps the meaning was deliberately ambiguous, for Rischbieth did fondly regard London as the heart of the Empire and thus an appropriate place for Australian feminists to make representations about reforms for Empire women. The vision of British and Dominions women combined in 'unity of action', as when Australian feminists lobbied the imperial conference on the issue of women's suffrage and married women's nationality, inspired Rischbieth and other Australian feminists. Their sense of British identity shaped their sense of who they were.

One of the early achievements of the Australian Federation of Women's Societies was to persuade Prime Minister W. M. Hughes of the principle that Australian women should be able to go as delegates to the League of Nations and in particular to secure his support for the appointment of its nominated candidate, Sydney playwright and temperance campaigner Marguerite Dale as (substitute) delegate in 1922, the first woman delegate to attend from any of the Dominions. Rischbieth, as we have seen, saw the appointment as an epoch-making event. Australian feminists, like others around the world, were ardent believers in the League of Nations, both because of its promise to secure international peace and because the Covenant recognised equality between the sexes. Feminist participation as delegates only increased their admiration. Stella Allen, a Melbourne journalist and delegate in 1924, returned enraptured. Said a press report:

> She had come back with an almost overwhelming sense of the importance of the League of Nations. In no other place in which she had been were women and men on such equal terms as in Geneva. The mental attitude was one of absolute equality.[47]

But the AFWV could not monopolise appointments. The woman delegate between Dale and Allen, in 1923, was the Melbourne historian Jessie Webb, the nominee of the National Council of Women.

The status of the Australian Federation of Women Voters as the representative voice of Australian women did not go uncontested. The National Council of Women protested long and loudly at Rischbieth's presumption. Harriet Newcombe wrote offering sympathy and support to Rischbieth in March 1924:

> I think that your difficulties with the N.C.W. are enough to try the stoutest heart and that you are indeed brave to stick to your guns as you do . . . N.C.W. publicly and privately assert that the Federation has no claim whatever to represent Australia.
>
> My dear love to you. The very thought of you puts life into me . . .[48]

Writing to Carrie Chapman Catt, president of the (renamed) International Alliance of Women for Suffrage and Equal Citizenship, in 1924, about a possible visit to Australia, Rischbieth advised:

> It is only fair to let you know that there has been some opposition in Australia from the National Councils of Women to another international body having a national auxiliary in the country, but I think women are feeling the need for such a body as the Australian Federation, and the difficulty mentioned will die a natural death . . .[49]

With the passage of time the two organisations adapted to each other's existence, both continuing to speak for the interests of women, but each forging a distinctive identity—the NCW tending to represent the point of view of professional women and the AFWV pursuing the feminist aim of complete equality of citizenship. Both organisations worked through affiliated societies and both adopted women's distinctive modes of doing politics: lobbying, writing submissions, organising conferences, promoting lecture tours, engaging in radio broadcasts and arranging deputations. The AFWV and its affiliated associations also supported the political campaigns of non-party feminists for parliamentary office.

In 1925, the British Dominions' Woman Citizens' Union reformed as the British Commonwealth League (BCL), its aim 'to secure equality of liberties, status and opportunities between men and women in the British Commonwealth of Nations'. That year it organised an important conference in London on women and citizenship, attended by delegates from Bermuda, India, Canada, South Africa, Britain, New Zealand and Australia, which was represented by Bessie Rischbieth, Chave Collison, Britomarte James and Edith Jones, the last two delegates of the Victorian Women Citizens' Movement. It discussed equal citizenship under the headings of Political Equality, Equal Moral Standard, Nationality, Slavery and Economic Equality, a combination of interests that reflected both the maternalist orientation of 1920s feminism as well as the discursive shift towards 'equality'. Thus in the economic field, the principle of equality required both equal pay for equal work as well as a demand for recognition of the value of women's work in the home.

The British Commonwealth League would provide an invaluable forum for Australian feminists abroad, who would prove ever more adept at exploiting English networks and publicity to further their cause. Australian feminists presented papers on the oppressed condition of Aboriginal people from 1927, when Constance Cooke addressed the BCL as well as the Anti-Slavery Society, and in 1930 Bennett's argument about the slavery of Aboriginal people, publicised by the *Manchester Guardian*, led ultimately to the appointment of the Royal Commission in Western Australia.

Post-suffrage feminists participated in a variety of international organisations and congresses. Their conviction that national, racial and class prejudices should be combated in the interests of human solidarity and international peace fostered a deep commitment to organising and participating in meetings with women from different nations and promoting education about different cultures and countries. Australian feminists have always been world travellers. Numerous Australian women went to overseas peace conferences in the post-war years, beginning with the International Peace Conference in 1919, attended by Cecilia John, Vida Goldstein and Eleanor Moore, honorary secretary of the Sisterhood of Peace which would become the Australian branch of the Women's International League for Peace and Freedom. Fond friendships strengthened political commitments. Goldstein and Street were close to Edith How Martyn while Bessie Rischbieth formed close links with Carrie Chapman Catt and Margery Corbett Ashby of the International Alliance of Women for Suffrage and Equal Citizenship. At the Alliance Congress in Rome in 1923, where Australia was one of forty-three nations represented, feminists resolved to affirm that it was the duty of all nations to work for friendly international relations, to demand the substitution of judicial methods for those of force; and to promote the conception of human solidarity as superior to racial, or national, solidarity. The Women's Service Guild subsequently resolved to recommend to the federal government that it establish a university in Canberra with a Chair in International Relations.

The same ideal of peace through international understanding informed the proceedings of the Pan-Pacific Women's Conference, established in 1928 under the auspices of the Pan-Pacific Union to promote friendship and equal citizenship between the women of Pacific nations. The first Pan-Pacific conference, held in Honolulu, was chaired by Australian science graduate and welfare worker Eleanor Hinder, then working with the Young Women's Christian Association in Shanghai. Conferences were then held every two years, with discussions organised around prepared papers and reading lists for specified topics. The conferences were in some ways the forerunners of Women's

Studies programs, paper givers expected to perform at a high level, being 'capable of viewing their subject in a philosophic light in relation to the social structure of their country as a whole or even of evaluating its international significance'.[50] There was considerable sensitivity about the representativeness of the Australian delegation, with Dr Georgina Sweet, chairman of the nominating committee, conferring at length with Rischbieth, who advised 'we shall have to be particularly careful to recognise the status of the industrially organised women in Australia', suggesting that Muriel Heagney should be consulted.[51]

The commitment to respect other cultures led many feminists to challenge racist nationalisms. In 1932, women delegates to the Pan-Pacific conference were asked to consider the topic 'National Policies Affecting International Relations—What Limitations on Nationalism Are Desirable?' and, in particular, the questions:

> Is national control of immigration, especially any exclusion policy, liable to endanger world peace or at least to create political, social, racial and economic complications? (eg the Australian racial attitude to Italian immigration.) Does your country exclude or limit the immigration of any racial or national type? If so, what justifications are given? What reactions have resulted among the people so treated?
>
> . . .
>
> Is a diversity in racial and cultural types to be regarded as an enrichment, producing the fusion and change out of which inventions, discoveries, improvements arise, or as a contamination of the group heritage?[52]

In 1934, the fourth Pan-Pacific Women's Conference met in Vancouver, chaired by Dr Georgina Sweet, national president of the Young Women's Christian Association in Australia. The theme was 'Practical Ways and Means of Promoting Peace'.

Feminists invoking the virtues of internationalism were among the earliest critics of the White Australia policy. The Women's Political Association in Victoria held a public meeting on the subject in June 1919, its organisers confident that Australians had become more 'Cosmopolitanised', more fully alive to the contradictions between the ideal of the 'brotherhood of man' and support for a restrictive immigration policy. In general women internationalists opposed socialist men, who defended the male living standard from cheap Asian labour.

'No one learns by isolation; Australia is large enough for all', said Mrs Griffin, adding, 'our moral superiority is a joke'. 'Does not Australia pride herself on being the land of experiments?' asked Clara Weekes. 'Why fear the experiment of admitting the Asiatics?'[53] In a paper called 'Australia and National Righteousness' given to the Australian Federation of Women Voters in 1930, Vida Goldstein pointed out that our 'Eastern neighbours' felt chafed by Australia's 'arrogant discrimination against them', and she urged those present 'to keep before the people the moral necessity of friendliness towards all races'.[54]

Eleanor Hinder, while working in China, sent a circular letter in the early 1930s to friends in Australia deploring the Australian tendency to identify exclusively with Europe:

> We are, as you know, very isolated with a population 98 per cent British in origin: we have a national religion—the White Australia policy, every organisation looks in affiliation to international groupings which centre in Europe. For the majority of the women of Australia, the women of Oriental countries simply do not exist . . .[55]

As an affiliate with the International Alliance of Women for Suffrage and Equal Citizenship, the Australian Federation of Women Voters sent a large contingent of delegates to its triennial congresses in Europe—Rome in 1923, Paris in 1926 and Berlin in 1929. The maternalist and moral orientations of the Alliance spoke to and shaped the goals of interwar feminism in Australia. In the early 1930s, however, Australian feminists from the United Associations in New South Wales—notably Jessie Street and Linda Littlejohn—sought a new alliance with the American-based group Equal Rights International (an offshoot of Alice Paul's American National Women's Party), which was established to assert the primacy of an equal rights approach to feminism. Traditionally the champions of women's difference—their distinctive needs, peculiar oppressions and different values—Australian feminists would increasingly focus on the goal of equality with men and in the process feminism itself became more assimilationist.

PART IV
EQUALITY WITH MEN

7
THE RIGHT TO WORK

INTERNATIONAL FRAMEWORKS FOR ACTION

In 1929, the Sydney feminist Linda Littlejohn travelled to an international conference in Berlin, organised at the suggestion of the British group Open Door Council, founded three years before. The Berlin gathering was attended by women from twenty-one countries, whose purpose was to establish a worldwide organisation, which they would name Open Door International for the Economic Emancipation of the Woman Worker (ODI). Its single goal was absolute equality for women and men in the paid workforce. More particularly, it aimed to mobilise opposition to all restrictive or protective regulations enacted specifically for women workers—relating, for example, to nightwork, maternity, weights, dangerous substances and processes—which, ODI thought, kept women in a position of inferiority as workers. Open Door International opposed the codification of such restrictions in various conventions of the International Labor Office (ILO).

Open Door International was not opposed to restrictive industrial regulations as such. Where they were based upon the nature of the work and not the sex of the worker, they could be constructive and beneficial to all workers as human beings. But, continued Linda Littlejohn in her report:

> [ODI] is opposed to special restrictions placed on women because they are women; since such restrictions do irreparable harm to women by lowering her status. Moreover, they maintain many employments and processes as monopolies for men; limit woman in her choice of employment; and so lower her rate of wages.

Such restrictions do not protect women. They do, in fact protect men, while inflicting serious economic injury on all women.[1]

Back in Sydney, a number of sympathetic women formed the Australian Open Door Council, of which Littlejohn became founding president. Some time later a separate branch was formed in Victoria, with K. A. Gilman Jones, secretary of the Victorian Women Citizens' Movement, as president. This became the Equal Status Committee, which sponsored Muriel Heagney to write her passionate advocacy of women's right to work in *Are Women Taking Men's Jobs?* in 1935.

At the same time, Jessie Street, Littlejohn's close colleague in the United Associations (UA), was involved in parallel political moves. Both had embarked on the equal rights road, forging international links independent of the International Alliance, of Women for Suffrage and Equal Citizenship network which was Bessie Rischbieth's power base although it was Rischbiethk who first introduced Street to Anne Kelter Wiley of the National Women's Party in Washington. In 1930, Street travelled to Geneva where she attended an 'At Home' hosted by Open Door International and a meeting to form a World Equality Group, soon to be renamed Equal Rights International (ERI). Its founding members were drawn from eight countries, although its guiding hand was Alice Paul, president of the National Women's Party in the United States. Its first office-bearers were Helen Archdale from Great Britain, chairman, and Jessie Street from Australia, vice-chairman. The aim of ERI was complete equality in the right to work. Geneva provided an exciting new political arena for feminist action.

The impetus for this international assertion of equal rights came from American feminists, on the Inter-American Commission of Women, including Alice Paul, who had long lobbied against restrictions on women's work. In both Britain and the United States, conflict over the wisdom of protective industrial legislation had become a divisive issue for feminists, and in the 1930s Australian feminists became caught up in that dispute. The target of Equal Rights International, as of Open Door International, was the International Labor Office.

In Geneva, Jessie Street joined in a deputation to Albert Thomas, secretary of the ILO office, stressing that 'women on the other side of the world' had experienced extreme difficulty as a result of such legislation, which was intended to be beneficial, but operated with quite the reverse effect. 'These women desired protection', she said, 'but only the protection which operated for men and women alike'.

When Street returned to Sydney, via Fremantle on the SS *Oronsay*, she was interviewed by the *Daily News*, which reported she had much to say regarding the status of women in other countries. She particularly stressed the fact that 'in Czechoslovakia women and men get equal pay for equal work'.[2] She was met at Fremantle by Bessie Rischbieth.

The other issue that prompted concerted feminist action in Geneva, this time at the League of Nations, was married women's loss of nationality rights. Australian feminists had campaigned abroad for recognition of married women's nationality rights, and thus citizenship rights, since at least 1910, when Australian and New Zealand women, led by Vida Goldstein, lobbied the imperial conference in London. Acting Prime Minister W. M. Hughes declined to take up the issue: it was a domestic matter, he said, not the business of 'self-governing Dominions'.[3] In response to the Dominions statesmen's rebuff, Dominions feminists set up the Australian and New Zealand Women Voters' Committee, specifically to lobby future imperial conferences. This was the genesis of the British Dominions' Woman Citizens' Union, which became the British Commonwealth League.

Following the Hague Nationality Convention's endorsement in 1930 of a code that ratified inequality of treatment between men and women, American feminists were successful in their request that the issue be discussed at the League of Nations Assembly in 1931, a session attended by the nominee of the Australian Federation of Women Voters, Dr Ethel Osborne, who had, as it happened, worked closely with the ILO as a specialist in women's industrial health. Osborne put the Australian feminist position that the Hague Convention should be overturned, but not until 1948 did Australian women gain the same nationality rights as men.

In 1932, the First Commission of the League of Nations considered the proposal presented by eight international feminist organisations, that 'Articles 8 to 11 of the Nationality Convention drawn up at the Hague in 1930 should be revised or supplanted by an entirely new convention based on sex equality'. The Hague Convention set an unfortunate precedent they said; to recommend that nation states ratify it as it stood would involve 'the recognition in the first code of international law of the old legal system, whereby a married woman has been forced to depend for her nationality on that of her husband'.[4] The campaign for equality in nationality was led by women delegates from the South American countries Chile and Colombia, but the

Canadian resolution urging support for the Hague Convention carried the day.

South American feminists continued their international campaign for equal nationality rights, but extended it, calling for a more general Equal Rights Treaty. In 1933, the governments of Cuba, Ecuador, Paraguay and Uruguay, meeting at the Seventh International Conference of American States in Montevideo, became the first to sign an Equal Rights Treaty, which stipulated 'the contracting states agree that upon the ratification of this Treaty, men and women shall have equal rights throughout the territories subject to their respective jurisdiction'.[5] Feminists were jubilant over this formal recognition of equal rights. Doris Stevens, the United States chairman of the Inter-American Commission on Women, proclaimed its historical significance. 'It is', she said, 'the first time in history that states have agreed to outlaw unequal treatment of their women by international action'.[6] The 1934 ERI general meeting hailed the 'great international victory for international feminism'.[7]

The Equal Rights Treaty, endorsed by ERI, had also been accepted by six other international feminist organisations—the International Council of Women, the International Alliance of Women for Suffrage and Equal Citizenship, the International Federation of University Women, the International Federation of Women Lawyers, the All-Asia Conference on Women and the Women's International League for Peace and Freedom. At its annual general meeting in Geneva in 1935, ERI, chaired in that year by Australian Linda Littlejohn, noted that it had been 'a momentous year for feminists': 'equality of the sexes has become a subject of major international importance'.[8] Littlejohn wrote to the secretary-general of the League of Nations anticipating an international convention on equal rights:

> The most cursory survey of the codes of law and of custom which regulate the conduct of the affairs of nations will suffice to show that women hold a position of marked inferiority to men . . .
> An international Convention embodying the principle of the equality of the sexes appears to be a suitable method of endeavouring to establish the maximum of equality between men and women in all matters of civil and political rights.[9]

As a result of feminists' 'systematic lobbying', the Montevideo Equal Rights Treaty and the nationality issue were placed upon the agenda of the sixteenth Assembly of the League of Nations. The

Women's Consultative Committee interviewed all delegates and lobbied international women's organisations. 'The rising tide of interest among women throughout the world in support of the equality campaign at Geneva is extraordinary', reported the Committee.[10] But the League of Nations deferred action.

Linda Littlejohn was one of Australia's most ardent advocates of equal rights. An executive member of the United Associations, she was well known as a passionate and tireless public speaker and broadcaster. She attributed her energy, as we have seen, to the power of feminism itself, 'a power that pushed the true feminist along'.[11] Her involvement with the women's movement began characteristically, with her contribution to founding the first day nursery in Sydney; she was also a life governor of the Crown Street Women's Hospital, a government-appointed member of the New South Wales Board of Health and, like so many feminists, a member of the League of Nations Union.

With the self-confidence that came from wealth, elegance and practised eloquence, Littlejohn was an inspiring lecturer and winning debater. In 1930 she presented around one hundred talks, to community organisations, to seminars, at churches, on radio. For three years, she spoke three times a week on the Sydney radio station 2GB, and she led the women's debating team that twice won the Radiola Cup which was awarded by Amalgamated Wireless. Like many other feminists of this generation, she was a keen international traveller, her crowded itineraries determined by political and professional commitments and made possible by personal wealth. In 1935, when the *Melbourne Herald* announced that 'our best known feminist is off to Europe', it added that she had a 'very good platform manner, a flair for clothes, a sense of humour, a gift for repartee'.[12] These were qualities that she would need in her capacity as international president of Equal Rights International, an organisation riven by personal and national rivalries, which had led to the forced resignation of the English president Helen Archdale.

In urging Australian feminism down a new road, in suggesting that maternalism was an outdated and dangerous species of sentimentalism and that equal rights was the only way to go, Littlejohn would find an unlikely political ally in Muriel Heagney, who had also attended the founding conference of Open Door International in 1929, in Berlin. They were an odd political couple, the upper class radio personality and the working class union organiser, but Heagney had her own reasons for making common cause with Littlejohn.

Heagney was a proud member of her class, fiercely loyal to the Labor party, passionately committed to feminism, but constrained by her male comrades to not speak its name. In the 1920s she had championed the right of mothers at home to an income of their own, but by the 1930s the time had come to change tack. Wounded by charges of collaborating with the class enemy in her advocacy of motherhood endowment, which was represented by Labor men as an attempt to undermine the male basic wage, and distressed by attacks on women's employment during the Depression, Heagney had decided that women must win their independence as wage earners in the labour market, working with men, not against them.

In Europe, in 1935, Littlejohn negotiated the difficult political tensions besetting feminists in their debates over the meaning of equality. In the same year as she was elected president of Equal Rights International she had attended, with four other Australian delegates (Amy Wheaton from Victoria and H. Taylor, E. Taylor and A. Stubbin from New South Wales) the fourth annual conference of Open Door International in Copenhagen. The conference discussed the world economic crisis and attacks on women's employment, recent ILO publications, equal pay for equal work and married women's right to earn, and reaffirmed that 'the right to work is the right to live'.[13] There was a long and lively debate about the policy implications of maternity for women workers, with delegates finally agreeing that it should be regarded as a woman's private business.

> Maternity can only be fairly and effectively protected when a woman is left in full possession of her rights as an adult human being. Neither marriage, nor pregnancy, nor childbirth, nor nursing a child are reasons for depriving her of the human right to decide for herself whether or not she shall engage in paid work. To refuse this right to a woman or to impose restrictions on her exercise of it, does not help her; and so it is not really protection, but is a serious attack on the economic interest of the woman earner.[14]

The ODI conference also discussed at length the Montevideo Equal Rights Treaty, with delegates arguing that feminists' initial jubilation had been too hasty. Since signing their agreement, many countries had in fact introduced restrictions on women's work, sometimes under the guise of 'protection'. Moreover, many feminist organisations that themselves subscribed to protective measures for women had endorsed the terms of the Treaty; however, in ODI's view, 'protective legislation and equal rights can never coincide', so that those at the meeting felt they were unable to endorse the Treaty as it stood.[15] Discussions at the Copenhagen conference continued into the social occasions and were also broadcast live on the national radio station. At the concluding dinner, held at the Royal Yacht Squadron, thanks were offered by international president Chrystal Macmillan to the Danish president, Julie Arenholt, in the form of a thoroughly modern woman's gift—an enamel, marcasite and coral cigarette case.

The new preoccupation with 'equality' in these international forums would lead to substantial change in direction in feminist policy in Australia. Quite suddenly, it came to be understood that women must win equality through disavowing sexual difference and by emulating men—taking their rightful place in the men's world of politics and the professions, in the mines and factories, working day and night if necessary, alongside men. In this scenario, motherhood was not so much valuable national work to be supported and protected, a distinctive womanly activity to be recognised and rewarded, but a handicap to be overcome: 'no woman shall be deprived of her position on account of her motherhood'.[16] In a major discursive shift, the woman as worker began to replace the woman as mother as the ideal feminist subject. Women demanded equal rights with men in their capacity as wage earners.[17]

Australian feminists had, since the winning of suffrage, developed a distinctive local program addressed to women's difference as mothers, as wives, as dependants, as domestic drudges, as victims of seduction. They looked to the state to create a society in which all women would be better protected and feel more secure—physically as well as economically—and in which women's distinctive work as mothers would be valued and appropriately rewarded. They had stressed the goal of economic independence for all women—for married and single women, Aboriginal and non-Aboriginal women, women working as home makers or in the paid workforce—seeing this as the essential precondition for women's freedom.

During the 1930s, as the feminist platform began to be reformulated to accommodate the new emphasis on women's right to work, the sameness of women and men as human beings, as workers and as citizens began to be highlighted. The effect was that men's lives became the standard against which feminists would measure women's progress, as their focus shifted from domestic relations to the conduct of public life.

The logic of this reorientation was that aspects of women's experience specific to women—childbirth, motherhood, sexual violation, the domestic servitude of the wife, birth control—would gradually disappear from the feminist agenda, to be discovered anew in the 1970s when Women's Liberation declared the personal to be political.

Feminists were caught up in the paradox that Joan Scott has suggested is constitutive of feminism: that so long as the citizen or worker or human being was defined in terms of the masculine condition, sexual difference would always pose a problem for women.[18] The resulting tensions between what have come to be called 'difference' and 'equality' approaches to securing justice for women were evident in the exchanges between the United Associations and Equal Rights International. For although it was feminists from the UA who joined the international push for equal rights, it was as if the implications of their initiative, for the condition of mothers, were not at first clear to them.

At the 1934 meeting of the ERI, policy discussions about motherhood, housekeeping and birth control were marked by considerable disagreement: was this peculiarly women's business really the concern of an organisation dedicated to equal rights? Whereas it was clear to some feminists that there *was* 'a close relation between the question of Birth Control and the equality of the sexes', the meeting refused its inclusion on the agenda 'on the grounds that it was not within the scope of the ERI which concerned itself with the legal rights and disabilities of women only'.[19] Discussions about mothers' rights to independence and liberty and the injustice of home makers receiving 'no wage whatsoever' (Jessie Street's phrase) were too difficult to be resolved: a committee was charged with drawing up a questionnaire seeking members' views.

The conceptual difficulties posed by sexual difference were evident in the tortuous wording of the questions:

> Considering the fact that maternity is a valuable and important contribution to Society, a service that can only be rendered by women, how can the question of equal rights be most justly interpreted taking into consideration this contribution that only women can give?
>
> Is it right to consider that any compensation, help or protection of maternity is incompatible with equal rights as these provisions are not for the benefit of woman but of the child, therefore for Society itself?

> Is maternity the private concern of the mother or is it in part the concern of Society?
>
> . . .
>
> Is it compatible with equal rights to provide training for housekeeping and needlework to girls and not to boys?[20]

Equal Rights International, influenced by the ideology of the American National Women's party, interpreted equality in ruthlessly individualist terms. Until the 1930s, Australian feminists operated in a different conceptual framework, one that highlighted human interdependence and looked to the state to secure social welfare. In their proposals for motherhood endowment, they had attempted to reconcile recognition of the importance of mothers' caring work with women's citizens' rights to equality and independence.

Thus the UA's replies to the ERI questionnaire reiterated Jessie Street's arguments in the UA leaflets, advocating payment to mothers in recognition of their distinctive service to the state, and payment to wives working in their own homes in recognition that modern democratic societies had outgrown 'the once universal system of payment "in keep" or "in kind" for services rendered'. Historical progress had specific consequences for women as 'homemakers', who had been 'deprived of their independence and liberty'.[21]

In refusing the American idea that feminist organisations had to choose between difference and equality, in continuing to argue for protection of women's distinctive interests alongside equality for women as workers and citizens, the UA insisted on a distinctive voice for Australian feminism. The platform continued to press for state remuneration of motherhood during the 1940s, even as it placed more emphasis on women's right to equality with men in the public domain. The 'Objects' of the UA were amended after 1935 to add the goal of the Equal Rights Treaty:

> To secure an amendment to the Constitution of the Commonwealth of Australia to provide that men and women shall have equal rights in Australia and all territories under the jurisdiction of the Commonwealth government.

But also included was Jessie Street's cherished aim: 'to secure economic independence for married women'.

ARE WOMEN TAKING MEN'S JOBS?

The shift in orientation of Australian feminism was a response not only to international developments, but also to radically changed economic and political circumstances in Australia—more specifically to changes in men's circumstances. Attacks on women in paid employment became common in Australia as the Depression deepened from the late 1920s until one in every three workers was left without a job. In these hard times, women workers were associated with waste and extravagance—and their very visibility, the visibility of their sexual difference, made them easy scapegoats for resentful men, who blamed men's unemployment on women taking their jobs.

To Keith Mackenzie, writing in the *Sydney Morning Herald* in 1934, the doctrine of 'masculinism' was Australia's 'only salvation'. Under the influence of 'feminism's shameless banner', women had stolen men's jobs. In the interests of the nation, women should 'refrain from entering the professions where they compete with men'. This would help the economy because the wages paid to married men would be spent on necessities for the family, such as food, clothing and furniture manufactured in Australia. 'We shall spend more on our home-grown bread and butter and boots and less on imported champagne and caviar and lipstick (not to speak of demoralising films and finery for the women demoralised by them)'.[22] Less would be squandered on imported feminine fripperies. Women were unpatriotic as producers and consumers. Writing in their defence, Jessie Street commented 'as for the accusation that the girls are "scarlet lipped" and "overdressed", if they are as described it must be that the employers prefer them so'. Women workers needed paid work just as much as men did; to sack women to make way for men would not 'cure unemployment, it will only shift the burden of it on to the shoulders of a class which is already handicapped by prejudice, custom and lack of status and opportunity'.[23]

Women workers were represented by male commentators as invaders, usurpers and thieves and as the destroyers of men's manhood. According to labour journalist Warren Denning, writing on 'The Economic Woman', women workers were doing two enormously harmful things: 'they are displacing men in whose sphere they have intruded, and they are not producing in the field where they were created to produce—that is, they are not making homes and bearing the children our nation so desperately needs'. For Denning, as for Mackenzie, women's entry into paid work was a trend that needed to be stopped:

> The women in manufacturing industry are almost entirely in ruthless and relentless competition with men. With a few negligible exceptions they are doing work which, individual for individual, can be done as well or better by men. They are taken into our factories because employers can get them cheap—that, almost entirely, is the only reason they are there.[24]

The new feminist emphasis on women's right to work clearly had local as well as international contexts. The sudden proliferation of men's attacks on women's employment forced feminists to articulate their right to work; rights thus come to be formulated in response to the denial of those rights by opponents. For example, in 1936, while the Australian Federation of Women Voters was holding its fifth triennial conference in Adelaide, the South Australian branch of the Labor party resolved that employment should be confined to those women who were in need and whose husbands or fathers were not in a position to keep them. The conference responded swiftly with its own resolution, affirming 'that the right to earn is the inalienable right of the individual whether man or woman'.[25]

That 'feminism' and 'anti-feminism' were locked into a dynamic discursive relationship was a point made by Nellie Lord in a small unpublished book written in 1934, described by her as 'my view of the position of women more especially Australian women'. But whereas feminism, for Lord, was a principle, anti-feminism was a policy.

> Perhaps the most frank expression of the objective of feminism was the pronouncement of the late Olive Schreiner 'We claim all labour as our province'. The slogan of the Anti-feminists would appear to be 'The woman's place is in the home' . . .
>
> When the Anti-feminist journalist repeats *ad nauseum* the dictum that 'the woman's place is in the home' he writes 'as one having authority'—and also as a scribe. He impudently presumes to dictate to every woman how she should be obliged to order her life without the slightest reference to her individual tastes or talents. He presumes to command what she shall do, and above all what she should not be permitted to do. Reduced to its simplest equation the dictum of the Anti-feminist signifies that one half of the community should be entirely reserved as domestic servants for the other half.[26]

No longer representing just one avenue to economic independence and freedom, paid work began to be defended as women's most fundamental right—and the right to work began to define feminism in new ways. Thus, when Jessie Street wrote as president of the UA to every member of the New South Wales parliament in 1940, demanding the repeal of the Married Women Teachers and Lecturers Dismissal Act passed in 1932, she reiterated an earlier claim that the legislation denied women teachers 'the right to marry', but added 'it also deprives a woman teacher who marries of the right to work'.[27]

Attacks on women in paid employment forced feminists to mobilise in defence of women's 'right to work'. In November 1933, Linda Littlejohn, as president of the UA, invited interested women to join the political fight:

> The right of woman to work for wages is endangered. We wish to discuss whether it is advisable to make a move to protect woman's right to be a wage earner. A woman individually can accomplish little, except perhaps endanger her own employment; but working through an organisation can accomplish much.[28]

In 1934, the UA formed a Professional and Business Women's Group with the aims: (1) to provide an opportunity for professional and businesswomen to examine and discuss present-day economic, social and political questions; (2) to provide a means whereby they could voice their opinions on these questions and through which they could exert their influence in reference to matters of vital importance to them; and (3) to generally promote and protect their interests.

In Melbourne, the Equal Status Committee, formed as a branch of Open Door International and chaired by K. A. Gilman Jones, asserted 'the unqualified right of women to work when and where they will on an equal footing with men'.[29] In her capacity as a member of the Committee, Muriel Heagney compiled her book on women's employment to respond to 'the current propaganda against women in industry, implying that women and girls were taking men's jobs and thereby becoming a contributory factor in general unemployment'.[30]

In the most systematic case made by an Australian feminist in defence of women's right to paid work, Heagney's book *Are Women Taking Men's Jobs?*, published in 1935, surveyed the extent, nature and conditions of women's work, especially in Victoria, and demonstrated the extreme sexual segregation of the labour market in Australia. 'The sphere of women's work appears to be more circumscribed in Australia than in other countries', she wrote. 'Of the 909 trades and callings listed by the Commonwealth Statistician, women are recorded in only 87, whereas, in America, for several decades the census returns show women working in all but thirty or forty of the total trades reported'.[31] She also demonstrated the appalling wages and conditions that characterised much women's work, pointing out that there had been no investigation into women's industrial conditions for over fifty years. Moreover, 'the position of women in industry' had also been virtually ignored by women's organisations in recent years.[32]

Are Women Taking Men's Jobs? was a sustained argument for women's right to paid employment on the same wages and conditions as men. Women, like men, had a right to a living wage, to be achieved through the implementation of the principle of the rate for the job. In the context of the labour movement for which she had long worked, Heagney had become convinced that the only way women would come to be accepted by trade unions as legitimate workers was if they ceased to be employed as cheap labour. In 1925, as a nominee of the Victorian Trades Hall Council, she participated in a government enquiry into the conditions of women workers in the firm of H. V. McKay. Heagney had also helped prepare the 1926 Clothing Trades Union case before the Arbitration Court for an equal minimum or basic wage for men and women in the industry. This case, she later explained, represented 'a departure from the policy of differential rates hitherto adopted, and reflects the modern viewpoint on the value of women's labour and social rights'.[33] The justification for women's claim was put with characteristic fervour as she pointed to the history of women's subjection:

> Primarily it was a demand for the right to complete economic independence for women workers and a frank declaration that a woman's contribution to production is equally valuable to that of a man. History teaches that in the most primitive societies woman enjoyed equality, but as our civilisation developed she lost all her rights, and sank deeper and deeper in subjection . . . Having plumbed the depths, she has gradually risen by ceaseless striving until in our day women enjoy equal rights in most spheres of life. The notable exception to this is the sphere of industry, but here too women are rebelling and demanding equality.[34]

But Judge Drake-Brockman, in hearing the case, was also mindful of history. He refused to depart from the precedents laid down by the Court, awarding clothing workers a woman's basic wage—approximately 55 per cent of the male basic wage.

Heagney set her arguments in an international context, providing extensive information about women's employment conditions in other countries, commending the progress of both the United States and the USSR. She reported on the conflict between different international feminist organisations regarding the wisdom of industrial protection for women workers, noting the view of the Women's Committee of the Labor and Socialist International that:

> The arguments put forward by non-industrial women in favour of the abolition of protective legislation for women workers have not been accepted by those who are qualified to speak on behalf of the women workers. It is the view of the women workers concerned that such legislation has helped to raise the status of women, and has been the means of protecting women workers in many industries from excessive exploitation.[35]

Interestingly, Heagney's own conclusion, in line with the Open Door International position repudiating protective legislation, represented a significant departure from labour movement traditions:

> After fifty years' experience of protective legislation introduced for women and gradually extended to cover all workers, we, in Australia have nothing tangible to show in the way of greater achievement than the workers elsewhere, consequently, concentration on organisation to secure the application of the principle of equality and occupational rates of pay for all grades of work appears to afford the only means of raising standards in this State and preventing discrimination against women workers on the ground of sex.[36]

In pointing to the facts of women's employment, Heagney emphasised that it was 'the driving force of stern economic necessity' that led so many women into the workforce, but she also insisted on the feminist principle: 'The right to work is no prerogative of men . . . Women's right to work rests not on her dependants, nor on the fact that she does or does not compete with men, but in the absolute right of a free human being, a taxpayer and a voter, to economic independence'.[37]

The defence of women's right to work led to a reinvigoration of the campaign for equal pay, for women could only claim the same jobs as men if they did not threaten to undercut men's wages. Equal pay was not only a right in itself, but also the necessary precondition of women's claim to all available occupations. In *Are Women Taking Men's Jobs?* Heagney had pointed out that the Australian women's wage rate was among the lowest in the world: 'In Australia, India, and France, the ratio is 52 per cent of the male rate, whereas in Great Britain it is 58 per cent, United States 59 per cent and Sweden 61 per cent'.[38]

In New South Wales, the alliance forged between the United Associations and the New South Wales Teachers' Federation, in particular between Jessie Street and Lucy Woodcock, contributed towards increased feminist involvement in industrial issues and the campaign for equal pay. In 1937, when the Sydney County Council stated its intentions to dispense with the services of married women, the UA sought legal advice about the feasibility of their plans 'in the industrial jurisdiction and also at common law'. They were advised that such dismissals would be illegal and that the Council would be liable to an action at common law for damages. At the same time, the UA sought advice from feminist lawyer Nerida Cohen on the most effective ways to work for equal pay, and on whether and how to put a case before the Commonwealth Arbitration Court. Cohen advised:

> In my opinion there are no legal limitations to prevent the Commonwealth Court of Conciliation and Arbitration from giving equal pay . . . Thus the increase in the Commonwealth female rate could in my opinion be obtained by an application to the Commonwealth Court in the same way as in the case of the State female rate provided the application is made in the case of a dispute extending beyond the limits of any one State.[39]

Feminists and trade union activists came together in 1937, when the New South Wales Clerks' Union, prompted by Heagney, convened an equal pay conference which was attended by fifty-three organisations, including public servants', hairdressers', rubber workers' and textiles' unions, the Communist party and feminist groups such as the UA and the Feminist Club. The conference was addressed by John Hughes, assistant secretary of the Clerks' Union, who affirmed their feminist goal: 'Equal pay means the establishment of economic independence for women and provides a basis upon which they can struggle to secure the consummation of full equality'.[40] The Council of Action for Equal Pay was formed to co-ordinate the subsequent campaign.

Meanwhile the policy of sacking female married workers continued to take its toll on individual women, including feminists. In 1940, Irene Greenwood, well known in Perth for her feminist broadcasts on Friday morning radio, was dismissed by the Australian Broadcasting Commission, along with other married women as a cost-cutting measure. She wrote on the effect on her life in a letter to Jessie Street:

> Strange how we realise the economic implications of cutting the married woman worker when we suffer ourselves. I earned £110 a year. This enabled me to educate my children to University and High School standard. (Both now have good permanent positions.) I lose the income, result, I look for a cheaper flat than the one I was able to have while earning. I cancel my life assurance, to give me £100 at 56 (or at death). Can no longer meet premiums. I fire my help who washed and cleaned weekly for me at 10/-. I have payments owing on a £25 portable typewriter, and certain furniture which previously I was able to afford easily. So there it is!
>
> In addition I must cancel all my subscriptions to overseas magazines and periodicals, and my library subscription, and what a loss this is to me, and to those who got the benefit of my readings over the air! I feel this last most keenly of all . . .[41]

Greenwood survived her reduced circumstances to become a leading feminist activist at home and abroad in the 1950s and was still active into the 1970s.

AN EQUAL PLACE IN HISTORY

In 1934, the chairman of Equal Rights International wrote to the secretary of the International Committee of Historical Sciences to urge that body to encourage member societies to provide 'fair and unified teaching on the subject of the Women's Movement'.[42] Feminists in Australia, since Louisa Lawson's time, had long been concerned to write women into the national history. In the 1930s, they were presented with three occasions on which to do this: in 1934, Victorians commemorated the centenary of settlement, as did South Australians in 1936; and 1938 was the sesqui-centenary of Australian settlement, which was predominantly a Sydney event. On each occasion, feminists claimed a place for women in the history of Australian settlement, conscious that in traditional accounts of the building of nations, women were usually invisible. In each State, a women's committee was formed to produce a collection of writing to inscribe women's place in the national memory.

The books (and associated memorial gardens) aimed to record the work of women as pioneers, as helpmates of men, desiring to honour those 'who made the great venture and came with their men-folk to this unknown land'. Having arrived in Victoria, as *The Centenary Gift Book* put it:

> Women did more than cook and sweep. They milked cows, dug for gold, sowed the corn, and even literally put their hand to the plough. They tended the sick and dying, they comforted the homesick and in every way passed down to the women of today their splendid heritage of courage and initiative.[43]

Such women were also eulogised in Mary Gilmore's 'Ode to the Pioneer Woman' in *The Peaceful Army*, edited by Flora Eldershaw in Sydney. With their 'endurance and courage' they 'made the land':

> For they were women who at need took up
> And plied the axe, or bent above the clodded spade;
> Who herded sheep; who rode the hills, and brought
> The half-wild cattle home—helpmates of men.[44]

The working of this new land was, then, central to the claims made by feminists self-consciously writing women into history. As we have already seen, however, the fact that pioneers were also dispossessors and despoilers—that women on the land proved their national virtue at the expense of Aboriginal women, whom they displaced—created considerable tensions in the production of these commemorative works. As literary nationalists, feminists became complicit in Australian racism.

Australian feminists, like their fellow-countrymen, were colonisers and colonised, both. Miles Franklin was a fierce feminist and passionate nationalist. 'And why should I care so passionately', she wrote about dying eucalypts in the back country, 'it is a burden'.[45] Defensive about the settlers' appropriation of Aboriginal lands, Franklin nevertheless felt that the greatest oppression was British condescension, and she used the occasion of the 1938 sesqui-centennial to excoriate Australians for their colonial grovelling to visiting scions of royalty and to castigate the feminist movement for its suffocating suburban respectability.

Franklin's Australian disgust at the official sesqui-centennial celebrations and the associated women's conference was poured into lively diary entries: 'such outrage to my sense of self-respect made me ill'. Why, she wondered, were such conferences opened by 'imperial imported parasites—nincompoops . . . representatives of over-lording privilege are set forth to display themselves for the slavering worship of the mere colonials'.[46] Even the women's memorial garden was to be opened by 'the "excellencies"': 'Surely some old woman from the outback, seamed and hard worked could more fittingly have done this?'.

The women's conference was organised around the theme of 'This Changing World' and speakers included a number of names prominent in the women's movement, such as Adelaide Miethke on 'This Changing World—Its Challenge', Bessie Rischbieth 'Forces Which Have Advanced or Hindered Women's Progress in Public Life', Linda Littlejohn 'Have Women's Organizations Served Their Purpose?' and Dame Enid Lyons 'The Mother and the Modern World'. Edith Waterworth moved the vote of thanks. It was the overbearing and overweight maternalism of the speakers that Franklin found hardest to bear. She described Dame Enid thus:

> a neat face spoiled by fat. She has no depth or originality but is a smart politician—just that—as much yes-no as George Reid . . . She talked and talked for an hour or more, on and on, and blew over it a vast wheeze from the bellows of motherhood . . . Other women condemned as freaks and perverts have gone before and made it possible for her thus to air herself on the public platform.[47]

For Franklin, the history of Australia was a history of female self-sacrifice. Men were inherently parasitic: 'there never was a man who achieved anything without some woman as potato to his willowslip, but they like to do it without acknowledgment'. Australian women would never win an equal place in history until they ceased to be 'a nation of charwomen'. 'The idea is that we must all grovel together on the kitchen floor.' To achieve an equal place in their society, Australian women would have to get up off the floor.

THE OPPORTUNITIES OF WARTIME

With the outbreak of war in 1939, Australian women saw a new opportunity to assume the responsibilities of their equal citizenship, many wanting to join the armed services. The war also gave new urgency to the equal pay issue as women began to fill jobs left by enlisting men. Everywhere the question was raised of what rate to pay the women replacing men. In 1940, the United Associations brought together all the women's organisations that had supported equal pay (twenty in all, including trade unions, feminist groups, State branches of the National Council of Women and the Young Women's Christian Association (YWCA)) in a combined application seeking permission to intervene in the basic wage enquiry then being conducted by the Federal Arbitration Court. Leave was granted, and Street and Nerida Cohen, who was to appear as Counsel before the Court, travelled to Melbourne.

When Cohen went before the Court to say that she wished to make an application regarding the basic wage 'in respect of women', the Chief Justice replied that as no reference had been made to the women's wage by any of the unions, the Court would not be able to hear her. Cohen was successful in winning an adjournment to consult the unions. A meeting was called by the Trades Hall Council where representatives of thirty-one unions were addressed by Cohen and Street, who argued that lower women's wages would drag down men's wages and result in male unemployment. The unions unanimously resolved to recommend to the Australian Council of Trade Unions (ACTU) that a simultaneous application by all the unions in industries in which women were, or might be, employed, be made to the Court in support of equal pay. The report to the UA emphasised the historical significance of the event:

> Although the application of the women's organisations was not heard on this occasion, some very important steps in the realisation of equal pay for women have been taken. This is the first occasion on which important women's organisations which stand for equal pay have publicly combined to support the claim for equal pay for women before the official tribunal of the country in whom is invested the power to grant the claim.[48]

Meanwhile, the Council of Action for Equal Pay pressed ahead under the leadership of Muriel Heagney, but by the end of the 1930s a destructive rivalry had developed between the two women leaders of the equal pay campaign. By 1941 they had broken completely, allegedly over a disagreement as to the timetable for the achievement of equal pay, but also possibly because Street had effectively upstaged Heagney in her intervention before the Arbitration Court.

During the 1940s, the UA pursued its broad equal rights strategy, while maintaining its advocacy of the rights of wives and mothers. The range of feminist concerns was evident in a lengthy questionnaire sent to candidates in the 1940 federal election. They were asked:

1. Are you in favour of amending the law to extend to married women the same right to establish their domicile as is enjoyed by single women and married and single men?
2. Will you support a move to bring pressure to bear on the British government to pass legislation to give to British women who marry foreigners the right to retain their British nationality?
3. Are you in favour of the Commonwealth instituting a scheme for the payment to mothers of child endowment in recognition of the value to the State of the work performed by mothers in bearing and raising children?
4. Are you prepared to eliminate all sex discrimination in the Public Service and other occupational spheres and to adopt the principle throughout of equal pay and equal opportunity for all men and women?
5. Are you prepared to introduce legislation to guarantee to women the right to decide for themselves when and where and in what occupation they shall work and to make it illegal to pass restrictions limiting the right to work of women?
6. Are you in favour of a proper proportion of women being placed on Commissions, Boards and Committees appointed by the Government?[49]

Increasingly, feminist political campaigns focussed on the restrictions imposed on women, on their disabilities, rather than on their need for protection from men. Increasingly, feminists demanded a right of access to men's world of politics and professional opportunity.

When Dr Lucy Gullett of the UA was asked in the early 1940s to give a talk on 'What Remains to be Done and How To Do It', her brief answers were 'Everything' and 'Unity'. The substance of her paper showed the extent to which feminism had changed orientation: no more talk about human welfare, mothers' rights and the economic independence of married women. Now the measure of progress was the extent to which women occupied positions in public life.

> Until we have women in juries helping the cause of justice, women in Parliament helping to make the laws under which they live, women on boards, women as Directors of Hospitals, women on Municipal Councils, women allowed to follow their vocations,

without interference, whether married or single and women having the same right to equality in wages as men, I think we can truthfully say that everything remains to be done.[50]

The outbreak of war also prompted feminists to assert their right as citizens to an equal share in the defence effort. Jessie Street wrote to the Minister for the Army:

> The women of the country are as anxious to help, and have as much right to help in the war effort as the men of the country. In the interests of the defence of the country, the brain power and general abilities of women should be used as well as the brain-power and abilities of men.[51]

More specifically feminists argued their right—as able-bodied citizens—to contribute to the active defence of the country.

The outbreak of hostilities had been followed by a flood of women volunteering for defence work, and numerous unofficial organisations had been formed to advance women's military ambitions. They designed and donned their own uniforms in a bid to gain recognition of their serious intent. They joined rifle clubs to prepare themselves for the practical defence of their country. In February 1941, Street advised members that for six months the UA had been training instructors: 'we have secured two rifle ranges and flat roofs suitable for drilling'. Believing that countries could best defend themselves against aggression when an army was supported by the active participation of the civilian population, Street advocated training in rifle clubs as an extension of citizenship appropriate for both sexes: 'we believe it to be of vital importance that able bodied men and women in Australia should learn the use of portable weapons of defence'.[52]

During 1941, the official auxiliaries to the armed forces were established—the Women's Auxiliary Australian Air Force Service, the Australian Women's Army Service, the Royal Australian Navy Service—and then in 1942 the Australian Land Army. Rates of pay were considerably less than for the men's services. In July, the president of the United Associations, Erna Keighley, wrote to the Minister for the Army urging that women in the auxiliary services be rendered eligible for all the benefits available to men—deferred pay, repatriation benefits, pensions and postal concessions. 'There is a growing discontent all over the Commonwealth at the discrimination against women in the defence forces', she wrote. If the discrimination applying to benefits were ended, the only question remaining for settlement would be the question of equal pay: 'we trust that the Government will soon give consideration to this most vital matter'.[53] In the event, women were successful in winning equal allowances and eligibility for repatriation benefits.

Wartime opened up new employment opportunities for women. They were drawn into industry, human and transport services and the auxiliaries to the defence forces in large numbers. Between 1939 and 1943, the number of women in the paid workforce increased by nearly 50 per cent, from 437 000 in July 1939 to a high of 646 000 in December 1943. Under the provisions of the Women's Employment Board (WEB), established in 1942 as a temporary wartime tribunal to determine appropriate rates of pay for women entering men's jobs, thousands of female workers earned unprecedently high incomes. Feminists were pleased that, under the guidelines established by WEB, women workers were able to prove their relative efficiency compared with that of male workers, even though they could never be classified as more productive than men. Women working in men's jobs could be awarded between 60 and 100 per cent of the male rate; most were awarded 90 per cent and thus took home much larger pay packets than before the war.

In this context of rapid change and with the public visibility of women at work never having been higher, their underrepresentation in parliament and public life seemed increasingly anomalous, a denial of women's equality as citizens. Women demanded right of entry into public office, but this was no longer conceptualised as offering protection to vulnerable women and girls, at risk in the public domain; a seat in parliament, on a board or commission were now matters of equal rights.

In 1942, the UA organised a celebration of the fortieth anniversary of women's suffrage in New South Wales. The invitation observed that with 'the infiltration of women into industry and their enrollment [sic] in the defence forces—in both of which fields they have proved their capabilities—it seems anomalous that they have little representation in Parliament'.[54] In the new discourse on rights, a seat in parliament was no longer an extension of citizenship, but a career opportunity denied to women. Careers were being made, as Miles Franklin observed, when she attended another function organised by the ALP Central Organising Committee and was forced to listen to a very long speech by Mrs Quirk, MLA, whose sartorial style spoke of newly acquired riches:

Mrs Quirk MLA tall and stout, real publican's widow figure. Majestically attired in an expensive black beaded gown and cape with white facings so well cut and she as expensively harnessed that her figure instead of gross became fashionable. Her coiffure and make-up, even to tinted nails, must have been the work of a professional . . . She had a thick sheaf of quarto sheets: on each of these was a sentence or two. She discoursed on each of these as texts for an incredible time and then laid it down so that her victims could ache with boredom because of the number still to be endured. She kept on for half an hour. People were sneaking out in ones, twos and fives. The MLA seemed quite oblivious of this.

Franklin's dispirited conclusion was that the female MLA was 'the equal as an empty windbag of any male, ignorant, self-seeking member of Parliament'.[55]

The following year nevertheless saw a concerted interstate effort to elect women to the federal parliament organised by the Women for Canberra movement. Not one woman had yet been elected to either the Senate or the House of Representatives—although they had been eligible since 1902 and many feminists had offered themselves as (mostly Independent) candidates. In 1943, nineteen feminists stood as Independents, none successfully. Jessie Street stood as an endorsed Labor candidate for the anti-Labor seat of Wentworth, and with UA support she came close to winning. In the event only two women were successful that year, each endorsed by one of the major parties—Enid Lyons, widow of ex-Prime Minister Joe Lyons, and United Australia party candidate for the House of Representatives seat of Darwin in Tasmania; and Dorothy Tangney, a Labor Senate candidate from Western Australia.

Lyons and Tangney interpreted their projects as political women in different ways. Lyons, the older of the two and a mother of eleven children, assumed the importance of her sex to her role as a politician: 'I have a very great faith in the good sense of my sex. I expect that I shall have a wonderful backing from women everywhere'. But she cautioned against high expectations: 'You must not expect me to be a superwoman. So many people seem to think that in the short period of one parliament, I shall be able to transform man and all his works'.[56] Tangney, the single career woman and member of the Labor party stated: 'I am not a feminist. I believe that women should work in harmony with men in the business of government as in every other aspect of work'.[57] In the event, Tangney was largely responsible for introducing in 1948 the feminist reform longest fought for: namely, married women's nationality rights.

The Women's Charter conference of 1943, initially billed as a National Women's Conference for Victory in War and Peace, was a big event. Meeting in Sydney in November, and attracting delegates from approximately ninety women's organisations, it was the largest, most representative women's conference yet held in Australia, in many ways a high point in the history of Australian feminism—even as Professor A. P. Elkin asked organiser Jessie Street, hopefully, whether 'the day for sex dicotomy [sic] was past'.[58] The conference addressed the diversity of women's lives and interests—as citizen, mother, home maker, wage earner, voluntary worker, member of the services, professional woman—and formulated a charter of rights for women in the post-war world. Questions dealt with included the care and status of mothers, the birth-rate, child care, community centres, employment, social security, moral standards, liquor, housing, equal rights and legal reforms. The resultant recommendations, which were revised and extended at the second 1946 conference, are discussed in more detail in the next chapter.

Twenty thousand copies of the Australian Women's Charter were printed and sent to members of State and federal parliaments, local government bodies and to the Charter Committees set up in each State. Follow-up conferences were held in Perth in 1943 and in Adelaide and Melbourne in 1944. Jessie Street, the chairman of the Federal Charter Committee, was invited to address meetings in New Zealand. Members of the Federal Committee included Ada Bromham, Isabel McCorkindale (as deputy chairman), Nerida Cohen, Mona Ravenscroft, Lucy Woodcock and Eve Higson. In March 1944, thirteen Committee members took the Charter to Canberra, where they were received by Attorney-General H. V. Evatt deputising for Prime Minister John Curtin, who was ill. Evatt and Street were old friends and mutually admiring political visionaries. They established a close working relationship, which led Street to join the Australian delegation to the conference that established the United Nations Organisation in San Francisco.

8
NO DISCRIMINATION ON THE GROUNDS OF SEX OR RACE

THE AUSTRALIAN WOMEN'S CHARTER AT HOME AND AWAY

In May 1945, Jessie Street joined the Australian delegation in the Liberator Bomber that flew them to the United Nations Conference on International Organisation in San Francisco. She was the only woman delegate and she took with her a copy of the Australian Women's Charter to show leaders of women's organisations in other countries, who reportedly expressed a desire to frame similar documents for their own nations. In the debates around the formulation of the United Nations Charter at San Francisco, Australian feminists played a decisive part in achieving the inclusion of a commitment to equality of the sexes in the founding documents.

As planned by the Charter Committee before Street's departure, sixty-six Australian women's organisations combined to sign the following cable to the Secretary-General of the United Nations Conference:

> Request United Nations International Conference Incorporate Into Post-War Plans The Democratic Principle Of Equality Of Status, Opportunity, And Reward For Men And Women, And Elimination Of All Discriminations Based On Sex.

This cable, together with those sent by the National Council of Women and the Australian Federation of Women Voters, were photostated and circulated to the national delegations by the Secretary-General. Street then joined Dr Bertha Lutz from Brazil in organising meetings of the women members of delegations, who campaigned to have the principle of equal rights for men and women incorporated into the United Nations Charter. 'If you read the Charter in its original form', said Street, 'you will see there is no reference whatever to women'.[1]

Writing from the Sir Francis Drake Hotel in San Francisco, a very busy Street kept feminists back home closely informed of developments: 'I have been put on three Committees, so I often have many meetings morning, afternoon and evening'.[2] Her main business was to work with Bertha Lutz in formulating an amendment to the draft Charter, which became Article 8: 'The United Nations shall place no restrictions on the eligibility of men and women to participate in any capacity and under conditions of equality, in its principal and subsidiary organs'.

The next month, in June, Street was still busy: 'The meetings are continuous—morning, afternoon and evening and . . . to bed so late that it is a real effort of will to get up in the morning'.[3] She was full of praise for Bertha Lutz; without her they would never have achieved anything so satisfactory for women in the Charter. 'I am quite satisfied' she reported.

> I am not easy to please as you know. Of course our resolutions must be put into effect—but that is for the future. We are building the framework—the machine to drive it remains to be seen.[4]

Street and Lutz and others also worked on the drafting of a resolution recommending that the Economic and Social Council set up a special Commission on the Status of Women, which would take over the work of the Consultative Committee that had liaised with the League of Nations in the late 1930s. The new body would study existing conditions and prepare reports on the political, civil and economic status and opportunities of women, with special reference to discrimination and limitations placed on them on account of their sex—and would devise ways for nations to make provision for assistance to mothers. This last clause was probably Street's, but the concern to incorporate an acknowledgment of sexual difference into definitions of human rights would prove increasingly problematic.

The Commission on the Status of Women, which was at first a Sub-Commission, was duly created, but there would be some dispute over who should take credit. In 1952, Muriel Tribe wrote to Street in London reporting that in the last *International Women's News* Bertha Lutz was crediting herself with being the originator of the proposal to create the Commission. Street replied that this was both 'ungenerous and egotistical'. She then recorded her version of events, which was generous to Lutz:

> It is quite true that Bertha Lutz moved the resolution and spoke excellently when doing so. This was important, but the resolution proposing the formation of a Commission on the Status of Women was the culmination of a campaign lasting several weeks, to get Article 8 into the [United Nations] Charter . . . Without the campaign to get the Article into the Charter it would have been quite futile to propose the formation of a Commission on the Status of Women . . . During the campaign a number of us, particularly Bertha Lutz (Brazil), Minerva Bernadino (Dominican republic) Amelia Ledon (Mexico) and myself canvassed nearly all the delegates and had daily consultations discussing the progress of the campaign and the difficulties that we encountered. After prodigious work we got the support of all the delegates except the US, UK and Cuba . . . We had a further consultation about proposing a Commission on the Status of Women and we drafted another resolution. This was the resolution that Bertha Lutz proposed . . . Bertha Lutz is now a member of the Status of Women Commission and will attend her first meeting on 24 March in Geneva when the Commission meets. Whatever the shortcomings of Berta Lutz may be, she is a good feminist and I think will put real drive into the Commission.[5]

For Street to call someone a 'good feminist' was the highest accolade.

Street travelled back to Australia via London, where she encountered extensive bomb damage, food shortages and social deprivation. 'I think Australia has set an example to the whole world with its plans for re-employment', she wrote. 'We are indeed a happy people.'[6] She caught up with feminist friends, including Margery Corbett Ashby. 'Mrs Rischbieth', she noted, 'is away'. Bessie Rischbieth had spent the war years in London and was one of the few Australians visited by fellow West Australian, Prime Minister John Curtin when he visited London during that time.

Street had meanwhile decided to resign as president of the United Associations. Writing to her 'dear fellow members' from Australia House, she commended the effectiveness of feminist politics in Australia, adding 'everything seems to be going so well that I am going to take the step of resigning . . . This is a mark of confidence in the present administration and not lack of or waning interest. Congratulations on the work you have done and the success you have achieved in the way of equal allowances and the improvements in married women's domicile rights'.[7] Clearly Street had other political plans; the prospect of endorsement as a Labor candidate in the 1946 election beckoned, and she had to organise the second Australian Women's Charter conference—to be held, like the first, in Sydney.

The 1946 conference was, like the 1943 one, a big event, attended by delegates from India, France, Ceylon and New Zealand, as well as from all States of Australia. Travel restrictions prevented delegates from the USSR, the United States and China from arriving. Kapila Khandvala brought greetings from the All India Women's Conference. Associated functions included an historical play, *Caroline Chisholm*, written by George Landon Dann and produced by Doris Fitton, depicting the life of a 'great Englishwoman, who worked against tremendous difficulties in Australia and England, to provide protection and security for single girls who had immigrated to Australia during the stresses and strains of its early colonisation period'.[8]

An exhibition of the work of Australian women artists, the first of its kind held in Sydney, was held at the Art Gallery of New South Wales. An historic Peace Procession saw hundreds of women marching through the streets of the city, applauded by thousands of onlookers. Marchers carried banners proclaiming peace, and floats represented different national communities—Chinese, Greek, Indian, Indonesian and Yugoslav. One float, designed by Sydney artist Nan Nortin, illustrated the theme of protest against war, with the figure of a mother holding two little children looking across at a hill studded with crosses. The march proceeded to Martin Place, where a wreath was placed on the Cenotaph by conference chairman Jessie Street.

The Australian Women's Charter report (1946–1949) noted 'with satisfaction' the Economic and Social Council's appointment of the Commission on the Status of Women, charged with examining and reporting upon the disabilities of women and making recommendations for the removal of these disabilities. An Australian Co-operating Organisation was established to provide a direct link between the Commission on the Status of Women and co-operating organisations in Australia, liaison work for which Street obviously felt well suited.

The Australian Women's Charter reaffirmed 'the need for the immediate application of the principle of equality as between men and women in all laws, regulations and usage'. Its numerous recommendations were organised under five headings (1. International, 2. Equality of Status, 3. Employment, 4. Family, Home and Community and

5. Social) and thirty-five sub-headings, and they self-consciously addressed the interests of women in their diversity—women in paid employment and women who worked in the home, mothers and wives, Aboriginal women and non-Aboriginal women, professional women, nurses, domestic workers and ex-servicewomen, rural and suburban women, young and old.

There were more than a hundred specific recommendations to government including the introduction of motherhood endowment (in addition to child endowment) as remuneration for the mother's work in the home; the introduction of jury service for women; the holding of a referendum to achieve an amendment to the Constitution guaranteeing women's equal rights, status and opportunity with men; the restoration of local option polls to control the distribution of liquor licences; the establishment of federal control of Aboriginal welfare; uniform grounds for divorce; the decriminalisation of prostitution; and the establishment of a national network of child care centres, as well as community centres combining libraries, playgrounds, nurseries and community kitchens.

Detailed attention was given to the oppression of Aboriginal people, recognising the diversity of conditions and needs of those living on missions and reserves, on pastoral stations and in towns and cities, specifically addressing their rights as parents, workers and potential citizens. Noting that the Commonwealth should take full responsibility for the welfare of Aboriginal people and that the conditions in which they worked left Australia open to the charge of 'slave labour', the Charter made eighteen separate recommendations, drawing on the extensive work with Aboriginal people carried out during the last two decades by activists such as Constance Cooke, Mary Bennett and Ada Bromham. Bennett and Bromham had continued to document the enslavement of Aboriginal workers and the ongoing removal of Aboriginal children during the 1940s.

The Charter accordingly recommended the payment in cash of total wages earned by Aboriginal workers and their right to earnings to be secured by law, the recognition of Aboriginal rights to industrial organisation for the improvement of wages and conditions, and the provision of appropriate training to enable Aboriginal people to enter professional occupations; and for 'tribal Aborigines', the allocation of reserves, such reserves 'to be inviolable, the land and natural resources to be the property of the Aborigines and adequate for their economic and cultural life'.

The Charter also recommended that legislative amendments be

made to recognise Aboriginal parents' custody rights; that the law controlling the guardianship of Aboriginal children contain the same provisions as the law controlling other children; that Aboriginal people not be removed to, or held in, institutions except by a magistrate's order, after they have appeared before a court; and that Aboriginal parents be given the same opportunity as other parents to appear before a court to offer evidence that they are suitable persons to have care and control of their children. In their emphasis on parental rights to custody, feminists were extending their campaigns for mothers' rights waged for more than forty years.

In the Charter's very comprehensive program for social and economic change, the demand for equal rights was complemented by a wide-ranging blueprint for reform in all areas of life. One noticeably new item on the feminist agenda was the call for the government provision of 'child care'. The new term expressed the perception of a new need. Previously feminists had campaigned for support for mothers in their work at home, for the provision of health services, the maternity allowance and motherhood endowment. The new call for 'child care centres' pointed to a separation of child care from motherhood and the idea that child care might be the province of experts, a significant shift in Australian feminist thinking. But child care was a precondition for equality in the public domain.

The government provision of child care was necessary to enable ordinary women to go out to work. Women needed to be freed, like men, from the responsibility of caring for others on a daily basis. The use of child care centres during the war had provided a precedent, when feminists had been able to argue that Australia's war effort was being impeded by the lack of adequate facilities. Advocates of the government provision of child care cited the cases of women such as Mrs B. Byles of Rozelle:

> Mrs B. Byles . . . has given up her job in a war factory because she thought her children were being neglected . . . She said 'I used to worry about the children, especially when I found they had not eaten meals I had prepared for them before leaving for work. I got badly behind with the housework, mending, washing and ironing. I'm satisfied that I can't do two jobs properly.'[9]

The establishment of centres run by professionally trained staff would solve Mrs Byles' difficulties and those of thousands of other women in her position.

A wartime survey of the Leichhardt and Balmain communities in Sydney found many mothers with pre-school-age children were willing to work in war industries if substitute care for their children were provided. The imperatives of the war effort enabled feminists to campaign for child care as a patriotic service: 'The immediate object is to release more women for war industries and reduce absenteeism among married women now working on war jobs'. The new arrangements set a precedent for the post-war order. And once again Australian feminists looked to the state to provide the preconditions for women's freedom and independence.

'Child care was a government responsibility', affirmed Lucy Woodcock, the president of the 'Care of the Child in Wartime Committee'. 'You have to gear everything to the war effort at present, but child care should become a permanent part of the educational system. It should be a government responsibility like State education'. The Australian Women's Charter recommended accordingly that the government:

> Subsidise a national scheme for the establishment of a network of child care centres wherever needed; and provide that governments, local councils and elected citizens' bodies in each State co-operate in the development and administration of these Centres in order to develop local interest and effort to the maximum;
>
> Expand the premises and staff of baby health centres so that they may serve in the dual capacity of baby health centre and day nursery;
>
> . . .
>
> Require all child care establishments to conform to standards recognised by the local health authorities, and the person in charge to possess the necessary qualifications.

The Australian Women's Charter was a comprehensive document in envisaging the range of changes necessary to bring about equality for women in social, economic and political life. In one area of life, however, feminists did not push for rights. For Australian feminists in the 1940s, sexuality remained the site of women's degradation.

Feminists imagined women as political and economic subjects, as mothers, workers and citizens, but not as desiring sexual subjects. They didn't incorporate sexual rights in the Charter and there were no recommendations concerning birth control. Rather, sex continued, in the Australian feminist tradition, to be seen as a source of degradation and exploitation, sexual desire as a condition that needed to be strictly regulated. The endorsement of the equal moral standard still meant that men as well as women should strive for 'purity'. Promiscuous girls needed 'rehabilitation'. Thus the Charter recommended:

> a widespread educational campaign on the necessity for self respect and for high and equal moral standards; the danger of promiscuity; the need for early treatment [of VD] and on the extent to which alcoholic beverages act as a contributing factor in the incidence of V.D. [and] the adoption of scientific methods for the rehabilitation of girls and women who have formed promiscuous habits.

The Charter also condemned state regulation of prostitution with its inevitable harassment of women, recommending that soliciting laws be abolished and replaced by general legislation against annoyance or molestation.

SEXUAL RIGHTS

In attitudes towards sexual relations a gulf had opened up between organised feminists, most of whom were in their fifties and sixties by 1946, and the self-consciously modern young women who pursued wartime possibilities of romance and sexual pleasure. The conditions of war—the new freedoms and mobility, the presence of hundreds of thousands of American servicemen, the atmosphere of danger and excitement, the access to new wages—had provided Australian women with unprecedented opportunity for sexual adventure, which many took up with alacrity. By the 1940s, women were thinking more about themselves.

'I expressed a desire', wrote one young Teachers' College student in her diary, '. . . for a Yank boyfriend. Melb. and in fact all Austr. is swarming with them—since Xmas—& I felt I'd missed life, not having even met one—Else and I spoke to some one night in the dark of Swanston St. but didn't pick them up as most girls do now'. A few weeks later she was pleased to record her own war victory:

> Anyway I can tell my Grandchildren at least that during those momentous days when Austr. was rapidly accumulating thousands

upon thousands of Yanks, when Melbourne went bad, & every girl discussed her 'pick-ups' I too had a little experience.[10]

In such 'experience' young Australian women were discovering a new source of self-fulfilment and personal liberation.

Feminists despaired at the foolishness of these silly girls or 'amateurs' as the press liked to dub them. The proliferation of vice in wartime cities simply strengthened the feminist conviction that girls and women must strive for chastity. Feminists remained determinedly anti-sexual in their politics, philosophy and platforms. Sex indulgence, it was assumed, was always harmful for women. Some blamed the proliferation of beauty contests which overemphasised the bodily part of woman's personality. But while the aging leaders of the feminist movement talked in terms of the dangers of seduction, vice and promiscuity, young women in pursuit of pleasure found it difficult to identify with such a self-abnegating politics. Speeches about self-control and chastity fell on closed ears. Commenting on the lack of response to the Women for Canberra movement, organisers lamented that young women 'were not seized with the seriousness of the matter'.[11]

World War II produced a social panic about the spread of venereal disease—newspaper editorials warned that the figures for venereal disease were rising with 'horrifying rapidity'—confirming feminists' worst fears about the dangers of 'promiscuity' and 'indiscriminate intimacy' for girls and women. Widespread publicity emphasised the high incidence of disease among young women, a 45 per cent increase in infection among sixteen- to twenty-year-old girls reported in Sydney in April 1943.

Just as bad from the feminist point of view was the prevailing double standard in the official apportioning of guilt: young women bore the brunt of the blame and the punitive treatment, often being sent to the Parramatta Girls' Industrial School (originally built for the reception of convicts). The double standard against which feminists had long protested was being enacted with a vengeance by vice squad raids and the widespread detentions of young women. National Security Regulations gave police new power to arrest these women on 'reasonable suspicion'. Ada Bromham, in 1943 national corresponding secretary of the Woman's Christian Temperance Union (WCTU) and member of the Australian Women's Charter Committee, complained that 'girl VD suspects were being hunted down by Gestapo methods'.[12]

The targeting of young women by the state and attacks on their morality by assorted male authorities prompted feminists to retaliate by blaming men, characterising them as seducers and perverts. Men were asked to own, and own up to, their lusts; women were innocent victims in need of protection. Jessie Street railed at men's exploitation of women and the state's collusion in trying to make 'sex indulgence' safe. In the *Daily Telegraph* she was reported as saying:

> Attention should be directed to the seducers of young girls instead of always to those seduced . . . What are we doing to protect our young girls? Hundreds of them have been seduced and infected with disease . . . Why is this evil allowed to flourish? Why is the flower of young womanhood, the future mothers of Australia, allowed to be debauched and diseased? One reason is that instead of trying to stamp out immorality and disease, those in control have tried to make sex indulgence safe. Never in history has there been any safe way of indulging promiscuity in sex. There is only one infallible way of preventing disease—chastity.[13]

Street then referred to recent meetings in Sydney called to discuss the alarming spread of venereal disease, where, almost without exception, the men had blamed immoral girls. This was ridiculous, according to Street. Rather, 'the blame for the seduction of girls and the spread of disease must be placed where it belongs—on the shoulders of the men concerned'. Perverts and debauchees, she said, should be removed from society: 'remove those who create the demand and the supply will not be called into being'. There was no possibility in this feminist conception of sexual relations for the play of female desire, of women as desiring sexual agents.

Women at large, however, seemed to be expressing their interest in sex at every opportunity, not only on the streets and in newspapers, but in response to surveys—such as that conducted by Dr V. H. Wallace in his birth control clinic in Melbourne—and in evidence to the national enquiry by the National Health and Medical Research Council (NHMRC) into Australia's falling birth-rate. That the Australian Women's Charter did not incorporate any recommendations to secure women's access to birth control is, in retrospect, remarkable. For during this time, when interviewed, Australian women said again and again how oppressed they felt by childbearing. It stopped them working, it prevented them from going out, it led to their husbands' unfaithfulness. Many women also mentioned that trams didn't permit prams.

For some forty years feminists had advocated voluntary motherhood, but this was to be achieved through men's sexual restraint. Feminists persisted with the idea that men could be persuaded to give up on sexual desire, but with little evident success, because by the 1940s women were making clear their need for contraceptives—to prevent unwanted pregnancies, to enable them to co-operate with their husbands, to avoid domestic drudgery, to avoid the resort to abortion. Moreover, by the 1940s good sexual relationships were deemed crucial to happy marriages. 'I believe a happy marriage is based on a happy sexual life between husband and wife', wrote one patient to Dr Wallace. 'Where there is a continual fear of pregnancy it is bound to cause discord.'[14]

Many young women, growing up as witnesses to their mothers' lives in the Depression, were determined not to live as they did. The memory of the drudgery and unhappiness weighed heavily. One woman wrote to Dr V. H. Wallace from Carrum on the outskirts of Melbourne: 'my mother had 10 children luckily 5 died . . . It is a great pity birth control cannot be taught free to the masses'.[15]

When the New South Wales parliament introduced legislation in 1946 to ban the advertising of contraceptives, however, feminists were forced to take a stand. Once again it was the action of those wanting to curb women's freedom that forced feminists into articulating a new right, not to contraception as it happened, but the 'right of free enquiry into and free discussion of a vitally important social question'. In a deputation to the Minister of Justice, seven women's organisations—the New Education Fellowship; the Hotel, Club and Restaurant Employees' Union; the Young Women's Christian Association (YWCA); the Sydney Business and Professional Women's Organisations; the United Associations (UA); the Australian Federation of Women Voters; and the Ironworkers' Union Women's Auxiliary—argued strongly in favour of the availability of information about contraceptives, which 'had saved the health and lives of untold numbers of women'.[16]

Ruby Rich, on behalf of the Australian Federation of Women Voters, declared with passion: 'I will circulate all the books by Dr Marie Stopes on which I can lay hands. I will go to jail if necessary. I will defy legislation which is merely a crude dictatorship'.[17] Rich had long been an advocate for birth control, speaking to conferences in London where she had spent much time in the 1930s, but Australian feminists were more likely to stress the health benefits for women than the possible enhancement of sexual pleasure. The New South Wales

Obscene and Indecent Publications Act limited, but did not ban outright, the advertising of contraceptives.

From the 1940s, non-party feminism became as closely identified with the interests of the working woman as it had once been with the vocation of the mother, yet there was little public recognition of the fact that the ability to limit childbearing was clearly a crucial precondition to equal participation in public life. Leaders of the twentieth century women's movement such as Ada Bromham, Jessie Street, Bessie Rischbieth, Ruby Rich, Jean Daley, Muriel Heagney and Linda Littlejohn were either childless or wealthy enough to employ private nannies. If leadership positions in public life were to be open to all women, then reproductive freedom and the provision of public child care would be as important as political and economic rights—yet once the war was over these ceased to be major feminist issues. Equal pay and equal opportunity—in work and in public life—were the big feminist themes in the 1950s and 1960s. But as feminism increasingly became the cause of those who desired to join the public world of men, other women were moved to express their disapproval of this new pursuit of self-interest. Thus did Dorothy Iremonger of Yass warn the leaders of the Women for Canberra movement to guard against 'a mere stampede for parliament of ambitious women'.[18]

COLD WAR POLITICS

Feminists were often moved to criticise the ambitions of other feminists. The history of Australian feminism was marked by a series of rivalries between strong women, who did their best to hide unseemly jealousy from view—but in the late 1940s conflict erupted into the public domain over Jessie Street's appointment to the United Nations Commission on the Status of Women. When the Australian Women's Charter movement set up links with women's organisations in other States, there was initially much support.

In Western Australia, the Women's Service Guild, chaired by Isabel Johnston, had at first greeted the initiative with enthusiasm. When alerted to these national and international developments, however, Bessie Rischbieth, still in London, was quick to caution West Australian feminists against the Charter Committee's duplication of the work of long-established feminist organisations, notably her own Australian

Federation of Women Voters. Back in Australia, she became more critical of the Charter movement's influence with the federal Labor government and persuaded her supporters to distance themselves from it.[19]

In November 1945, Rischbieth and Street were among four Australians who attended a conference in Paris where the leftist World Federation of Democratic Women was formed. It was there that Rischbieth's opposition to the totalitarian ideology of Communism— and to Jessie Street as its seeming exponent—crystallised. In a radio address on her return to Australia, having been exiled in London by the war, Rischbieth made a speech on the theme of 'Democracy at the Crossroads', in which she urged Australians to become active in defending their democratic institutions (parliament, the right to vote, civic responsibility) against the methods of the Soviet order (suppression of free speech, the imposition of uniformity and domination from the top). Her outspoken defence of civil society came logically to one who had, from the 1920s, proclaimed the 'new citizenship' to be 'an evolutionary force'. For Bessie Rischbieth, as theorist and activist, feminist citizenship required civil society.[20]

On Jessie Street's appointment as Australian delegate to the UN Commission in 1947, Bessie Rischbieth and Isabel Johnston led a deputation of protest to Prime Minister Ben Chifley, recommending that future appointments be made by the Commonwealth government and not the Department of External Affairs; that is, not by Minister H. V. Evatt. When Rischbieth heard that the Australian Women's Charter Committee was to become the co-ordinating agency linking the Commission on the Status of Women with Australian feminists, she protested directly to Evatt, disputing the legitimacy of the Charter Committee's claim to be representative of Australian women's organisations: 'We do not consider it the best channel to use to get together women of all shades of thought and opinion'.[21]

In Bessie Rischbieth's increasingly anti-Communist view, Jessie Street, in her evident sympathies with the Soviet Union, had put herself beyond the pale. In the context of the Cold War, the personal rivalries and leadership ambitions of Australian feminists were sharpened by larger ideological conflicts, and life generally became very unpleasant for those deemed to be Communist sympathisers. When the Australian Labor party moved to expel members of proscribed organisations, Street—who was a member of both the New South

Wales Peace Committee and the Russia Friendship Society—resigned her membership of the Australian Labor party in disgust.

In the context of the Cold War, feminism was increasingly identified with subversive forces, threatening the stability of family and community. It was blamed for the rising tide of divorce and family breakdown, the proliferation of unmarried motherhood, women going out to work, and men's loss of power. Arguing against the appointment of women to the New South Wales Marriage Guidance Council, the Attorney-General said men did not like being pushed around by women. With younger women showing little interest in feminism, the number of paid-up members of the UA fell into decline (less than 200 in the early 1950s) and the secretary, Caroline Scrimgeour, despaired at the climate of hostility to feminism: 'The cause of equality of status is so unpopular with the press etc that we can expect no attractive publicity through them'.[22]

THE RIGHT TO NON-DISCRIMINATION

In 1947, Street took her place on the Commission on the Status of Women, which elected her as vice-chairman. Among the first items on the agenda was a consideration of the Draft Declaration of Human Rights, to which she, together with the chairman, Bodil Begtrup from Denmark, proposed a number of feminist amendments. The range of their proposed amendments points again to the paradox inherent in feminist politics, in the attempt to extend the category 'human' to have it apply to women. On the one hand, feminists needed to outlaw sexist discrimination; on the other, they wanted to draw attention to the importance of sexual difference. So, for example, they proposed that male pronouns and nouns be avoided where possible to make it clear that human rights applied 'without discrimination to the female sex'. They objected to the original declaration that 'all men are brothers' and had the wording of Article 1 changed to read that all human beings should act towards one another 'in a spirit of brotherhood'. In Article 2, the Declaration made a commitment to recognising rights without distinction:

> Everyone is entitled to all the rights and freedoms set forth in this Declaration, without distinction of any kind, such as race, colour,

sex, language, religion, political or other opinion, national or social origin, property birth or other status.

This was gratifying to feminists, but at the same time they wanted to draw attention to the particularity of the human rights abuses suffered by women, which could not be rectified unless specified and explicitly addressed.

Women were affected by different kinds of ill treatment than were men. 'Among the most common injustices suffered by women who are suspected of promiscuity is to be arrested without warrant, to be subjected to forcible physical examinations, to be detained without a trial or sentence and to be registered as prostitutes', explained Street. 'No woman should be subjected to any curtailment of civil rights by reason of the fact that she is suspected of being, or is, a prostitute.' She suggested the addition of a specific clause to the Declaration—'No woman shall be deprived of her personal liberty or be subject to arbitrary and unauthorized arrest by laws or regulations passed under the pretext of protecting health and morals'—but was assured that the general wording of Articles 3 and 5 sufficed.

When Street proposed that the clause prohibiting slavery be extended to prohibit 'white slavery', again the general wording of Article 4 was thought to be sufficient. Committed to abolishing distinctions based on sex, the architects of the Draft Declaration resisted incorporating specific rights for women. Thus Bodil Begtrup's suggestion that the Declaration of Human Rights should recognise the 'rights of motherhood' was also refused; instead Article 25 stipulated that 'motherhood and childhood are entitled to special care and assistance'. Mothers were considered not as political subjects with rights, but as a group akin to children, in need of social care.

Ironically, this refusal of the idea that child-bearers were rights-bearers occurred just at the moment when large groups of mothers in Australia were about to robbed of their children—Aboriginal mothers being joined by large numbers of non-Aboriginal unmarried mothers who were also deemed unfit to raise their own children. At the very moment when the rights of mothers needed to be defended on a large scale, feminism in Australia, encouraged by the international focus on 'non-discrimination', shifted its attention to gender relations in the public domain.

Within the conceptual framework of non-discrimination, feminist interpretations of equality became more assimilationist. In their opposition to distinctions based on sex, feminists perforce embraced masculine norms and priorities as their own. Feminism came to be defined as the demand that women be treated like men. This was reflected in various proposals for a bill of rights or blanket bill, such as that proposed in Western Australia by distinguished lawyer and legal adviser to the Women's Service Guild Margaret Battye, who designed a bill to eliminate all sexual discrimination in Australian law. A symposium was held to discuss her proposal in September 1949, addressed by West Australian Senator Dorothy Tangney; however, when she submitted it to Prime Minister Chifley he said it should be referred to State Premiers, and there it lapsed.

To encourage women to participate in parliamentary politics, feminist organisations again established Women's Model Parliaments (they were first tried out in Vida Goldstein's day) with prominent women appointed to the offices of Speaker and Governor. In Western Australia, one hundred women became members within a week of the parliament's formation in January 1946. They were invited to choose their party membership, but the identity of the parties differed significantly from those already in existence. They included the Monetary Reform party, the Electoral Reform party, the International party, the Social and Moral Reform party, the Home-Makers party and the WA Development party, the last-named proving easily the most popular and thus forming the government. In Victoria, the League of Women Voters, formed in 1945 from an amalgamation of Women for Canberra, the League of Women Electors and the Victorian Women Citizens' Movement, also organised a Women's Model parliament in 1946, which encouraged the participation of senior school girls as well as women interested in a career in politics. Inspired to make a bid for the real thing, three members stood in that same year for state parliament and two for local government, but none was successful.

Feminism in the 1950s concentrated on the achievement of formal equality with men in the public domain in campaigns for equal pay, equal opportunities in the workforce, the right to sit on juries and boards and the right to sit in parliament. In 1951, the United Associations asked candidates in the forthcoming federal election whether they would agree:

1. To grant women equal pay, status and opportunity in the Commonwealth Public Service, thereby giving an impetus to outside bodies to follow suit.
2. To rescind sec. 49 of the Commonwealth Public Service Act

and sec. 170 of the Commonwealth Bank Act, 1945, both of which forbid the employment of women after marriage regardless of their ability.
3. To appoint a proportion of women to Boards created by the Government, particularly where such Boards affect the welfare of women and children.
4. To appoint a proportion of women on delegations to overseas Conferences, such as the UN Organisation in its various departments and the ILO.
5. To unify and thus simplify the Divorce laws of the Commonwealth.
6. To hold a Referendum to provide for a Blanket Bill giving women equal rights, status and opportunity with men and stipulating that any sex discriminations embodied in any laws or regulations be invalid.[23]

But they also supported moves to secure the payment of maintenance to deserted wives, attempts by civilian widows to have their payments increased and the moves to standardise divorce under Commonwealth jurisdiction, a goal finally realised in 1957.

Feminist campaigns for the rights of Aborigines and ethnic minorities also reflected the new emphasis on the principle of non-discrimination. During the war, feminists had been to the fore in a campaign to rescue Jews in Europe from the 'process of extermination' being carried out by the Nazis. In Tasmania, the local branch of the League of Nations Union wrote in November 1943 to the Prime Minister of 'the desperate need to take immediate action towards their relief' and sent a copy of the resolution to Jessie Street, who in turn contacted thirty organisations in Sydney, calling on them for support.[24] Street arranged a deputation to Canberra to ask that the government immediately accept another 8000 Jewish refugees, as previously agreed at the Evian conference in 1938.

In 1949, the United Associations became involved in several clashes with the Minister for Immigration, Arthur Calwell, over the deportation of non-Europeans who had entered the country during the war. The UA took up the case of Demetrios Georg Gelis of the Greek Seamen's Union and that of the Malayan A. S. B. Amjah, whose case was represented to the UA as one of discrimination against an Australian woman: 'Mrs Amjah and her family are being discriminated against. If Mrs Amjah had married a white man—no matter how mean, brutal, slovenly or drunken he might have been—there would have been no discrimination against her'.[25] Minister for Immigration Arthur

Calwell was, however, unmoved and reiterated his belief in the necessity of discrimination:

> I am unable to agree to the adoption of the suggestion put forward by your organisation as I am firmly of the opinion that by doing so the homogeneity of our European population would inevitably be destroyed and there would be brought to this country the strife and problems that are the invariable lot of States having mixed populations.[26]

In 1949, the UA also began a campaign to persuade the Kempsey Council in New South Wales to end its policy of excluding Aboriginal people from the public swimming pool: 'This action of the Kempsey Council violates every principle of the UN Charter to which Australia contributes'. As the UA explained to the town clerk, its members had

> concerned themselves with this matter because one of the Objects of our Association is the removal of discriminations which operate unjustly against individuals. In this we ally ourselves with that clause of the UN Charter which affirms 'there shall be no discrimination on account of race, colour, creed or sex'.

In response, the Aboriginal Welfare Board assured the UA that 'the Board in furthering its policy of assimilation was anxious that Aboriginal children should have every opportunity in association with other children and that it was felt their attendance at the baths afforded an excellent opportunity in this regard'.[27]

When Jessie Street was living in London during the early 1950s, in the context of the Cold War, she was approached by the Anti-Slavery Society to join their Australian sub-committee and, more specifically, to follow up a story sent to them by Mary Bennett about the conditions of Australia's indigenous people. Street became passionately involved in the campaign for Aboriginal reform and determined to take a case against Australia to the United Nations. Convinced that basic human rights were being denied to Aboriginal people, Street wanted to bring Australia to account, but came to the conclusion that an Australia-wide body was needed to put the case.

Until that time Aboriginal rights groups were all State-based. Street wrote to potential allies in Australia—Ada Bromham, then in Queensland, Shirley Andrews in Melbourne, Ann Waters and Pearl Gibbs in Sydney—suggesting that if the subject of Aboriginal rights were 'to be brought before the United Nations . . . it would help considerably if you had an all Australian organisation'. Shirley Andrews was pleased to report that a new indigenous organisation, the Aboriginal Australian Fellowship, had been formed in Sydney by Pearl Gibbs, from Dubbo and an activist of South Sea Islander descent, Faith Bandler. As a delegate of the Fellowship, Bandler was crucial in winning the support of feminists for the dismantling of the discriminatory apparatus of the Aborigines Protection Act.

Back in Australia, in 1957, Street undertook an extensive tour of the country to examine the conditions of Aboriginal people at first hand, after which she wrote a lengthy report. In Sydney, she helped launch the petition calling for a referendum to secure Commonwealth responsibility for Aboriginal welfare. The wording of the preamble to the petition, written in her hand, echoed the United Nations emphasis on non-discrimination:

> believing that many of the difficulties encountered today by Aborigines arise from the discrimination against them in two sections of the Commonwealth Constitution, which specifically exclude Aborigines from the enjoyment of their rights and privileges enjoyed by all other Australians . . .

In the same year, veteran campaigner Mary Bennett published her book *Human Rights for Australian Aborigines*, to 'publicise the principles of the Universal Declaration of Human Rights which do not apply to Australian Aborigines', with a preface commending her expert knowledge by her old friend Ada Bromham.

Also in 1957, in Perth, Bessie Rischbieth went before the Constitution Review Committee to make the same case for federal responsibility for Aboriginal affairs that she had made for the past thirty years. The federal Constitution denied Aboriginal citizens rights: 'Our very federal Constitution prevents our national Government from taking legislative measures in relation to the welfare of . . . Aborigines at all except in Territories directly under their control'. Aborigines needed 'a more secure place in their own country'.

WORKING CLASS WOMEN REGROUP

One women's organisation that attracted a number of Aboriginal women into its membership was the Union of Australian Women

(UAW), formed in 1950 as a revamped version of the left-wing New Housewives' Association, which had operated as a sort of women's auxiliary to the Communist party. The Union of Australian Women was an organisation for working class women, including those who worked as housewives and mothers in the home, as well as women in the paid workforce, trade unionists and the wives of trade unionists. It worked closely with affiliated groups such as the Seamen's Women's Committee, the Miners' Women's Auxiliaries and the Waterside Workers' Women's Committees.[28]

The UAW's concern with the economics of daily life, domestic conditions and the welfare of children placed it in the distinctive Australian tradition of labour movement feminism, which had promoted motherhood endowment in the 1920s. It was appropriate, therefore, that Labor stalwart Henrietta Greville, by then eighty-nine years of age, was asked to speak at the inaugural meeting. Greville's earlier feminist advocacy of the independence of the married woman had no echoes, however, in the deliberations of the Union of Australian Women, whose commitment to solidarity with the men of their class precluded an identification as feminist and made it wary of sex antagonism.

The organisation was initially most concerned about the high cost of living, conducting numerous campaigns around prices and wages. It was most active in its local communities—localities—urging better facilities for families in new post-war suburbs and supporting women as candidates in municipal elections, but there was also effective co-ordination between local and national campaigns. One of its best-supported initiatives was the Mother and Child campaign, launched in 1956 with the specific goal of securing an increase in Child Endowment, a payment that as Jessie Street noted, had given many mothers their 'first taste of economic independence'. In July 1958, nearly 300 women converged on Canberra from all over Australia bearing petitions with 30 000 signatures calling for an increase in Child Endowment and the Maternity Allowance. Although successive Liberal party Ministers refused to commit themselves, in 1959 for the first time the Maternity Allowance was extended to Aboriginal women.

In its grass roots work in local communities, the Union of Australian Women became involved in several campaigns to assist Aboriginal families, and Aboriginal women also joined the organisation, especially in North Queensland where Gladys O'Shane and Muriel Callope were active in the Cairns branch. In New South Wales, Pearl Gibbs was a member of the New South Wales Management Committee for several years.

In Newcastle, Barbara Curthoys, secretary of the Newcastle branch of the Union of Australian Women, and others supported Aboriginal families on the reserve at the Purfleet Mission Station: managers were withholding payments of rent claimed by the New South Wales Aborigines Welfare Board, which had burnt down their original homes. A meeting organised by Elsie Allen and Marjorie Maher, Aboriginal women living on the reserve, led to a protest campaign waged in conjunction with the Union of Australian Women and the Newcastle Trades Hall, asking for improvements to the housing in return for rent. They were not successful in the short term, but such activism was part of the longer struggle that was eventually successful in having the whole tyrannical apparatus of 'protection' dismantled; by the late 1960s the laws governing New South Wales reserves were changed and the Aborigines Welfare Board was dissolved.

Although most of the members of the Union of Australian Women were housewives and mothers, there were growing numbers in the organisation—as in the society at large—who combined domestic responsibilities with paid work, with larger numbers of married women entering paid employment throughout the post-war period. The wartime operation of the Women's Employment Board had set a precedent for increasing women's wage rates. In 1949, women workers achieved a small victory when, following submissions from women's organisations, the Arbitration Court set the female basic wage at 75 per cent of the male rate. When employer groups applied in 1952 to have the rate reduced to 60 per cent, women's organisations responded by putting the case for equal pay. The president of the United Associations, Caroline Scrimgeour, placed a full-page article in the Union of Australian Women's journal *Our Women*, titled 'Woman as a Citizen', in which she stated that unequal wages constituted 'the most glaring example of inequality of status in present day Australia'.

There were significant differences between the claims advanced by women's organisations, however. Older feminist groups argued, as they had done for some thirty years, for an individual wage—the rate for the job—to be supplemented by child and motherhood endowment. The Union of Australian Women, however, mindful of their men's investment in the family wage, argued for a wage to support a husband and wife, regardless of whether workers actually had wives. Their support of a wage for a couple highlighted the political difference between their organisation—based as it was in the labour movement and in communities in which the majority of women were housewives—and feminist organisations, which had always made claims for women as individuals, who as citizens had a right to economic independence.

Throughout the 1950s women's organisations and trade union women continued to campaign for equal pay, focussing on submissions to industrial courts as well as to parliaments. In 1956, when three Australian delegates—Esther Taylor, a clothing worker and member of the Bronte branch of the Union of Australian Women; Cecilia Shelley, secretary of the Hotel, Club and Caterers' Union in Western Australia for thirty-four years; and Kath Williams, organiser of the Liquor Trades Union and secretary of the Victorian Trades Hall Council Equal Pay Committee—attended the International Conference of Working Women in Budapest, they were farewelled by Lucy Woodcock, former vice-president of the Teachers' Federation and president of the United Associations.

Teachers in New South Wales were finally successful in winning equal pay in 1958, when the State government passed the Equal Pay Act for workers on State awards performing essentially the same work as men and New South Wales became 'an equal pay State'. In the same year, the Australian Council of Trade Unions submitted to women's pressure and convened a national conference on equal pay and working conditions in Sydney. They also presented a petition to the Minister for Labour and Industry, Harold Holt, signed by 62 000 people, urging the government to honour its decision to implement the 1951 International Labor Office (ILO) convention on equal pay.

For the majority of women workers, however, equal pay and equal opportunity were elusive goals. Trade union women and feminist organisations kept up their campaigns during the 1950s and 1960s, when an upsurge in the demand for labour saw a softening of traditional opposition to married women working. Finally, in 1966, the federal parliament passed legislation removing the marriage bar in the Commonwealth public service and banks, thus opening up new opportunities for women seeking permanency and promotion. Feminists in the 1950s and 1960s, labouring in an often hostile environment, did the essential groundwork for the successful equal pay cases between 1969 and 1974.

Feminist campaigns in the 1950s and 1960s were also finally successful in winning the citizen's right that proved most elusive to women—the right to sit on juries, the right, that is, to sit in judgment on men, the right that seemed to be the most threatening of all. In New South Wales, Kate Dwyer and Annie Golding had led a deputation to the Attorney-General asking that he grant this right as early as 1904. In 1951, the Jury Act was passed allowing New South Wales women to perform jury service, but only if 'appropriate facilities' were available in the courts. In 1977, further legislation required women to serve, but they could still claim exemption if they were pregnant or caring for children. By that time, women were liable for jury service in all States, but were allowed more grounds for exemption than men—in Victoria, for example, until 1975, they were entitled 'as of right' to be excused. In Queensland, which had been the first State to admit women to jury service (from 1923), a District Court judge agreed to a request from a man in 1991 not to be tried by women jurors, because as a Christian man it went against the teaching of the Bible: to have women sit on the jury was an abomination of God. The Attorney-General later quashed this decision.

9
AN END TO WOMAN'S ROLE

'THE BAR ROOM SUFFRAGETTES'

The first questions the police asked Ro Bognor when they found her and Merle Thornton chained to the foot rail of the public bar at the Regatta Hotel in Brisbane were: 'where were her children?' and 'who was looking after them?'[1] Bognor and Thornton had gone there, in March 1965, to protest against the Queensland law that prevented women from being served alcohol in public bars. Upon being refused a beer, they took a dog chain and very large padlock from a bag and chained themselves to the rail, an action that sparked enormous media interest and presaged a new phase in the history of feminism. For one of the main reasons these 'wives of University lecturers' were criticised was their lack of feminine decorum: their defiant demand for a drink had flouted the prevailing code of womanly respectability. Feminism was becoming intemperate and brazen.

The women's demand to be allowed to drink in public bars, alongside the men, represented a sharp break with a feminist tradition that had been closely allied with the temperance movement and that had cultivated the respectability expected of exemplary citizens. Barbara Curthoys called her study of the Union of Australian Women *More Than a Hat and Glove Brigade* to signal its sometimes militant purpose, but its mode of attire in fact suited its mode of doing politics. The organisation operated very much in the tradition of the polite deputation presenting properly constituted petitions, its sartorial style denoting its respect for political convention and institutional ritual.

Thornton and Bognor had themselves initially adhered to convention by presenting their case for drinking rights in a deputation to the

Minister for Justice, but without result. Their next action, their dramatic occupation of that men-only space, was deliberately transgressive and disruptive, a radical departure from older forms of Australian feminist politics. At the same time, however, the demand for 'the right to put their elbow on the bar and foot on the rail alongside men' (as the *Sunday Truth* put it)[2] could be seen as an extension of the established feminist agenda, the logical next step in the assimilationist project pursued under the banner of equal rights for some thirty years.

Merle Thornton, mother of two, was a post-graduate student in Philosophy at the University of Queensland. Why should she be prevented from joining her colleagues after work for a drink? 'Imagine yourself the businessman, worker, academic, politician', she said, 'who couldn't go down to the bar for a drink with the others after the conference, to celebrate the completion of a big job, or just because you felt like it'.[3] In Australia, the pub was an extension of the workplace. The exclusion of women from the space of the allegedly 'public' bar effectively discriminated against them as citizen-workers. 'Think of the women struggling for first class citizenship', said the 'bar-room suffragettes' who were also members of the ALP, 'the journalists who can't pick up bar gossip; the businesswomen who can't make contacts in the bar; the women at various conferences and meetings who can't adjourn to the bar with others'.[4]

Merle Thornton knew that the logic of equal rights for women entailed a refusal of special protection, the sort of protection allegedly being offered by hotels in the parlours and lounges set aside for 'ladies' (where, perversely, given women's lower wages, higher prices prevailed). She outlined her opposition to 'Victorian protective patronage' in a press release, condemning legislation that set out 'to protect women who don't want to be protected'. It was said that bar-room talk was 'not nice' and women should be shielded from it, but 'such protectiveness was catastrophic to women':

> To protect women against their will from certain conversation or social situations is to treat them as mental children. Treating people as mental children is a quick way to make them into mental children.[5]

Women had the rights of adults and it was 'a principle of prime importance that all normal adult citizens, irrespective of race or sex, should be treated in exactly the same way under the same law'. 'There is wide agreement on this principle', she added, 'which is incorporated in the United Nations Charter of Human Rights'.⁶ Her reference to the United Nations was echoed by supporters as when 'Shandy' wrote to the press:

> The Charter of the United Nations stands for human rights and fundamental freedoms for all without distinction in race, sex, language or religion. Good luck to the two young ladies who have drawn our attention to the drinking law which is contrary to this charter by discrimination against women.⁷

One of the most disturbing aspects of the case, it seemed, was that the women were mothers. In pursuing their own selfish interests these women were neglecting their primary obligations to their children. 'Would the ladies feel any guilt if some person had kidnapped one of their children while they were chained to the bar?' asked Frederick White of Banyo in a letter to the paper.⁸ In the Queensland State parliament, the Labor member for Sandgate wondered whether the neglected children should not be committed to the care of the welfare authorities. Journalists visited the women's suburban homes where they were relieved to find happy families and attentive mothers, in one case supervising the children's homework. Earlier feminist achievements thus rebounded on their successors; the cause of 'neglected children', once feminists' reason for entering public life, was now invoked to discredit the demands of their modern-day successors.

Correspondents to the newspapers also worried that the women's desire to drink was a sign of impending licentiousness and moral chaos. One woman from Townsville wrote indignantly:

> How proud your daughters will be that you gave them the right to grog-up; but why stop there?
> How about the free sale of marijuana or free love camps?⁹

Other women said they felt ashamed and degraded by the women's actions—as, no doubt, would have earlier feminists such as Rose Scott, Vida Goldstein and Ada Bromham, the latter of whom died in that same year, after a lifetime of activism, aged eighty-five.

Meanwhile Thornton and Bognor used the opportunity created by the extraordinary press interest to expand on their political program. In a pub crawl, prompted by an investigating ABC television 'Four Corners' crew, ten women visited a number of city hotels, carrying bottles of beer in their handbags. Thornton proclaimed the event a great victory for women's rights: 'It is not just the right to drink in bars we are seeking. We are after equal educational opportunities for women, equal job opportunities and equal treatment in every direction'. To that end she established the Equal Opportunities for Women Association, whose first meeting attracted about thirty people, mainly, the newspaper reporter noted, married women.[10]

The transformation of the protest in the pub into an extraordinary media event spoke to the deep anxieties generated by the prospect of women's social and sexual freedom. At the same time, the women's action also pointed to the changed nature of the feminist vision of equality. Desiring to follow men into the public bar, these young, educated, married women seemed ready to throw off the old constraints of dignity and decency. Worst of all, they seemed to be shrugging off the duties of motherhood. Both in the threatened response of those who asked about the women's maternal responsibilities and in the women's seeming indifference to them, it became evident that it was the 'role' of mother that kept women in their place. Once lauded by feminists as valuable national work, worthy of political recognition and remuneration, motherhood now came to be seen as the major barrier to women's freedom.

TAKING ACTION

In chaining themselves to rails in pubs, these 'bar-room suffragettes' were self-consciously connecting themselves to a feminist tradition of militancy (albeit an English one), signalling a need to move beyond the polite political practice of petition and deputation. In 1969, in Melbourne, Zelda D'Aprano invoked the same tradition of the English suffragettes when she drew attention to women's campaign for equal pay by chaining herself to the Commonwealth Building. After a meeting with Dianne Sonenberg of the Victorian Employed Women's Organisational Council (VEWOC), D'Aprano—a working class mother, trade unionist and Communist, with years of experience working in factories—decided the time had come for dramatic action. She recalled her decision in her autobiography *Zelda*:

> After having a chat about all of these aspects, we both agreed that something more than just talking was needed to draw attention to the pay injustice meted out to women and more positive action was required. We began to fantasise women

chaining themselves up like the suffragettes did and jokingly asked ourselves where women could chain themselves to make their protest effective.[11]

In the event, D'Aprano went ahead with the protest alone and, as in the Brisbane case, the chaining became a media event, attracting press, radio and TV coverage. It was followed by a similar episode, when D'Aprano was joined by two teachers, Thelma Solomon and Alva Giekie. This time the protest took place in front of the Arbitration Court, which had earlier that year heard a claim for equal pay by the Administrative and Clerical Officers' Association of the Commonwealth public service and the Meat Employees' Union, for whom D'Aprano worked and whose advocate R. J. Hawke, was later to become president of the Australian Council of Trade Unions and then Labor Prime Minister.

Four long-established women's organisations had been given leave to intervene in the case—the Australian Federation of Business and Professional Women's Clubs, the National Council of Women, the Australian Federation of Women Voters and the Union of Australian Women—and their presence in the Court was a reminder of the continuities of feminist activism, even as the older groups were about to be decisively forgotten.

With the 1969 equal pay decision, feminists secured, after decades of struggle, an important symbolic victory, even though it was limited in effect. The Arbitration Commission awarded equal pay, but only for equal work, strictly defined. As the *Sydney Morning Herald* declared the next day: 'Few women to benefit from wage decision'.[12] The judgment did not apply to work that was essentially or usually performed by females; that is, to the vast majority of women workers. It was instructive, however, and led to immediate feminist demands for access to the full range of men's occupations, in particular young women's right to take apprenticeships in traditionally male trades.

In Melbourne, D'Aprano, Giekie and Solomon, disappointed with the lack of interest shown in the equal pay issue by women trade unionists more generally, decided the time had come to form an organisation of 'women prepared to be militant in the cause of women'.[13] They met Bon Hull, then aged in her fifties, who offered her home for a meeting in March 1970, when the Women's Action Committee (WAC) was formally established, its name indicating the importance attached to 'action' by the emerging movement.

Equally important was the refusal of a constitution and hierarchical organisational structures.

D'Aprano had personally endured the effects of masculine ambition in the trade union movement. 'I was particularly vocal on the matter', she recalled.

> My experience had taught me that these type [sic] structures lead to power positions and, once you have positions of power, you have people fighting each other to obtain the power, glory and status that is created by these positions . . . I had learnt this lesson the hard way and shuddered at the thought of women becoming like men in their scramble for power.[14]

Members of the Women's Action Committee joined other Melbourne and interstate women at a national conference in May 1970, at the University of Melbourne. The gathering was organised by the Carlton Women's Liberation Group, which included university activists such as Liz Elliott, a brilliant and beautiful medical student and Martha Scott (later Macintyre), then a school teacher unionist and later a distinguished anthropologist and—like Liz Elliott in 1970—a member of the Communist party. Women's Liberation, Melbourne-style, was more closely connected to working class activism and trade unionism than its university-based Sydney counterpart—although History student Sue Bellamy attempted to make good the lack by taking a job in a factory and, in the socialist tradition, writing about the lives and attitudes of fellow workers, especially migrant women, in a widely-circulated paper on 'Factory Work'.

About 100 women from Sydney, Adelaide and Brisbane attended the 1970 Melbourne conference on 'female conditioning'. Papers were delivered by Margaret Greenland on 'Women and Education', by Coonie Sandford on 'Factors Affecting Women in the Workforce', and by Liz Elliott on 'The Family', in which she stressed the role of the housewife in capitalism as a consumer of 'wasteful consumer goods' and the divisive effects of male supremacy in the working class:

> Women Liberation's task was to attack this crippling form of false consciousness among workers in actions around issues affecting not only the public workforce and public education, but we must also find ways of reaching housewives.[15]

Throughout Australia, universities provided the right environment for the emerging movement to develop ideas, activism and ambition.

At Macquarie University in New South Wales, for example, a leaflet announced the formation of a group in January 1970, inviting newcomers to join over half a million women in Australia, Great Britain and the United States 'QUESTIONING and ACTING TO CHANGE the present roles of men and women and the present notion of "masculine" and "feminine" activities and abilities'.[16]

From the 1960s, increasing numbers of young women had embarked on a higher education that promised them equality in the professions and public life. With formal rights taken for granted, they came to conclude, in the Marxist conceptual framework in which most operated, that ideology constituted the main barrier to equality— not the ideology of the ruling class so much as 'the ideology of sexism'. Many of the first recruits to Women's Liberation had become politicised by the new left political movements associated with the protest against conscription and the war in Vietnam and with opposition to imperialist capitalism; and they equated their quest for 'liberation' with the nationalist struggle being waged by the Vietnamese. 'We are fighting too', announced a leaflet produced for the 1970 moratorium march by the Glebe group. 'Just as the people of South East Asia are fighting for the right to govern their country, the Women's Liberation movement asserts that women must fight the pressures in our society which prevent us from determining our own lives.'[17]

In Sydney, especially, Women's Liberation emerged in the context of these mobilisations of the new left. Women marched in the streets, attended political meetings and drank in pubs alongside men, and they discovered the ambiguous pleasures of a sexual freedom symbolised by the Pill and facilitated by the temporary absence of life-threatening venereal disease. By the 1960s syphilis and gonorrhoea could be treated with antibiotics, and HIV was still in the future.

But in these heady days of sexual and political freedom that marked the late 1960s, many also discovered that their male lovers, brothers and comrades treated them with the condescension and contempt reserved for inferiors. Men might call loudly for the (socialist) revolution, but outspoken women were abused as castrating bitches—as Kate Jennings, future poet and writer-in-exile in New York, well knew, when she used an anti-war rally at the University of Sydney, in September 1970, to denounce the men in the movement for their oppressive attitudes towards women. 'Watch Out!' she warned you may meet a real castrating female or you'll say I'm a manhating bra-burning lesbian member of the castration penis-envy brigade, which I am. I would like to speak.[18]

A sympathetic witness, 'Gale' (Kelly), reported her pleasure at the assault on radical men's arrogant pride:

> Who was to know . . . that Kate Jennings' little old pebble of a speech . . . was to turn into such a boulder which landed with a God-almighty splash right in the middle of the 'lefties-aren't-we-marvellous-altogether millpond' . . . Kate was the only woman to speak . . . Members of WL stood alongside while she took the mike . . . My observation was that it was the only speech that everyone did listen to . . . Me, my stomach caved in at the realisation that here was not a gathering of people who wanted a new society, a new lifestyle, liberty for all. That sea of males—guffawing, sniggering and calling out bed suggestions, was quite happy with the power structure—it suited them fine.[19]

In Sydney, the first Women's Liberation Group was formed when some friends, including the American Martha Ansara and the recently returned Coonie Sandford, distributed a leaflet at the Vietnam moratorium in December 1969, announcing that the inaugural meeting of the Women's Liberation Group would be held on 14 January at 64A Druitt Street, next to the Town Hall. The message in the leaflet, called 'Only the Chains Have Changed', was that women were oppressed by the ideology of 'woman's role' and the imperative of femininity, by the idea that women should be 'sweet, attractive, submissive, understanding, dependent and defenceless'.[20] Women's unpaid labour surely benefited the capitalist class, the same class waging the imperialist war in Vietnam, but women were also exploited by their male comrades; women needed a movement to secure their own liberation.

Women's Liberation arose from, and reacted against, the masculinist dynamics of the new left. Early leaflets in Sydney echoed the demands then being voiced in new left circles in the United States, and American writings began to circulate among sympathetic readers in Australia with little apparent regard for copyright—Gale Kelly authored a pamphlet called 'The Myth of the Vaginal Orgasm', which reproduced much of the text of the article of the same name written by Anne Koedt. Margaret Benston's article, 'The Political Economy of Women's Liberation', on the 'material basis' of 'women's oppression' (published in the US *Monthly Review* in September 1969) and Linda Gordon's 'Families' (published in

US Women: A Journal of Liberation also in 1969), attacking the nuclear family as chaining women to their reproductive role and perpetuating exploitation, were regularly photocopied, as was Pat Mainardi's 'Politics of Housework' from *Notes from the Second Year*. For all its self-conscious commitment to action, Women's Liberation was an intensely literary movement. In Adelaide, Dawn Rowan, who helped set up the first women's counselling service, remembers sitting up in bed devouring the literature after her first Women's Liberation meeting: '"Why I want a wife", "Christian oppression in the family", "The Myth of the Vaginal Orgasm" and "The Politics of Housework". I needed no more convincing'.[21]

That sex and power were defined in terms of each other was the radical message offered by Kate Millett in her influential book *Sexual Politics*, first published in the United States in 1969 and extensively publicised in Australia during 1970 and 1971. It was an especially powerful text for those who came to Women's Liberation at universities, offering historical and literary analysis of a kind never before encountered in Arts degrees, as well as a structuralist 'theory of patriarchy'. It also offered a powerful critique of heterosexuality and inspired meetings around the country to debate the question: 'Are Our Sex Lives Political?'.

Millett's riveting first chapter showed the ways in which (hetero)sexual relations, as depicted by four male modernist writers, were as deeply oppressive of women as any other aspect of society; that far from constituting a liberating experience, sex could be the site of women's most intimate and profound humiliation at the hands of men. In this writing coitus became 'a charged microcosm of the variety of attitudes and values to which culture subscribes'. Modernist sexually explicit writing—the writing many young women were taught to admire in university English courses—was characterised by a profound misogyny. Millett's book provided a new language of analysis and coined the term 'sexism', with conscious reference to 'racism', speculating that 'sexism may be more endemic in our society than racism'.[22]

As the title *Sexual Politics* suggests, Millett analysed the relations between men and women in terms the left best understood, as political relations. She coined a new analytical description: present-day society 'like all other historical civilisations is a patriarchy'. Patriarchy's chief institution was 'the family', but women's oppression was also secured through economic structures and the education system. And although intensive socialisation produced widespread consent to male domination, it also relied on the exercise of force: in particular, the sexual violence most completely realised in the act of rape.[23]

Millett's book offered 'theory', which began to be seen as of crucial importance for determining appropriate action. In Melbourne, the Women's Action Committee, in calling their first public meeting in August 1970, invoked an older discourse on the necessity of combating discrimination: 'Join the women of England and America to protest against exploitation and discrimination of women'. The list of speakers and topics pointed to the continuities in the history of Australian feminism: Mrs D. Sonenberg (VEWOC) on the 'result of the equal pay case—what now?'; Mrs G. Clarke (educationalist) on 'equal education'; Mrs Julia Dahlitz (LL.B.) on 'legal discrimination'; and Glen Tomasetti (folk singer), whose song 'Don't Be Too Polite Girls' set the new tone for the movement. Mrs Jan Harper, a tutor in the Sociology department at La Trobe University, spoke in the language of her discipline on 'the changing role of women in society'.[24] The speakers' marital and occupational status indicated such changes. Women now comprised one third of the paid workforce and 56 per cent of those women workers were married.

The real break with women's movements of the past was evident in their demand for 'abortion law reform', proposed at that meeting by Dr E. Janover of the Progressive Reform party. Women's right of sovereignty over their bodies—the sanctity of women's bodies—had long been espoused as a fundamental feminist principle, but at the cost of denying women's sexuality. In the new 1960s context of sexual liberation, feminists sought not to make men chaste, but to make themselves sexually free by asserting the right to sexual pleasure without the consequence of maternity. An activist in the National Abortion Action Coalition called 'Jenny' told *Vashti's Voice* about how her personal experience of having an abortion had made her 'a committed feminist':

> What right has any church or government, or anyone else . . . to decide whether or not a woman should have a child. Women have the right to control their own bodies. If we can't decide if and when to have children then we can't decide anything . . . It's disgusting that we are criminals in the eyes of the law . . . Society wants to keep women slaves to their biology.[25]

The rights to abortion, free contraception and child care were central to the new libertarian vision of equality. 'Abortion on demand' was a powerful slogan, expressing women's right to self-determination and the expectation that male politicians should not deny this women's right. 'ONLY STRONG ACTION WILL SHAKE THESE BRUTAL SADISTIC MEN OFF OUR BACKS', said the Sydney *Women's Liberation Newsletter* in September 1970.[26]

Form postcards, also published by Women's Liberation in Sydney and addressed to the Prime Minister, asked for the removal of the 27.5 per cent luxury tax from the contraceptive pill ('the present tax puts the "pill" in the same category as a fur coat—surely a distortion of priorities?') and expressed the 'urgent need for government sponsored, free, day-care centres open to all children'.[27] In a letter to potential supporters, the Balmain group explained the significance of the campaign for adequate child care centres: 'Women's Liberation feels that the inferior position of women in society today is due to the fact that all women are expected to take responsibility for housework and child-rearing, regardless of their individual talents'.[28]

In Melbourne, Women's Action Committee campaigns attacked discrimination: letters were sent to firms discriminating against women in the hiring of staff, to banks discriminating against women in the provision of home loans and to the sponsors of TV programs screening what began to be called sexist advertising. Action became more confrontational when WAC members took tram rides for which they paid only 75 per cent of the regular fare, highlighting to the attendant press the unfairness of women's lower wage rates. The range and vitality of Women's Liberation activism in the early 1970s were remarkable, as if years of pent-up energy were being released. In Melbourne, specialist action groups included the Women's Abortion Action Campaign (WAAC), the Equal Pay Committee, Community Controlled Childcare, Working Women's Committee, Women Prisoners' Action Group, the Teachers' Action Group, a Stewardess Rights Group, Children's Books, Women as People Group, Gay Women's Group and a Nurses' Group.

The Women Prisoners' Action Group published an exposé of the degrading and exploitative conditions in Fairlea and spelt out the need for 'human conditions': 'adequate food and medical care, right to protest, freedom from mail and literature censorship, standard working conditions and wages—and an open enquiry into Fairlea and the whole legal and penal system'.[29] In Box Hill, women began writing children's books as a first step towards building the new society; and suburban groups in Waverley, Burwood and Cheltenham continued the tradition of occupying the public bar of the local pub. In mid-1972, a women's centre was opened in Melbourne at 16 Little LaTrobe Street to co-ordinate both the proliferating campaigns and a range of do-it-yourself courses, including self-defence and 'how to wire fuses and 3 point plugs'.

Preparations began for the next equal pay case. In October 1972, Sylvie Shaw, on behalf of the Women's Liberation movement, joined representatives of the long-established Union of Australian Women and the National Council of Women in making submissions to the Arbitration Commission National Wage case to secure recognition for 'equal pay for work of equal value'. The submission referred to Australia's international obligations, invoking the principle of non-discrimination as enunciated by the United Nations Declaration of Human Rights, the General Assembly's Declaration on the Elimination of Discrimination Against Women in 1967 and the International Labor Office's Convention 100 concerning 'equal remuneration for work of equal value'. The court in Little Bourke Street was 'filled to capacity with women',[30] who also turned out in large numbers in Sydney, on 15 December, to hear the successful outcome. The election earlier that month of a Labor government (after the party had spent twenty-three years in opposition)—which intervened in support of equal pay, with Mary Gaudron arguing the case—was itself taken to be a sign of the impact of the women's movement in setting a new political agenda.

Members of the new movement gave inordinate amounts of time to political activity, to research and organisation, to writing and collating newsletters, to speaking at public meetings. Looking back at the diversity and creativity of political action, one is astonished at women's energy and élan. There were ongoing protests about the refusal of hotels to serve women in public bars, and in Melbourne a demonstration was held against Christmas as simply an occasion for the intensification of women's exploitation: 'there is nothing joyful about it but damn hard work and exhaustion . . . It means stuffing the turkey and "getting stuffed"'.[31] Women from the suburbs took to the streets dressed in black, overburdened with shopping, pushing prams containing cash registers to signify that it was only capitalists who benefited from the ritual of Christmas Day. In Sydney, the Bread and Roses group organised a public meeting in 1971 to discuss Mothers' Day, calling for 'Crèches not Chrysanthemums'.

Another popular target for activists was beauty contests, competitions that portrayed women as 'sex objects' and paraded them before judges 'like cattle'.[32] In the new sexualised femininity forged in the 1930s and the 1940s, a youthful beauty had become an imperative for all girls and women. In a 1970s leaflet entitled 'The Mask of Beauty' the author, Stannard Una, denounced this tyranny and the fact that 'little girls not only look endlessly at beautiful women, they hear and read about them too'.[33] Television advertising and other media images were identified as major culprits.

A 1971 Monash University leaflet blamed advertisements for the narrow definition of 'women's role'; even worse were the women's pages of newspapers which 'by their very existence discriminate, they are directed to the housewife and her role is mirrored as one of consumer, sex symbol and slave'.[34] That women's pages might speak to women's desires and interests and even afford them pleasure was an idea that could not be entertained by these impatient critics of 'mass media myth'. WAC members attended the Miss Teenage Quest with placards that asked 'What Use is a Beauty Queen?' and answered 'To Decorate the Boss's Office' and 'Good Breeding Stock', 'But Never Given Equality'. Protests against beauty contests extended into high schools and universities, with an intervention organised against Miss Coburg High in 1973.

WAC couched its aims for the most part in the language of 'equality'—economic equality, social equality, equal education—joined by the demand for abortion law reform. It thus represented a continuation of a much older feminist movement, its assumption about the importance of equal access to paid employment stemming from the 1930s, but there was more attention now to the range of barriers to equality at work. Hence the demand for increased child care facilities, an end to the differentiation between boys' and girls' school curricula, the need to encourage girls to undertake apprenticeships in male trades, the establishment of retraining centres for women returning to work after raising children, the provision of paid maternity leave and part-time work.

Femininity itself was identified as a major obstacle to equality at work, in particular women's adherence to 'the wife-mother role'. In her paper on 'Women in the Workforce', Coonie Sandford had stated that women must 'attack the wife-mother role, because it is the role which is the main oppressor of women, both in the public economy and at home'.[35] Femininity and the wife-mother role were the product of the pernicious processes of 'conditioning'. 'Is this conditioning the fundamental cause of the main problems confronting women in the workforce?' asked a publicity leaflet for a national Women's Liberation conference on women at work in Melbourne in 1971. Women's Liberation routinely denounced femininity in all its manifestations, especially women's use in advertising as 'sex symbols', their treatment as 'sex objects' and their position as stay-at-home mothers. They demanded a change of attitudes as well as new state services—access to birth control, abortion and child care—so that women could slough off the burden of the feminine role. Everywhere women expressed a deep yearning 'to develop their full potential'. Social expectations cramped and stifled women. So women declared war on society.

The condition of liberation to which women aspired was often imagined as an emulation of the existential freedom thought to be enjoyed by men. In this sense, Women's Liberation represented a radical extension of the assimilationist project of earlier feminisms. The 'liberation of women', wrote 'Joan' in the Melbourne *Women's Liberation Newsletter*, 'meant the acceptance of women by society . . . on the same basis as men. In other words as people'. To be fully human was to be like a man. Others, like the author of the Adelaide Women's Liberation Manifesto, argued that real individuality would only be possible if men as well as women were liberated from their prescribed roles:

> Accordingly, the freeing of woman from her subservient role, the assertion of her freedom as an individual, must *simultaneously* involve an attack on the male *role*. Men must have demonstrated to them the destruction of human relations that they perpetuate in clinging to their dominance as males.[36]

But would women assert their freedom?

THE GREAT AWAKENING

Germaine Greer's *The Female Eunuch*, published in England in 1970, and a best-seller in Australia following her publicity tour in 1972, incited women—in terms that echoed Simone de Beauvoir's call in *The Second Sex* of some twenty years before—to take on the responsibility of their freedom and renounce the complicity of passivity. In contrast to Kate Millett's structuralist account of 'patriarchy', *The Female Eunuch*, like *The Second Sex*, espoused a determinedly individualist credo. Whereas de Beauvoir's title seemed to characterise women as citizens, Greer's saw women as de-sexed, castrated like the black man in Eldridge Cleaver's *Allegory of the Black Eunuch*, which she cites in her chapter on 'The Stereotype'. Greer wanted women to assert their virility.

Although working and writing in England, the formative influence of Australian libertarianism was evident in her insistence that women forgo political agendas in order to concentrate on personal rebellion: 'The first exercise of the free woman is to devise her own mode of revolt, a mode which will refect her own independence and originality'.[37] Invoking the example of Nora in Ibsen's *A Doll's House*, Greer urged women to be courageous:

> The woman who realizes that she is bound by a million Lilliputian threads in an attitude of impotence and hatred masquerading as tranquillity and love has no option but to run away, if she is not to be corrupted and extinguished utterly. Liberty is terrifying but it is also exhilarating. Life is not easier or more pleasant for the Noras who have set off on their journey to awareness, but it is more interesting, nobler even.[38]

In its account of women's oppression, *The Female Eunuch* introduced its many readers to a new vocabulary that would become standard for Women's Liberation for the next twenty years or more.

There they learnt that girls were 'conditioned' from a young age to accept the precepts of femininity, that they must adhere to the 'stereotype' of the Eternal Feminine, that women were treated as 'sex objects' for men's delectation and abuse, that men's dominance was maintained by the imposition of 'sex roles' and that society functioned because of women's unremitting self-sacrifice. Greer was expressly suspicious of political platforms ('It is not a question of telling women what to do next')[39] and although her readers built on her analysis to decide appropriate political action—protesting against beauty contests and the depiction of women as 'sex objects' in advertising, for example —they took to heart her insistence that first and foremost women must exercise their will to reassess their own lives.

This theme was echoed in Janey Stone's article in the first edition of *Vashti's Voice* in July 1972: 'Only in a society where no roles are prescribed and any individual is free to develop full potential, can one begin to be liberated'. She identified three stages in Women's Liberation activism: first, the development of an analysis of women's oppression; second, '[overcoming] on a personal level some of the handicaps that are the result of our conditioning . . . the passivity, the feelings of inferiority and inadequacy'; third, 'action on specific issues'. Liberation involved 'self-activity' said Stone, echoing Greer:

> Liberation is not something that can be given to you. You must be actively involved in determining what liberation is for you, in the struggle to control your own life, in the struggle for your liberation.[40]

Change began with oneself. Hundreds of women took the advice and walked out on their marriages, changed their names, formed new households and began their lives anew. To the north east of Melbourne, the Eltham group was pleased to report that they were able to offer support to a number of local 'Noras': 'three have left their husbands, two are moving into communal situations'. Social change seemed elusive, 'but it is good to see changes in our own lives and the socialisation of our children'.[41]

To ease the passage of women wanting to leave the marital home but with nowhere to go, 'half-way houses' or 'women's shelters' were set up by women who sometimes volunteered their own houses for the cause. Such women's refuges were one of the characteristic forms of community action taken by Women's Liberationists during the early 1970s, initially staffed and wholly supported by women's unpaid labour and fund-raising. In Sydney, Elsie Women's Refuge was set up in November 1973 'for women and children who have nowhere to sleep' by a collective including Anne Summers, Margaret Power, Carol Baker and Jennifer Dakers. By January the following year, Elsie Women's Refuge was advertised more specifically for any woman 'needing to escape a violent home, needing advice and friends when faced with the legal, welfare, health system'.[42]

In Perth, the Nardine refuge was set up by volunteers from the Women's Centre Action Group, including Michel Kosky, Diane Fruin and Penny Fogarty, providing resources and organising a 24-hour roster. The refuge was envisaged as for 'women who need to get out of their marriage "homes", but have nowhere to take the kids while they look for their own place, and existing facilities in Perth cannot cope with their needs'.[43] Initially, letters were sent to 'wealthy individuals in the community asking for donations or household goods'. Once established, the volunteers at 'Nardine' provided the women seeking help not just with a temporary home, but also with advice about claiming maintenance, applications for public housing and counselling regarding domestic violence.

By 1974, most refuges were about to apply for government funding; but regardless of greater support, they were never able to accommodate all the women who needed their help. Perth feminists also established a Women's Health and Community Centre, envisaged as providing women with a combination of child care, health services, information and general support:

> We need a place where women can come, safe from being put down or humiliated or made into objects or treated as defective stereotypes. We are not bodies, but people encased in bodies, and doctors don't understand this and won't while they continue to be mainly men (or acting in a male frame of reference).[44]

The challenge was to invent new frames of reference, new forms of knowledge, new modes of living.

10
LIBERATION ON OUR OWN TERMS

REVOLUTION NOT REFORM

In a reflection on the goals of the Women's Liberation movement in August 1973, 'Ky' cautioned against reformist action becoming an end in itself and suggested that activists should always ask themselves: 'what does our action contribute to a feminist revolution?'.[1] The conception of social change that animated Women's Liberation in the early 1970s was ambitious. No longer interested in enjoying the fruits of 'full citizenship'—the cherished goal of interwar feminists—Women's Liberationists hungered for 'revolution', for the overthrow of existing social and political structures. They aimed at social and personal transformation, not the acquisition of political power. There was no desire to enter parliament, and little interest in conventional politics and the agendas of the major parties. In an article on the necessary relationship of feminism to socialism, 'Kathy' observed that with the removal of discrimination and equality in employment there would be more women in leading positions in business and government. 'Is this what we are looking for?' she asked. 'Have women who have "made it" helped the status of women?'[2]

Women's Liberation espoused 'revolution' in at least two senses. On the one hand the movement called for an end to the inequalities of capitalism, on the other for the overthrow of 'patriarchy', but the transformations had to begin with oneself. 'We are the revolution now.' Women's Liberationists often joined their critique of the seductions of reform to an espousal of separatism in one form or another.

In an influential article called 'How Can We Get What We Want', Sue Bellamy, a post-graduate student in Sydney, warned of the huge dangers of placing 'our hopes in parliamentary procedure and legislative change'. Rather, women had to work within their own 'newly created frameworks', explore our own consciousness and develop a 'New ARTICULATENESS'.

> We have to create our own channels, our own forms, set up our own groups (everything from general discussion groups to self-management for 'prostitutes')—and begin at last to explore our own consciousness . . . Think for yourself! Self management must begin with the individual before self management can begin among women in society . . .
> This is the beginning of a new school of experience—Liberation On Our Own Terms . . . Set yourself the goal of liberation, and don't stop—don't stop to play parliamentary games to the point where you lose sight of why you began the fight.[3]

University students were keen on revolution. Reflecting on the development of Women's Liberation in Canberra, Susan Eade (Magarey), then a married post-graduate student at the Australian National University (and later to become founding editor of *Australian Feminist Studies*), pointed to the similarities between Women's Liberation and other women's activism, but also to the important differences:

> . . . unlike earlier traditional women's groups or new groups formed within the women's movement, the Women's Liberation Group saw all its efforts as directed ultimately towards the total transformation of the whole society, indeed of all societies. Women's Liberation meant commitment to social revolution.[4]

What was revolutionary was the attack on sex roles, and more radically, the family. Some Australian activists read and quoted the early onslaught on the 'nuclear family' by American history student, Linda Gordon, first printed in *US Women: A Journal of Liberation* in Fall 1969, in which she said that abolishing the family was the key to achieving total social transformation. Thus at the 1971 Sydney conference—also attended by women from Melbourne and Adelaide—'Juanita' declared:

> Any movement seeking a change in women's roles attacks the family structure upon which capitalism rests and poses demands which capitalism cannot meet . . . The struggle for Women's Liberation is revolutionary because of this.[5]

In their commitment to 'revolution', Women's Liberationists brought together a Marxist political analysis and a counter-cultural faith in the possibility of personal renewal. The goal of revolution was welcomed by idealistic students, but also by veterans of the Communist party, such as Judy Gillett, Mavis Robertson, Joyce Stevens, Eileen Capochi, Zelda D'Aprano and a younger comrade, Carmel Shute, who eagerly embraced the new women's revolution. But Marxist analysis was no longer enough; to understand and address the specificities of women's condition (and conditioning) the independent insights of feminist theory were necessary.

Writers such as Millett and Greer, together with Eva Figes in *Patriarchal Attitudes*, Shulamith Firestone in *The Dialectic of Sex*, Juliet Mitchell in *Woman's Estate*, the contributors to the anthology *Sisterhood is Powerful* and the articles by Mainardi, Koedt and Gordon provided feminists with an analytical language which bound the women's movement together, across Australia and around the world. Their ideas were discussed, replicated and circulated by local interpreters in numerous newsletters and journals such as *Mejane*, *Vashti's Voice*, *Scarlet Woman* and *Refractory Girl*.

New recruits to the movement were urged to read, analyse, reflect, an injunction that lay the basis for the first courses in Women's Studies. The first meeting house of Women's Liberation in Perth, at 97 Rokeby Road, Subiaco, was commended in March 1973 for its 'informal atmosphere', but also for 'our own library [with] books and magazines for sale' including *The Female Eunuch* and *Sexual Politics*. It was 'an excellent venue for stimulating discussions'.[6] Students were informed that a university branch of Women's Liberation had also been formed, with Pat Giles and Elke Bettenay listed as contacts. Meanwhile, Cheryl Meinck, who edited a special Women's Liberation edition of the university magazine *Pelican* which contained a centrefold of four naked men and an article on 'Kunt power', was being prosecuted for obscenity.

The new discourse on 'sex roles' and 'conditioning' became the crucial medium of that new feminist political form, the consciousness raising (CR) group, the initiation ground for fresh recruits. From the early 1970s, these groups sprang into existence all over the country, each a small unit in a grand movement. For many women these gatherings were enormously productive, providing relief from feelings of personal failure, isolation and frustration. Problems with lovers, husbands and children, conflict over housework, money and sex were not theirs to bear alone. A new interpretative framework enabled women to make sense of their lives in terms that weren't demeaning. In the Melbourne suburb of Waverley 'they questioned [their] conditioning and shared experiences, thus furthering [their] understanding of women in society'.[7]

Women found a voice, and in the intensity of the reciprocal exchanges a basis was laid for friendships which often lasted a lifetime. Women who had spent most of their lives courting the admiration of men—whether at universities, at work or in their families—shared a new sense of solidarity with their sex. They discovered the pleasures of women's company. The joys of 'sisterhood' dominated many accounts of the fondly remembered 'Sorrento weekend' in November 1972, when Victorian groups met together on the Mornington Peninsula: 'To many of us it was a unique experience, the feeling of friendship, companionship, love, sisterhood amongst women was something we had never known before'.[8] And Sylvie Shaw in the Melbourne *Women's Liberation Newsletter* summed up the year with a tribute to 'sisterhood': 'what came out of 1972 was not the action or demonstrations . . . it was the feeling of being part of a growing awareness, of a developing movement and of knowing the real significance of sisterhood'.[9]

There were also numerous tensions, however, as women attempted to discuss painful private experiences with often judgmental 'sisters' who had to be cautioned against impatience: 'for one night try and put yourself in the position of someone without six months consciousness raising experience'.[10] At the end of 1972, it was reported from Glenroy in Melbourne that there was 'a lack of response to CR by some members' and 'clashing of personalities and alienation between some of the members'.[11] In the absence of formal organisation and procedure, domination, intimidation and the silencing of the less confident could occur unimpeded. Jo Freeman's article on 'The Tyranny of Structurelessness', first published in the United States in 1970 and widely photocopied thereafter, found a receptive audience.

Old hands were continually urged to be understanding towards newcomers: 'there is a tendency to be intolerant and inconsiderate to new members . . . we tend to forget how we thought and reacted before we knew about CR. The how-can-anybody-possibly-not-see-what-to-us-is-so-obvious attitude'.[12] There were concerns about the development of a 'hierarchy of consciousness'. 'We talk about "raising" consciousness as if it's climbing a ladder', wrote 'Marie' (Rowan) in the *Women's Liberation Newsletter*, 'with the notions of status and superiority in that sort of imagery. Uneasily we have tried to find new words to express the idea—stages, levels, degrees'.[13]

Lesbian women critiqued the heterosexism that informed the

functioning of CR groups, the assumption that lovers were men and thus absent from these women-only discussions. How might they discuss their sexual relationships when their female lovers were part of the group? CR groups also tended to assume that men were the enemy, an odd assumption to women for whom the racism of other women was a major problem and for the increasing number who felt that their motherhood was unacceptable. CR groups bound women together, but they also exposed the limits of shared experiences and values. Latent antagonisms or resentments could smoulder unspoken and unresolved.

CR groups were in any case considered not an end in themselves, but one stage on the path to liberation. Analysis was necessary to self-transformation, but it was also meant to prepare the way for action and outreach. Cheryl Meinck described this process in Perth:

> Women's Lib. in Perth began like that—exploded into life as we discovered our common oppression. By exchanging experiences, we gained a feeling of confidence, of solidarity and a rising anger at the roles we were being forced to play. We had meetings, guerilla theatre and group action—all concerned with two vital aspects of change
>
> (I) educating ourselves
> (II) educating others (especially those with the power to change our situation).[14]

Reading groups were important for education, but they could also breed restlessness. In Melbourne some anarchist women formed WIZ, because of frustration at 'lack of direct confrontation activity with the mass of women'. They determined to 'go out into the the suburbs east and west [to] communicate with women' and to this end they distributed 750 Women's Liberation manifestos in the Malvern shopping area and 'zapped' the bookstores that sold pornographic literature.[15] They remonstrated with chemists, assumed to be Catholic, who refused to stock contraceptives and demonstrated at Maxwell's electrical stores to draw attention to their sexist advertising. When, on another occasion, books in city bookshops were plastered with stickers saying 'this oppresses women', the *Sun* newspaper reported that 'the women libbers have turned militant' and 'the sex war has come to Melbourne'.[16]

Armed with the new truths about 'conditioning' and 'sex roles', Women's Liberationists went like missionaries to convert the unliberated masses in the suburbs. In late 1973, three members of the Watsonia CR group and two members of the South Yarra group went to speak to a Watsonia Mothers' Club meeting, attended by about forty women and four men. Although their talk presented 'the least controversial of feminist ideals', it provoked much indignation and hostility among their women listeners, who took the criticism of the system as 'personal insults' and insisted that 'they loved being wives and mothers, that they never discriminated between their male and female children, that they never took barbiturates, that they could go out to work if they wanted to . . . The men, of course, were disgusting'. Despite their initially unpromising reception, the visitors were confident in the end that they had struck a chord and were pleased that some of the women came to speak to them at the end of the meeting, 'mostly . . . to express support'. 'It was a very valuable experience', they concluded, 'to feel the common bond of feminism with "unliberated" women'.[17]

As debate within the women's movement proliferated so did disagreements, especially concerning the relative importance of class and gender and sexuality in determining women's oppression. There was fierce political debate about whether men or capitalists were the real enemy, one contributor suggesting helpfully that it would be better to stick to the term 'oppressor', because 'enemy' implied 'destruction and that is not our object in regard to the male sex'. Generally it was agreed that capitalism and patriarchy created a 'double oppression' for women, both locking them into 'woman's role'.[18] Women were conceptualised as consumers *and* sex symbols, unpaid workers *and* sex objects. Arguments about these issues dominated the national women's conference on socialism and feminism in Melbourne in October 1974, attended by over 600 women, and the early confidence in the natural unity of women gave way to anxiety about the destructive and 'counterrevolutionary' effects of ideological division.

Ideological orientation was as often as not signified sartorially and was thus all the more confronting. There was a tension between Women's Liberation's stated aim to create a mass women's movement and the rapid consolidation of a particular style, look and self-presentation, which served to emphasise the difference between themselves and 'unliberated' women, creating in the view of one Melbourne eastern suburbs group, an 'us and them' attitude which left suburban women feeling threatened.[19]

At the end of 1974, one angry contributor to the Melbourne *Women's Liberation Newsletter* denounced at length the hypocrisy and 'idealistic shit' of the movement's cant about sisterhood. T. Kristin had gone along to the Women's Liberation centre full of expectation, but immediately felt unwelcome:

> Many of my sisters sized me up at a glance, labelled me 'MIDDLE-CLASS' and deposited me in the appropriate pigeon hole. I've learned to accept my lesbian sisters firstly as other women, and not to dare to define their sexuality for them, or to feel threatened by it, yet I feel bitterly resentful when the depth of my feminist conviction is questioned because I can love a man. I'll never forget the humiliation I felt when I took my two kids to the centre, because I had nobody to leave them with, and two of my sisters sat only inches away from me discussing how much they disliked kids.

Kristin was not about to forfeit her right to a place in the women's movement, however, and feminism had given her the strength to assert herself:

> I AM A FEMINIST . . . IT IS MY CENTRE AND MY MOVEMENT . . . never again will my father, brother, husband, son, lover, boss, or any other man make me feel inadequate or ashamed because I don't live, look, feel or think the way they would like me to. NEITHER WILL MY SISTERS.

A movement that had been born in the desire to be free from the imposition of social roles had quickly developed its own set of prescriptions. But Kristin would have none of it:

> When any of you can show me where it is written down in black and white that I have to live on the dole in Brunswick with a commune of socialist radical lesbians who've had three abortions apiece in order to be a true feminist, then I'll get out of women's liberation. Till then we're going to have to share it.[20]

Marie, from Bayswater, was more easily put off. She wrote of going to the Women's Liberation centre and being 'confronted with a large group of women whose appearance was so new to me'; she felt 'conspicuous' and that she had nothing in common with the women there because of the 'dress and general appearance of a lot of the women'.[21]

NOT A DIRTY WORD: RECLAIMING REFORM

Feminists identifiably middle class, professional and respectable felt more comfortable in the Women's Electoral Lobby, formed in Melbourne early in 1972. The proposal to concentrate feminist energies into a lobbying group came from Beatrice Faust, well educated, libertarian in sympathies and experienced in political activism, notably in campaigns for abortion law reform and the liberalisation of censorship. Faust had read an article in the United States feminist magazine called *Ms*, (the new form of address recommended for women because it did not distinguish the married from the unmarried). The American report told of a feminist survey of presidential candidates carried out to ascertain their views on women's issues. Unaware that this mode of doing politics had been standard for Australian feminists since the turn of the century, Faust set about to persuade a hand-picked group of women to support this apparently novel approach. She approached 'women who knew the system, wanted change, but did not object to structure'. 'We must confine ourselves to issues that can be solved by legislation', Faust insisted, and lobby the relevant politicians.[22]

From the beginning, journalists such as Sally White at the *Age* were crucial in winning publicity for the new organisation's campaigns which focussed for the most part on access to work, government provision of child care and reproductive freedom. The mainstream media seemed to embrace WEL with relief, reassured that some feminists, at least, looked familiar and sounded reasonable, not posing a threat to the family or men's sexual prerogatives. Sally White attributed WEL's extensive media coverage, which reached into the rural press as well as the metropolitan papers, to WEL's more polite and considerate approach:

> The response has proved that Women's Lib is not a dirty word to the media, if they are approached in the correct way. Overpushing and non-understanding of the media is the surest way to antagonise people, who, after all, haven't the time to waste on useless, thoughtlessly presented material.[23]

Faust was similarly dismissive of Women's Liberation's political capacity: 'they were hopeless. They spent their time hating men'.[24] Yet it seems clear that it was the very disorder and anxiety provoked by Women's Liberation that created the space for WEL to flourish and explains the friendly response of the press. There were 164 articles on WEL in Australian newspapers in 1972, only three of them unfavourable.

WEL's greatest triumph was its effective intervention in the 1972 federal election in December, when members interviewed candidates of all parties on a number of specific issues relating to women and had the results published in a special lift-out section of the *Age*. A number of politicians remained defiant in their refusal to please, but most quickly read the writing in the increasingly supportive press. Labor men (Bill Hayden, Gough Whitlam) generally scored highest, while Liberal Prime Minister William McMahon scored a dismal one point out of a possible forty.

WEL's intervention in the political process was effective in reinstating women as an electoral force, a political bloc united in their demands, and the fact that WEL's campaign in 1972 coincided with the first defeat of the Liberal party in twenty-three years made it appear even more powerful. The pent-up desires of women and Labor to embark on a program of reform were mutually reinforcing, and once in federal government the Labor party proceeded to enact measures to make the aspiring public woman's path easier. In the ensuing years, feminism became more closely identified with Labor and Labor with feminism than had ever been the case—the few Liberal feminists, such as Eve Mahlab, being the exceptions who proved the rule.

WEL and Women's Liberation worked together on a number of projects during the early 1970s, forging an uneasy alliance in which Women's Liberationists barely concealed their scorn with WEL's desire to engage in conventional politics, while members of WEL professed impatience with the radicals' preoccupation with theory and self-knowledge. At a meeting of the ACT branch of WEL in March 1973, there was a frank exchange of views on what WEL and Women's Liberation thought of each other: 'This brought out a variety of attitudes and hostilities which could be summed up by saying that some WEL members felt they were being patronised by WL and some WL members felt that WEL needed more consciousness raising'.[25]

In Sydney, Adelaide and Hobart the revolutionary refusal of reform proved, for a time, relatively stronger; the lofty attitude of the intellectuals in the Hobart Women's Action Group in particular provoked resentment among their reform-oriented sisters. But in all cities, many women were members of both WEL and Women's Liberation, and the two strands of the women's movement often worked together pursuing common goals such as equal pay and equal rights in education and employment—as when they combined in Melbourne to pressure the Tramways' Union to admit women as tram drivers, and when they demanded that women be admitted to the Administrative Division of the Victorian public service.

Reformists and revolutionaries also came together on International Women's Day (IWD), reinvigorating the march that commemorated the action of the sweated workers who took to the streets in New York in 1908. In 1973, the Melbourne IWD Committee borrowed money to bring an Aboriginal woman speaker, Pat Miller (O'Shane), from Sydney to address the rally. For Women's Liberation, the IWD march provided a real opportunity to build up a 'significant force fighting for women's rights', but these warriors also worried that traditional demands for 'equality' could be too easily accommodated into patriarchal society, as had happened in the USSR.

Some respectable members of WEL, on the other hand, found their initiation into the politics of disruption exhilarating, as Joyce Nicholson, a middle class mother of four, recalled. First there had been the nervousness that accompanied her first demonstration at the public service exams:

> Nor will I forget my exhilaration and amazement at my first International Women's Day march in March 1973, when WEL and the women's movement generally was at its height. There was a big participation. This was an occasion when WL took the lead and young, forceful women, with microphones, told us what to do. 'Sit' they shouted, and we sat. 'March' they said, and we marched. 'What do we want?' they shouted, and 'What do we want?' we shouted in unison. 'Equality'. 'When do we want it?' 'Now'. Everything they chanted we chanted after them. As we surged up Bourke Street, we passed the theatre where *Alvin Purple*, a sexist film was showing. 'Fuck Alvin Purple', they shouted. 'Fuck Alvin Purple', I shouted, never having used the word before . . .[26]

Involvement in WEL was personally liberating for middle class women like Joyce Nicholson, but it was also a lot of hard work, especially for those like Katy Richmond, Winsome McCaughey and Julie Dahlitz in Melbourne and Edna Ryan, Helen Coonan, Jocelyn Scutt and Eva Cox in Sydney, who researched and drafted submissions and policy on everything ranging from child care, to equal pay, to divorce, to rape. One of WEL's most significant achievements in these years was Edna Ryan's successful submission to the Arbitration Commission in 1974 for an adult minimum wage, which finally put paid to the concept of the (male) family wage.

WEL members were influential in shaping the new Family Law Act in 1975 (which instituted fault-free divorce) and in having the value of women's domestic work taken into account in the distribution of assets on the breakup of marriage. In Sydney, the Rape Law Reform Action Group, including Di Graham and Kerry Heubel, produced a Draft Bill on Rape and Other Sexual Offences, which was crucial in bringing about the criminalising of rape in marriage in that State in 1981. Other States followed the New South Wales example in defining 'lack of consent' in terms of the WEL Draft Bill, 'a first', according to Jocelyn Scutt, 'for Australia and the common law world'.[27] The activism of WEL and other women's groups around issues of domestic violence was responsible for bringing about legislation providing for 'non-molestation', 'intervention' or 'family violence' orders to prohibit violent husbands from inflicting violence against family members or approaching them at home or work; although the effectiveness of the laws—or at least their implementation—has been questioned, as women continue to be assaulted or killed in their homes or when trying to leave them.

WEL's professionalism made it an extremely effective political organisation operating in the long-established feminist tradition of non-party politics; appropriately when the Australian Federation of Women Voters wound up in 1982, WEL took over its status as Australian affiliate with the International Alliance of Women. Like its predecessors, it acquired an image of moderation and respectability (and regularly held discussions on what made an effective lobby group). WEL was image-conscious, and its nervousness about lesbianism was one source of tension with Women's Liberation groups in the early days of their relationship. The rights of lesbians were not, initially, on the WEL agenda and lesbian women had to spend much time and energy asking their straight sisters to deal with their 'heterosexual chauvinism'.[28]

SEXUAL POLITICS

'I do enjoy a good fuck', wrote Kate in the Melbourne *Women's Liberation Newsletter* in September 1973. 'Living at home I really had been some sort of eunuch. Inside sexual urges dominated me as they had been suppressed for so long . . . When I left I let go with a big bang . . . I chose my partners . . . I followed my feelings and fucked when I wanted to and let myself enjoy it.' Kate's narrative of her sexual life had distinct echoes of Greer's treatment of sexuality in *The Female Eunuch*, including her use of the same metaphor of castration. An assertive attitude towards sexual relations had been commended by Greer as fundamental to women's liberation. Passivity was death. Kate's story of sexual liberation depended on Greer's, but it also moved beyond it:

> I met a girl. She is gay. All her friends are gay. I had been frightened to meet a gay person, a lesbian face to face . . . They were there, laughing, alive . . . To me the living essence of all that I had read and really dug in Women's Liberation literature . . . that it's about changing human relationships, learning to love ourselves and other women. This must be where a revolution begins.[29]

Kate was one of thousands of women who came to love other women in the context of Women's Liberation. Tasmanian feminist Shirley Castley has recalled that her involvement in three different types of feminist project (the intellectual, the bureaucratic and the international) was inextricably related to her falling in love with three different women: 'You meet someone and fall in love with them and you spark off each other and you do really interesting, new, exciting, fantastic and satisfying things'.[30]

Lesbianism, unlike male homosexuality, was not illegal, but that didn't mean that lesbian women were free from social discrimination. On the contrary, lesbianism was heavily stigmatised and many women feared declaring themselves because of the likely consequences at home, in the street and in the workplace. Lesbian women were deprived of basic civil liberties and denied the daily freedoms—to kiss and cuddle one's lover in public, for example—taken for granted by other women. More serious was the likelihood of losing one's job or one's children in a custody dispute. The worst oppression, however, according to a paper by Jocelyn Clarke and Laurie Bebbington presented at the national women's conference on feminism and socialism attended by over 600 women in October 1974, was the 'internal violence' created by secrecy.[31] Social attitudes needed to be challenged and discrimination on the grounds of sexual orientation declared illegal. But first lesbians had to convince heterosexual feminists to confront their own prejudices and privilege, and initially there was considerable reluctance.

The combination of the new feminist assumption that sexual pleasure was women's right—one of the last rights to be claimed by feminists in Australia—with the critique of sex roles, provided a conducive environment for the expression and exploration of lesbian desire. The critique of femininity and the family that characterised Women's Liberation owed much to lesbian women, who saw clearly the relationship between dichotomous 'sex roles' and 'compulsory heterosexuality', as the American poet Adrienne Rich would call that dominant institution. In any case, what could be more appropriate to feminism than the (emotional, social, physical) love of women. As Beverley Kingston put it in an article in 1974, the women's movement in its critique of marriage and motherhood offered lesbians new 'validity', but even as she warned against the imposition of a new orthodoxy ('The range of choices . . . will not be expanded by utterly destroying heterosexual monogamy as one of them'),[32] lesbianism began to be represented by some as correct political practice, as well as a legitimate expression of sexual desire.

'Radicalesbians' joined the proliferating women's groups and heterosexual women found themselves increasingly accountable for the seeming perversity of their desire. In Melbourne, the group initiated by Laurie Bebbington, Sue Jackson, Jocelyn Clarke and Di Otto created an important space for lesbians in Women's Liberation, but as elsewhere the increasing visibility of lesbians did not go uncontested. Many self-identified 'suburban' women, as we have noted, wrote of feeling uncomfortable with women who dressed so differently. Tensions escalated when Zelda D'Aprano expressed her misgivings about the increasing presence of lesbians in the women's centre, who 'seemed to find it necessary to huddle together in couple situations while they almost constantly displayed their affections towards their partners'. Moreover, it was perplexing that 'some of the lesbian women who are feminists found it necessary to wear men's clothing'. Zelda worried that the numbers of lesbians in Women's Liberation would come as a great shock to ordinary women 'and more than likely turn them away from the movement'.[33]

Her remarks prompted heated replies; a long debate ensued with participants explaining that lesbianism meant putting women first, but also urging feminists to accept their differences while remembering they shared a common political project. The issue of dress and gendered style again pointed to the dilemmas of feminist politics in a masculinist society. Refusing to dress like a woman, 'Chev' insisted, was not a matter of copying men, but a resistance to 'sex-stereotyped roles' and a 'challenge to sexual objectification'. Once again feminists were caught in the classic paradox: refusing femininity they perforce emulated the masculine. Freedom and equality were only imaginable in terms of the very structures of sexual difference that oppressed them.

One of the most trenchant attacks on homophobia in the women's movement was penned by the Hobart Women's Action Group, whose personal experience of ostracism (being told as lesbians to remain invisible so as not to alienate other women, being told they were a media problem) was interpreted as having more general theoretical significance for feminism. In a paper to the Mt Beauty conference in 1973, (which was reprinted in *Refractory Girl*), the Group castigated Women's Liberation for its sexist attitudes and discriminatory structures.

In a pioneering discussion of the implications of 'difference' in the women's movement, the authors argued that consciousness raising and sisterhood were 'heterosexually based institutions' that refused to acknowledge lesbian difference. The hope that lesbianism might disappear into an inclusive bisexuality was seen as a typical Australian response to minorities, 'a happy society envisaged as one in which everyone will eventually behave in the same way'. For all its talk of revolution, they charged, Women's Liberation in many ways emulated the assimilationist ideals of the wider society. Differences between women—whether deriving from class, race, ethnicity or sexuality—were denied or wished away, usually theorised as extra degrees of oppression, rather than as different kinds.[34] A similar critique of the Women and Politics conference in Canberra was made by Jill Matthews, Bertha Harris, Liz Fell and visiting US scholar Charlotte Bunch. The invisibility of the 'lesbian feminist agenda' at the conference was taken to be part of 'a slow movement towards the greater respectability of feminist topics'.[35]

'Radicalesbians' determined to make their difference clear—to their sisters and to the world. Styles of self-presentation—especially the abhorrence of feminine adornment—signified a defiance of sex role stereotypes. Lesbians championed new sorts of relationships, family forms and communal housing arrangements. Many women jettisoned husbands and suburban conventionality to embrace the new life. An account of two Sydney radical feminist households, accompanied by happy photographs and based on interviews, was included in the special 'lesbian issue' of *Refractory Girl* in 1974.

Members of the households declared that they were bonded by a different perspective: 'Wanting to relate to the women's movement in different ways. Most of us are involved in Radicalesbians, not all of us, but I'd say that all of us are involved with the women's movement'.

As lesbians, they thought their considerable 'energies' should be conserved for women: 'I think that because we are lesbians we're directing hardly any of our energies toward men, and we have all our energies for each other'. 'I was living in a household with straight women', averred another, 'and if women are relating to men, they tend to direct their energies more towards the men than to themselves—to the other women'. The fluidity and ebullience of the households were emphasised:

> At Canterbury Castle there are eight of us in the main part of the house. There are two other radical lesbians in the flat attached to the house. We expect another in about two weeks, making eleven of us.
>
> Here at Crystal Street we get so many visitors—there's a continuous exchange of people. We've got people from Melbourne, Adelaide, Newcastle, Canberra, New Zealand. Nine live here permanently, plus three or four permanent visitors whose faces you'd probably see if you came round here any time, plus numerous permanent visitors floating in and out.

Canterbury Castle was set up as a response to the overcrowding at Crystal Street, when one night thirteen people arrived from 'a trek around the bars' and another fifteen turned up from Melbourne: 'There were so many people in this room! Everyone was screaming and shouting—screaming "I want to move out"'.[36]

Such houses and the broader lesbian feminist culture they supported provided important affirmation for lesbian relationships. Radicalesbian conferences were complemented by dances and concerts; politics was permeated with pleasure. Heterosexual women occupied more troubled ground. Although early libertarian texts such as *The Female Eunuch* had exhorted women to 'embrace the penis', and the basic demand for access to abortion and contraception assumed women's interest in straight sex, the dominant message about men's treatment of women as sex objects and the increasing focus on rape as paradigmatic of heterosexuality put heterosexual women on the defensive.

Straight sisters were more comfortable invoking the old feminist right to say 'no' than in affirming their desire to say 'yes', for how could one admit to having pleasure with the oppressor. Indeed, those who presented themselves as sexually liberated might be charged with the worst form of false consciousness, as deluded 'victims of the most successful male chauvinist campaign yet'. Some diehards continued to insist, however, that one could be a 'true feminist' without hating men. Indeed, one could have 'happy relationships with men' while still maintaining a 'determination to fight for Women's Liberation'.[37] But the defensive tone was telling.

In 1977 conflict again erupted in Melbourne on the publication of an article by a seventeen-year-old 'bi-sexual' who compared the difference between lesbian and heterosexual practice as the difference between driving automatic and manual cars. Lesbians found especially offensive the statement that 'automatics (homosexuals) are good for learning on, until confidence is established and a woman can progress onto the real thing (ie heterosexuality)' and denounced the young woman as 'abnormal'. Angry at such 'patriarchal labelling' Bon Hull, a founding member of the Women's Action Committee, announced that she was ceasing her subscription to the *Women's Liberation Newsletter*. 'Our struggle', she wrote 'was about understanding and eliminating sex-roles and the crippling effect labels had on us by a patriarchal society, which has forcibly decided what behaviour patterns are normal and/or abnormal'.[38]

The women's movement was intent on changing ideas about what was normal, especially in sexual relationships. Some had begun to point to the similarities between 'normal' sexual intercourse and rape, which from 1973 increasingly became a focus of feminist political activity. Feminist discourse became more noticeably concerned with the dangers for women of male power, and an initial response was to organise classes for self-defence. In November 1973, the Melbourne *Women's Liberation Newsletter* ran an editorial advising that women needed to 'take positive steps towards protecting themselves' by learning self-defence and attack: 'Although feminist ideology opposes violence and aggression, as long as violence is perpetuated against women . . . *we have no choice* but to learn the skills of the aggressor in our defence'.[39] During the next month a rape crisis group was established by WL in Melbourne and the following year a phone service to provide counselling was set up.

In Sydney, in 1974, International Women's Day focussed on the theme of violence with a forum on 'rape, violence in marriage, violence against children, the law and violence, coping with violence, alternatives to violence'. Throughout Australia women's refuges were joined by rape crisis centres, which from 1975 received government funding. In 1976, Australian Women Against Rape was formed at a national conference of rape crisis centres. Declaring that 'women are men's property and thus incapable of determining their own sexuality',

Women Against Rape demanded the criminalisation of rape in marriage and changes to court procedure so that a victim's previous sexual history would be declared inadmissible evidence.[40] Volunteer workers at rape crisis centres did advocacy work with women victims, accompanying them to the court and hospital, providing information about pregnancy and venereal disease testing. Activists spray-painted porn shops seeking 'to connect the porn industry, violence against women and children with violent societal attitudes to women expressed as RAPE'. From the late 1970s women also took to the streets to 'Reclaim the Night' and outraged the masculine custodians of national memory by trespassing on the sacred sites of Anzac Day rituals to commemorate the women raped in war. Women Against Rape collectives specifically drew attention to the connections between militarism and male violence against women and children, while also pointing to the connections between nationalism and the cult of manhood.

ABORIGINAL AND 'OTHER' WOMEN

On the Australia Day weekend in 1973, Bon Hull took a trip to Palm Island off the Queensland coast to see for herself the plight of Aboriginal people in this 'island paradise turned into a concentration camp'. She described the system of 'detention and punishment' administered by a 'patriarchal white society' which inculcated black women with the skills necessary for domestic servitude: 'There they are taught domestic work which should train them nicely to become more docile and passive . . . They become in reality slaves. For they have no control of any wages they may earn from white employers'.[41]

Bon Hull urged that 'we women' could become 'agitators of our complacent society for the situation of our black sisters' who, because of their colour, 'were trampled on and suffer discriminations that leave us appalled'. To be effective advocates, however, white women would need to 'listen and learn from the courageous ones who refuse any longer to accept their humiliations . . . what they want and demand for their people should have our whole support'. Because the Queensland Aborigines and Torres Strait Islanders Affairs Act denied black Australians the right to control their lives, they should be abolished: the 'women of the world must unite against all oppression'.[42]

Contrary to the critical representations of feminists who came after them, those in the 1970s women's movement agonised about their own privilege and the clear differences in condition between women—the fact that working class, Aboriginal and migrant women were worse off than most—and they were always keen to bring them into their ranks. Women's Liberation in Canberra was especially aware of the middle class nature of the movement: unlike in Adelaide and Sydney, 'the vast majority were young married women, mostly with children and tertiary educated'.[43] They were rebuked at a Sydney conference: 'a lot of you sisters are still buggered up by your class, and while you refuse to recognise this you are buggering up the whole movement'.[44]

Pat Eatock was thus a welcome recruit. Arriving from Sydney, she joined Canberra Women's Liberation and stood in the federal election in 1972 as a black liberation candidate, when she was also involved with the Tent Embassy. Her involvement with Women's Liberation left her, as many Aboriginal women, with feelings of ambivalence, but she vividly recalled the elation of the early days in the Bremer Street Women's House, where she camped for six weeks with her daughter:

> The atmosphere at Bremer Street in 1972 was electric. Hardly an evening passed without some sort of meeting, with twenty to sixty women. Consciousness-raising was a twice weekly event. General meetings, action groups, and the embryonic Women's Electoral Lobby had a weekly time and space. Days were filled with the comings and goings of newsletter production, the preparation of leaflets, classes in screen printing, the establishment of the feminist library, or just dropping in.
>
> I was an active participant. Not only by choice, but also because I couldn't go to bed until the meetings ended.[45]

The inconvenience of her homelessness, she thought, might have prompted Canberra feminists to establish a female refuge. In 1973, Eatock addressed the WEL national conference, attended by 350 delegates, on the subject of 'Aboriginal women'. The conference resolved that the social security system should adopt a policy of 'positive discrimination' towards migrant and Aboriginal women, that a fact-finding tour of Aboriginal settlements be conducted, that the notorious Queensland Act be revised, that fringe and city dwelling Aborigines be taken up as an area of WEL action.[46] Canberra WEL tried to make good its failings by widening its membership to include 'unionists, migrants, Aborigines'. In Melbourne, in the same year, Pat Miller (O'Shane) and Cheryl Buchanan were invited to speak to white women's liberation about black women's liberation, and *Vashti's Voice* published Destiny Deacon's poetry.

Being of the left, Women's Liberationists were acutely aware that in a capitalist society some groups of women were more oppressed than others, but it was this way of conceptualising the issue that proved to be a problem. The different experiences of working class, migrant or Aboriginal women were theorised as a matter of double or triple disadvantage, as different degrees of oppression rather than different kinds. So convinced were feminists in their analysis of the sources of women's oppression—sex-roles, conditioning and stereotypes—that it was inconceivable that other factors might be more important to other groups of women: too much work for working class women, cultural and linguistic oppression for migrant women and the loss of land and children for indigenous women. Indeed, as it happened, it was the very 'radicalism' of Women's Liberation in attacking motherhood and the family that made it so inappropriate as a politics for indigenous women, whose families had been systematically smashed for decades. It was earlier forms of maternalist feminism—oriented to affirming the rights of mothers— that had spoken more directly to the specific needs of most Aboriginal women.

The relevance of the feminist politics of Women's Liberation to Aboriginal women was questioned by Pat O'Shane in an important intervention in *Refractory Girl* in 1976, in which she stressed the ways that different historical experiences shaped different priorities. O'Shane asked feminists to reflect on the particularity of their aims:

> So far as the women's movement is concerned it is necessary for women involved to examine carefully whether or not their aims as white women are necessarily those of black women.

The most urgent priority for Aboriginal people—men as well as women—was to address the effects of dispossession and the destruction of Aboriginal communities and culture. Land rights as well as medical, legal and educational services were on top of their political agenda. Her article was accompanied by a photograph showing a demonstration of Aboriginal women and children bearing placards with the messages 'Land = Self-Respect=Justice=Health=the Future=Life!!' and 'You Stole Our: Land. Culture. Self-Respect. Now You Steal Our Kids!!'[47]

O'Shane made two other points about the different political subjectivities of Aboriginal women: first, that they regarded racism as a worse oppression than sexism; and second, that Aboriginal men were not their enemy, that they must fight for their rights in solidarity with their men, not in opposition to them. In any case, Aboriginal women were already active in a wide range of community activities—in visiting prisoners, looking after children, in land rights groups, in working for their people's rights.

In New South Wales, Pearl Gibbs had played a formative role, with Faith Bandler who was of South Sea Islander descent, in establishing the Aboriginal-Australian Fellowship, whose main purpose was to abolish the 'protectionism' of the Aboriginal Welfare Board, of which Gibbs was a member. In Victoria, Margaret Tucker helped establish the United Council of Aboriginal and Islander Women, of which she was president during the 1960s. Pat O'Shane came from Cairns in North Queensland, where Aboriginal women had been active in the local branch of the Union of Australian Women in campaigns for improved housing and education. And in Brisbane, the poet Kath Walker (Oodgeroo Noonuccal) led the campaign for a Yes vote in the 1967 referendum on Aboriginal citizenship. In the 1970s, the Victorian Council of Aboriginal and Islander Women helped to start Aboriginal health services, hostels for girls and legal services. In New South Wales, the Black Women's Action Committee produced the journal *Koori-Binna*, a black Australian news monthly.

Attuned to the importance of class, Marxist feminists regularly berated their more idealistic sisters about the self-delusion in the concept of sisterhood, pointing out in 1977 that 'class and race differences meant that women experienced different forms and degrees of oppression'—but their only conclusion was to reiterate the importance of a class-based analysis.[48] In their ebullient self-confidence, feminists of all varieties failed to grasp that Aboriginal women had their own priorities and traditions of activism. Although feminists were keen to 'reach out' to Aboriginal women, they were slow to comprehend that, for the most part, Aboriginal women couldn't see the point in joining the white women's movement. They were more interested in liberating their own people.

WOMEN'S LIBERATION AS WOMEN'S STUDIES

Whereas members of the Women's Electoral Lobby set their sights on entering political parties, the bureaucracy and parliament, Women's

Liberationists extended their emphasis on analysis, explanation and the generation of new knowledge into the intellectual project that became Women's Studies. Reading lists lengthened and discussion groups became more formalised in new courses established in colleges of advanced education and universities, such as Flinders University in Adelaide, where the first Women's Studies course was begun in 1973. Young women who were often post-graduate students when Women's Liberation swept across the land—Sue Higgins (now Sheridan), Susan Eade (now Magarey), Ann Curthoys, Jill Matthews, Marilyn Lake, Patricia Grimshaw—were among those who pioneered the academic project of researching and teaching about women's lives, pursuing questions about the nature of women's oppression, its social, historical and philosophical bases and the nature of the established knowledges that demeaned or marginalised women. Historian Judith Allen was appointed to the first Chair in Women's Studies, established at Griffith University in Queensland.

Many of the early practitioners of Women's Studies were historians, seeking explanations for women's subordination in the historical processes of industrialisation, the sexual division of labour, the structuring of public life, in ideologies of the family and sexuality. The oppression of women was at first assumed to be an historical question. The first books to emerge from Women's Liberation in Australia were national histories, seeking explanations for Australian women's alleged status as the 'doormats of the Western world' in the peculiar character of our national history, its convict origins and its subsequent fashioning as a 'working man's paradise'. Anne Summers' *Damned Whores and God's Police*, Beverley Kingston's *My Wife, My Daughter and Poor Mary Ann*, Miriam Dixson's *The Real Matilda*, and *Gentle Invaders* by Ann Conlon and Edna Ryan, were all published in 1975. New feminist journals—*Refractory Girl* and *Hecate*—also published feminist research. Academic studies were joined by those produced by contemporary and veteran activists at the Women and Labour Conferences, initiated in 1978, which in their bringing together of academics and labour movement women were distinctive to Australian feminism. The resulting publications, including *Women, Class and History* (1980), edited by Elizabeth Windschuttle and *Worth Her Salt* (1982), edited by Margaret Bevege, Magaret James and Carmel Shute, provided valuable new resources for a burgeoning field of study. They were complemented by literary anthologies such as the *Penguin Anthology of Australian Women's Writing* (1988), edited by the entrepreneurial Dale Spender, which made a wider range of women's writings, past and present, accessible to new audiences.

As the intellectual project of understanding women's oppression led to more direct interrogations of the construction of knowledge and the ways in which meaning is produced, so the work of philosophers such as Moira Gatens and Elisabeth Grosz and the proliferating field of Cultural Studies became more influential among students of what would increasingly be referred to as 'sexual difference'. By the 1980s, Women's Studies courses had been established at most institutions of higher education, providing a new generation of young women with the words and ideas and confidence—the voice—to counter the oppressions they still encountered in their university courses as well as in their daily lives.

11
THE INSTITUTIONALISATION OF FEMINISM

FRENZY IN CANBERRA

Australian feminists have always looked to the state to effect a redistribution of resources between men and women and to provide the security and protection in which women and girls might live in independence and freedom. The state was called on to provide a buffer between tyrannical, too powerful men and defenceless, vulnerable women. During the first two decades of this century, feminists were successful in having a large number of women appointed to a range of 'protective' positions—as police, magistrates, doctors, welfare workers, factory inspectors and gaol wardens. Feminism wrote its agenda into state policy through legislation and the creation of new institutions such as children's courts, women's hospitals and maternal and infant welfare centres. During the middle decades of the century, feminists continued to lobby, with less success, for the appointment of women to government boards, juries, commissions, and State and federal parliaments.

It was in the 1970s and 1980s, however, that the institutionalisation of feminism reached its apotheosis, with whole programs and complex administrative machinery established by governments—federal and State—to promote the status of women, equal opportunity, non-discrimination and finally, affirmative action. In this period we see the emergence of what we might call 'state feminism'.

From the early 1970s, there had been renewed demands for women to be admitted to the higher echelons of the public service, but it was the appointment of one woman in particular, at the very highest level, which symbolised the new era inaugurated by the election in 1972 of the reforming Labor government led by Gough Whitlam. Personally sympathetic to feminist aspirations (he scored well in the Women's Electoral Lobby (WEL) survey), Whitlam consolidated his support in the women's movement, soon after taking office, with three highly symbolic measures: he removed the luxury tax from contraceptives, introduced paid maternity leave for Commonwealth public servants and introduced a supporting mothers' benefit to enable single women to keep their children. His was a permissive vision of equality.

In 1973, in a blaze of publicity, Whitlam appointed Elizabeth Reid as his adviser on women's affairs. Selected from an impressive short list of eighteen applicants, Reid was in many ways an unexpected choice. A philosopher and tutor at the Australian National University, intellectual in disposition, Reid adapted quickly to the challenge of turning theoretical ideas into public policy. Hailed in the media as a 'super girl', she became the prototypical 'femocrat', the term invented for the distinctly Australian type of feminist bureaucrat, a label attached (often with pejorative intent, depending on the user) to the hundreds who entered the federal and State public service in the 1970s as part of the project to translate feminist ideals into government policy.

Their brand of feminism was the liberal version espoused by the Women's Electoral Lobby, with its readily expressed demands for government-subsidised child care, equal employment opportunity, equal access to education, free contraceptives and safe abortion on demand. Whereas many in Women's Liberation were philosophically opposed to any engagement with patriarchal institutions and uninterested in pursuing formal power—seeing traditional politics as part of the problem, rather than the solution—feminists associated with WEL were eager to enter the parties and parliaments.

When, in the process, they forged careers as public servants, as lobbyists, as politicians and later as corporate executives, they confirmed the views of the more suspicious of their sisters, that their feminism was merely a means of self-advancement, equal opportunity the occasion for a breezy opportunism. The dominant politics of the Women's Liberation movement in the 1970s was anarchist, individualist and revolutionary, with many expressing opposition to co-option by the state and disapproval of feminists who bought into masculine perks and the privileges of office in the name of women. Inevitably, as time passed, a number of the most vocal critics of this alleged feminist perfidy themselves embraced the perks of office and the pleasures of power.

Those who entered the institutions and thereby institutionalised feminism argued that this was the logic of their political commitment. They were part of the rush to reform that characterised the early 1970s in Australia. The broader political context, created by proliferating social movements (environmentalism, Gay Liberation, Aboriginal rights) and the timely election of a radical Labor government, were conducive to expectations of radical renewal, as Lyndall Ryan, a femocrat in the 1970s and later founding director of Women's Studies at Flinders University, recalled: 'The years 1973–75 produced an aura of revolutionary government, prepared, even anxious and eager to try new approaches, new ideas and new structures'.[1] Feminists were keen to put their new ideas to government, and indeed to join the government.

Sarah Dowse, who enjoyed a distinguished, if brief, career as a femocrat before resuming her career as a writer, explained feminists' practical options in these terms:

> We have to decide whether we are going to change society or whether we are going to develop small enclaves of alternative ways of living which will eventually self-destruct through depletion of energy. If we want to be in a position to help all women who need to free themselves from domestic tyranny we have to devise strategies for extending services on a scale large enough to have a genuine impact.[2]

Dowse became Head of the Women's Affairs Section of the Department of Prime Minister and Cabinet in 1974, replacing Reid as Prime Minister's Adviser at the end of 1975.

For the term of the Whitlam government, however, Elizabeth Reid was the public face of state feminism and she quickly became a local celebrity, with journalists publishing her views on any subject on which she cared to reflect—marriage, sex, men, love, motherhood, masturbation. As the first such appointment arising from the Women's Liberation movement, Reid was forced to bear the burden of very high expectations and face the hostility that arose from the resentment, disapproval and jealousy of many in the women's movement. Initially, though, she received gratifying support from women at large.

Working in the beginning with just one assistant, Louise Lake, also from the Philosophy department at ANU, she travelled across the country during 1973–74, seeking women's views on what they needed to improve their conditions at home, in education and in employment.

Her high profile made her a focal point of collective anticipation. She later recalled the pressure:

> We talked in factories, in housing centres, on farms, in schools, at women's meetings, in dairies, in gaols, in universities—in short wherever women were. I was deluged with letters invariably beginning: 'thank God at last there is someone to whom I can talk, someone who might listen and understand'. In a short time I was receiving more letters than anyone else in government other than the Prime Minister.[3]

Reid and her staff worked long hours, at the frantic pace of the newly empowered, determined to improve conditions for the mass of women. Their achievements were impressive, establishing as they did the basis of significant feminist programs, securing Commonwealth underwriting of the delivery of a range of new women's services—women's refuges; rape crisis centres and women's health centres; child care; working women's centres; equal opportunity policies in education, training and employment and housing programs. Reid stressed the idea that all areas of government had an impact on women's lives, that all Cabinet submissions should be examined for their effect on women.

Within a couple of years, 'Superfem', as she was dubbed by cartoonist Robyn Coopes in *Refractory Girl*, was joined in the rapidly expanding Commonwealth public service by other feminist university graduates, keen to join this experiment in reform. The new recruits included many of those who had also applied for the adviser's job—Susan Ryan, who would become a Labor Senator and Minister for Education, was appointed to the International Women's Year Secretariat, and Lyndall Ryan joined the Priorities Review Staff and then Women's Affairs, while Daniela Torsh joined the Schools Commission as Executive Officer to the Committee on Social Change and the Education of Girls. Marie Coleman was appointed Chairman of the Social Welfare Commission and later, in 1976, Director of the Office of Child Care. Other feminists went to work in the areas of health, employment, education, social security, the Women's Affairs Section of the Department of Prime Minister and Cabinet and in various Ministerial offices.

A priority area for feminists was child care, for without affordable quality child care, women would not be able to win equality with men in the workforce or public life. Whereas once feminist policy sought to recognise sexual difference—by advocating motherhood endowment, for example—motherhood was now a handicap to be overcome, a hindrance in the way of equality with men. The provision of child care was central to this liberal feminist vision, but its advocates clashed with the supporters of an older style of 'pre-school education', who favoured the idea that young children needed only a few hours kindergarten or pre-school, two to three days a week, a pattern of education that depended on mothers staying at home. Between 1972 and 1975, the two lobbies were locked into an unseemly fight for funding, with feminists initially outmanoeuvred by the more experienced bureaucrats in the Department of Education, so that by mid-1975 the children's services program had committed most of its very substantial funds to pre-schools.

But the government commitment to child care was firmly in place, and under the new Liberal government the balance in spending shifted away from pre-school education. A larger proportion of funds went into recurrent expenditure on child care (salaries, for example) which enabled newly established centres to maintain properly trained staff. At the same time, the types of child care services diversified, with funds allocated to school holiday programs, after-school care, Aboriginal children's services and child care in women's refuges. Between 1973 and 1980, some 30 000 new Commonwealth-subsidised child care places became available. Child care came to be seen by the women's movement as the working woman's basic right, while the rising voice of economic rationalism supported it as the means to move women off welfare benefits.

One of the major and long-lasting achievements of the femocrats was to secure federal funding for the services established voluntarily by the Women's Liberation movement—especially women's refuges, health centres, rape crisis centres and child care. Indeed, Marian Sawer, the leading scholar of women and public policy in Australia, has suggested that in their creative development of policy machinery and government-funded services, unrivalled in any other country, these femocrats effected a 'quiet revolution'.[4] Working from inside the public service, they acted with initiative, speed and flair to wrest money from established budgets for services that had never before existed. For example, the Community Health Program was identified as a source of funding for women's refuges; later their support became institutionalised in the Supported Accommodation Assistance Program, and the number of refuges funded by government increased from twenty-one in 1975, to ninety-six in 1980 and 190 by 1988. Hundreds of women were thereby assisted, as Sarah Dowse had hoped, to escape 'domestic tyranny'.

Community health centres were also started with federal government aid—for example, the Leichhardt Community Women's Health Centre in Sydney opened in 1974 and the Hunter Region Working Women's Centre at Mayfield in 1976. By the end of the decade the Commonwealth government funded six women's health centres across Australia. Gradually State governments assumed responsibility for these services, so that in New South Wales, for example, by the mid-1980s, the government supported nineteen women's health centres, including the Jilmi Aboriginal Women's Health Centre in Nowra.

The feminist funding that really attracted public attention, however, was the $2 million set aside for a grants' program for International Women's Year (IWY) in 1975, the result of Elizabeth Reid convincing the Prime Minister that he should take feminism seriously. '$2 Million for the Sheilas: Surprisingly It's Not a Joke' ran the *Age* headline on 1 January.[5] The allocation of grants was administered by a specially appointed International Women's Year Secretariat advised by a National Advisory Committee, comprising women from within the bureaucracy and outside, representing a range of interests, convened by Reid. The hostility of some sections of the women's movement towards Reid and other feminists who now 'walked the corridors of power', 'playing men's games' was unleashed at a very angry meeting of around 200 women in Balmain Town Hall, in January 1975, protesting at IWY grant decisions.

The critics, including Anne Summers and Mavis Robertson, were outraged that several Women's Liberation projects had been overlooked in favour of non-feminist proposals. Unable to attend the meeting, Reid sent her friend and member of the National Advisory Committee, Shirley Castley. It was an unpleasant experience, as Castley made clear in her report:

> The aggressiveness and hostility which I encountered was fairly vicious and allowed no place for proper dialogue . . . Basically, the meeting was an excuse for them to go to the national press and TV to criticize IWY—the reasons for them wishing to criticize IWY are simply that *they themselves had not been funded*. There was no possibility that their hostility could be deflected into useful debate either at that meeting or, I suspect, at any other time. The women's movement is dead; long live Women![6]

The issue of IWY grants highlighted the contradictions of feminism as a representational politics, with the self-styled leaders of Women's Liberation insisting that femocrats account to them, while femocrats themselves, employed by the government, considered they must serve the much larger constituency of Australian women. Mavis Robertson, for example, argued that funding should go primarily to Women's Liberation groups, because they were the ones committed to change.

Despite the conflict over spending priorities, much was achieved by the IWY program. Seeding and longer term grants made possible many creative, valuable and long-lasting projects, ranging from the Working Women's Centre established by the Australian Council of Salaried and Professional Associations at the behest of Sylvie Shaw, the ABC's 'Coming Out Show' (later, 'Women Out Loud', now closed down), the Schools Commission's report *Girls, Schools and Society*, the history research project directed by Dr Kay Daniels and published as *Women in Australia An Annotated Guide to Records* and the Women's Film Fund. In the public eye, however, IWY came to symbolise feminism as excess, equated with the extravagance attributed to the Whitlam government in general, cited as evidence that taxpayers' funds were being wasted on extremist and/or trivial causes.

Elizabeth Reid's account of the opening of the controversial 'Women and Politics' conference in mid-1975, attended by some 800 women, evokes well the scandal that came to attach to IWY (and the government), as well as the diversity of women involved and the divisions opened up between them. Her description of the reception in Parliament House suggests the transgressiveness of *carnivale*:

> Aboriginal women demonstrated outside, criticising inadequate representation of their concerns in the programme. Labor women stood behind the Prime Minister during his opening speech with placards denouncing the decisions recently taken by him on East Timor. His speech was interrupted when the Aboriginal women proceeded into the hall chanting and singing. Women from the women's movement wearing men's suits [invitations from PM&C had stated appropriate dress was lounge suits] mingled in the audience with farm women, factory workers, church women . . . The statue of King George V in King's Hall was draped with a placard reading 'Women and Revolution, not Women and Bureaucracy' and 'lesbians are lovely' and similar slogans were written in lipstick on the mirrors in the men's toilets. The press, accustomed to sensationalising every possible aspect of my work, and my beliefs, had a heyday.[7]

Under constant attack from within and without the women's movement, Reid was exhausted from over-work. The decision to move her from the Prime Minister's Office into the Department of Prime Minister and Cabinet provided the occasion for her resignation, after which she went to live and work overseas.

In many ways the work of the femocrats represented a continuation of the older non-party tradition of feminist politics, pioneered early in the century, for entrenching feminism in the bureaucracy made it independent of the fate of particular parties. In the 1970s, they developed a distinctive mode of bureaucracy, as proposed by Sarah Dowse in a paper to the Women and Politics conference—the centre–periphery or 'wheel' model, with the hub in the major co-ordinating department and spokes in functional departments, with policy separated from program delivery. Installed in the bureaucratic machinery of government, the programs developed a life of their own, so that the implementation of policy intiatives continued, if in more straitened circumstances, when the Labor government was removed from office in controversial circumstances in 1975. Indeed, because feminist programs had been put in place, many developments reached fruition under the less sympathetic Liberal government, led by Malcolm Fraser, which replaced Labor. Fraser still had to answer to a continuing and outspoken women's movement. One of the crucial preconditions for the exercise of feminist power in political institutions, as Sarah Dowse perceptively noted, was the continuous pressure from an independent women's movement.

Under the leadership of Sarah Dowse in the Women's Affairs Branch of the Department of Prime Minister and Cabinet from December 1975, the 'wheel model' of feminist policy machinery began to be implemented in the federal bureaucracy. An American-born member of Canberra Women's Liberation, a mother of four and (like Reid) separated from her husband, Dowse first worked as a journalist with the Australian Information Service in 1973, before transferring to work with Elizabeth Reid in the Women's Affairs Section, later to become a Branch. Dowse was theoretically informed and politically astute and she persuaded Prime Minister Fraser to support her plan for the establishment of women's policy units across a range of different departments, thereby laying 'the groundwork', according to Lyndall Ryan, 'for the future of feminism in the bureaucracy'.[8]

Fraser wrote to the Ministers for Health, Education, Social Security, Aboriginal Affairs, Immigration and Ethnic Affairs, Environment, Housing and Community Development and to the Attorney-General, asking them to consider establishing women's policy units 'to give proper consideration to the concerns and rights of women in the formulation of policy and the administration of programs'. Most complied, with ten new policy units being established (in addition to the Women's Affairs Branch and the Women's Bureau, which had existed since 1966 in the Department of Employment and Industrial Relations) to initiate reforms and monitor existing departmental programs for their effects on women.

The Equal Employment Opportunity Unit established in the Public Service Board in 1975, headed by inaugural convenor of Canberra WEL Gail Radford, was upgraded to a Bureau in 1978, setting a precedent for similar machinery in State bureaucracies. A Women's Welfare Issues Consultative Committee was established in December 1976 to advise the Social Security Minister. The Fraser government was the first to allocate a portfolio to Women's Affairs, announcing the appointment of a Minister Assisting the Prime Minister in Women's Affairs in June 1976, the first appointment being Tony Street and the next, Ian McPhee.

Developments in Canberra were complemented by activity in the States. Sex-discrimination legislation was passed first in South Australia in 1976 and then in Victoria and New South Wales in 1977, but Canberra remained the major source of funding for feminist initiatives. In 1978, the National Women's Advisory Council was established as a new channel of communication between the wider community of women and the Women's Affairs Branch of the federal government, with the effective and well-liked Beryl Beaurepaire, vice-chairman of the Victorian Liberal party, in the chair and Aboriginal, migrant, rural and trade union women among the members.

Beaurepaire was a staunch feminist and able to use her influence in the Liberal party to ensure the defeat in federal parliament of the Lusher motion, which proposed to cut medical benefits for abortions. Granted a research budget, the National Women's Advisory Council was also able to conduct and sponsor a number of valuable research projects with migrant women and mothers of disabled children, looking at women's economic circumstances and the aged. It also provided ongoing funding to the Working Women's Centre in Melbourne.

With the proliferation of services and programs for women and the implementation of equal opportunity measures in the public service, the ranks of femocrats swelled. In many ways the femocratic project can be seen as a continuation and fruition of the bid by post-suffrage feminists early in the century to create a woman-friendly Commonwealth, establishing state services to secure women's independence and freedom; and in both cases the political programs led to the widespread recruitment of women personnel into government service.

By the early 1980s, women had made dramatic inroads into Commonwealth and State bureaucracies, reaching positions of unprecedented seniority. Between 1975 and 1982, the number of permanent women officers in the Second Division of the Commonwealth public service had increased from two to twenty-seven, at which time women comprised one quarter of the Third Division and one half of the Fourth Division. Equal opportunities seemed to be within the reach of women—especially if they were white, English speaking, and tertiary educated.

Although the Women's Electoral Lobby was avowedly non-party in its politics, the particular definition of equality favoured by its members, which rested on the disavowal of sexual difference and the promotion of equality in the workforce, led to a close identification with the Labor party, which proved, in turn, increasingly responsive to feminist demands. Whereas once Labor women such as Jean Daley and Muriel Heagney had refused the label feminist, seeing it as the preserve of middle class women, Labor women now enthusiastically adopted feminism as their own cause.

Women members of the ALP demanded appropriate representation as political candidates and on party structures. Before the 1970s, most successful women political candidates had represented conservative parties; by the late 1980s the pattern had changed. In 1989, there were fifty-three Labor party women MPs in Australian parliaments compared with twenty-one Liberal and nine National party women.

The year 1990 saw the election of Australia's first women premiers—Carmen Lawrence in Western Australia and Joan Kirner in Victoria—both Labor politicians and self-proclaimed feminists. It was in the relatively new Australian Democrats that women fared best, however. The first party to be led by a woman, (the feisty and forthright Janine Haines, elected leader in 1986) the Democrats could boast a higher proportion of women as parliamenary representatives than any other party and all but one of their subsequent leaders have been women.

Perhaps the most distinguished of the new federal politicians was Susan Ryan, whose political career, bringing feminism and Labor party policy together, was paradigmatic of the state feminist project. It was fitting that Ryan as Minister Assisting the Prime Minister on the Status of Women presided over the passage of the federal government's first Anti-Discrimination Act in 1984 (she had introduced a private member's bill in 1981) and the Affirmative Action (Equal Employment Opportunity for Women) Act in 1986. This legislation, largely drafted by Chris Ronalds, in many ways marked a turning point, but it was also the culmination of the long campaign for equality at work, initiated by Muriel Heagney with the publication of the book *Are Women Taking Men's Jobs?* in 1935.

Ryan was another founding member of Canberra Women's Electoral Lobby—by the 1980s WEL had come to look like a veritable feminist employment agency—and like Elizabeth Reid, a post-graduate student at the ANU, where she had graduated with a Master of Arts degree, in English Literature, in 1973. An applicant with Reid for the first position as Adviser to the Prime Minister, she joined the IWY Secretariat. In 1974, she was elected to the ACT Legislative Assembly; in 1975 she became an ALP Senator. In 1983, the election of the Hawke Labor government heightened feminist expectations of a renewed commitment to improving the status of women.

Ryan as Minister for Education and Minister Assisting the Prime Minister on the Status of Women, like Elizabeth Reid ten years before, bore the burden of these expectations. She was assisted in this task by Dr Anne Summers, Head of the Office of the Status of Women (OSW) between 1983 and 1986. Summers had been an activist and theorist in the women's movement since the 1970s, when she had been a founding member of the Sydney collectives that established the journal *Refractory Girl* (in 1973) and Elsie female refuge (in 1974). Her influential history of Australian women *Damned Whores and God's Police* (published in 1975) had won her public recognition and a Ph.D. degree and helped to establish her reputation as writer and journalist, which would assist her in the work of publicising the work of the OSW in Canberra.

Anne Summers and Susan Ryan—both intellectually able and long-experienced activists—proved an effective combination in translating feminist ideals into public policy during the 1980s. The new Labor government led by Bob Hawke signalled its commitment to the project of anti-discrimination by ratifying the United Nations Convention on the Elimination of All Forms of Discrimination Against Women in 1983—with two significant reservations: one maintaining the existing exclusion of women from combat or combat-related duties; the other exempting Australia from the provision of paid maternity leave, which was generally only available to Commonwealth and State public servants.

The following year, in 1984, the government translated its commitment into legislation, passing the Sex Discrimination Act, which outlawed discrimination on the grounds of sex, marital status and pregnancy in employment, education and the provision of services and also made sexual harassment unlawful in employment and education. The outlawing of sexual harassment represented the realisation of the long-cherished feminist goal of protecting women and girls from men's sexual licence. The commitment of feminists such as Rose Scott and Vida Goldstein to the 'equal moral standard' and their conviction that women could never be equal as citizens, while men treated them as 'creatures of sex' (or 'sex objects' as Women's Liberationists would say), was finally inscribed in legislation regulating sexual behaviour at the workplace.

To cement links between the broader women's movement and the OSW, the government established a new body, the National Women's Consultative Council (NWCC) to replace the National Women's Advisory Council. A new 'Consultation and Assistance' program of funding was negotiated by Summers to support women's organisations and projects aimed at improving the status of women—the biggest program of its kind since 1975. Grants were made to WEL, the Federation of Business and Professional Women, the National Council of Women, the Young Women's Christian Association, the Catholic Women's League and the Movement for the Ordination of Women, ironically helping to render more vocal the women's organisations which still felt entitled to call femocrats to account. Endorsed by the Labor party, yet answerable to the women's movement, Susan Ryan's job as a feminist government Minister was fraught with the contradictions inherent to institutionalised feminism.

The federal Sex Discrimination Act was supplemented in 1986 by the Affirmative Action Act, which required companies employing over 100 employees and institutions of higher education to implement affirmative action programs that would address structural disadvantage and act to remove barriers to equality. However, the legislation was weakened in response to concerted opposition, especially on the part of business interests, in an increasingly market-oriented economic climate.

Companies and universities were required to report annually on their programs, but the only sanction for non-compliance was being named in federal parliament. The legislation did, however, lead to a proliferation of job opportunities in the field of equal opportunity itself and the promotion of some women into the professions and middle management. Those who benefited from the new employment and political opportunities were those best positioned to take advantage of them. Meanwhile, the majority of women workers remained segregated in low paid, insecure jobs in factories, offices and homes. In their own homes, women continued to perform the vast majority of unpaid domestic labour. Many were becoming exhausted and ill as a result of their double or triple load. And in their homes, as well as outside, women were still vulnerable to systematic male violence.

The background of male violence against women, publicised in the 1980s by state-sponsored feminist surveys, seemed to make a mockery of women's bid for equality. What was the point of equal rights if women lived in daily fear of abuse, intimidation and assault? How was men's violence to be curbed? In 1987, under the ambit of the National Agenda for Women, the federal government funded a three-year $1.6 million National Education Campaign. As in many areas, the feminist movement was effective in changing understandings, so that individual acts of violence came to be seen as part of a gendered pattern, expressions of systematic 'violence against women'—which became the focus for the National Committee on Violence Against Women established in 1992, and the New South Wales Premier's Council on Violence Against Women formed in 1996. The influence of feminist discourse is evident in the 1992 Position Paper of the National Committee on Violence Against Women, which describes the fear of violence as a 'powerful weapon in the oppression of women'[9] and in the introduction in the 1980s of new censorship controls of film and video materials. But challenging understandings would seem to be easier than ending the patterns of violence and their disabling effects on women.

Patterns of work also seem resistant to change. The very success of liberal feminist measures enshrined in equal employment opportunity and affirmative action legislation has highlighted their limitations in dealing with the entrenched sexual division of labour on which the organisation of paid work is based. The rhythms of work assume the worker to be masculine—independent, autonomous and free from domestic responsibilities. Affluent women could deal with the resultant contradictions by employing nannies and other private help, but most female workers, now required to earn their living as well as keep house, are overworked and underpaid. Equal employment opportunity programs could not by themselves remedy fundamental class, ethnic and racial inequalities, often grounded in long histories of oppression. The highly visible success of some beneficiaries of state feminism—

dubbed by Mary Kalantzis 'the EEO industry'—simply increased the resentments and anger of those unable to share in the advancement.[10]

INSTITUTIONALISING DIFFERENCE, INSTITUTIONALISING POWER

Feminist policy-making was necessarily a politics of representation; feminists deciding on an agenda for 'women's affairs' had to presume that they represented 'women'. But which women? As feminist theorists Denise Riley and Judith Butler have pointed out, such claims always spark a chain of refusals.[11] Claiming to speak for women, feminists inevitably courted objections from all sorts of women that they didn't speak for them. 'It was the stated aim of the Office of the Status of Women to improve the status of all women in Australia', wrote Gisela Kaplan in *The Meagre Harvest*, a critical study of the women's movement in these years. 'One must ask who "the women" are.' In speaking about the relationship, or lack of it, between migrant women and the Australian women's movement, German-born Kaplan wrote with feeling about her and others' sense of 'exclusion'.[12] Non-English-speaking-background women were marginalised and patronised by an elite of Australian-born women of Anglo-Irish descent, who largely comprised the women's movement and were certainly its public face.

For Kaplan, recalling feminism in the 1970s and 1980s conjured up the remembered pain of rejection, which she saw as representative of the experience of women like her: 'I know of no single immigrant woman of NESB [non-English-speaking] background who is a stranger to the experience of ostracism and exclusion by other women and by feminists'.[13] Hers, too, was inevitably a politics of representation, seeking to speak for those whom feminism had ignored. But Kaplan also points out that the institutionalising of identity politics which occurred in these years, the reconceptualisation of ethnicity as a matter of cultural difference rather than economic disadvantage, consolidated differences between women. Ethnic Community Councils were authorised to speak to government on behalf of ethnic communities, but they were overwhelmingly dominated by men. In deciding that migrant women be 'dealt with' by the Office of Multicultural Affairs, rather than the Office of the Status of Women, governments 'structurally cemented in the division between women of non-English-speaking and women of Anglo-Celtic background'.[14]

Many groups of migrant women have, however, shaped the politics of the Australian women's movement in ways that are obscured by an account of simple 'exclusion', which places all agency with 'Anglo' women. In Melbourne, the Women's Group of the Federazione Italiana Lavoratori Emigrati e Famiglie (FILEF) was effective in articulating the needs of working women, especially migrant women's need for information in their own languages about health, child care and safety issues. The Working Women's Centre opened in Melbourne in September 1975 with IWY funds, with Mary Owen from WEL as Industrial Research Officer and Sylvie Shaw as Publicity Research Officer, also employed two part-time migrant liaison officers fluent in Greek, Italian and Spanish. The Centre's first publications included a multilingual poster and a Discussion paper on the particular needs of migrant women. A multilingual paper called *Women at Work* with articles written in Italian, Greek, Turkish, Spanish, Arabic and Serbo-Croatian as well as English, discussed subjects such as women's rights, industrial health, pregnancy and dismissal, child care, international developments and workers' compensation. The increase in subscriptions, from around 6000 in 1977 to 13 000 in 1982, suggests the usefulness of the paper.[15]

The Working Women's Centre and the Working Women's Resource Centre in Adelaide also produced multilingual leaflets on issues such as outwork and sexual harassment. In 1977, the Working Women's Charter called for an end to 'discrimination on the basis of sex, race, country of origin, age, religious or political belief, appearance, marital status or sexual preference'. It also called for 'attention to the needs of migrant women workers', child care, maternity leave, parental leave for family emergencies, access to health services and research into women's health and occupational health, information on sex education, contraception and abortion. It could be argued that it was migrant women who maintained the visibility of working class women—factory women—in feminist politics into the 1980s, who continued to remind femocrats that class exploitation and working conditions were feminist issues.

An application for an IWY grant was successful in winning funds to form the Australian Migrant Women's Association in 1975. As a result of continuous pressure on government, migrant women forced an acknowledgment of their distinctive needs by the Galbally Report into Post Arrival Programs and Services, which led to the National Women's Advisory Council conducting a series of consultations with migrant women across the community, in workplaces, hospitals and community centres; their conclusions were published in the book *Migrant Women Speak*. In 1979, a Migrant Women's Co-ordinator was appointed in the Department of Immigration and Ethnic Affairs and a number of new measures were implemented, such as the extension of the Home Tutor Scheme, which facilitated women's access to English language classes.

With the election of the Hawke Labor government in 1983, the resources allocated to serving the needs of migrant women expanded and policy became more focussed. The new Women's Emergency Services Program made refuges for migrant women a priority; and people attending courses under the Adult Migrant Education Program were given free child care. There were new appointments in Canberra, and migrant women joined the ranks of sisters in suits. German-born Ursula Doyle and Dutch-born Frederika Steen, appointed to head the Women's Desk in the Department of Immigration and Ethnic Affairs, in 1984, established links with women in different ethnic communities and gave priority to persuading them to avail themselves of the services and resources provided by government. Steen became a valuable contact point for the emerging migrant women's groups, but she also made women's concerns more visible to the men who ran Ethnic Affairs.

Following the example first set by the Migrant Women's Speak Out in New South Wales in 1982, Steen organised a national conference in February 1985 of over one hundred women from community and government organisations across Australia, to determine priorities for federal and State Ministers for Immigration/Ethnic Affairs. The nature of the four priority areas highlights not only the divergences, but also the similarities, between migrant women's priorities and those espoused by 'mainstream' groups such as WEL. Their priorities were improved health, safety and working conditions for the female immigrant workforce; improved access to language classes, education, training and retraining for immigrant women; improved access to culturally appropriate child care; and improved services for aged and aging immigrant women.

Following this conference, participants were inspired to form a number of new migrant women's organisations, such as the Immigrant Women's Resource Centre in New South Wales and the Migrant Resource Centre in Brisbane. With the assistance of Frances Milne, executive officer of the Federation of Ethnic Community Councils of Australia (FECCA), a national women's network was established to secure greater representation of migrant women on state feminism's new peak body, the National Women's Consultative Council, and to persuade government to hold separate consultations with immigrant women.

The Minister then responsible for the Office of the Status of Women, Susan Ryan, responded with a grant to bring together around 200 women from thirty different ethnic communities at a meeting in Melbourne. One outcome was the formation in 1986 of the Association of Non-English-Speaking-Background Women, chaired by Matina Mottee, erstwhile vice-president of the New South Wales Immigrant Women's Speak Out Association, who had been active in the Greek community and the refuge movement.

Pressure for increased representation on the NWCC continued, with the result that by 1988 four of its nineteen members were women from non-English-speaking backgrounds, including Mottee; Bruna Pasqua, the woman deputy chairperson of the Federation of Ethnic Community Councils; and Cora Gatbonton, a Filipina activist from Queensland. With this new membership, Marian Sawer has observed, the NWCC 'became the only Commonwealth body outside the area of multicultural affairs where NESB representation was in proportion to the NESB component of the population'.[16] State feminism could at last make some claim to be representative, at least in terms of people's ethnic backgrounds.

Matina Mottee saw her work on the National Women's Consultative Council as enabling a two-way exchange: 'I believe that they influenced me but I believe that I influenced them'.[17] From the 1980s, migrant women's groups have increasingly drawn on state support to set up their own culturally appropriate women's services, such as Action for Family Planning in Melbourne which argued that contraception was 'an industrial issue'.[18] Its change of name in 1991 to Women in Industry and Community Health reflected its broader interest in promoting the wellbeing of migrant women workers.

Forced in large numbers to use refuges (constituting 41 per cent of Sydney refuge users by the early 1990s), many immigrant women have yet felt uncomfortable with the refuges' cultural assumptions about family, men and the management of conflict. Italian-born women have advocated strategies that enable women to stay in their own homes and devised community-based ways of shaming the perpetrators of violence. The Vietnamese Women's Association in New South Wales, founded in 1984, lobbied successfully for funding to build Mimosa

House, an Indo-Chinese women's refuge in the western suburbs with six bilingual staff who speak Vietnamese, Cantonese, Mandarin, Lao, Thai and Khmer. Therese Ngoc Le Dang explains how their community attempts to resolve conflict:

> Women, victims of domestic violence, are often advised by workers of the mainsteam refuges to take legal action against their husbands. But in our policy we avoid that, because sometimes it is not only the husband's fault, sometimes it is the woman's fault as well. We try to let them interact, to bring them to counselling, and to console them and to reconcile . . . We would only advise them to go to take legal action if we have no other alternative.[19]

Immigrant women working in women's services also spend much time educating their communities about women's rights as they are legally defined in Australia, and fending off angry men resentful of feminist interference in their family affairs. Immigrant women often act as mediators between their communities, feminists and the state. In all sorts of ways and in numerous places, immigrant women have challenged, shaped and extended Australian feminism's engagement with the state, while often remaining ambivalent about their relationship with feminism.

If immigrant women tended to conceptualise their relationship with feminism as one of 'exclusion' and 'marginalisation', Aboriginal women have been more likely to speak of its 'irrelevance'. The focus of organised feminism on career opportunities, sexist discrimination and abortion law reform, for example, did not speak to indigenous women concerned about high levels of infant and maternal mortality in their communities, the ravages of alcohol and the effects of losing their land, children and culture. Feminist critiques of the family and woman's role were insensitive to the fact that Aboriginal women had had their children forcibly removed for decades by the state. Whereas an earlier generation of feminists, in the 1930s, had been among the leading critics of the policies of child removal, their successors in the 1970s seemed oblivious to both the existence of the policies and earlier feminist opposition to them.

Aboriginal people had cause to regard the state with hostility. The historical institutionalisation of indigenous people, the policies of segregation and dispersal, the coercion enacted under the guise of 'protection' until well into the 1960s, all these experiences led indigenous people to flee the power of the state. At the Black Women's Meeting at the Women and Politics conference it was noted that while white women wanted access to abortion, black women wanted an end to 'forced sterilisation' and support for rebuilding family and community life. As historian Jackie Huggins has written, 'while many white women have won their fight to get out of their kitchens, Black women are still fighting to get in, but this time tailored to their own specifications'.[20] The institutionalisation of feminism, the implementation of public policy oriented to achieving an equal position for women in public life, simply highlighted for many Aboriginal women its character as 'racially privileged', as white, Western and individualist.

Women's Liberation groups often reached out to Aboriginal women in the early 1970s, inviting them to speak and join the cause, but it did not occur to these groups that they might not be interested. In emphasising the oppressions of sexism, feminists could not see that racism might be a more destructive force for Aborigines and Torres Strait Islanders; nor did they appreciate that their expectation that Aboriginal women should join their movement might be seen as 'assimilationist'. Pat O'Shane had asked 'Is There Any Relevance in the Women's Movement for Aboriginal Women?' in 1976 and Marcia Langton made the same suggestion speaking to the Australian Women's Trade Union conference in the same year. She also suggested that, in its critique of masculinity, feminism could be divisive and destructive for the Aboriginal community. As Elizabeth Williams quietly observed: 'Often the women's movement is unable to see where importance lies'.[21]

By the 1970s there was a renewed focus in Aboriginal activism on land rights and self-determination, and black women were prominent in the Tent Embassy protest outside Parliament House, when they graphically made the point that in their dispossession they were exiles in their own country. With the establishment of Land Councils, following the first land rights legislation in 1976 under the Fraser government, Aboriginal women were forced to argue that their responsibilities as traditional landowners should also be recognised. The initial procedures for making land claims operated within white masculine paradigms, which privileged men's knowledge and participation.

Aboriginal women pointed out that they had obligations as cultural custodians which were often overlooked by white officials assessing claims; Pitjantjatjara women, for example, decided that they must make people aware of their links to, and responsibilities for, their country, travelling first to hearings in Adelaide and then across Australia performing ceremonies and making videos to publicise their obligations to the land. They formed the Ngaanyatjarra Pitjantjatjara

Yankunytjatjara Women's Council in 1980 to serve as a forum for 3000 Aboriginal women, from twenty-five member communities in South Australia, Western Australia and the Northern Territory, providing an autonomous space for women, who could also make direct input into the general Land Council.

The Women's Council has assisted in acquiring funding for women-only vehicles to enable women to attend meetings, to conduct ritual business, and to collect material for hunting and art production; the registering and protecting of women's sacred sites at Uluru; the research and planning of the Congress Alkuru birthing centre in Alice Springs; and support for women to participate in public debate at national conferences. The Council employs sixteen women full-time, who have worked in community outreach projects including Disability Employment Support, Domestic Violence, Commonwealth Respite For Carers, Nutrition Support for Young Mothers and Babies and Aged Care Support Services.[22] This model of organising was replicated in other parts of the country. A Central Australian Women's Council formed in 1983 and in New South Wales the Western Women's Council was formed in 1984.

Invited to reflect on Aboriginal women's relationship to the white women's movement, Lilla Watson, the first Aboriginal woman to be employed as an academic at the University of Queensland, commented: 'There was and is no question that I support in strongest terms women's liberation, whether it be for black or white women. Simultaneously it must be recognised that these two groups—black women and white women—will take two very different roads'.[23] Throughout Australia, Aboriginal women proved Watson's assessment correct as they took their own roads in setting up health, media, educational and legal services for their communities. In New South Wales, for example, Shirley Smith was a leading organiser of the Aboriginal Health Service, and in Alice Springs Freda Glynn was crucial to establishing the local media network, CAAMA.

Indigenous women developed their own strategies to deal with alcohol abuse and domestic violence and they have sometimes joined with non-Aboriginal women in securing government funds for refuges: in New South Wales, for example, two Aboriginal-controlled women's refuges, Cawarra at Mt Druitt and Ngala at Moree, were opened to support Aboriginal and non-Aboriginal women in crisis; while the Wirraway Women's Housing Co-operative provided emergency shelter and alternative accommodation in the area so that women do not need to leave their own country. But it was sometimes at women's refuges, when fleeing domestic violence, that Aboriginal women experienced the hurt of racist discrimination from the non-Aboriginal workers.

The women's movement attempted to bring Aboriginal women on board, often not recognising, as Jackie Huggins has pointed out, that Aboriginal women were, for good reason, reluctant to engage with a discourse they had no part in shaping.[24] From Canberra, femocrats instigated numerous meetings and conferences, in the late 1970s and early 1980s, which recommended the appointment of an Aboriginal women's taskforce to work with the National Women's Advisory Council. In 1981, Pat O'Shane—the first Aboriginal teacher in Queensland and the first Aborigine to be admitted to the Bar in New South Wales—was appointed to the Office of Women's Affairs, conducted further talks about setting up the taskforce, and arrived at the following terms of reference. The taskforce would: 'enquire into the involvement of Aboriginal women in land rights, health, housing, education, employment, legal aid, culture and child care (with particular reference to the adoption and fostering of Aboriginal children); and make recommendations to the Commonwealth on what action may be taken to meet any identified needs'.

O'Shane departed to head Aboriginal Affairs in New South Wales (the first Aboriginal woman to take charge of a government department), but discussions continued between the Office of Women's Affairs and a group of Aboriginal women in Canberra, including Marcia Langton, Eleanor Bourke and Aileen Buckley. Guidelines for the taskforce were drawn up, as were specifications for the position of leader, which was finally filled in July 1983 with the appointment of Phyllis Daylight from Queensland, then employed as education officer for the Department of Education and Youth Affairs in Darwin. She was assisted by Mary Johnstone from Yass and a number of women employed as regional co-ordinators under the Community Employment Program, to carry out consultations among some 200 communities across Australia.

In 1984, a national conference attended by around 100 indigenous women was held to review the work of the taskforce; the first national conference of indigenous women ever held, it was regarded as being of great historical significance in fostering a national perspective among Aboriginal and Islander women. The conference resolved that the National Advisory Council and the Department of Aboriginal Affairs recognise the status of women as landowners, demands being reiterated all over the country. They also drew attention to their specific housing and health needs. The Aboriginal Taskforce report, *Women's Business*, was launched in 1985, but there was no government response until 1989, by which time its author Phyllis Daylight had died.

There were more positive developments in the Department of Aboriginal Affairs, where an Aboriginal Women's Unit was set up in 1984; it was made permanent in 1986 when it was upgraded to the Office of Aboriginal Women, with a staff of five in the central office supplemented by a network of women's co-ordinators in State and Territory offices. In 1986–87 funding was provided for a Women's Initiatives Program to enable Aboriginal women in remote communities to establish resource centres, refuges and health and information services, supplemented by a further $1.6 million in 1988, most of which was administered by State women's co-ordinators. Priority was given to proposals for Aboriginal women to run their own services, to promote opportunities for women to pass on their cultural heritage to their children, to facilitate reunions of Aboriginal people separated from their families by past welfare practices, to support audio-visual productions and to provide multilingual information packages on government services.

In some States, Aboriginal women were active on the Women's Advisory Councils, especially in the Northern Territory and Western Australia; they were being given back 'the power of voice', as Laurel Winder, chair of the Aboriginal and Islander Congress of Western Australia, put it.[25] It is significant perhaps that Aboriginal women achieved this voice through the Aboriginal Affairs bureacracy rather than in the Office of the Status of Women, confirming the impression that the institutionalisation of feminism worked to entrench the power of white women.

In 'A tidda's manifesto', Catrina Felton and Liz Flanagan have recently argued that the

> elevated status that White women have enables them to secure the resources to control feminism . . . Generally speaking White feminists have not recognised or challenged the implications of racism or the historical and political discrimination that Koori women face . . . That is why many Koori tiddas view feminism as simply another White politically controlled institution, established to benefit White women, first and foremost.[26]

Accustomed to representing themselves as the oppressed, many white feminists have had difficulty in recognising their own racial (and class) privilege, as the beneficiaries of Aboriginal dispossession and the power of whiteness in a racist society.

These different assessments of the meaning of state feminism in Australia during the 1970s and 1980s—the tensions between proud narratives of femocrat achievement and denunciations of feminist complicity in racist oppression—are not easily reconciled, for there is surely truth (as well as desire) in both accounts. Histories always contain, and cannot expect to resolve, such incommensurate narratives. Perhaps it is better to hold on to the gap in communication and listen for what it can tell us. Feminism *is* historically embedded in white/Western/liberal culture. Recognising that the relationship between Anglo and Aboriginal women is a matter not just of benign 'difference', but also of power, historically and structurally entrenched, is to recognise, as Ien Ang has said, that 'complicity' is a structural inevitability. Feminism has empowered white women, but its gains were not reserved for white women. Insofar as it is an emancipatory project that advances the interests of some women in the name of all women, its claims to representation will always be contested.

But rather than castigate feminism for its inability to deliver social justice on all fronts, for its failure to become the natural political destination for all women, it would be probably more apt to accept, as Ien Ang suggests, that feminism is a limited project, providing a limited political home, that it is a politics of partiality. Ang teaches Cultural Studies in Western Sydney and has written about the meaning and implications of being 'Asian' and 'feminist' in Australia. In an essay on '"Other women" and post-national feminism', Ang suggests that feminists give up on their conceit of 'representation', that they jettison the ambition of inclusion in favour of an acceptance of partiality:

> While a politics of inclusion is driven by an ambition for universal representation (of all women's interests), a politics of partiality does away with that ambition and accepts the principle that feminism can never ever be an encompassing political home for all women, not just because different groups of women have different and sometimes conflicting interests, but, more radically, because for many groups of 'other' women other interests, other identifications are sometimes more important and politically pressing than, or even incompatible with, those related to their being women.[27]

Ang's point about the limited and partial nature of feminism as a political project is important, but rather than the metaphor of the 'limited home', I would prefer to think of feminism as an open house, even if a temporary abode. Not all will want to visit and some won't stay—but hopefully most women will feel free to take up residence and rearrange the house and contents as they see fit. As self-styled 'young feminists' are wont to say, they must refurbish the house of feminism to suit themselves.

CONCLUSION

At LaTrobe University I teach a post-graduate class on the history of feminist thought, and when students come to read classics such as Mary Wollstonecraft's *Vindication of the Rights of Women* (published in 1792) and Simone de Beauvoir's *The Second Sex* (1949), they still gasp with the shock of recognition. The analyses of these long-dead writers sound so contemporary; their rendering of the female condition so true! When Wollstonecraft writes of women 'smiling under the lash at which [they] dare not snarl' and de Beauvoir observes that 'the fact of being a man is no peculiarity. A man is in the right in being a man', the students exclaim that 'yes, that's right, but why is this still the case? We know that so much has changed in women's lives'.

The history of Australian feminism over the last one hundred years is undoubtedly a record of political achievement leading to major changes in the relations between the sexes; women have succeeded in campaigns for fundamental political, civil and economic rights. They have won voting rights and the right to hold public office; they have won access to universities and professional careers; they have established wide-ranging health services for women, including hospitals, maternal and infant welfare clinics and community health centres; they have secured the appointment of women to positions as police officers, gaol wardens, doctors and magistrates, to protect women from what is now called sexual harassment; they have achieved equal custody and property rights for mothers and challenged governments to extend basic citizen rights to Aboriginal people; they have secured a degree of economic independence for women, in benefits such as the Maternity Allowance and Child Endowment, the removal of the marriage bar in employment and the formal recognition of equal pay. By establishing women's refuges, feminists have made it easier for women to leave violent relationships; by securing a pension for sole parents, they have made it easier for mothers to establish independent households; by winning substantial government funding for child care centres, they have enabled thousands of women with children to enter paid work and thus to support themselves.

Germaine Greer has recently observed that women's lives are now better, but harder. Women have more options than they did one hundred years ago; more paths are open to those who wish to pursue them; the female sex is able to live more independently than in previous times, but we pay a high price and carry a heavy load. Women have taken on the world, but the world is still, by and large, structured on men's terms. Women have won equal opportunity and the formal right of equal pay, but the organisation of the workplace is still geared to the masculine experience of autonomy, mobility and freedom from domestic responsibilities. Thus, every ten years or so, there is an outburst of protest from 'working mothers' at the contradictions of their lives, the utter impossibility of their predicament. 'Goodbye Supermum' proclaimed a recent weekend magazine cover, whose inside story detailed the stressed lives of overworked, exhausted mothers. 'Supermum is not dead', observed one casualty, 'she is the living, walking dead'.

The headlines to such stories are written as if they are recording a recent discovery, but the plight of the 'working mother' has long been a cause of feminist concern in Australia and it remains so. It was the socialist friend of women, writer and organiser William Lane, who named women 'the weary sex' in his late nineteenth century novel *The Workingman's Paradise*, and labour women's organiser Lilian Locke-Burns who coined the slogan 'One Woman One Job' in support of the campaign for motherhood endowment in the 1920s. Providing mothers with an income from the state would enable them to reduce their working hours, without reducing them to a condition of dependence on men. Despite a prolonged campaign forged by a cross-class alliance of non-party feminists and labour movement women activists, their goal of economic freedom for mothers remained unrealised, the challenge posed to the relationship of marriage too revolutionary. When feminists next turned their attention to devising ways of winning economic independence for mothers they focussed on the provision of government child care, but it soon became clear that the definition of 'normal working hours' was oppressive of those who did not share men's taken-for-granted condition of absenteeism from domestic responsibilities. Equality with men, on men's terms, began to look like an ill-conceived goal.

In Britain, in the 1970s, socialist feminists promoted a new political platform that had as its centrepiece a 25-hour week for all workers, necessary if everyone were to combine paid work with caring and other social responsibilities. In Australia, in 1977, the Working Women's Charter called for maximum working hours to be set at thirty-five hours a week. Canadian feminist theorist Mary O'Brien, in her book *The Politics of Reproduction*, published in 1981, envisaged gender equality in terms of a restructured working day; and Frigga Haug, in Germany, called for a policy of affirmative action that would see men systematically incorporated into caring and other socially useful, but unpaid labour. In 1986, I pointed to the centrality of 'the question of time' to women's oppression in a symposium on 'the future of socialism' in Australia (an idea that was still thinkable), published as *Moving Left* and edited by David McKnight, and as I write, sociologist Lois Bryson, reporting on the Women's Health Australia study, has called for a six-hour day for mothers in paid work, to safeguard their physical and mental health. Women's excessive workload has been a feminist issue for decades.

One symptom of the contradictions involved for women seeking freedom in a man-made world is the rapidly declining birth-rate; it has been estimated that around one third of women now in their twenties will not bear children. Another is the number of women dependent on the sole parent pension—in 1996, 320 300 women, comprising around 93 per cent of all recipients, lived on this government benefit. Yet another expression of the contradictions in women's lives is their desire for shorter working hours. In 1996, 53.8 per cent of women were in the paid labour force, 21 per cent working part-time; at the same time 73.7 per cent of men were in the paid labour force, only 7.6 per cent working part-time.

Women are thus three times more likely than men to be employed part-time, but in a society where longer working hours remain the norm, and indeed are encouraged, part-time workers are locked into a position of economic and social subordination. One effect, then, of the contradictions of women living in a man's world is their comparative poverty; whereas nearly half of all women have a gross weekly income of less than $200, only 27 per cent of men do. Of men and women in the workforce, men earn on average $714.50 per week, women $468.30 per week. Real equality between the sexes therefore requires a systematic reduction in the normal working week, a redistribution of resources and responsibilities. A limit on working hours thus remains a high-priority feminist issue, especially as the recent deregulation of the labour market and spread of enterprise bargaining have made organised bargaining and collective political intervention—which worked to Australian women's benefit—ever more difficult. So, while a small number of women have been encouraged to climb the corporate ladder, the contradictions between the organisation of public and private life for the mass of working women have become ever more acute. Affordable, quality, government-funded child care remains crucial to negotiating these conflicts, as does generous provision of parental and sick leave by employers.

Work defined and paid as part-time locks wives into a condition of economic and psychological dependence on husbands, which is at odds with the independence taken to be the right and precondition of the exercise of citizenship in a democratic polity. All women's and girls' capacity for independence is further undermined by their physical insecurity, their daily vulnerability to male violence, in the home and on the streets. Women, of course, are not alone in their vulnerability to violence, but it is overwhelmingly men who are the perpetrators of violence and women who are the victims of their sexual and domestic assaults. Women live in fear of male violence in our society and order their movements, design their houses and plan their timetables in the light of that fear. Their freedom of movement and expression is quite severely curtailed as a result.

Feminist campaigns have addressed the threat male violence poses to women in various ways, aiming both to prevent assaults and provide greater protection for women at risk, through the introduction of 'restraining orders', television campaigns to change understandings of what is deemed to be appropriate male behaviour, the provision of telephone counselling services and rape crisis centres, and the outlawing of rape in marriage. Feminists have also promoted the virtues of self-defence for women, emphasising the importance of freeing women from their status as the protected sex, which continues to be constituted through their exclusion from combat duties in the armed forces and, on the home front, through the advice of police that if they want to be safe from serial killers women should not venture out at night unaccompanied by a man. To become—in the words of the Woman's Christian Temperance Union in 1913—'mistresses of themselves' women must achieve not just economic independence, but also the capacity for self-protection, learning to view our bodies as vehicles of empowerment, rather than sources of weakness. The state could make an important contribution to securing women's right to independence as citizens by making self-defence classes for girls mandatory in the school curriculum. We also need to secure recognition of women's right to avail ourselves fully of the defence of self-defence in law.

In the long history of feminism, the nature of women's demands has varied enormously, as sometimes they have sought recognition of their sexual difference, at other times asserting women's rights as human beings. As American historian Joan Scott has written, this oscillation between demands based on sameness and those based on difference is inherent to feminist politics, a sign of the constitutive contradictions of feminism's engagement with liberal individualism. To quote Scott:

> In the age of democratic revolutions, 'women' came into being as political outsiders through the discourse of sexual difference. Feminism was a protest against women's political exclusion; its goal was to eliminate 'sexual difference' in politics, but it had to make its claims on behalf of 'women' (who were discursively produced through 'sexual difference'). To the extent that it acted for 'women', feminism produced the 'sexual difference' it sought to eliminate. This paradox—the need both to accept and to refuse 'sexual difference'—was the constitutive condition of feminism as a political movement through its long history.[1]

In other words, feminism had to operate within terms not of its own choosing, and do politics in a masculine political system not of its own making. Feminists had to refuse sexist discrimination, even as they demanded recognition of the significance of sexual difference. Little wonder that the goals of 'freedom' and 'independence' and 'equality' proved as elusive as they were mesmerising.

In its latest DIY mode, feminism seems to have given away politics completely, announcing its project as one of 'attitude' and 'individual practice'. In her introduction to the collection *DIY Feminism*, Kathy Bail recommends the virtues of 'disorganised feminism', her contributors part of a generation that wants feminism to be feisty and fun. In her hymn to the pleasure of individual pleasure and her rejection of platforms and manifestos, Bail tells us that the do-it-yourself-for-yourself feminists whose reflections she has collected 'want to be identified through their interests and passions—such as music, publications or business—before their gender'. She acknowledges that most adhere to a broad feminist agenda: 'They advocate equality in pay and educational and employment opportunities, and the right to abortion and affordable child care; they are concerned about the high incidence of rape and domestic violence. But that doesn't mean they will readily call themselves feminist'.[2] Or organise to achieve social transformation. There is a defensive tone in Bail's writing that can't help but draw attention to her generation's ambivalence towards organised feminism. They are the daughters who must make it on their own.

In reviewing the long history of feminism in this country one is struck again and again by the creativity and energy of feminists of all generations, their gusto and stamina and ebullience and courage. And the pleasure they took in their politics. From the heady confidence of the Women's Federal Political Association meeting in Melbourne, soon after Federation through the middle years of the gatherings of the 'wild, wild women' of the United Associations in Market Street, Sydney,[3] to the explosion into life of Women's Liberation in Perth in the 1970s to the transgressive cavortings at the Women and Politics conference in Canberra in 1975, feminists—as Linda Littlejohn suggested in 1931—have derived momentum from the movement itself. It must be hoped that Australian women will be so passionately moved again.

NOTES

Introduction

1 *Dawn* 21 January 1931.
2 Publicity leaflet, 'Mrs Linda Littlejohn Leader of Australian Women's Movement', Rischbieth papers, NLA MS 2004/4/306(a), National Library of Australia.
3 *Dawn* 21 January 1931.
4 Quoted in Ruth Teale ed. *Colonial Eve Sources on Women in Australia 1788–1914* Oxford University Press, Melbourne, 1978, pp. 168–9.
5 'Release Heather Osland: Information'. Release Heather Osland Campaign.
6 Quoted in Judith Allen '"Our deeply degraded sex" and "The animal in man"': Rose Scott, Feminism and Sexuality 1890–1925' *Australian Feminist Studies* 7&8, Summer, 1988, p. 68.
7 Marilyn Lake 'The Independence of Women and the Brotherhood of Man' *Labour History* 63, November 1992, p. 3.
8 ibid., p. 13.
9 Pamphlet, *Income for Wives* . . . United Associations of Women (UA) papers, ML MS 2160/Y4481, Mitchell Library.
10 League of Women Voters, South Australian branch papers, MS SRG 116/7/1, State Library of South Australia.
11 Report of 1936 Conference of Australian Federation of Women Voters, UA papers ML MS 2160/Y789.
12 Walker to *Advertiser* 20 June 1974, cutting, League of Women Voters, South Australian branch papers, MS SRG 116/7/1, State Library of South Australia.
13 *Dawn* 14 November 1922.
14 *Dawn* 12 December 1923.
15 Germaine Greer *The Female Eunuch* MacGibbon & Kee Ltd, London 1970, p. 42.
16 Rose Scott, speech on womanhood suffrage, March 1892, Scott papers, ML MS 38/38, Mitchell Library.

17 *West Australian* 12 February 1921.
18 Jill Roe 'Chivalry and Social Policy in the Antipodes' *Historical Studies* 22, 88, April 1987, p. 405.
19 Rose Scott, correspondence, 13 April 1904, Scott papers, ML MS 38/41.
20 Royal Commission appointed to Investigate, Report and Advise upon Matters in relation to the Condition and Treatment of Aborigines, 1935, Minutes of Evidence, p. 557.

Chapter 1

1 Louisa Lawson 'Divorce Extension Bill or The Drunkard's Wife' *Dawn* 1 March 1890.
2 Carlotta Smith 'Louisa Lawson A Poet and the Mother of a Poet' *Life* 1 January 1920, Lawson papers, ML MSS A 1895, Mitchell Library.
3 Louisa Lawson 'First Public Speech', Lawson papers, ML MSS A 1898.
4 See Olive Lawson ed. *The First Voice of Australian Feminism: Excerpts from Louisa Lawson's The Dawn 1888–1895* Simon & Schuster, Sydney, 1990.
5 *Republican* 1, 1, 4 July 1887.
6 Louisa Lawson Scrapbook, vol. 1, Lawson papers, ML MSS A 1895.
7 ibid.
8 *Dawn* 1 November 1897.
9 *Dawn* 1 July 1889.
10 ibid.
11 Quoted in Audrey Oldfield *Woman Suffrage in Australia A Gift or a Struggle?* Cambridge University Press, Melbourne, 1992, p. 136.
12 Lawson 'First Public Speech', op. cit.
13 Oldfield op. cit. p. 140.
14 Ada Throssell to Sir John Forrest 27 June 1898, WA Premier's Department, Acc. 1496, 686/1898.
15 Mrs G. O. Ferguson to Sir John Forrest 11 July 1898, WA Premier's Department, op. cit.
16 Suzanne M. Marilley 'Frances Willard and the Feminism of Fear' *Feminist Studies* 19, 1, Spring 1993.
17 Oldfield op. cit. p. 117.
18 Quoted in Alison Alexander 'The Public Role of Women in Tasmania 1803–1914', PhD thesis, History department, University of Tasmania, 1989, p. 236.
19 ibid., p. 238.
20 McAulay papers, Tasmanian State Archives, NS 331/9.
21 Rose Scott Reply to Miss Badham, c.1895, Scott papers, ML MSS 38/38 Mitchell Library.
22 Rose Scott Speeches and Notes 1892–1918, Public Address, March 1892, Scott papers, ML MSS 38/38.

23 Rose Scott Speeches and Notes re literature, 1893–1903, Scott papers, ML MSS 38/26.
24 Rose Scott Reply to Miss Badham, op. cit.
25 Judith Allen *Rose Scott Vision and Revision in Feminism* Oxford University Press, Melbourne, 1994, p. 76.
26 ibid., ch. 3; Rose Scott Speeches and Notes, 1892–1918, March 1892, Scott papers, ML MSS 38/38.
27 Scott 'Why Women Want the Vote', Scott papers, ML MSS 38/38.
28 *Dawn* 1 July 1890.
29 Rose Scott Speeches and Notes, March 1892, Scott papers, ML MSS 38/38.
30 Lawson 'First Public Speech', op. cit.
31 Reproduced in Judy Mackinolty and Heather Radi eds *In Pursuit of Justice Australian Women and the Law 1788–1979* Hale and Iremonger, Sydney, 1979, p. 106 and Jan Roberts *Maybanke Anderson Sex, suffrage and social reform* Ruskin Row Press, Sydney, 1997, p. 68.
32 Marilyn Lake 'The Politics of Respectability Identifying the Masculinist Context' *Historical Studies* 22, 86, April 1986, p. 126.
33 Quoted in Patricia Grimshaw 'Bessie Harrison Lee and the Fight for Voluntary Motherhood' in Marilyn Lake and Farley Kelly eds *Double Time Women in Victoria 150 Years* Penguin, Melbourne, 1985, pp. 141–2.
34 ibid., pp. 143–4.
35 ibid.
36 Lake 'Politics of Respectability', op. cit., p. 129.
37 ibid., p. 128.
38 Quoted in Roberts op. cit., p. 70.
39 ibid., p. 67.
40 ibid., p. 74.
41 Lois 'What Have We Done With the Vote!' *Sydney Morning Herald* 27 May 1914, p. 7. My thanks to Jan Roberts for this reference.
42 Roberts op. cit., pp. 60–1.
43 Rose Scott Letter re public demonstration to show gratitude to Sir John See and Sir William Lyne for enfranchisement, Scott papers, ML MSS 38/38.
44 Janice Brownfoot 'Annette Bear-Crawford' in Heather Radi ed. *200 Australian Women* Redress Press, Sydney, 1989, pp. 59–60.
45 Oldfield op. cit., p. 149.

Chapter 2

1 Rose Scott Letter re public demonstration . . . Scott papers, ML MSS 38/38, Mitchell Library.
2 Rose Scott Speech, March 1892, Scott papers, ML MSS 38/38.

3 See Judith Smart 'Modernity and Mother-heartedness: Spiritual and Religious Meaning and Influence in Australian Women's Suffrage and Citizenship Movements 1890s–1930s'. Unpublished paper.
4 Rose Scott on the Women's Political Education League, 10 June 1904, Scott papers, ML MSS 38/41.
5 Rose Scott Speeches and Notes re literature, 1893–1903, Scott papers, ML MSS 38/26.
6 Bessie Rischbieth to Carrie Chapman Catt 24 November 1924, Rischbieth papers, NLA MS 2004/7/62, National Library of Australia.
7 Letter, 23 May 1913, Rischbieth papers, NLA MS 2004/1/7.
8 *Dawn* 14 November 1924.
9 *Woman's Sphere* 10 July 1903.
10 'Women's Political Attitude The Value of a Non-Party Basis of Action' *Dawn*, Monthly Organ of the Women's Service Guild of Western Australia, 12 April 1921.
11 Leaflet, 'Something You DON'T Know', United Associations of Women (UA) papers, ML MSS 2160/Y789, Mitchell Library.
12 Leaflet, 'United Associations of Women Aims and Objects', UA papers, ML MSS 2160/Y4481.
13 Report of Australian Federation of Women Voters conference, 1936, UA papers, ML MSS 2160/Y789.
14 *Dawn* 12 February 1921; *West Australian* 12 February 1921.
15 *West Australian* 12 February 1921.
16 Rose Scott to Dr Crossley 23 December 1922, Rose Scott correspondence, Scott papers, ML MSS 38/20X.
17 Rose Scott 'Why Women Want the Vote', Scott papers, ML MSS 38/38.
18 Vida Goldstein, Women's Federal Political Association of Victoria, 'Why Women Should Use the Vote', Scott papers, ML MSS 38/39.
19 Dianne Davidson *Women on the Warpath Feminists of the First Wave* University of Western Australia Press, Nedlands, 1997, pp. 83–4.
20 ibid.
21 Goldstein, 'Why Women Should Use the Vote', op. cit.
22 Scott to Inspector-General of Police 4 February 1904, Scott papers, ML MSS 38/20X.
23 Women's Political Education League (WPEL) Presidential Report, 1904, ML MSS 38/43.
24 ibid.
25 Minutes, WPEL meeting, 2 November 1903, Scott papers, ML MSS 38/40.
26 C. H. Spence to Scott 8 May 1906, Scott papers, ML MSS 38/21.
27 Newspaper clipping on visit to Sydney of Edith Cowan, Scott papers, ML MSS 38/20X.
28 *Dawn* 14 November 1921, 14 August 1923.
29 *Woman Voter* 10 March 1913.

30 *Dawn* 14 May 1924.
31 'Statement of Conditions of Work for Women Police in South Australia', League of Women Voters papers, MS SRG 116, South Australian Archives.
32 *Woman Voter* 26 August 1914.
33 WPEL Annual Report, 8 November 1905, Scott papers, ML MSS 38/41.
34 ibid.
35 *Woman Voter* quoted in Carmel Shute 'Heroines and Heroes: Sexual mythology in Australia 1914–18' in Joy Damousi and Marilyn Lake eds *Gender and War Australians at War in the Twentieth Century* Cambridge University Press, Melbourne, 1997, p. 29.
36 Joy Damousi 'Socialist women and gendered space: Anti-conscription and anti-war campaigns 1914–18' in Damousi and Lake op. cit. pp. 265–8.
37 Shute op. cit., p. 28.
38 Davidson op. cit., p. 62.
39 ibid., p. 63.
40 *Dawn* 12 January 1921.
41 *Dawn* 12 May 1921.
42 *Dawn* 14 November 1922.
43 Report of the Leeds Suffrage Association, Overseas Suffrage Literature, Scott papers, ML MSS 38/39.
44 South Australian Women's Non-Party Association, 'Women's Work for Child Welfare in South Australia', League of Women Voters papers, MS SRG 116, South Australian Archives.
45 *Dawn* 13 June 1921.
46 *Dawn* 12 January 1921.

Chapter 3

1 Jean Daley 'Woman to Woman' *Woman's Clarion* July 1927.
2 Sarah Benton 'Gender, Sexuality and Citizenship' in Geoff Andrews ed. *Citizenship* Laurence & Wishart, London, 1991, p. 161.
3 Quoted in Anne Summers *Damned Whores and God's Police* Penguin, Ringwood, 1975, p. 358.
4 Vicky Pierce 'The Lowest Common Denominator—Children, State and Society, Tasmania 1896–1920', BA Hons thesis, History department, University of Tasmania, 1983, pp. 32–3.
5 Royal Commission on Childhood Endowment or Family Allowances, Minutes of Evidence, *Commonwealth Parliamentary Papers* 1929, vol. II, pp. 1116, 1134.
6 Lilian Locke-Burns 'State Provision for Mother and Child' *Labor Call* 19 June 1919.
7 *Argus* 5 September 1912.

8 *Age* 6 September 1912.
9 ibid.
10 *Woman Voter* 9 October 1912.
11 Ada Bromham to *West Australian* 20 February 1931.
12 *Dawn* 14 January 1923.
13 ibid.
14 *Dawn* 14 April 1923.
15 ibid.
16 ibid.
17 ibid.
18 ibid.
19 *West Australian* 20 February 1931.
20 Muriel Heagney 'Report of Investigation into the Position of the Unmarrried Mother' 26 April 1923. 'Has the Maternity Allowance Failed?' *Labor Call* 22 May 1924.
21 ibid.
22 Quoted in Gail Griffin 'The Feminist Club of New South Wales 1914–1970: A History of Feminist Politics in Decline' *Hecate* xiv, 1, 1988.
23 Dame Janet Campbell 'Report on Maternal and Child Welfare in Australia' *Commonwealth Parliamentary Papers* 1929–30–31 vol. II, p. 6.
24 See Helen Jones *In Her Own Name Women in South Australian History* Wakefield Press, Adelaide, 1986, pp. 178–9 and Margaret Allen, Mary Hutchison and Alison Mackinnon eds *Fresh Evidence, New Witnesses* South Australian Government Printer, Adelaide, 1989, pp. 222–3.
25 *Non-Party News* September 1924 quoted in Allen et al. op. cit., p. 222.
26 Jones op cit., p. 236.
27 ibid., p. 180.
28 Heather Radi 'Whose Child?' in Judy Mackinolty and Heather Radi eds *In Pursuit of Justice Australian Women and the Law 1788–1979* Hale and Iremonger, Sydney, 1979, p. 128.
29 ibid.
30 Millicent Preston Stanley *Whose Child?* stage copy, Millicent Preston-Stanley Vaughan papers, NLA MS 9062/1, National Library of Australia.
31 ibid.
32 Radi op. cit. p. 128.

Chapter 4

1 Quoted in Judith Allen '"Our deeply degraded sex" and "The animal in man": Rose Scott, Feminism and Sexuality 1890–1925' *Australian Feminist Studies* 708, Summer 1988, p. 68.
2 Judith Allen *Rose Scott Vision and Revision in Feminism* Oxford University Press, Melbourne, 1994, esp. ch. 2.

NOTES

3 Paper: 'The Economic Independence of the Married Woman', Miscellaneous speeches and notes, Rose Scott papers, ML MSS 38/40, Mitchell Library.
4 Letter, 19 May 1913, Rischbieth papers, NLA MS 2004/1/6, National Library of Australia,
5 Letter, 23 May 1913, Rischbieth papers, NLA MS 2004/1/7.
6 Letter, 3 July 1913, Rischbieth papers, NLA MS 2004/7/1913.
7 Letter, 18 July 1913, Rischbieth papers, NLA MS 2004/1/12.
8 Letter, undated, Rischbieth papers, NLA, MS 2004/1/11.
9 Grant McBurnie 'Angela Booth: The Importance of Being Well Bred' in Marilyn Lake and Farley Kelly eds *Double Time Women in Victoria 150 Years* Penguin, Ringwood, 1985, pp. 312–21.
10 Angela Booth *The Necessity for Woman Awakening to her Political Civic Duties An address by Mrs James Booth given before the Liberal Educational Society* Pritchard Bros., Adelaide, 1914, p. 6.
11 Lesbia Harford 'Untitled', April 1915, reprinted in Marilyn Lake and Katie Holmes *Freedom Bound II: Documents on Women in Modern Australia* Allen & Unwin, Sydney, 1995, p. 27
12 Vida Goldstein 'Venereal Disease' *Woman Voter* 10 March 1914.
13 Quoted in Meredith Foley 'The Women's Movement in New South Wales and Victoria 1918–38', PhD thesis, History department, University of Sydney, 1985, p. 252.
14 Jean Daley 'Independence' *Woman's Clarion* February 1925.
15 Bennett to Rischbieth April 1932, Rischbieth papers, NLA MS 2004/12/23.
16 Lilian Locke-Burns 'State Provision for Mother and Child' *Labor Call* 19 June 1919.
17 ibid.
18 See, for example, Joy Damousi 'Marching to Different Drums' in Kay Saunders and Raymond Evans eds *Gender Relations in Australian Society Domination and Negotiation* Harcourt Brace Jovanovich, Sydney, 1992. See also Susan Magarey 'The Politics of Passion: Sex and Race in the New Australian Body Politic' *Australian Feminist Studies* 12, 25, April 1997.
19 Muriel Heagney 'Child Endowment' *Labor Call* 1 February 1923.
20 Nelle Rickie, letter to editor, *Labor Call* 6 March 1924.
21 'A Call to the Women of Australia to Demand an Honourable Native Policy', Rischbieth papers, NLA MS 2004/12/197.
22 United Associations of Women pamphlet, *Income for Wives: How It Can Be Managed or The Economic Independence of Married Women*, United Associations of Women (UA) papers, MS 2160/Y4481, Mitchell Library.
23 Edith Jones, delegate to conference of representatives of missions, societies and associations interested in the welfare of Aborigines to consider the Bleakley report, Rischbieth papers, NLA MS 2004/12/506.

24 *Dawn* 16 August 1927.
25 Daley op. cit.
26 E. Lee Conway, Letter to editor, *Labor Call* 5 July 1923.
27 Rose Scott 'The Future of the Race' *Woman Voter* 15 July 1914, cited in Marilyn Lake and Katie Holmes eds *Freedom Bound II: Documents on Women in Modern Australia* Allen & Unwin, Sydney, 1995, pp. 18–19.
28 Street to Edith How Martyn 9 July 1934, Street papers, NLA MS 2683/3/41.
29 How Martyn to Street 22 August 1934, Street papers, NLA MS 2683/3/50.
30 McBurnie op. cit.
31 For the full letter see Lake and Holmes op. cit., pp. 104–5.
32 Daley op. cit.
33 Muriel Heagney Letter to editor, *Labor Call* 1 February 1923.
34 Women's Industrial Convention, Minutes, p. 3 Melbourne University Archives.
35 ibid., p. 18.
36 Heagney 'Child Endowment', op. cit.
37 Letters to editor, *Labor Call* 1 March 1923, 26 April 1923.
38 Letter to editor, *Labor Call* 6 September 1923. See also Joy Damousi 'Socialist Women in Australia c. 1890–1918', PhD thesis, History department, Australian National University, 1987.
39 Royal Commission on Child Endowment, Minutes of Evidence, p. 1116.
40 Daley op. cit.
41 *Labor Call* 6 September 1923.
42 ibid.
43 Letter to *Labor Call* 26 April 1923.
44 Letter to *Labor Call* 28 February 1924.
45 Editorial, 'Labor Women', *Labor Call*, 7 April 1921.
46 'ALP Easter Conference, 1923' *Labor Call* 26 April 1923.
47 *Woman's Clarion* December 1924, February 1925, March 1926.
48 Diane Kirkby *Alice Henry The Power of Pen and Voice: The Life of an Australian-American Labor Reformer*, Cambridge University Press, Melbourne, 1991.
49 *Woman's Clarion* May 1925.
50 *Woman's Clarion* July 1925, August 1925. See also Kirkby op. cit., pp. 190–3.
51 *Woman's Clarion* March 1926.
52 Royal Commission on Child Endowment, Minutes of Evidence, pp. 1135–7.
53 ibid., p. 923.
54 ibid., pp. 344–5.
55 ibid., pp. 906–16.
56 ibid., pp. 915–16.

57 ibid., p. 8.
58 Royal Commission on Child Endowment, Majority Report, Commonwealth Parliamentary Papers, vol. 2, 1929, pp. 1343–4.
59 Royal Commission on Child Endowment, Minority Report, p. 1392.
60 Pamphlet, No. 1, *Income for Wives How It Can Be Managed or The Economic Independence of Married Women*, UA papers, MS 2160/Y4481.
61 Jessie Street radio broadcast, 1 November 1936, NLA, MS 2683/3/641–3, Street papers, National Library of Australia.
62 Pamphlet, *Woman as a Homemaker*, UA papers, ML MS 2160/Y4481.
63 *Daily Telegraph* 29 January 1943.
64 Pamphlet, No. 2, *The Justice of Equal Pay and Equal Opportunity*, UA papers, ML MS 2160/Y4481.

Chapter 5

1 *Dawn* 16 March 1932, 20 April 1932.
2 *West Australian* 7 May 1932, Rischbieth papers, NLA MS 2004/12/351, National Library of Australia.
3 Travers Buxton to Dr Basedow, MHR, 13 February 1929, Anti-Slavery Society papers, Rhodes House, Oxford, MS Br.Emp. S22/G374.
4 Harris to Rev. C. E. C Lefroy 9 December 1929, Anti-Slavery Society papers, op. cit.
5 Harris to Bryce 15 October 1928, Anti-Slavery Society papers, op. cit.
6 Harris to Bryce 20 January 1930, Anti-Slavery Society papers, op. cit.
7 Travers Buxton to Rev. C. E. C. Lefroy 31 December 1929, Anti-Slavery Society papers, op. cit.
8 *Dawn* 14 May 1925.
9 *Dawn* 16 April 1925.
10 Bennett to John Harris 2 June 1930, Anti-Slavery Society papers, op. cit.
11 Report of 1929 conference of representatives of missions, societies and associations interested in the welfare of aborigines, Rischbieth papers, NLA MS 2004/12/506.
12 ibid.
13 Bennett to Harris 30 May 1930, Anti-Slavery Society papers, op. cit.
14 Harris to Bennett 6 September 1928, Anti-Slavery Society papers, op. cit.
15 Harris to Cooke 7 June 1929, Anti-Slavery Society papers, op. cit.
16 Reprint from *Manchester Guardian*, Rischbieth papers, NLA MS 2004/12/304. See also Bennett to H. W. Nevinson 7 June 1930, Anti-Slavery Society papers, op. cit.
17 *Dawn* 16 July 1930.
18 Buxton to Cooke 10 November 1930, Anti-Slavery Society papers, op. cit.
19 *Dawn* 17 December 1930.

20 ibid.
21 Constance Ternente Cooke 'The Status of Aboriginal Women in Australia', Anti-Slavery Society papers, Br. Emp. S22 G 378, Rhodes House, Oxford.
22 Constance Cook to John Harris 6 October 1930, Anti-Slavery Society papers, Br. Emp. S22 G374, Rhodes House.
23 Bennett to Rischbieth 9 December 1930, Rischbieth papers, NLA MS 2004/12/4.
24 Rischbieth to Pearce 24 March 1931, Rischbieth papers, NLA MS 2004/12/6.
25 Bennett to Rischbieth 19 December 1931, Rischbieth papers, NLA MS 2004/12/22.
26 Bennett to Rischbieth April 1932, Rischbieth papers, NLA MS 2004/12/23.
27 ibid.
28 ibid.
29 *West Australian* 7 May 1932, cutting, Rischbieth papers, NLA MS 2004/12/351.
30 *West Australian* 26 May 1932, 21 June 1932.
31 *West Australian* 21 June 1932.
32 ibid.
33 *West Australian* 26 June 1932.
34 Chief Secretary's Department, 'Allegations by Mrs M. M. Bennett in regard to native slavery' MS 166/32, Battye Library.
35 M. M. Bennett 'The Aboriginal Mother in Western Australia in 1933', Rischbieth papers, NLA MS 2004/12/218.
36 ibid.
37 ibid.
38 'Women of Note' *Dawn* October 1930.
39 *Daily News* 4 June 1933, cutting, Chief Secretary's Department, op. cit.
40 *West Australian* 11 December 1933.
41 Neville to Minister 12 December 1933, Chief Secretary's department, op. cit.
42 Bennett to Rischbieth 20 September 1933, Rischbieth papers, NLA MS 2004/12/50.
43 Bennett to Rischbieth 18 October 1933, Rischbieth papers, NLA MS 2004/12/57.
44 Report of the Royal Commission appointed to Investigate, Report and Advise upon matters in relation to the Condition and Treatment of Aborigines, Western Australian Parliamentary Papers, Minutes of Evidence, pp. 557–8.
45 ibid., p. 560.
46 ibid., pp. 561–76.
47 The petition is reproduced in Marilyn Lake and Katie Holmes eds *Freedom*

Bound II: Documents on Women in Modern Australia, Allen & Unwin, Sydney, 1995, pp. 63–7.
48 ibid., pp. 539–40.
49 ibid., p. 536.
50 ibid., p. 537.
51 ibid., pp. 215–16.
52 ibid., p. 216.
53 ibid.
54 ibid., p. 221.
55 ibid., p. 225.
56 Neville to State general secretary, Women's Service Guild, 15 June 1933, Rischbieth papers, NLA MS 2004/12/42.
57 Royal Commission appointed to Investigate . . . Aborigines, Western Australian Parliamentary Papers, Minutes of Evidence, p. 300.
58 Bennett to Buxton 22 August 1936, Anti-Slavery Society papers, MS Br. Emp. S22/G378.
59 Bennett to Harris 7 March 1937, Anti-Slavery Society papers, MS Br. Emp. S22/G377.
60 Bennett to Harris 20 October 1935, Anti-Slavery Society papers, MS Br. Emp. S22/G377.
61 ibid.
62 Mary Fullerton 'A Fantasy' in Frances Fraser and Nettie Palmer eds. *Centenary Gift Book* Robertson and Mullens, Melbourne, 1934, p. 46.
63 Cooke to Buxton 9 July 1935, Anti-Slavery Society papers, MS Br. Emp. S22/G377.
64 Cooke to hon. sec., Women's Centenary Committee 10 June 1935, Cooke papers, GRG 52/32/73, South Australian Archives.
65 Cooke to Buxton 20 November 1935, ibid.
66 Daisy Bates 'Our Pioneer Women and Our Natives' in Louise Brown Beatrix de Crespigny, Mary P. Harris, Kathleen Kyffin Thomas, Phebe N. Watson eds. *A Book of South Australia Women in the First Hundred Years* Rigby, Adelaide, 1936, p. 94.
67 Bennett to Jones 5 December 1936, enclosed in letter from Jones to Harris 30 December 1936, Anti-Slavery Society papers, MSS Br. Emp. S22/G378.
68 ibid.

Chapter 6

1 Women's Service Guild, Annual Report, *Dawn* 14 June 1924.
2 Jill Vickers 'Feminist Approaches to Women in Politics' in Linda Kealey and Joan Sangster eds *Beyond the Vote: Canadian Women and Politics* University of Toronto Press, Toronto, 1989, p. 23.
3 *Dawn* 12 April 1921.

4 *Dawn* 14 May 1923.
5 *Dawn* 12 January 1921.
6 *Dawn* 12 April 1921.
7 Leaflet, 'United Associations of Women, Aims and Objects', UA papers, ML MS 2160/Y4481, Mitchell Library.
8 *Dawn* 14 November 1921.
9 Paper, 'Australian Federation of Women's Societies (for equal citizenship)', p. 13, Rischbieth papers, NLA MS 2004/6/18, National Library of Australia.
10 ibid., p. 4.
11 Women's Political Educational League (WPEL), report of meeting, 10 June 1903, ML MS 38/40, Mitchell Library.
12 'United Associations of Women, Aims and Objects', op. cit.
13 Ada Bromham election address, *Dawn* 12 February 1921.
14 Judith Smart 'Eva Hughes' in Marilyn Lake and Farley Kelly eds *Double Time Women in Victoria 150 Years* Penguin, Ringwood, 1985, p. 183.
15 Judith Smart 'Jean Daley and Mary Brodney' in Lake and Kelly, op. cit., p. 286.
16 *Sydney Morning Herald* 24 August 1948, cutting, UA papers, ML MS 2160/Y789.
17 Scott, letter, 13 April 1904, Scott papers, ML MS 38/41, Mitchell Library.
18 ibid.
19 WPEL, President's Address, August 1904, ML MS 38/43.
20 'Women and Party Politics' *Woman's Sphere* 10 July, 1903.
21 ibid.
22 WPEL meeting, 12 March 1903, ML MS 38/40.
23 W. A. Holman to Scott 19 July 1909, Scott papers, ML MS 38/20X.
24 Goldstein in *Christian Science Monitor* 4 December 1918, cutting, Rischbieth papers, NLA MS 2004/4/144.
25 Bessie Rischbieth 'Women in Public Life' *Dawn* 12 January 1921.
26 UA leaflet, UA papers, ML MS 2160/Y789.
27 British Commonwealth League, Report on Conference on Citizen Rights of Women, 1925, p. 40, Fawcett Library, London.
28 *Dawn* 14 June 1924.
29 Questionnaire, UA papers, ML MS 2160/Y789.
30 UA to J. B. Chifley 10 November, 1941 UA papers, ML MS 2160/Y789.
31 Goldstein in *Woman Voter* 8 September 1910, Rischbieth papers, NLA MS 2004/4/175.
32 Geoff Browne 'Eleanor Glencross and Ivy Weber' in Lake and Kelly op. cit., p. 350.
33 *Dawn* 16 April 1925, 14 May 1925.
34 *Dawn* 20 April 1927.
35 *Dawn* 12 August 1921.
36 *Dawn* 22 October 1930.

37 Harriet Newcombe to Rischbieth 25 August 1915, Rischbieth papers, NLA MS 2004/4/28.
38 Circular letter, Rischbieth papers, NLA MS 2004/5/45.
39 ibid.
40 Waterworth to Rischbieth 3 April 1919, Rischbieth papers, NLA MS 2004/5/52.
41 Annie Carvosso to Rischbieth 10 April 1919, Rischbieth papers, NLA MS 2004/5/57.
42 H. Bennett to Rischbieth 18 April 1919, Rischbieth papers, NLA MS 2004/5/59.
43 Newcombe to Miss King 24 July 1921, Rischbieth papers, NLA MS 2004/4/13.
44 Newcombe to the Officers of the new Federation of Australian Women's Societies 31 October 1921, Rischbieth papers, NLA MS 2004/5/34.
45 Newcombe to Rischbieth 14 July 1921, Rischbieth papers, NLA MS 2004/4/12.
46 Newcombe to Rischbieth 31 October 1921, Rischbeith papers, NLA MS 2004/5/34.
47 Newspaper report, Rischbieth papers, NLA MS 2004/4/302.
48 Newcombe to Rischbieth 19 March 1924, Rischbieth papers, NLA MS 2004/4/15.
49 Rischbieth to Catt 24 November 1924, Rischbieth papers, NLA MS 2004/7/62.
50 Georgina Sweet to Mrs Carlisle McDonnell 30 April 1929, Rischbieth papers, NLA MS 2004/6/22.
51 Rischbieth to Sweet 4 January 1929, Rischbieth papers, NLA MS 2004/6/69.
52 'National Policies Affecting International Relations' *Bulletin of the Pan-Pacific Union*, 154, 1932, p. 10. UA papers, ML MS 2160/Y792.
53 *Woman Voter* 3 July 1919.
54 Goldstein 'Australia and National Righteousness', Rischbieth papers, NLA MS 2004/4/248.
55 Hinder, circular letter, 12 February 1930, Rischbieth papers, NLA MS 2004/4/17.

Chapter 7

1 Muriel Heagney *Are Women Taking Men's Jobs?* Hilton and Veitch, Melbourne, 1935, p. 174.
2 *Christian Science Monitor* 30 October 1930, cutting and *Daily News* 2 December 1930, cutting, Equal Rights International (ERI) papers, Box 331, Fawcett Library, London.

3 *Woman Voter* December 1910, Rischbieth papers, NLA MS 2004/4/178, National Library of Australia.
4 *Christian Science Monitor* 7 November 1932, cutting, ERI papers, Fawcett Library.
5 Montevideo Equal Rights Treaty, Article 1, ERI, United Associations of Women (UA) papers, ML MS 2160/Y790, Michell Library.
6 *Christian Science Monitor*, 24 January 1934, cutting, ERI papers, Fawcett Library.
7 Minutes, ERI general meeting, 9 September 1934, ERI papers, ML MS 2160/Y790.
8 Summary Report of Women's Consultative Committee, UA papers, ML MS 2160/Y790.
9 Littlejohn to Secretary-General League of Nations (undated), UA papers, ML MS 2160/4790.
10 Women's Consultative Committee, Information Bulletin, 1 June 1935, UA papers, ML MS 2160/Y790.
11 *Dawn* 21 January 1931.
12 Linda Littlejohn, Publicity Leaflet, Rischbieth papers, NLA MS 2004/4/306(a).
13 Open Door International (ODI), pamphlet, 1963, UA papers, ML MS 2160/Y4481.
14 Littlejohn report in Heagney op. cit. pp. 174–5.
15 ibid. p. 175.
16 ERI, Meeting Agenda, 10 September 1934, UA papers, ML MS 2160/Y790.
17 ODI submission to 16th Assembly of the League of Nations, quoted in Heagney op. cit., p. 177.
18 Joan Scott *Only Paradoxes to Offer* Harvard University Press, Cambridge, Boston, 1996.
19 ERI, minutes of meeting, 9 September 1934, UA papers, ML MS 2160/Y790.
20 ERI Maternity and Housekeeping Questionnaire (undated) UA papers, ML MS 2160/Y790.
21 Resolutions for ERI from UA (undated), UA papers, ML MS 2160/Y790.
22 Quoted in Patricia Grimshaw, Marilyn Lake, Ann McGrath and Marian Quartly *Creating a Nation* Penguin, Ringwood, 1996, p. 251.
23 Street to *Sydney Morning Herald* 20 February 1934, Street papers, NLA MS 2683/38, National Library of Australia.
24 Warren Denning 'The Economic Woman' *Australian National Review* 1 July 1938.
25 Australian Federation of Women Voters, report of proceedings, p. 4, UA papers, ML MS 2160/Y789.

26 Nellie Lord 'Feminism and Anti-Feminism', UA papers, ML MS 2160/Y790.
27 Street, circular letter, 23 April 1940, UA papers, ML MS 2160/Y789.
28 Littlejohn, circular letter, 15 November 1933, UA papers, ML MS 2160/Y789.
29 Heagney op. cit., p. 12.
30 ibid. p. 8.
31 ibid., p. 14.
32 ibid., p. 189.
33 ibid., p. 34.
34 ibid., p. 35.
35 ibid., p. 171.
36 ibid., p. 188.
37 ibid., p. 12.
38 ibid., p. 31.
39 Nerida Cohen, opinion on equal pay, 29 October 1937, UA papers, ML MS 2160/Y790.
40 Hughes quoted in P. Johnson 'Gender, class and work: the Council of Action on Equal pay campaign in Australia during World War 2' *Labour History* 50, May 1986, p. 132.
41 Irene Greenwood to Jessie Street 2 October 1940, Street papers, NLA MS 2683/3/159.
42 ERI, minutes of general meeting, 9 September 1934, UA papers, ML MS 2160/Y790.
43 Frances Fraser and Nettie Palmer eds 'Foreword', *Centenary Gift Book* Robertson and Mullens, Melbourne, 1934.
44 Frances Eldershaw ed. *The Peaceful Army* Ringwood, Penguin (Reprint), 1988, p. 2.
45 Miles Franklin diaries, June 1937, exercise book no. 3, ML MS 364/4, Mitchell Library.
46 Franklin diaries, February 1938, exercise book no. 2, ML MS 364/4.
47 ibid.
48 Report of application to the Federal Arbitration Court, UA papers, ML MS 2160/Y789.
49 UA circular letter to candidates, 9 September 1940, UA papers, ML MS 2160/Y789.
50 Lucy Gullett, 'What Remains to be Done . . .', UA papers, ML MS 2160/Y790.
51 Street to Minister F. M. Forde 13 March 1942, Accession no. 508/1, file 339/701/228, Australian Archives.
52 Street to members, UA, 20 February 1941, UA papers, ML MS 2160/Y789.

53 Erna Keighley to Minister F. M. Forde 31 July 1942, UA papers, ML MS 2160/Y789.
54 Circular, 7 August 1942, UA papers, ML MS 2160/Y789.
55 Franklin diaries, 28 August 1942, ML MS 364/4.
56 *Sydney Morning Herald* 21 October 1943.
57 *Daily Telegraph* 8 October 1943; 'Debuts in Canberra' in Marilyn Lake and Katie Holmes eds *Freedom Bound II: Documents on Women in Modern Australia* Allen & Unwin, Sydney, 1995, pp. 92–3.
58 Professor A. P. Elkin to Jessie Street, 19 November 1943, Street papers, NLA MS 2683/3/315.

Chapter 8

1 Street to 'dear fellow members', 16 May 1945, United Associations of Women (UA) papers, ML MS 2160/Y793, Mitchell Library.
2 ibid.
3 Street to 'dear fellow members', 5 June 1945, UA papers, op. cit.
4 Street to 'dear fellow members', 10 June 1945, UA papers, op. cit.
5 Tribe to Street 14 January 1952; Street to Tribe 5 February 1952, UA papers, op. cit.
6 Street to 'dear fellow members' 27 August 1945, UA papers, op. cit.
7 ibid.
8 'News Review', Street papers, NLA, MS 2683/3/694.
9 *Daily Telegraph* 10 June 1943.
10 Quoted in Marilyn Lake 'Female Desires: the Meaning of World War 2' in Joy Damousi and Marilyn Lake eds *Gender and War: Australians at War in the Twentieth Century* Cambridge University Press, Melbourne, 1995, p. 60.
11 ibid., p. 72.
12 *Daily Telegraph* 7 October 1943.
13 *Daily Telegraph* 20 May 1943.
14 Letter from J. C. Newport to Dr Wallace 28 November 1943, Wallace collection, University of Melbourne Archives.
15 Letter to Dr Wallace 12 November 1943, Wallace Collection, op. cit.
16 *Sydney Morning Herald* 26 March 1946.
17 ibid.
18 Dorothy Iremonger to *Sydney Morning Herald* 12 February 1943.
19 See Dianne Davidson *Women on the Warpath: Feminists of the First Wave* University of Western Australia Press, Nedlands, 1987, pp. 197–204.
20 Bessie Rischbieth 'Democracy at the Crossroads', report of radio broadcast, kindly provided by Dame Rachel Cleland.
21 Dianne Davidson *Women on the Warpath*, p. 215.
22 Secretary to members, 14 May 1950, UA papers, ML MS 2160/Y789.

23 UA to candidates, 12 April 1951, UA papers, ML MS 2160/Y789.
24 League of Nations Union, Tasmanian branch, to Street 25 November 1943, Minister for External Affairs to Street 24 January 1944, *Hebrew Standard* 10 February 1944, cutting, UA papers, ML MS 2160/Y791.
25 Norman Paling to UA 4 August 1949, UA papers, ML MS 2160/Y791.
26 Calwell to Street 1 September 1949 UA papers, ML MS 2160/Y791.
27 C. L. Scrimgeour to Minister for the Interior, 6 September 1949, and to Aboriginal Welfare Board 4 October 1949, Aboriginal Welfare Board to UA 18 October 1949, UA papers, ML MS 2160/Y791.
28 This account is based substantially on Barbara Curthoys and Audrey McDonald *More Than a Hat and Glove Brigade The Story of the Union of Australian Women*, Bookpress, Sydney, 1996.

Chapter 9

1 *Telegraph* 1 April 1965.
2 *Sunday Truth* 11 April 1965.
3 Pamphlet *Women are Members of the Public*, c. 1965. (copy given to author by Ro Bognor)
4 *Sunday Truth* 4 April 1965.
5 Pamphlet, *Women are Members of the Public*, op. cit. Also quoted in 'Women in Chains' *Woman's Day* 10 May 1965.
6 ibid.
7 *Telegraph* 5 April 1965.
8 *Telegraph* 11 April 1965.
9 ibid.
10 *Courier Mail* 5 April 1965.
11 Zelda D'Aprano *Zelda* Spinifex, Melbourne (new edition), 1995, p. 171.
12 Quoted in Edna Ryan and Anne Conlon *Gentle Invaders Australian Women at Work* Penguin, Ringwood, 1989, p. 151.
13 D'Aprano op. cit., p. 175.
14 ibid., p. 191.
15 Report on Women's Liberation Conference, 16–18 May 1970, Women's Liberation Conferences 1970–74, First Ten Years Collection (FTYC), Sydney.
16 'Now!' The Macquarie University Group of the Australian Women's Liberation Movement', 1 January 1970, FTYC.
17 'We are fighting too', Glebe group, 1970, FTYC, Archive of Women's Liberation, Sydney.
18 Kate Jennings, Leaflet. 'Watch Out . . .', 1 September 1970, FTYC.
19 Sydney *Women's Liberation Newsletter* October/November 1970, FTYC.
20 'Only the Chains Have Changed', 15 December 1969, FTYC.
21 Quoted in Chilla Bulbeck *Living Feminism The Impact of the Women's*

Movement on Three Generations of Australian Women Cambridge University Press, Melbourne, 1997, p. 129.
22 Kate Millett *Sexual Politics* Granada, London, 1970, pp. 23, 39.
23 ibid., p. 25, 33, 44.
24 Leaflet, 'Women's Action Committee', Bon Hull papers, Melbourne Women's Liberation Archives (MWLA).
25 'Abortion' *Vashti's Voice* 2, 1972, Vashti Collective papers, MWLA.
26 Sydney *Women's Liberation Newsletter* September 1970, FTYC.
27 Women's Liberation Postcards, 1 January 1970, FTYC.
28 Balmain group, letter, 24 July 1970, FTYC.
29 Vivien Altman 'Fairlea' *Vashti's Voice* 1, 1972, Vashti Collective papers, MWLA.
30 Melbourne *Women's Liberation Newsletter*, 1 November 1972; Submission to the Equal Pay/National Wage Case, 1972 Women's Liberation Movement MWLA.
31 Melbourne *Women's Liberation Newsletter* December 1972, MWLA.
32 'The Selling of Sex', Bon Hull papers, MWLA.
33 Stannard Una 'The Mask of Beauty', Women's Liberation Collective papers, 23A/08/03/46, MWLA.
34 Adri Palamara 'The Hand That Cradles the Rock', Bon Hull papers, MWLA.
35 *Women at Work* booklet, FTYC, Women's Liberation Publications, Sydney, 1/6.
36 Cited in *Liberation* 4, June 1971, reprinted in Marilyn Lake and Katie Holmes eds *Freedom Bound II: Documents on Women in Modern Australia* Allen & Unwin, Sydney, 1995, pp. 148–54.
37 Germaine Greer *The Female Eunuch* Macgibbon and Kee, 1971 (2nd edition), p. 20.
38 ibid., p. 19.
39 ibid., p. 21.
40 Janey Stone 'Who Are We? Where Are We Going?' *Vashti's Voice* 1, 1972, Vashti Collective papers, 37/1/1/1, MWLA.
41 'Group report', Melbourne *Women's Liberation Newsletter* February 1973.
42 Sydney *Women's Liberation Newsletter* November 1973; leaflet Elsie Women's Refuge, SFB/Elsie/44, FTYC.
43 Women's Liberation of Western Australia, June 1974, Murdoch University. See also records at the Lespar Library, Darlington, WA.
44 ibid.

Chapter 10

1 *Women's Liberation Newsletter* August 1973, Marie Rowan papers, 68/4/3, Melbourne Women's Liberation Archives (MWLA).
2 ibid.

NOTES

3 Sue Bellamy 'How Can We Get What We Want', Glebe group, 1 November 1970 First Ten Years Collective (Archive), (FTYC) Sydney.
4 Susan Eade (Magarey) 'And Now We Are Six: a plea for women's liberation' *Refractory Girl a journal of radical feminist thought* 13/14, March 1977, p. 3.
5 Juanita Keig 'Building a Mass Movement for Women's Liberation', 30 January 1971, Women's Liberation Conferences, FTYC, Sydney.
6 Liberation Information, 1 March 1973, Murdoch University.
7 Melbourne *Women's Liberation Newsletter* April 1973, Marie Rowan papers, op. cit.
8 'Week-end at Sorrento', Marie Rowan papers, op. cit.
9 Melbourne *Women's Liberation Newsletter* December 1972, Marie Rowan papers, op. cit.
10 Melbourne *Women's Liberation Newsletter* September 1972, Marie Rowan papers, op. cit.
11 Melbourne *Women's Liberation Newsletter* December 1972, Marie Rowan papers, op. cit.
12 ibid.
13 Melbourne *Women's Liberation Newsletter* September 1973, Marie Rowan papers, op. cit.
14 Melbourne *Women's Liberation Newsletter* 1 January 1973, Marie Rowan papers, op. cit.
15 Melbourne *Women's Liberation Newsletter* July 1973, Marie Rowan papers, op. cit.
16 ibid.
17 Melbourne *Women's Liberation Newsletter* September 1973, Marie Rowan papers, op. cit.
18 'The Women's Movement', Melbourne *Women's Liberation Newsletter* May, June, July 1973, Marie Rowan papers, op. cit.
19 General meeting Report, Melbourne *Women's Liberation Newsletter* April 1977, Marie Rowan papers, op. cit.
20 Melbourne *Women's Liberation Newsletter* December 1974, Marie Rowan papers, op. cit.
21 Marie, 'A letter from Marie from Bayswater', Melbourne *Women's Liberation Newsletter* March 1976, Marie Rowan papers, op. cit.
22 Faust quoted in Joyce Nicholson 'The Women's Electoral Lobby and Women's Employment: Strategies and Outcome', MA minor thesis, Women's Studies, University of Melbourne, 1991, pp. 24–5.
23 ibid., p. 27.
24 ibid., p. 23.
25 *Women's Electoral Lobby (WEL) ACT News* 2, 15 March 1973, Canberra, p. 228.
26 Nicholson, op. cit., pp. 35–6.

27 Jocelynne A. Scutt 'Legal activism' in Barbara Caine ed. *Australian Feminism A Companion* Oxford University Press, Melbourne, 1998, p. 450.
28 Canberra WEL report on national conference, June 1972, FTYC.
29 Kate 'I think I must forget about men' Melbourne *Women's Liberation Newsletter* September 1973, Marie Rowan papers, MWLA.
30 Interview with Shirley Castley, 8 March 1997, Hobart.
31 Jocelyn Clarke and Laurie Bebbington 'Lesbian Oppression and Liberation', Sue Jackson papers, 06/04/02, MWLA.
32 Bev Kingston 'Lesbianism and Feminist Theory' *Refractory Girl* 5, summer, 1974, p. 5.
33 Zelda and Maureen 'Sisters Speak and response to Sister Speak', Melbourne *Women's Liberation Newsletter* April 1976, Marie Rowan papers, 68/5, MWLA.
34 Hobart Women's Action Group 'Sexism and the Women's Liberation Movement', *Refractory Girl* Summer 1974 pp. 30–33.
35 Charlotte Bunch 'What is Lesbian Feminism?' *Vashti's Voice* Autumn 1976, Vashti Collective, 37/01/05.1, MWLA.
36 'radicalesbian lifestyle' *Refractory Girl*, Summer 1974, pp. 12–15.
37 Diane 'Brunswick', Melbourne *Women's Liberation Newsletter* May 1974, Marie Rowan papers, 68/4/4, MWLA.
38 Bon Hull 'Dear Newsletter Collective' Melbourne *Women's Liberation Newsletter* September 1977, Marie Rowan papers, 68/4/4, MWLA.
39 Women's Liberation Newsletter Collective 'Our Thoughts' Melbourne *Women's Liberation Newsletter* November 1973, Marie Rowan papers, 68/4/4, MWLA.
40 'Australian Women Against Rape', Melbourne *Women's Liberation Newsletter* March 1976, Marie Rowan papers, 68/4/4, MWLA.
41 Bon Hull 'La Dolce Vita on Palm Island', *Vashti's Voice* 3, March 1973, pp. 9, 18.
42 ibid.
43 Bif Macdougall 'On organisation', paper for Sydney conference, January 1971, Sydney FTYC, 71/14.
44 Louise E. King, conference paper, 30 January 1971, Sydney conference, FTYC, 71/19.
45 Pat Eatock 'There's a Snake in My Caravan' in Jocelynne A. Scutt ed. *Different Lives* Penguin, Ringwood, 1987, p. 25.
46 WEL Canberra, report of national conference, January 1973, NLA MS 3683/4/1, National Library of Australia.
47 Pat O'Shane 'Is There Any Relevance in the Women's Movement for Aboriginal Women?' *Refractory Girl* 12, September 1976, pp. 31–4.
48 Marxist-Feminist Conference Collective, 11 June 1977, FTYC.

Chapter 11

1 Lyndall Ryan 'Feminism and the Federal Bureaucracy 1972–83' in Sophie Watson and Rosemary Pringle eds *Playing the State: Australian Feminist Interventions* Allen & Unwin, Sydney, 1990, p. 74.
2 Sarah Dowse quoted in Ryan op. cit., p. 81.
3 Elizabeth Reid 'The Child of our Movement: A Movement of Women' in Jocelynne A. Scutt ed. *Different Lives* Penguin, Ringwood, 1987, p. 15.
4 Marian Sawer *Sisters in Suits: Women and Public Policy in Australia* Allen & Unwin, Sydney, 1990, p. xiv. I am indebted to Sawer's comprehensive account for much of the information in this chapter.
5 ibid., p. 18.
6 Shirley Castley, report of meeting, 27 January 1975, public meetings file, FTYC, Sydney.
7 Elizabeth Reid quoted in Marian Sawer, *Sisters in Suits*, op. cit., p. 15.
8 Ryan op. cit., p. 81.
9 Quoted in Gail Mason 'Violence' in Barbara Caine ed. *Australian Feminism A Companion* Oxford University Press, Melbourne, 1998, p. 343.
10 Mary Kalantzis 'Ethnicity meets gender meets class in Australia' in Watson and Pringle op. cit. p. 39.
11 Denise Riley *Am I That Name? Feminism and the Category of Women in History* Macmillan, London, 1988; Judith Butler *Gender Trouble Feminism and the Subversion of Identity* Routledge, New York, 1990.
12 Gisela Kaplan *The Meagre Harvest* Allen & Unwin, Sydney, 1996.
13 ibid., p. 128.
14 ibid., p. 124.
15 Anna Pha 'Working Women's Centre: Its First Five Years', Minor Thesis, MA (Industrial Relations), University of Melbourne, 1982, p. 15.
16 Sawer op. cit., p. 119.
17 Quoted in Chilla Bulbeck *Living Feminism The Impact of the Women's Movement on Three Generations of Australian Women* Cambridge University Press, Melbourne, 1997, p. 162.
18 'AFP as an industrial project' in Marilyn Lake and Katie Holmes eds *Freedom Bound II: Documents on Women in Modern Australia* Allen & Unwin, Sydney, 1995, p. 172.
19 ibid., p. 160.
20 Jackie Huggins ' "Firing On In The Mind": Aboriginal Women Domestic Servants in the Inter-War Years' *Hecate* 13, 2, 1987/88, p. 23.
21 Elizabeth Williams 'Aboriginal First, Woman Second' in Scutt op. cit., p. 72.
22 Anna Cole, Julia Burke, and Winnie Woods 'Ngaanyatjarra Pitjantjatjara Yankunytjatjara Women's Council' in Caine *Australian Feminism* op. cit., p. 466.

23 Lilla Watson 'Sister, Black is the Colour of My Soul' in Scutt op. cit., p. 51.
24 Jackie Huggins 'A Contemporary View of Aboriginal Women's Relationship to the White Women's Movement' in Norma Grieve and Ailsa Burns eds *Australian Women Contemporary Feminist Thought* Oxford University Press, Melbourne, 1994.
25 Sawer op. cit., p. 139.
26 Catrina Felton and Liz Flanagan 'Institutionalised Feminism: A Tidda's Perspective' *Lilith a feminist history journal* 8, Summer, 1993, p. 55.
27 Ien Ang 'I'm a feminist but . . . "Other" women and post-national feminism' in Barbara Caine and Rosemary Pringle eds *Transitions New Australian Feminisms* Allen and Unwin, Sydney, 1995, p. 73.

Conclusion

1 Joan Wallach Scott *Only Paradoxes to Offer: French Feminists and the Rights of Man* Harvard University Press, Cambridge, 1996, pp. 3–4.
2 Kathy Bail ed. *DIY Feminism* Allen & Unwin, Sydney, 1996, p. 6.
3 See the words of the UA song 'Wild, wild women' in Marilyn Lake and Katie Holmes eds *Freedom Bound II: Documents on Women in Modern Australia* Allen & Unwin, Sydney, 1995, pp. 99–100.

INDEX

Aboriginal Affairs (Department of), 273–4
Aboriginal and Islander Congress, 274
Aboriginal-Australian Fellowship, 250
Aboriginal Health Service, 250, 272
Aboriginal Land Councils, 271–2
Aboriginal Welfare Board, 208, 250
Aboriginal Women's Unit, 274
Aborigines
  citizenship, 6,14, 118, 250
  dispossession, 15, 22, 123, 132–3, 271, 275
  land rights, 15, 249–50, 271–3
  parents' custody rights, 82–3, 118, 126, 196
  removal of children, 14, 83, 195–6
  rights, 91, 93–4, 110–13 passim
  women see women, Aboriginal
Aborigines' Protection League, 133
abortion, 201, 223–4, 226–7, 237–8, 245, 254, 261, 267, 270–1, 282
Ackerman, Jessie, 25–60
Action for Family Planning, 269
Adelaide Women's Liberation Manifesto, 227
Adult Migrant Education Program, 268
Affirmative Action Act (Equal Employment Opportunity for Women) Act (1986), 264
alcohol, 12, 24, 26, 54, 65–6, 148, 150, 198, 214, 270, 272
Allen, Elsie, 211
Allen, Judith, 30, 87, 251
Allen, Stella, 159
American servicemen in Australia during World War II, 198–9

Amjah, A.S.B., 208
Andersen, Dr Margaret, 71
Anderson, Francis, 56
Anderson, Maybanke, 36
Andrews, Shirley, 14, 208–9
Ang, Ien, 15, 275
Ansara, Martha, 221
Anti-Discrimination Act (1984), 262
Anti-Liquor Leagues, 65
Anti-Slavery Society, 14, 112–15, 117, 130, 161, 208
Anti-Suffrage League, 42
Archdale, Helen, 168, 171
Are Women Taking Men's Jobs?, 10, 168, 176, 178–9, 181, 263
Ashby, Margaret Corbett, 193
Ashton, Lizzie, 35
assimilation policy, 208
Association for the Protection of Native Races, 115
Association of Non-English Speaking Background Women, 269
Australasian Home Reading Union, 38–9
Australian Aboriginal Fellowship, 209
Australian and New Zealand Women Voters' Committee, 155, 169
Australian Council of Trade Unions (ACTU), 185, 212, 218
Australian Federation of Business and Professional Women, 218
Australian Federation of Societies for Equal Citizenship, 50
Australian Federation of Women's Societies, 154, 158–9
Australian Federation of Women Voters

(AFWV), 7–8, 10, 50–3, 76–7, 81, 94, 118, 124, 127, 131–4, 142, 144, 150, 154, 159–60, 163, 169, 177, 191, 201, 203, 218, 241
Australian Feminist Studies (journal), 232
Australian Highway (journal), 91
Australian Imperial Force, 65
Australian Labor Party (ALP), 7, 27, 38, 41, 44, 73–6, 91, 101–4, 105, 143, 145, 151, 172–3, 177, 188–9, 203–4, 215, 239, 262–4
Australian Land Army, 187
Australian Migrant Women's Association, 267
Australian National University (ANU), 232, 254–5, 263
Australian Women's Army Service, 187
Australian Women's Charter, 191, 194, 197, 199–200, 202–3
Australian Women's Charter Conference (1943), 190
Australian Women's Charter Conference (1946), 194
Australian Women's Charter Report (1946–1949), 194
Australian Women's National League (AWNL), 90, 143
Australian Women's Suffrage Society, 42
Australian Women's Trade Union Conference, 271

baby health centres, 53, 69, 197
Badham, Miss Edith, 28
Bail, Kathy, 281–2
Baillie, Helen, 131
Baillie, Dr Mabel, 76
Baines, Jennie, 63
Baker, Carol, 229
Baker, E.H., 105
Bandler, Faith, 14, 209, 250
Barrett, Dr Edith, 79
basic wage, 78, 98, 104–5, 172, 179–180, 185, 211
Battye, Margaret, 206
Beadle, Jean, 143–5
Bear, Annette (later Bear-Crawford), 43–4
Bear, John Pinney, 43
Beaurepaire, Beryl, 261
beauty contests, 199, 225–6, 228
de Beauvoir, Simone, 228, 277
Bebbington, Laurie, 242–3

Begtrup, Bodil, 204–5
Bellamy, Sue, 219, 231
Bennett, Mary (Montgomerie), 5, 14, 51, 91, 110–16, 118–25, 128–31, 134, 195, 208–9
Benston, Margaret, 221
Bent, Thomas, 44
Bernadino, Minerva, 193
Besant, Annie, 51
Bettenay, Elke, 233
Bill of Rights (or 'Blanket Bill') proposal, 206–7
Birks, Rosetta, 40
Black Women's Action Committee, 250
Bland, Professor F.A., 108
Bleakley, J.W., 113–14
Board for the Protection of Aborigines, 82
Boelke, Dr Grace, 70
Bognor, Ro, 10, 214
Booth, Angela, 89–90, 144
Bourke, Eleanor, 273
Bread and Roses group, 225
British Commonwealth League (BCL), 113, 114, 122, 124, 160, 169
British Dominions' Women Suffrage (later Citizenship) Union, 155
Bromham, Ada, 5, 11, 14, 51, 53–5, 56, 65, 66, 74, 76, 79, 94, 111, 118, 121, 125, 126, 131, 134, 140, 143, 144, 151, 190, 195, 199, 202, 208, 209, 216
Brown, Dr Vera Scantlebury, 70
Bruce, Stanley Melbourne, 103–4, 141
Bryce, Mrs, 131
Buchanan, Cheryl, 248
Buckley, Aileen, 273
Bull Ant (magazine), 32, 34
Bulletin (magazine), 32, 34
Bunch, Charlotte, 244
Buxton, T.H., 116

CAAMA, 272
Call to the Women of Australia, A, 110, 119, 122
Callope, Muriel, 210
Caldwell, Robert, 40
Calwell, Arthur, 207–8
Campbell, Dame Janet, 81, 82
Capochi, Eileen, 233
'Care of the Child in Wartime Committee', 197

INDEX

Carlton Women's Liberation Group, 219
Carvosso, Annie, 156, 158
Cass, Dorothea, 122
Castley, Shirley, 242, 258
Catholic Women's League, 263
Catt, Carrie Chapman, 50, 160, 161
Centennials, 132
Central Australian Women's Council, 272
Central Methodist Mission, 43
Chief Protectors of Aborigines, 83, 113, 122, 127, 130
Chifley, Ben, 203, 206
child care, 5, 15, 190, 195, 196–7, 202, 224, 226, 227, 230, 238, 240, 254, 256–7, 267, 268, 273, 278, 280, 282
child endowment, 10, 12, 98, 101, 104, 106, 108, 149, 151, 186, 195, 210, 277
child welfare, 39, 55, 66, 67, 68, 79, 81, 149, 156
Child Welfare Association, 156
Child Welfare Bureau, 68
children
  custody rights, 2, 3, 6, 15, 62, 72, 73, 82, 84–6, 118, 126, 196
  'neglected', 72, 83
  removal of, 14, 83, 195–6
Children's Books (Action Group), 224
Chinese-Australia Friendship Society, 54
Christison, Robert, 111
citizenship, 6, 14, 50, 51, 55, 61, 62, 66, 75, 87, 93, 97, 118, 139–48, 154, 155, 156, 158, 160, 161, 169, 184, 187, 188, 215, 231, 250, 264, 280
  mother-citizen, 10
Clark, Caroline, 67, 73
Clarke, Jocelyn, 242, 243
Cobbe, Frances Power, 36
Cohen, Nerida, 181, 185, 190
Cold War, 14, 202–4, 208
Coleman, Marie, 256
Collison, Chave, 114, 160
Coming Out show, 259
Commission on the Status of Women, 14, 192–3, 194, 202–4
Communist party, 99, 181, 210, 219, 233
Community Controlled Childcare, 224
Community Employment Program, 273
Community Health Centres, 258, 277

Conlon, Ann, 251
consciousness raising (CR), 233–6, 239, 244
contraception, 90, 95–6, 220–2, 223, 245, 267, 269
  The Pill, 220
Convention on Slavery, 94, 114, 115
Cook, Constance, 5, 14, 51, 110, 111, 112, 114, 115, 116, 117, 123, 124, 130, 131, 133, 134, 140, 161, 195
Coonan, Helen, 240
Cooper, Leontine, 26
Couchman, Elizabeth (May), 143
Council of Action for Equal Pay, 10, 74, 181, 185
Council on Violence Against Women (New South Wales Premier's), 265
Country Women's Association (CWA), 81, 122
Cowan, Edith, 11, 37, 51, 55, 60, 79, 102, 152–3
Cox, Eva, 240
Crimes (Girls' Protection) Amendment Act (1910), 147
Crowley, F.K., *New History of Australia*, 6
Curthoys, Ann, 251
Curthoys, Barbara, 211, 214
Curtin, John, 104, 106, 144, 190, 193
Cuthbertson, Margaret, 71

Dahlitz, Julie, 223, 240
Dakers, Jennifer, 229
Dale, Marguerite, 8–9, 68, 150, 159
Daley, Jean, 5, 56, 72, 75, 78, 91, 94, 96, 102, 103, 144, 151, 202, 262
Damned Whores and God's Police, 251, 263
Daniels, Dr Kay, 259
D'Aprano, Zelda, 10, 217–19, 233, 243
Davey, Dr Constance, 68
Dawn (journal), 20, 21, 22, 23, 36, 61, 66, 77, 94, 112, 115, 124, 125, 147, 153, 155
Dawn Club, 21
Daylight, Phyllis, 273, 274
Deacon, Destiny, 249
Deakin, Alfred, 55
Democrats (Australian), 262
Department of Immigration and Ethnic Affairs, 268
Derham, Freda, 42

difference
  cultural, 118, 266–76 passim, 266, 275
  sexual, 118, 173–4, 176, 192, 204, 244, 256, 262, 281
divorce, 150, 204, 207, 240
  grounds for, 195
Dixson, Miriam, 251
DIY Feminism, 281
DIY feminists, 281–2
Doll's House, A, 29, 228
domestic work, 11, 241, 265
Dowse, Sarah, 255, 257, 260
Doyle, Ursula, 268
Draft Declaration of Human Rights, 204
Dugdale, Henrietta (later Dugdale Johnson), 23, 45
Dwyer, Kate, 101, 213

Eade, Susan (later Magarey), 232, 251
Eatock, Pat, 248
economic independence, 88, 89, 91, 92, 95, 96, 98, 103, 105, 106, 173, 175, 210, 278, 280
Egan, Melba, 126
Elliot, Liz, 219
Ellis, Dr Constance, 76
Equal Employment Opportunity (EEO), 261, 263, 265, 266
Equal Employment Opportunity Unit, 261
equal moral standard, 95, 96, 111, 148, 160, 199, 264
equal pay, 5, 16, 90, 97, 99, 150, 180, 181, 185, 188, 202, 206, 211, 212, 218, 225, 239, 240, 277, 278
Equal Pay Act (1958), 212
Equal Pay decision (1969), 218
Equal Pay decision (1972), 225
equal rights, 4, 163, 167–90 passim, 191–213 passim, 215, 239
Equal Rights International (ERN), 1, 163, 168, 170, 171–2, 174, 175, 182
Equal Rights Treaty (Montevideo), 170, 172
Equal Opportunities for Women Association, 217
equal opportunity, 202, 206, 212, 253, 254, 256, 278
Equal Pay Committee, 224
Equal Status Committee, 168, 178
Ethnic Community Councils, 266

eugenics, 96
Evatt, H.V., 190, 203

family endowment, 104, 106
Family Law Act (1975), 240
family wage, 5, 55, 99, 100, 105–66
Faust, Beatrice, 238
Federal Convention (1897), 27, 39, 40
Federation of Business and Professional Women, 264
Federation of Ethnic Community Councils of Australia (FECCA), 268, 269
Federazione Italiana Lavoratori Emigrati e Famiglia (FILEF), 267
Fell, Liz, 244
Female Eunuch, The, 11, 227–8, 233, 242, 245
femininity, 221, 226
feminism
  see also woman movement, women's liberation, and women's movement
  activism, 3, 4
  anti-conscription, 63–4
  difference, 15, 118, 163, 173–5, 192, 204, 244, 256, 266–76 passim, 275–81
  discrimination, 191–2, 204–9
  equality, 2, 4, 5, 45, 89, 163, 173, 175, 205, 206, 217, 240, 244, 279
  institutionalised, 253–76 passim
  interdependence, 12, 55
  limits of, 15, 175–6
  non-party, 10, 13, 52, 61, 67, 75–7, 84, 98, 103, 105, 140, 141, 145, 148–9, 151, 152, 154, 160, 260, 278
  post-suffrage activism, 9–16, 49–163 passim
  racism, 183, 222, 274, 275
  revolutionary, 231–2, 239
  'state', 253–66 passim
Feminist Club, 10, 52, 66, 80, 81, 105, 140, 147, 157, 181
'femocrats', 254, 257, 260, 261, 264, 273, 275
Ferguson, Mrs G.O., 26
Few Hours in a Far Off Age, A, 23
Figes, Eva, 233
film censorship boards, 12
Firestone, Shulamith, 233
Fisher, Andrew, 56, 75

INDEX

Fogarty, Penny, 229
Forrest, Sir John, 25
Francis, May, 78
Franklin, Miles, 183–4, 188–9
Fraser, Malcolm, 260
Free Kindergarten Union, 38
Freeman, Jo, 234
Fremantle Labor Women's League, 143
From a Victorian to a Modern, 73
Fruin, Diane, 229
Fullerton, Mary, 132

Galbally Report, 267
Gatbonton, Cora, 269
Gatens, Moira, 252
Gay Women's (Action) Group, 224
Gentle Invaders, 251
Gibbs, Pearl, 14, 208, 209, 210, 250
Gieke, Alva, 218
Giles, Pat, 233
Gillett, Judy, 233
Gilman, Charlotte Perkins, 36, 51, 87, 88, 154
Gilmore, Mary, 183
Girls, Schools and Society, 259
Glencross, Eleanor, 102, 144, 151
Glynn, Freda, 272
Golding, Annie, 101, 213
Golding, Kate, 41
Goldstein, Vida, 13, 24, 37, 44, 49, 53, 57, 63, 64, 76, 90, 120, 144–6, 147, 151, 154–5, 161, 163, 169, 206, 216, 264
Goode, Agnes, 84, 102
Gordon, Linda, 221, 233
Graham, Di, 241
Green, T.H., 55
Greenland, Margaret, 219
Greenwood, Irene, 181–2
Greer, Germaine, 11, 227–9, 233, 242, 278
Greville, Henrietta, 5, 91, 210
Griffin, Mrs, 163
Grimshaw, Patricia, 251
Grosz, Elizabeth, 252
Guillaume, George, 73
Gullett, Dr Lucy, 186

Habitual Criminals Bill, 62
Haines, Janine, 262
Halley, Dr Gertrude, 68
Harford, Lesbia, 90
Harper, Andrew, 38
Harper, Jan, 223

Harris, Bertha, 244
Harris, Sir John, 112, 114, 117
Harrison Lee, Bessie, 32–4, 39
Harvester judgment (1907), 55
Haug, Frigga, 279
Hawke, R.J., 218
Hayden, Bill, 239
Heagney, Muriel, 1, 10, 56, 74, 80, 92, 97–100, 102, 104, 162, 168, 171–2, 178, 180–1, 185, 202, 262–3
Hecate (journal), 251
Henry, Alice, 61, 102–3
heterosexism, 234, 244
Heubel, Kerry, 241
Higgins, H.B., 56
Higgins, Sue (later Sheridan), 251
Higson, Eve, 190
Hill, Ernestine, 121
Hinder, Eleanor, 70, 116, 161, 163
Hodge, Margaret, 155
Holder, Frederick William, 40
Holman, May, 152–3
Holman, W.A., 146
Holt, Harold, 212
homophobia, 244
Hooton, Henrietta, 145
Hotel and Caterers' Union, 97, 212
Hotel, Club and Restaurant Employees' Union, 201
Hotson, Kathleen, 64
Housewives' Association, 81
Huggins, Jackie, 271, 273
Hughes, Eva, 143
Hull, Bon, 218, 246, 247
Hughes, W.M., 85, 159, 169

identity politics, 266
Iles, Mrs, 51
Immigrant Women's Resource Centre, 268
Immigrant Women's Speak Out Association, 269
infant mortality rate, 67, 70, 80, 270
Infants Protection Act (1904), 43, 62, 147
Inter-American Commission of Women, 168
International Alliance of Women, 241
International Conference of Working Women, 212
International Labor Office (ILO), 150, 167–9, 212, 225

International Peace Conference (1919), 161
International Woman Suffrage Conference, 44
International Women's Day (IWD), 240, 246
International Women's Suffrage Alliance (IWSA) (later the International Alliance of Women for Suffrage and Equal Citizenship and later again the International Alliance of Women), 63, 67, 155, 157, 160–3, 170
International Women's Year (IWP) (1975), 15, 258, 267
Ironworkers' Union Women's Auxiliary, 201
Itinerants' Society, 27, 37

Jackson, Sue, 243
James, Britomarte, 154, 160
Jennings, Kate, 220–1
John, Cecilia, 63, 161
Jones, Edith, 14, 69, 93, 110, 112–15, 124, 132, 134, 152–3, 160
Jones, K. A. Gilman, 168, 178
Jones, Rev. John, 112
Johnston, Isobel, 203
Johnstone, Mary, 273
Joyner, Mrs, 119
Jull, Dr Roberta, 68–9
Juvenile Smoking Suppression Act (1903), 147

Kalantzis, Mary, 266
Kaplan, Gisela, 266
Karrakatta Club, 37
Katz, Alicia, 64, 100
Keighley, Erna, 187
Kelly, Gale, 221
King, Helen, 61
King, Jane, 26
King, M., 158
Kingston, Beverley, 243, 251
Kingston, Charles, 40
Kirner, Joan, 262
Koedt, Anne, 221, 233
Koori-Binna, 250
Kosky, Michel, 229
Kristin, T., 236–7
Kropinyeri, Matthew, 83

Labor Call (journal), 74, 93, 95, 101
Labor Party *see* Australian Labor Party
Labor women, 64–5, 73–7, 91, 98, 101–4, 143–5, 152, 259, 262
Labor Women's Conference, 144
Labor Women's Organisation, 65
'lady doctors', 60
Ladies' Social Purity Society, 24
Lake, Louise, 255
Lane, William, *The Workingman's Paradise*, 278
Langton, Marcia, 271, 273
Lavender, Bella, 37–8, 39
Lawrence, Carmen, 262
Lawson, Louisa, 19, 22–3, 28, 31, 36, 41, 49, 58, 182
League of Nations, 8, 68–9, 94, 114–15, 132, 139, 150, 157, 159, 169, 171, 192
League of Nations Assemblies, 68, 149, 169
League of Nations Union, 68, 139, 147, 207
League of Women Voters, 7–8, 152, 206
Leavitt, Mary, 25
Ledon, Amelia, 193
Lee, Mary, 24–5, 40
lesbianism, 241–6
Lewis, Sarah, 97
Liberal Party, 143, 210, 239, 261
Limitation of Offspring, 42
Lindsay, Norman, 56
Littlejohn, Linda, 1–2, 140, 148, 150, 163, 167–8, 170–2, 184, 202, 282
Locke-Burns, Lilian, 44, 56, 74, 91–2, 143, 278
Longman, Irene, 79, 105–6
Lord, Nellie, 177
Love, Courtship and Marriage, 42
Lowe, Annie, 45
Lusher motion, 261
Lutz, Bertha, 191–3
Lynch, Lena, 104
Lyne, William, 41
Lyons, Dame Enid, 184, 189
Lyons, Joseph, 114, 189

McAulay, Ida, 27, 37
MacCallum, M.W., 78
McCaughey, Winsome, 240
MacDonald, Amelia, 65, 141
McDonald, Louisa, 38

INDEX

Mackellar, C.K., 146
McKorkindale, Isabel, 190
McLennan, Hector, 40
McMahon, William, 239
McNeilly, Charlotte Elizabeth, 2
McPhee, Ian, 261
Maher, Marjorie, 211
Mahlab, Eve, 239
Mainardi, Pat, 233
Maloney, Dr William, 42, 45
Manning, Sir William, 38
March of Australian Women, 7
marriage, 2, 35, 87, 91, 99
   'companionate', 33–4
   conjugal rights, 19, 33, 93
   legal status of women within, 4, 10, 19, 93
   nationality rights within, 149, 169–70, 190
   rape within, 15, 35
   rights of women within, 3, 19
   sexual violence within, 20, 35
Marriage and Heredity, 33
Marriage Guidance Council, 204
Married Women's Property Act, 39, 149
Married Women Teachers' Committee, 148
Married Women Teachers and Lecturers Dismissal Act, 149, 178
Martel, Nellie, 41
Martyn, Edith How, 161
masculinity
   reform of, 31–6, 40
Maternal and Infant Welfare Centres, 15, 227
maternal mortality, 80–2, 270
maternity, 75–6, 172
maternity allowance, 10, 71, 75–82, 101–2, 149, 210, 277
   see also motherhood endowment
maternity benefits, 12, 15
maternity leave, 254, 263, 267
Matthews, Jill, 244, 251
Meagre Harvest, The, 266
Meinck, Cheryl, 233, 239
Mejane (journal), 233
men, white
   sexual relations with Aboriginal women, 111
Men's League for Women Suffrage, 4
Miethke, Adelaide, 133, 184
Migrant Resource Centre, 268

Migrant Women Speak, 268
Migrant Women's Speak Out, 268
Mill, John Stuart, 36, 40
Miller, Emma, 26, 64
Millet, Kate, 222–3, 233
Milne, Frances, 268
Miners' Women's Auxiliaries, 210
Minns, B.E., 32
Mitchell, Juliet, 233
Montefiore, Dora, 21, 73
Moore, Eleanor, 161
Moreley, Rev. W., 115
Morrison, Annie, 126
Moseley, Henry, 124, 130
mothers
   rights as, 56, 72–86 *passim*, 103
   unmarried, 75, 80, 204
Mothers' and Babies' Health Association, 67
Mothers' Pension Fund, 74
mothers' schools, 69
motherhood, 20, 29, 50, 86, 145, 173, 205, 217, 256
   voluntary, 2, 33, 39, 200–1
motherhood endowment, 5, 12, 91–2, 98–9, 101, 103–4, 106, 108, 149, 195, 211, 256, 278
Mottee, Matina, 269
Movement for the Ordination of Women, 264
Ms (magazine), 238
Mulcahy, Ellen, 97
Muller, Charles, 26
Munro, James, 43
Murdoch, Walter, 56
Muscio, Mildred, 104, 106
My Wife, My Daughter and Poor Mary Ann, 251

Nannup, Emily, 126
National Abortion Action Coalition, 233
National Agenda for Women, 265
National Committee on Violence Against Women, 265
National Council of Women (NCW), 9–10, 58, 61, 70, 74, 76–9, 97, 104–5, 133, 140, 156–7, 159–60, 185, 191, 218, 225, 264
National Education Campaign, 265
National Health and Medical Research Council (NHMRC), 200

Nationalist Party, 11, 55, 102
National Women's Advisory Council, 261, 264, 267, 273
National Women's Consultative Council (NWCC), 264, 269
Neglected Children and Juvenile Offenders' Act (1905), 82, 147
Neglected Children's Department (VIC), 73
Neville, A.O., 122, 124, 130
New Education Fellowship, 201
New Left, 221
New Protection, 56
Newcombe, Harriet, 155, 158
Ngaanyatjarra Pitjantjatjara Yankunytjatjara Women's Council, 271–2
Nicholls, Elizabeth, 25, 157–8
Nicholson, Joyce, 240
Non-English Speaking Background (NESB), 266–7, 269
Non-Party News (journal), 194
Nortin, Nan, 194
Nurses (Action) Group, 224

O'Brien, Annie, 64
O'Brien, Mary, 279
O'Shane, Gladys, 210
O'Shane, Pat, 14, 240, 248–50, 271, 273
O'Sullivan, E.W., 146
Office of Aboriginal Women, 274
Office of Multicultural Affairs, 266
Office of the Status of Women (OSW), 263, 266, 269
Onslow, Madeleine, 37
Open Door International (ODI), 1, 10, 167–8, 171–3, 178, 180
Osborne, Ethel, 169
Osland, Heather, 2–4, 16
Otto, Di, 243
Owen, Mary, 267

Pankhurst, Adela, 63–5
Pan-Pacific Women's Conferences, 70, 116, 123–4, 161–2
Parade of Mothers, 66
Pasqua, Bruna, 269
Paul, Alice, 168
Payment for Women's Work, The, 89
Pearce, George, 118
Pearson, C.H., 38

Pengelly, Ann, 7–8
Piddington, A.B., 98
police matrons, 59
Police Offences Amendment Act (1908), 147
policewomen, 148, 151, 161
Polini, Emilie (Patricia Mary Ellis), 82, 84–5
Politics of Reproduction, The, 279
Power, Margaret, 229
Presbyterian Ladies College, 37–8
Prisoners' Detention Act (1908), 147
Professional and Business Women's Group, 148, 178
Professional Women Workers' Association (NSW), 70, 81
Progressive Reform Party, 223
prostitution, 30, 123, 129, 198
  de-criminalisation, 195

Queen Victoria Hospital for Women, 44, 76
Queen's Willing Shilling Fund, 44
Queensland Women's Suffrage League, 26
Quirk, Mrs, 188–9

Racial Hygiene Centre, 81
Racial Hygiene Congress (1929), 96
Radford, Gail, 261
Rae, Arthur, 41, 146
Rape Crisis Centres, 15, 247, 256–7, 280
Rape Law Reform Action Group, 241
Ravenscroft, Mona, 190
Real Matilda, The, 251
Reclaim the Night, 247
Reed, Carrie, 42
Refractory Girl (journal), 233, 244, 249, 251, 256, 263
refuges, 15, 19, 229–30, 246, 248, 256–7, 269, 272, 273, 277
Reid, Elizabeth, 254, 256, 258–9, 260, 263
Reid, George, 35
Rich, Ruby, 96, 124, 201–2
Richmond, Katy, 240
Rickie, Nelle, 78, 93, 99, 100–2
Rischbieth, Bessie, 5, 7, 9, 50–1, 53, 56, 64–6, 77, 88, 91, 118–19, 125, 127, 130–1, 134, 141–2, 144–5, 154–62, 168–9, 184, 193, 202–3, 209

INDEX

Roberts, Florence, 5, 87
Robertson, Mavis, 233, 258–9
Rounsevell, William, 50
Rowan, Dawn, 222
Royal Australian Navy Service, 187
Royal Commission, Western Australian (1934), 14, 124–31 passim
Royal Commission on Aborigines (1913–14), 83
Royal Commission on Health (1925), 80
Royal Commission on the Basic Wage (1919), 98
Royal Commission on the Constitution (1927), 113
Rural Workers' Union case, 97
Ryan, Edna, 240, 251
Ryan, Lyndall, 255–6, 260
Ryan, Susan, 256, 262–4, 269

St George's Reading Circle, 37
Sandford, Coonie, 219, 221, 226
Sappho, 90
Sawer, Marian, 257, 269
Scaddan, John, 58
Scarlet Woman (journal), 233
Schenk, Rev., 119, 121
Schenk, Mrs, 119
Scott, Martha (later Macintyre), 219
Scott, Rose, 5, 11, 13, 20–1, 26, 28–31, 36, 38, 41, 44, 49–51, 53, 56–7, 59–60, 62, 87–8, 94–5, 107, 145–7, 216, 264
Scott-Griffiths, Jennie, 64
Scrimgeour, Caroline, 211
Scullin, Prime Minister, 79
Scutt, Jocelyn, 240–1
Searle, Ethel, 27
Second Sex, The, 227, 277
Seery, Mrs, 101
Sex Discrimination Act (1984), 263–4
'sex slavery', 30, 88, 95, 119
sexual division of labour, 251
sex education, 95
sexual harassment, 62, 264, 277
Sexual Politics, 222, 233
sexual rights, 11, 14, 17, 197–202 passim
sexuality
 feminism and, 7, 33, 56–7
Shaw, Sylvie, 225, 234, 259, 267
Shelley, Cecelia, 212
Shute, Carmel, 233

Sisterhood of International Peace, 64, 161
Slavery Convention, 94
Smith, Shirley, 272
Smyth, Brettena, 33, 42
Socialist and Communist Women's Group, 100
Society for the Prevention of Cruelty to Women and Children, 44
Solomon, Thelma, 218
Sonenberg, Dianne, 217, 233
Spence, Catherine Helen, 39–40, 60, 67–8, 153
Spender, Dale, 252
Stanley, Millicent Preston, 52, 66, 80, 82, 85, 102, 144, 150, 152
State Children's Bill (the Neglected Children and Juvenile Offenders Act) (1903), 62, 147
State Children's Council, 67
Steen, Frederika, 268
Stevens, Joyce, 233
Stewardess Rights Group, 224
Stirling, Dr Edward, 40
Stone, Janey, 228
Stopes, Marie, 201
Stout, Lady Anna, 155
Street, Jessie, 5, 10, 14, 51, 54, 65, 96, 104, 106–7, 140, 144, 157, 161, 163, 169, 174–8, 181–2, 185, 187, 189–94, 200, 203, 205, 207–9
Street, Tony, 261
Suffrage, 9–12, 19–45 passim
 men's role in, 44
Summers, Anne, 229, 251, 258, 263–4
Supported Accommodation Assistance Program, 257
supporting mothers' benefit, 254
supporting parent benefit, 16
Sweet, Dr Georgina, 162
Sydney Business and Professional Women's Organisations, 201
Sydney Women's Literary Society, 38

Tangney, Dorothy, 189–90, 206
Taylor, Esther, 212
Teachers' Action Group, 224
temperance movement, 32, 65
Tent Embassy, 248, 271
Testator's Family Maintenance and Guardianship of Infants Act (1916), 73
Theatrical Employees' Union, 99

Theatrical Managers' Association, 99
theosophy, 51, 141
Thornton, Merle, 10, 214–16
Thorp, Margaret, 63, 70
Throssell, Ada, 25
Tomasetti, Glen, 223
Torsh, Daniela, 256
Tribe, Muriel, 192
Triennial Convention of the Australasian Woman's Christian Temperance Union, 155
Tucker, Margaret, 250
Turner, Ethel, 36

Union of Australian Women (UAW), 212, 214, 218, 225, 250
   Aboriginal participation in, 210
   Mother and Child campaign, 210
United Associations (of Women) (UA), 1, 5, 7, 10, 51–3, 76, 94, 107–8, 124, 140, 142–4, 148–50, 154, 157, 163, 168, 171, 174–5, 178, 181, 184, 187–9, 193, 201, 206–8, 211–12, 282
United Australia Party, 108, 143
United Council for Women Suffrage, 43–4
United Council of Aboriginal and Islander Women, 250
United Nations Charter, 191–3, 216
United Nations Conference (1945), 191

Vallence, May, 125, 128, 131
Vashti's Voice (journal), 223, 228, 233, 249
venereal disease (VD), 20, 56–8, 90, 95–6, 198–200
Victorian Council of Aboriginal and Islander Women, 250
Victorian Employed Women's Organisations Council (VEWOC), 217
Victorian Lady Teachers' Association, 43, 97
Victorian Trades Hall Council, 99, 179, 212
Victorian Woman's Suffrage Society, 23, 42
Victorian Women's Citizens' League (VWCM), 9, 14, 69, 76, 93, 113, 152, 154, 160, 168
Vietnam War, 220–1

Vietnamese Women's Association, 269
Vindication of the Rights of Women, 277
violence
   against women, 247, 265, 280
   domestic, 230, 241, 272–3, 282

waged work, 4, 74, 176–82 *passim*, 184–8, 279–80
   part time, 4, 279–80
   women, 176–82 *passim*, 184–8, 211
wages,
   adult minimum, 240
Wallace, Lizzie, 101
Wallace, Dr V.H., 96, 200–1
Walker, Ellinor, 7–8, 11
Walker, Kath (Oodgeroo Noonuccal), 250
Warmadean, Mary, 126
Waters, Ann, 208
Waterside Workers' Women's Committees, 210
Waterworth, Edith, 140, 151, 156
Watson, Lilla, 272
Webb, Jessie, 159
Weber, Ivy, 152
Weekes, Alice, 97
Weekes, Clara, 97, 163
welfare state, 11, 49, 55, 58–9
Western Australian Aborigines Act, 119
White Australia Policy, 76
   feminist opposition to, 76, 162
White, Sally, 238
Whitlam, Gough, 239, 255, 259
Whose Child? (play), 82, 85
'Who's For Australia League', 145
Willard, Frances, 36, 49
Williams, Agnes, 26
Williams, M. Jamieson, 78, 94, 158
Williams, Kath, 212
Winder, Laurel, 274
Windeyer, Margaret, 41
Wise, B. R., 146
Wives' and Mothers' Union, 108
WIZ, 235
Wolstenholme, Maybanke (later Andersen), 21, 36, 38–40
woman movement , 19–20, 22, 24, 33, 35, 40, 41, 44, 73
   see also women's movement
   Aboriginal rights, 54, 110–35 *passim*
   maternalism, 12–13, 20, 49–71 *passim*, 72–86 *passim*, 92–3, 160

INDEX

nationalism, 182
protectionism, 26, 56-8, 62-3, 110-35 passim, 200
reforms, 20
Woman Voter (journal), 61, 155
Woman's Christian Temperance Union (WCTU), 9, 23-7, 32, 35, 44, 49, 58, 61, 65-6, 94, 152, 157-8, 199, 280
Woman's Clarion (journal), 5, 72, 91
Woman's Sphere (journal), 36, 51, 145
Woman's Suffrage Journal, 36
Woman's Voice (journal), 35-6, 38
Womanhood Suffrage League (WSL), 21, 28, 35, 39, 41, 73
women, Aboriginal, 110-35 passim, 270-6 passim
  custody rights see also Aborigines, parents' custody rights, 82-3
  sexual abuse of, 113-14, 116-17, 120
Women Against Rape, 246-7
Women and Economics, 87, 89
Women and Politics Conference (1975), 244, 259-60, 270, 282
Women as People (Action Group), 224
Women Citizens' Association, 78
Women in Australia, An Annotated Guide to Records, 259
Women in Industry and Community Health (WICH), 269
Women Prisoners Action Group, 224
women, white
  elected to parliament, 11, 80, 142, 152
  political candidates, 7, 11, 13
Women for Canberra, 151-2, 189, 199, 201
Women Caterers' Union, 97
Women Public Servants' Association, 97
Women Typists' Association, 97
Women Voters' Association, 52
Women's Abortion Action Campaign (WAAC), 224
Women's Action Committee (WAC), 218-19, 223-4, 226, 246
Women's Action Group (Hobart), 239, 244
Women's Advisory Councils, 274
Women's Affairs, 255-6, 260-1, 273
Women's Auxiliary Air Force Service, 187
Women's Bureau, 261

Women's Business (Aboriginal Task Force Report), 274
Women's Centenary Committee, 133
Women's Central Organising Committee, 104
Women's Charter, 191-8 passim, 202
Women's Charter Conferences, 10, 190, 194
Women's Club, 66
Women's Electoral Lobby (WEL), 13, 24, 237-41, 248, 250, 254, 261-4, 267, 268
Women's Emergency Services Program, 268
Women's Employment Board (WEB), 188, 211
Women's Federal Political Association, 44
Women's Film Fund, 259
Women's Franchise League, 37
Women's Health and Community Centre (Perth), 230
Women's Health Centres, 256
Women's Immigration Auxiliary Council, 68
Women's Industrial Convention (1913), 97
Women's Initiatives Program, 274
Women's International League for Peace and Freedom, 64, 161, 170
Women's Legal Status Act (1918), 60
Women's Liberation, 5-8, 14, 174, 219-30 passim, 231-52 passim, 254, 255, 257-8, 271, 282
see also women's movement, feminism
  critique of the family, 232, 249, 270
  female conditioning, 219, 226, 229, 233, 235, 249
  'radicalesbians', 243-5
  sex objects, 225, 227-8, 236, 245, 264
  sex roles, 14, 232, 233, 235, 243, 249
  sexual freedom, 220
  women's 'roles', 214, 217, 221, 226-7, 236
Women's Liberation Newsletter, 227, 232, 234, 236
Women's Literary Society, 36
women's movement
  see also feminism; woman movement; women's liberation

315

and Aborigines, 21–2, 27–8, 161, 195, 207–9, 247–50, 270–6 passim
age of consent, 8, 12, 15, 25–6, 40, 57, 150
internationalism, 167–75
and migrant women, 207–8, 248–9, 261, 266–76 passim
relations with Aboriginal women, 270–6 passim
Women's National Movement, 54
Women's Non-Party Association (of South Australia) (WNPA), 7, 9, 61, 67, 84, 111, 140, 153, 155, 157–8
Women's Non-Party Political League, 10, 140
Women's Organising Committee (of the Australian Labor Party) (WOC), 75, 101–2
Women's Peace Army, 63
Women's Political and Social Crusade, 143
Women's Political Association (formerly Women's Federal Political Association) (WPA), 57–8, 61, 63, 76, 89, 97, 140, 145, 162, 282
Women's Political Education League (WPEL), 51, 57, 59, 62, 94, 140, 145–7
Women's Post and Telegraph Association, 97
Women's Progressive Association, 41
Women's Service Club, 52
Women's Service Guild (WSG), 9, 14, 20, 50, 54, 58, 60, 64–69, 76, 79, 94, 110, 115, 118, 122, 125, 128, 139, 141–2, 145, 147, 149, 153, 155, 157, 161, 206
Women's Social and Political Union (WSPU), 88, 154–5
Women's Studies, 11, 161–2, 233, 250–2
Women's Suffrage League (WSL), 40, 140
Women's Trade Union League, 103
Women's Union of Service, 81
Women's Welfare Issues Consultative Committee, 261
Woodcock, Lucy, 188, 190, 197, 212
Workers' Educational Association, (WEA), 5, 90–1
working class women, 74, 209–13 passim
'working mothers', 74, 278
Workingmen's Political League, 43
Working Women's Centre, 15, 259, 261, 267
Working Women's Centres, 256
Working Women's Charter, 267, 279
Working Women's Committee, 224
Working Women's Resource Centre, 267
Working Women's Trade Union, 25
World War I, 54, 63–5, 69, 100
anti-conscription, 63–4
World War II, 14, 184–90 passim, 198–9

Young, Jeanne, 153
Young Women's Christian Association (YWCA), 68, 70, 161–2, 185, 201, 264